GOVERNING BY VIRTUE

Governing by Virtue

*Lord Burghley and the Management
of Elizabethan England*

NORMAN JONES

OXFORD
UNIVERSITY PRESS

OXFORD
UNIVERSITY PRESS

Great Clarendon Street, Oxford, OX2 6DP,
United Kingdom

Oxford University Press is a department of the University of Oxford.
It furthers the University's objective of excellence in research, scholarship,
and education by publishing worldwide. Oxford is a registered trade mark of
Oxford University Press in the UK and in certain other countries

© Norman Jones 2015

The moral rights of the author have been asserted

First Edition published in 2015
Impression: 1

Published in the United States of America by Oxford University Press
198 Madison Avenue, New York, NY 10016, United States of America

British Library Cataloguing in Publication Data
Data available

Library of Congress Control Number: 2015932987

ISBN 978-0-19-959360-6

Printed and bound by
CPI Group (UK) Ltd, Croydon, CR0 4YY

Acknowledgments

This book has been long in gestation, and it has benefited from the kindness and generosity of many people and institutions. I have been their friend and client, and, as any good early modern person knew, those patronage categories are interchangeable, but both demand loyalty and thanks.

On the meta level several institutions and benefactors have given me the opportunity to research, think, and write over the past decade. My home institution, Utah State University, has given me opportunities, and used its resources to make them happen. I thank my colleagues who helped me find the balance between teaching, research, and administration: Provost Raymond Coward, Dean Gary Kiger, and Dean John Allen lead that group. Dan McInerney, Associate Department Head in History and interim head during my sabbatical in 2008–9, along with Monica Ingold and Diane Buist, helped make my administrative life flexible enough to keep writing and research as a regular part of my weeks. The librarians of the USU Merrill-Cazier Library deserve my deep thanks. Jennifer Duncan, in particular, arranged the acquisition of the *State Papers Online* and *Cecil Papers*, databases without which this book could not have been written. She was helped in this by the generosity of the Tanner Charitable Trust, whose endowment of the USU libraries paid the bill.

After forty years of research, my debts to other scholars are huge, and their numbers are legion. The notes speak to the size of those debts, but there are some people who have been active in shaping this manuscript. Dr Susan Cogan read an early version and gave it a very useful critique. Sun Chao of Fudan University did the same. Long conversations about early modern governmental practice with Len Rosenband helped sharpen my arguments, and Bob Mueller has always been there to explain the arcana of the royal household. Robert Tittler has helped me keep to the historical straight and narrow, and taught me to see in new ways.

The list can go on and on, but none of these helpful colleagues is to blame for a book that is forced to make large generalizations and which dwells on cases. Those choices are all mine. And if I do not recognize all the work of my many colleagues, I want to stress that this book is, as much as possible, built on my experience in the manuscripts over many, many years. Sometimes I have reached conclusions on my own, from the evidence that others have reached. If I knew of their discoveries, I have cited them, but I have clung to my principle of checking the primary sources.

This book is an extended meditation on the connections between values and actions, administrative structures, and the needs and desires of those living within them. It explores the intersections between theory, processes, and life. I call it my department head's book, since it was heading the USU History Department for eighteen years that taught me to think about systems that depend on the virtues and values of those who run them, rather than on hard reporting lines. I came to see myself as the modern analog of a petty baron among other petty barons, sometimes known as full professors. We are a hard group to lead, but a powerful one. I thank my colleagues in History for suffering through my learning, and for teaching me so much. In particular, I have appreciated the tutelage of Ed Glatfelter.

All modern scholars are the recipients of patronage from individuals and institutions. Two have been especially important in the writing of this book. The Principal and Fellows of Jesus College, Oxford, elected me a Visiting Senior Research Fellow for 2008–9, housing me, feeding me, and teaching me while I used Oxford's splendid research facilities and tested my ideas on friends, especially Susan Doran and Paulina Kewes. The Huntington Library has given me several fellowships across my career, and the one in 2012 was especially important because it was there that this book really jelled. I deeply appreciate the encouragement the Huntington's directors of research, Roy Ritichie, and Steve Hindle in his stead, have given me. A grant from Utah State University's Mountain West Center for Regional Studies gave me the opportunity to spend time in the National Archives, completing essential work on the records of the Court of Wards.

This book is a product of the twenty-first century, built upon digital databases that did not exist when I began thinking about it in 2002. All of us working in this field have seen these databases change our practice, letting us return *ad fontes*. The *Early English Books Online* put the Short Title Catalog on our desks in full text versions. I had the opportunity to work with Thompson Gale as an advisor on the *State Papers Online [SPO]* project, which gave me early access to this marvelous tool, now published by Cengage. The *State Papers Online* provided access to two thirds of Lord Burghley's papers. One part, deemed to be about affairs of state, resides in the National Archive of the UK; the part of no interest to the state or the family was sold off, to become the Lansdowne Manuscripts in the British Library. The final third remained in the family, at Hatfield House. When those, known as the *Cecil Papers*, were digitized by ProQuest, it became possible to reunite Lord Burghley's archives with a few keystrokes. Now, research that would have taken weeks of running between Kew, Euston, and Hatfield can be done instantly.

These new tools are all based on the old manuscript calendars, however, so searching them is not always productive. But what they do make possible is the examination of actual manuscripts. As far as possible, this book was built on the principle that I should read the manuscript rather than depend on others' uses of the manuscript or on the calendars. A consequence has been a much richer understanding of the period, since many important documents were hidden under vague calendar entries. It is an axiom of Elizabethan historians that great scholars have drowned in Burghley's archive, but thanks to digitization we can much more easily find our way through his records of the period. They are even more voluminous than the calendars indicated, but we can work much faster, on a much broader front.

After I had begun work on this book my wife, Lynn Meeks, died in 2006. From the ashes of that loss arose the Phoenix of a new life with Cecile Gilmer, who married me in 2008. She is my most enthusiastic supporter in this work, and without her I doubt it would have been done. I dedicate it to her with my deepest love and thanks.

Logan, UT

October 15, 2014

Contents

List of Illustrations

List of Abbreviations

Bacon, *Works*	James Spedding, Robert Leslie Ellis, and Douglas Denon Heath, eds, *The Works of Francis Bacon*, 15 vols, <http://onlinebooks. library.upenn.edu/webbin/metabook?id=worksfbacon>
BL	British Library, London
BL Lansd.	British Library, Lansdowne Manuscripts
Collins	Arthur Collins, ed., *The Life of the Great Statesman William Cecil Lord Burghley*, London: 1732. Collins edited the anonymous life of Burghley written by one of his employees
CP	The Cecil Papers, the online digital collection of the manuscripts at Hatfield House calendared in HMC, Salisbury
Elyot, *Governor*	Thomas Elyot, *The Book Named the Governor*, ed. S. E. Lehmberg, New York: Dutton, 1970
English Reports	*The English Reports*, Edinburgh: W. Green and Sons, 1900–
Hartley, *Proceedings*	T. E. Hartley, ed., *Proceedings in the Parliaments of Elizabeth I*, 3 vols, Leicester: Leicester University Press, 1981–95
HEH	Henry E. Huntington Library, San Marino, CA
H&L	P. L. Hughes and J. F. Larkin, eds, *Tudor Royal Proclamations*, 3 vols, New Haven: Yale University Press, 1969
HMC	Historical Manuscripts Commission
HPT	History of Parliament Trust, *The Commons 1558–1603*, <http:// www.histparl.ac.uk/research/members/members-1558-1603>
Naunton	Robert Naunton, *Fragmenta regalia, or Observations on Queen Elizabeth Her Times and Favorites*, ed. John S. Cerovski, Washington, D.C.: The Folger Shakespeare Library, 1985
Parker Correspondence	John Bruce and Thomas Perowne, eds, *Correspondence of Matthew Parker, Archbishop of Canterbury*, Cambridge: Cambridge University Press for the Parker Society, 1853
Strype, *Annals*	John Strype, *Annals of the Reformation and the Establishment of Religion*, Oxford, 1824, 4 vols
TNA	The National Archives of the UK, Kew

Introduction

When I was a doctoral student working under Sir Geoffrey Elton in the 1970s the political world of the Tudors was understood to be a very top-down place. Scholars of the mid-twentieth century were interested in the emerging nation state and sought signs of its development. They understood that institutional and organizational sophistication were necessary to the more modern forms of the state that emerged in the seventeenth century, so they sought signs of it in Tudor government. In addition, many were seeking the roots of the English parliamentary democracy.

Sir Geoffrey Elton's *Tudor Revolution in Government* (1954) epitomized this search for centralizing government, but it was not alone. Sir John Neale and Wallace Notestein argued for a sort of organic maturation of Parliament during Elizabeth's reign that was another sign of the birth of modern English government, complete with a Loyal Opposition. C. H. Williams had written on the *Making of the Tudor Despotism* in the 1920s. Elton rejected his vision of a fascist Henry VIII, but Joel Hurstfield felt compelled to ask, "Was there a Tudor despotism after all?" in 1967. In essence, he attacked the notion that Tudor people consented to their government's orders, comparing some of the acts of the Reformation Parliament to that of the German Reichstag in 1933, granting Hitler total power.[1]

A mediating school of thought appeared in the work of Penry Williams and Wallace MacCaffrey, both of whom recognized that if there was a top, there also must have been a middle. Williams's superb study of the Council of Wales shows his understanding clearly, as does MacCaffrey's *Shaping of the Elizabethan Regime*, which emphasized the creation of a ruling team. Nonetheless, they saw royal power as real and important. As Williams wrote in his *Tudor Regime*, "The strength of Tudor government lay in a skilful combination of the formal and the informal, the official and the personal."[2]

These were men whose political understanding was forged in the 1930s and 40s and whose sense of government was that it ran naturally toward centralization and totalitarianism of one sort or another. Of course, some hoped for such a thing. Marxist historiography of the era posited a rising middle class and an aristocracy in crisis to explain the politics of the later sixteenth and early seventeenth centuries. For them, not surprisingly, issues of power among the landowning and acquiring

---

[1] Joel Hurstfield, "Was There a Tudor Despotism after all?" *Transactions of the Royal Historical Society*, 5th ser., 17 (1967), 83–108.

[2] Penry Williams, *The Tudor Regime* (Oxford: Clarendon Press, 1979), 462.

classes were at the core of discussions of politics. The "rising" gentry necessarily were pushing out the "declining" aristocracy in the work of Lawrence Stone, Hugh Trevor-Roper, and R. H. Tawney (although Tawney did note that the aristocracy and the gentry tended to meld together when viewed closely).[3]

The storm over the gentry slowly moved away, but one of its legacies was a much greater attention to local history and "subaltern" groups such as Puritans and Catholics, as well as ethnic and linguistic minorities who had felt the oppression of the royal despotism. They were discovered to be much more complex actors than had been assumed, people with their own cultures and opinions, just like the rest of the nation. Moreover, they lived in local contexts much more than a national one.

The intellectual historians of Tudor England in the mid-twentieth century had discovered another sort of Tudor reality, the "commonwealth." Late Henrician and Edwardian thinkers had conjured the idea out of their Protestant approaches to governance, Erasmianism, and a commitment to godly social improvement. These thinkers were seeking to establish God's true order in a state providentially freed from papal corruption. The "commonwealth men" became a staple of studies of Edward VI's reign. Geoffrey Elton made an effective attack on the concept in 1979, badly damaging the idea that they made up a party in Edward VI's era.[4]

Elton did, however, insist that the ideas associated with the commonwealth men were taken up in Elizabeth's reign by the "men who thought coolly, secularly and constructively about the problems of the commonweal and who faced the practical tasks involved in turning aspiration into action." When Sir William Cecil got control of the state, and brought back into government his Cambridge colleagues such as Sir Thomas Smith, Edwardian humanist/evangelical ideas were applied to governance, but without the religious fervor associated with Edwardian commonwealth preachers like Hugh Latimer.[5]

Elton's article banished discussions of the commonwealth men from most of the literature, though Winthrop Hudson, whose work influenced Elton's article, demonstrated his point about the carryover from Edwardian to Elizabethan governing circles. In an elegant little work entitled *The Cambridge Connection and the Elizabethan Settlement*, Hudson explored how the early Elizabethan governors were shaped by their Cambridge educations, and how that, in turn, shaped the Elizabethan settlement. They shared common values, rather than forming a party, and those values came to be applied in Elizabeth's reign.[6]

---

[3] R. H. Tawney, "The Rise of the Gentry, 1558–1640," *The Economic History Review*, 11, no. 1 (1941), 1–38. Lawrence Stone, "The Anatomy of the Elizabethan Aristocracy," *The Economic History Review*, 18, no. 1/2 (1948), 1–53. H. R. Trevor-Roper, "The Elizabethan Aristocracy: An Anatomy Anatomized," *The Economic History Review*, new ser., 3 (1951), 279–98. R. H. Tawney, "The Rise of the Gentry: A Postscript," *The Economic History Review*, 2nd ser., 7 (1954–5), 97.

[4] For a review of the historiography, as well as a critical attack on the concept, see G. R. Elton, "Reform and the 'Commonwealth-Men' of Edward VI's Reign," in G. R. Elton, *Studies in Tudor and Stuart Politics and Government*, vol. 3, *Papers and Reviews, 1973–1981* (Cambridge: Cambridge University Press, 1983), 234–53. Chapter DOI: <http://dx.doi.org/10.1017/CBO9780511560514.007> accessed Dec. 28, 2013.

[5] Elton, *Studies*, vol. 3, 253.

[6] Winthrop S. Hudson, *The Cambridge Connection and the Elizabethan Settlement of 1559* (Durham: University of North Carolina, 1980).

Separately (although Hudson and I did have tea and talk about these things) I had reached a similar conclusion in my *Faith by Statute: Parliament and the Settlement of Religion, 1559.* To me, it was clear that the early Elizabethan leaders were bent on the restoration of parts of the Edwardian settlement of religion, not on creating something new.[7]

In the vein established by Elton and Hudson, Catharine Davies brought back the issues concerning the commonwealth men without reviving their party in her study of the defense of the Reformation in Edward's reign. Importantly, she explored conceptions of governance, the roles of magistrates, and related issues in ways that make it easy to link them to the magistrates who later ran Elizabeth's England.[8]

These works reminded me that the conceptions of duty and magisterial virtue used by the Elizabethans had their roots in late Henrician and Edwardian experience and education, modified by the humility induced by the reign of Philip and Mary. When Edward VI died, God, wrote Sir John Cheke, took "the measure of their impiety, that the more heavy severity of divine justice may be exercised upon them."[9] The Edwardian Protestants were humbled by a hard lesson that they would not forget.

In the 1990s work on the state in early modern England emphasized the role played by semi-independent local authorities and local people who used the state as a tool to solve particular local issues. Patrick Collinson remarked that these local governors were not simply subjects of the Crown. They were citizens of a commonwealth that functioned only because of their sense of civic duty. To express this, he coined the description of Tudor England as a "monarchical republic" in which traditions of popular participation sat somewhat uneasily alongside the sovereign authority of the Crown.[10]

John McDiarmid brought together a number of authors to consider Collinson's "monarchical republic" thesis. The results are mixed, but by making the argument more subtle the contributors, especially Ethan Shagan and Peter Lake, demonstrated the limits of the concept, since law and religion must be put back into our understanding of the Elizabethan political mind—which undermines the classical republicanism of the monarchical republic.[11] There was a great deal of monarchy and very little republicanism in Elizabeth's state, in part because its very nature was rooted in the contractual nature of late feudal monarchy.

Contractual concepts of service created a "public sphere" of a particular sort for the Elizabethan magisterial classes. Given the necessity of negotiation between the

[7] Norman Jones, *Faith by Statute: Parliament and the Settlement of Religion, 1559* (London: Royal Historical Society, 1982).

[8] Catharine Davies, *A Religion of the Word: The Defence of the Reformation in the Reign of Edward VI* (Manchester: Manchester University Press, 2002).

[9] Hastings Robinson, ed., *Original Letters Relative to the English Reformation... Chiefly from the Archives of Zurich* (Cambridge: Parker Society, 1846), vol. 1, 144.

[10] Patrick Collinson, "De Republica Anglorum, or History with the Politics Put Back" and "The Monarchical Republic of Queen Elizabeth I," in Patrick Collinson, *Elizabethan Essays* (London: Hambledon Press, 1994), 1–30; 31–58.

[11] John F. McDiarmid, ed., *The Monarchical Republic of Early Modern England: Essays in Response to Patrick Collinson* (Aldershot: Ashgate Publishing, 2007).

monarch and the ruling classes, it was important to Elizabeth to influence the opinion of the public that mattered. Burghley understood this instinctively, and from his first days in office was using polemics, sermons, tracts, proclamations, legislation, progresses, public punishments, and other tools to influence the general understanding of events and support for royal policies.[12] Peter Lake and Steven Pincus have convinced us to take the concept of the "public sphere" back into the Reformation era; Lord Burghley would have agreed, understanding the need to create shared ideas about national issues, such as the Catholic threat. The realm's leaders had to be convinced to defend it from the threats Burghley was defining, be they foreign, religious, or stiff-necked, grasping, greedy landlords, by enforcing the laws.

Steve Hindle has argued forcefully that law was a lever in the hands of people who sought to use the Crown in their own interest, increasing the power of the state from the grass roots up. As he says, early modern English governance was not arcane or remote. It was a process in which subjects were intimately involved and one which they learned to manipulate and even change in their own interest. "The early modern state did not," he says, "become more active at the expense of society; rather, it did so as a consequence of social need."[13]

Michael Braddick and John Walter have argued in a similar fashion. They downplay the institutions of the state, stressing instead the importance of the network of local officeholders who were instrumental in creating and evolving the ways in which the Crown's central agencies worked. These agencies were set in a hierarchy that might appear to be distinct, but they were experienced as part of an organic local order. Together they created the basis for the early modern "power grid." Individuals' placement on this three-dimensional grid was determined by the number of hierarchies in which they participated and the degree to which their ranking within those separate hierarchies was mutually reinforcing.[14]

Braddick carried this argument into his important book *State Formation in Early Modern England, c.1550–1700*. Observing that the state was actually a network of agencies exercising distinctively political power, with varying and imprecise forms, he called for the study of the state's authority in the localities. He rejected the idea of linear state building that had concerned his predecessors and studied "state formation," tracing changes in the form of the state wrought by "the net effects of the uses made of state power by innumerable individuals and groups."[15]

Marjorie McIntosh, looking at local authority in the entirety of England from 1370 to 1600, found a similar picture, after applying her rigorously statistical analysis

---

[12] Peter Lake, "The Politics of 'Popularity' and the Public Sphere: The 'Monarchical Republic' of Elizabeth I Defends Itself," in Peter Lake and Steven Pincus, eds, *The Politics of the Public Sphere in Early Modern England* (Manchester: Manchester University Press, 2007), 59–60.

[13] Steve Hindle, *The State and Social Change in Early Modern England, c.1550–1640* (New York: St Martin's Press, 2000), 16.

[14] Michael J. Braddick and John Walter, eds, *Negotiating Power in Early Modern Society: Order, Hierarchy and Subordination in Britain and Ireland* (Cambridge: Cambridge University Press, 2001), 38–9.

[15] Michael Braddick, *State Formation in Early Modern England, c.1550–1700* (Cambridge: Cambridge University Press, 2000), 96.

of local law enforcement. English society, she discovered, had a set of core values that were widely held throughout the society. These included preserving the harmony and tranquility of communities, enforcing good order and discipline, and developing appropriate responses to common issues such as poverty. Underpinning these values were the magistracy's concerns about personal credit, good name, honor, and control of dangerous elements. By Elizabeth's reign, she says, the great social dislocations of the first half of the sixteenth century were coming to an end, with "the working through and resolution of many of the tensions that resulted from these changes, including the formulation of a revised Protestant English ideology."[16]

Across the Channel (in a scholarly as well as a literal sense) discussions of early modern government were influenced by late twentieth-century political experiences. The creation of multi-national entities like the EU and the surprising resurgence of claims for local autonomy among Europe's ethnic and linguistic minorities made people think about the early modern political mosaics of the Holy Roman Empire and the Spanish Empire. H. G. Koenigsberger forcefully introduced the idea of early modern composite states in 1975, an idea that was taken up in the 1990s with some enthusiasm by students of continental monarchies and by historians of seventeenth-century Great Britain. By Koenigsberger's definition, Tudor England/Ireland/Wales was a composite state to which Scotland was added. These "constitutional" monarchies preserved large amounts of local autonomy even while being ruled by monarchs who claimed central authority. Across Europe, states were composed of numerous subordinate political communities that were linked to the center, be it monarchical, republican, or some other form of government, through distinctive contractual combinations of rights and obligations.[17]

It was a satisfying enough construct that J. H. Elliott elaborated on composite states in *Past and Present*, and Conrad Russell used it to explore the causes of the English Civil War.[18]

Meanwhile, economic historians and sociologists have observed identifying patterns which, although they come from very different sets of data, confirm the interlinked nature of culture and politics. Craig Muldrew, setting out to reconstruct the economic practices of early modern England, describes the "culture of credit." He begins by noticing that the rapid economic growth in the mid-Tudor period was joined to the economic ethics taught by humanist texts. It was a credit system that was interpersonal and informal, requiring that people perform their promises. This, he says, also gave rise to huge amounts of litigation over unfulfilled obligations. Hundreds of thousands of law suits per annum were filed beginning in the 1550s, peaking in the period 1580 to 1640. This explosion only tapered off once new credit structures were adopted.[19] This litigation arose

[16] Marjorie Keniston McIntosh, *Controlling Misbehavior in England, 1370–1600* (Cambridge: Cambridge University Press, 1998), 209–13.

[17] H. G. Koenigsberger, "Monarchies and Parliaments in Early Modern Europe: *Dominium Regale* or *Dominium Politicum et Regale*," *Theory and Society*, 5, 2 (1978), 191–217.

[18] J. H. Elliott, "A Europe of Composite Monarchies," *Past and Present*, 137 (1992), 48–71. Conrad Russell, *The Causes of the English Civil War* (Oxford: Oxford University Press, 1990).

[19] Craig Muldrew, *The Economy of Obligation: The Culture of Credit and Social Relations in Early Modern England* (London: Macmillan Press, 1998), 2–3.

because the classes engaged in these exchanges needed the stability that came from rule of law to protect their own positions.

Of course, litigation was only possible for people who had a system to use, which made the legal structures of the realm doubly important. Historians of parliament and of the law have been suggesting that the legal institutions of Elizabeth's era were still entangled in the older traditions of the feudal state, even though the courts were increasingly royal in nature. As Christopher Brooke observes, the writing of William Fleetwood, on "tenures," a commentary on that classic of English law Littleton's *Tenures*, and William Lambarde's study of Saxon law, put land use at the heart of the law. They knew it was rooted in feudal service (except, perhaps in Kent), and that the duties of service had been evolving. Peasants were turning into freeholders and nobles into copyholders, while the Queen continued to collect her dues from them. As the monarch granted use of land to men who could not supply military service, seigneurialism was declining, and the power of the monarchy was being asserted.[20]

This process matured in the seventeenth century. In Elizabeth's reign it was still in negotiation, aided by the revamped use of feudal legal structures like the Court of Wards and Liveries.

By the same token, Elizabethan conceptions of parliamentary service were more rooted in older ideas of duty, honor, and consultation with the powerful, rather than in a sense of political action. Although parliamentary statute law was increasingly important, parliament's real importance had to do with granting the Queen supply, a concept squarely rooted in older ideas of the relationship between monarch and magistracy.

Douglass North, in a more abstruse and sometimes historically inaccurate study, makes the argument that this legalism was a necessary stage of economic development as we move "from fragile to basic to mature natural states." He locates an important phase of this movement in England in the reign of Elizabeth, noting that Burghley used the Court of Wards as a tool of social cohesion not revenue, and that it was an era in which we see the elites embracing the institutionalization of the legal structures that aided them in their pursuit of secure tenure of property.[21]

Peter Bearman, in a dense sociological study of Norfolk, develops an argument that the county elites of Norfolk were, until late in Elizabeth's reign, bound together by kinship and other local relationships. The generation that came to power later in her reign (he says 1580, but I would put the date in the mid-1570s) organized itself around religious rhetoric instead, changing their understandings of their places in county and national government. As men in Norfolk participated in the structures of the state mediated through the court, they shifted their allegiances to national and religious identities that went beyond the local. Insisting that this was a long, multi-generational, process, he shows how

---

[20] Christopher Brooke, *Law, Politics and Society in Early Modern England* (Cambridge: Cambridge University Press, 2008), 334–41.

[21] Douglass C. North, *Violence and Social Orders: A Conceptual Framework for Interpreting Recorded Human History* (Cambridge: Cambridge University Press, 2009), 27–30; 73.

new patterns of gentry identity were strong enough to account for their patterns of participation in the English Civil War.[22]

Political scientists have contributed to this conversation by asking about the impact of the Reformation on "composite" early modern states. As Daniel Nexon shows, the Reformation stressed these systems by creating now sorts of cross-institutional alliances.[23]

The complex nature of these composite states, with their highly variable systems of local rule, required, as Thomas Risse observes, trust between magisterial groups, making maintenance of that trust a key job of early modern rulers. If it broke down, the state itself became ungovernable.[24] That is why religion was such a dangerous toxin. It could undermine solidarity and mutual trust. England and other early modern states had insufficient "state capacity" to exert direct control, so their governments worked through social trust developed by personal contact. Therefore, it took on tangible forms expressed through marriages, common institutions such as universities and the court, and a myriad of small social exchanges among the ruling classes. Essentially, trust was maintained through regional, family, legal, and other sorts of memberships that allow social cohesion in the ruling classes to flourish. Maintaining trusting relations between the elites was part of the royal managers' jobs.

In my own work, I have seen confirmation of these observations.[25] The dependence on conceptions of magisterial virtue gave them a sense of membership in the ruling elite. Conceptions of morality and the role of the godly state shifted significantly over the course of the era, but the shifts could be weathered because the trust and solidarity remained. Politically, the Reformation taught the Crown the necessity of cooperating with local authorities through existing structures, reinvigorating institutions like parliament, while giving the monarchy more influence through extensions and rationalizations of land holding and local power. Over several generations, these evolving relationships rearranged the power structure as England became increasingly Protestant. The Reformation gave Elizabeth a unique place in God's providential design, increasing her need to maintain the cooperation of the magisterial classes in order to do her divine duty.[26]

The emphasis on the importance of negotiated government in English historiography has taken the focus off of the role of the royal state. Although Geoffrey Elton showed Thomas Cromwell and other proto-bureaucrats improving the agencies of central control as part of the "Tudor revolution in government," the new

---

[22] Peter S. Bearman, *Relations into Rhetorics: Local Elite Social Structure in Norfolk, England, 1540–1640* (Rutgers, NJ: Rutgers University Press, 1993), 5–11.

[23] Daniel H. Nexon, *The Struggle for Power in Early Modern Europe: Religious Conflict, Dynastic Empires, and International Change* (Princeton, NJ: Princeton University Press, 2009), 5–6.

[24] Thomas Risse, "Vertrauen in Räumen begrenzter Staatlichkeit: Eine politikwissenschaftliche Analyse," in Jörg Baberowski, ed., *Was ist Vertrauen? Ein interdisziplinäres Gespräch* (Frankfurt: Campus, 2014), 127–46.

[25] Norman Jones, *The English Reformation: Religion and Cultural Adaptation* (Oxford: Blackwell Publishing, 2002). Norman Jones, *God and the Moneylenders: Usury and the Law in Early Modern England* (Oxford: Basil Blackwell, 1989).

[26] Elliott, "Composite Monarchies," 59.

historiography now pays little attention to them. The Crown looks strangely passive in current Tudor historiography.

This is odd, especially when you take into account what Steven Ellis has been saying about the Tudor border administrations, in which the Crown plays an active and destabilizing role.[27] Seen from Ireland, Wales, and the Northern Marches, the Reformation was just one part of the Tudor policy of centralization, uniformity, and cultural imperialism introduced by Henry VIII. By 1603 the Tudor state had brought the "borders" under much greater central control.[28]

This raises the question of what role the monarchy played in the nation. We have learned that the court was the focus of Tudor government, and that Elizabeth's court was distinctive. And it is obvious that Elizabeth was a very powerful presence in her state. Yet her power had to be transmitted beyond the court through men like Burghley, Leicester, Essex, and lesser men and women who served her, and, because it was transmitted orally, it is very hard to trace. As Natalie Mears observes, Elizabeth organized the political discussion and used various counselors depending on her desires.[29] When she made up her mind, if she did, her men of business had to carry out her will—though they sometimes worked hard at getting her to will the things they thought she should.

Reading my colleagues and meditating on my own discoveries led me to write this book. If the Elizabethan state was less a state than a composite formation, how did it work? If you were Elizabeth, how did you manage this unwieldy system as a monarch endowed by God with authority over everyone, but with little bureaucracy and no army? What role did personalities play in Elizabeth's state? Was temperament and proclivity important in understanding how Elizabethan England worked?

Given that my colleagues were describing historical reality in the Tudor state, there must have been a corresponding managerial reality that shaped the behavior of the Queen and her managers. Lord Burghley, in particular, became the focus of this study because he managed on Elizabeth's behalf, with her permission, according to his own instincts. I also focused on Burghley because his administrative archive is the main source of our knowledge of the Elizabethan state. We are forced to see it as he saw it because we have to use the papers he collected and annotated with such enthusiasm. The very shape of Elizabethan research is based on the way his office organized his papers, which, in itself, is a clue to the way he saw the state.

Insofar as I can, I have gone back to the manuscripts in writing this book. I made it a rule to use the primary sources whenever I could, and if I used printed editions I sought to check them against the originals. Moreover, as anyone who has worked in Elizabethan history knows, the calendars are very poor for much of the reign and many of the collections, so I had to look at manuscripts to find out what was actually in them. A single line of description in the *State Papers Domestic* can

[27] Steven G. Ellis, *Tudor Frontiers and Noble Power: The Making of the British State* (Oxford and New York: Oxford University Press, 1995).

[28] Steven Ellis, "Centre and Periphery in the Tudor State," in Robert Tittler and Norman Jones, eds, *A Companion to Tudor Britain* (Oxford: Blackwell Publishing, 2004), 133–50.

[29] Natalie Mears, "The Council," in Susan Doran and Norman Jones, eds, *The Elizabethan World* (London: Routledge, 2011), 63.

describe eighty folios. In the *Calendar of Lansdowne Manuscripts*, an eighteenth-century calendar, entries can tell us more about eighteenth-century ideas of history than the content of a manuscript, as when one John Castle was dismissed as "a crazy Puritan." Crazy he may have been, but Puritan he was not, as you can see when you read the manuscript of his poem "Canticle Compiled for the Comfort of that Right Blessed Virgin Elizabeth."[30]

The result is a work that unapologetically depends on new readings of the sources and on my instinctual grasp of the contexts in which the documents are placed, based on many years of using them. Nonetheless, I apologize to those whose works I perhaps should have cited. A book of this scope is forced to leave out many important conversations.

I was also constrained by missing historiography. I was forced to explain governmental structures before I could talk about them, finding, in many cases, very little modern scholarship on major sectors of the royal government, such as the Court of Wards. Condensing and explaining these, I discovered, was no easy task, and one that few others have taken on. So this is my attempt to make sense of rulers who were making choices according to their conceptions of duty and honor within England's governmental systems and processes. Cicero observed that virtues and actions are conjoined, and so they are in this book. You cannot talk about values without describing processes and actions, and you cannot understand actions without explaining processes and values.

The management of the state turned around conceptions of political duty and the reciprocal duties of the monarch and the magistracy, and we can see these in operation by looking at various issues confronting Elizabeth and Burghley. Thus this book is organized into studies of various points and issues of management. Chapters are devoted to the interplay between the gentlemen charged with enforcing the law and the Queen's interests and needs; the raising and spending of money; defense, and religion. Preceding these are chapters on the political culture of this magisterial world, the value systems on which voluntary participation in government rested, and the way Burghley understood and deployed those values. It was important to portray the tight little world of the ruling classes and how they managed up and down within it; how perceptions of state actions and duties were manipulated; and how Burghley gathered the information he needed to do his work.

This system of magisterial virtue, resting on divine will as understood through the classics, scripture, and English law, limited the possibilities of the monarch, and ensured the flexibility of the magisterial classes as they employed the dull tools of the state. These limitations meant that much of the change that slowly crept into the Elizabethan state was driven from below, by magistrates who wanted to use the royal power for their own benefit, rather than from above. Burghley and Elizabeth had a tiger by the tail and they moved carefully, avoiding too much offense and accepting the limitations the system gave them. In the process, they allowed the evolution of the fluid concept of the "ancient" constitution that troubled Stewart England.

---

[30] Lansd. 99/fols 70–4v. *A Catalogue of the Lansdowne Manuscripts in the British Museum: With Indexes of Persons, Places and Matters*, 191.

1

Managing Elizabethan England

For no man holds land simply free in England, but he or she that holds the Crown of England: all others hold their land in fee, that is upon a faith or trust, and some service to be done...

Sir Thomas Smith, *De republica Anglorum*

Although it was greatly expanded by the Tudors, the remit of royal government remained narrow. Its primary job, as Elizabeth and Burghley saw it, was to keep the queen's peace within the realm while defending it from external enemies. As the lord of all the landlords, the Queen owed them peace and justice, and they owed her service and support.

Their England was a proprietary state, technically owned by the monarch, but administered by those who held the usufruct of the property. This created a particular sort of relation between the Queen and those who held the property. As Sir Thomas Smith, that touchstone of all discussions of the Tudor constitution, explained:

> For no man holds land simply free in England, but he or she that holds the Crown of England: all others hold their land in fee, that is upon a faith or trust, and some service to be done to another Lord of a Manor, as his superior, and he of an higher Lord, till it come to the Prince and him that holds the Crown.... He that holds the land most freely of a temporall man... holds by fealty only, which is, he shall swear to be true to the Lord, and do such service as appertains for the land which he holds of the Lord. So that all free land in England is holden in *fee* or *feodo*, which is asmuch to say as in *fide* or *fiducia*: That is, in trust and confidence, that he shall be true to the Lord of whom he holds it, pay such rents, do such service, and observe such conditions as was annexed to the first donation. Thus all save the Prince be indeed not *viri domini*, but rather *fiduciary domini*, and *possessores*.[1]

As Smith says, owing services in return for land (or a corporate charter) from the monarch created the core relationship between the Crown and the magisterial classes. It also created the points of leverage and contact between them. Landlords, trustees of the Queen, served as governors and soldiers at the order of the monarch. And the monarch demanded service, as well as in rents, fees and duties. Moreover, the monarch was pledged to look after the orphans of those owing knight service as tenants *in capite*. Or, to be more precise, the Queen had the right to manage the

---

[1] Thomas Smith, *De republica Anglorum: The Maner of Gouernement or Policie of the Realme of England* (London, 1584), 111–12.

property on their behalf and bestow them in marriage, in the interest of their common good. As Smith is careful to point out, this was a contractual arrangement, in which the stakeholders worked together.

Smith translated the Latin *res publica* as "common wealth," not "republic," since commonwealth catches the nature of government by shared responsibility better than "republic." He defines it as a form of social contract founded on mutual benefit: "A society or common doing of a multitude of freemen collected together and united by common accord and covenants among themselves, for the conservation of themselves aswell in peace as in war."[2] Smith probably would have us notice that he says they are "freemen" who come together in their common interest, rather than "the people." For, as Elyot insisted in his *Boke Named the Gouernour*, and Smith confirmed, the common people did not participate in government. Elyot cites the use of the word "commons" in vulgar English to demonstrate that "There may appear like diversity to be in English between a public weal and a common weal, as should be in Latin, between *Res publica*, and *Res plebeia*."[3] In short, England was a common weal, in which the social orders were created and arranged by God, preventing the chaos of a republic.[4]

In that common weal there were many sorts of governance, since it was a composite state. The Kingdom of England and the Kingdom of Ireland, the Duchy of Lancaster, the Stanneries of the West Country, the Palatinate of Durham, the Channel Islands, corporate boroughs, the Marches of Wales and the Presidency of the North, assize courts, leet courts, the commissions of the peace, and for nearly anything else—the list can go on and on. What they all had in common was the mix of men who ran them. They appeared in many different venues, all because of the powers they had in their locales.

To understand the management of the Elizabethan state, we must recognize the conceptions of status and duty shared by the magisterial classes in this divinely organized common weal. It was their sense of owed service and joint responsibility that made it function, giving the central state what leverage it had over the localities.

Steve Hindle has nicely summarized the miracle of Tudor government. Observing that the Elizabethan state had only about 1,200 paid officials, he comments:

> Much of Tudor governance was, perforce, carried out by amateurs who volunteered their service out of a combination of desire for national or local recognition of their honor and prestige and of an ethos of public duty which was derived partly from the tradition of classical republicanism mediated through the humanist curricula of grammar schools and universities and partly from indigenous habits of political participation in the institutions of manor, parish and county.[5]

The monarchy was to use its authority as the greatest landowner and the legitimator of local power to maintain the reciprocal obligations built into feudal contracts, legal rulings, and, increasingly, statute law. In its self-concept the Elizabethan government was less a monarchical republic than a composite feudal federal monarchy

---

[2] Smith, *Republica*, 10.   [3] Elyot, *Governor*, 2.   [4] Elyot, *Governor*, 6.
[5] Steven Hindle, "County Government in England," in Robert Tittler and Norman Jones, eds, *A Companion to Tudor Britain* (Oxford: Blackwell Publishing, 2004), 98.

whose use of Parliament was the ultimate expression of both the monarch's inability to rule without the support of the powerful, and of the powerful peoples' need of binding arbitration for their own good.

Governance took place in a world in which place, personal connection, trust, honor, and expertise were granted authority that never appeared on an organizational chart. To put it another way, the great chain of being was its organizational chart, enforced only by the angels. Largely informal, it depended heavily on the will, knowledge, and motivation of a few hundred gentlemen and nobles for its effectiveness. It was shaped by law and custom, but the understanding of these on the part of the ruling classes determined what could actually be accomplished.

In social science jargon, the Elizabethan state depended upon "social knowledge." Widely used now to catch the ephemeral but powerful ways in which the internet builds communities, it is also called the "wisdom of crowds." Social knowledge is defined as common understanding and practice that is a result of the connections between the individual members of society, resident in no single one of them. It is a form of knowledge acquired by imitation, which makes it very hard to document, but it is, nonetheless, real.

Consequently, in any discussion of Elizabethan government we must recognize that it was effected through overlapping formal and informal networks, networks that were based on the ruling community's sense of its duty and purpose. Most importantly, the act of governing, and of political leadership, was personal. Successful rule in the pre-bureaucratic, pre-statist systems required individuals to bear their shares of the common responsibility.

It was about what sociologists have dubbed the "density of acquaintanceship." People, networked through institutions such as families, parishes, colleges, local governments, and courts, were able to engage in collective action. The density of these acquaintanceships in the ruling class provided the social capital that allowed it to deal with and initiate social change through collective action. Moreover, your importance in the system was determined more by where you were situated in the network of acquaintanceship than by mere demographic status—although in a deferential, hierarchical society, those of lesser status but great connection always had to pay deference even as they influenced action.[6] Politically and economically, it depended heavily on a "culture of credit," in which standing and reputation were at the heart of social responsibility.[7]

William Cecil gives us a fine picture of how this social system of governance worked. In June of 1569 he was pondering how to defend the realm from dangerous invaders and prevent civil wars like those raging in France and the Low Countries. The resulting document is entitled "A necessary consideration of the perillous

---

[6] My thanks to my colleagues for introducing me to network theory: John C. Allen, Susan E. Dawson, Gary E. Madsen, and Chih-Yao Chang, "A Social Relationship Response to a Proposed Coal-Fired Power Plant: Network Theory and Community Change," *Community Development Journal*, 39, 1 (2008), 35–49. See also Paul D. Maclean, *The Art of the Network: Strategic Interaction and Patronage in Renaissance Florence* (Durham, NC: Duke University Press, 2007), 1–34.

[7] Craig Muldrew, *The Economy of Obligation: The Culture of Credit and Social Relations in Early Modern England* (London: Macmillan Press, 1998), 2–7.

state of this time." Heavily corrected and interlined in Cecil's own spidery hand, it presents a stark sketch of the weakness of the Crown. Written just before the Northern Rebellion in 1569, it is eloquent in its expectations of the magisterial classes.

His propositions were two. First, that all nations who accept the authority of the Bishop of Rome feel it is their duty in conscience to persecute "with all violence" the recusants in their midst. It follows that states that will persecute their recusant citizens will also attack neighboring nations which do not recognize papal authority.[8] Second, England is their greatest enemy, and so their natural target. No monarchy in Christendom was a greater loss to Rome, or a better model for reformation, than England. So what should be done?

"And herein the first and principal mean to prevent these perils with the assistance of Her Majesty," he says, must be to "use the speedy force of her own assured good subject," by boosting their readiness. Mustering that force and boosting its readiness required him to build a system that relied upon powerful local influences.

His solution rested on the voluntary creation, led by nobles, bishops, knights, and the leading men in each locality, of interlinked oaths of association.[9] The men at the top of the pyramid of authority would swear to defend the Queen and pledge to contribute money. This money was entrusted to a particular person in every shire, who would keep it to use for the defense of the realm whenever the Queen or her council called for it.

In turn, these leading men would invite lesser men—merchants, clothiers, farmers, householders, mayors and their ilk—to subscribe and contribute, too. Those who agreed to sign and pay were to be secretly noted in a book, along with those who refused. The refusals were to be categorized into two kinds, recusants of conscience and recusants who simply did not have the means to contribute.[10]

In short, when England faced such a crisis, the Queen could call upon every gentleman to do his duty and make a voluntary contribution. There is no call to build an army, raise taxes, or do any of the other things we might think a state could do when faced with such danger. Instead, we have the assumption that the nobles and gentlemen will see to the organization of the defense if asked.

We get a sense of this after the Northern Rebellion had been suppressed, when Cecil drafted a thank-you note for the Queen to send to certain gentlemen of Northumberland. She had heard of their good and faithful service from the Lord Warden, the Governor of Berwick, and the earl of Sussex. Expressing her appreciation of their faithful service, she asked for their continued fidelity.[11] Set against the background of the trials and retaliations being carried out on their neighbors who had rebelled, this is a telling gesture.

The use of the word "fidelity" in the letter to the Northumbrians reminds us of Smith's observation that every man holds his land "in trust and confidence, that he shall be true to the Lord" who gave it. It also requires us to notice the concept of

---

[8] TNA SP 12/51/fols 9–13.

[9] I suspect that this 1569 document contains the theoretical seeds of what became the Bond of Association in 1584.

[10] TNA SP 12/51/fols 9–13.   [11] CP 157/140.

"trust." The rhetoric of governance invoked trust and friendship all of the time. Thousands of orders from the Queen and council were addressed to "right trusty and well beloved" subjects. More strikingly, letters from the Privy Council to local commissioners were signed by the councilors as "Your Loving Friends," changing direct orders into friendly requests. The council's trust in its friends to carry out its orders was sometimes abused, but the pretence of trust and friendship was maintained.

A superb example of this ironic call on trust and friendship is the 1591 letter from the Privy Council to "our loving friends the Sheriff and Justices of peace of the county of Norfolk," rebuking them for dereliction of duty. It has been eight months, the loving councilors say, since the justices received their order to investigate purveyances in the county. "Whereas we greatly marvel, considering the usual complaints made in parliament we do therefore again will and require you...that presently you do proceed to the diligent execution and performance of the full effect of...our former letters." They sign it "Your Loving Friends."[12]

Tudor political culture was displayed in several rhetorical streams. These streams had their sources in feudal honor, the common law, Christian morality, and humanist values. In a world in which there was limited direct coercion, these values, like that of trust, had to be announced and reinforced frequently by all of the actors, from the Queen down to schoolteachers, homilists, catechists, and mothers.

Perhaps the easiest way to see these overlapping rhetorics is to look at politics as mid-Tudor people did, as being about individual morality, not political values. They judged good and bad actions in the context of an individual's virtue, in accord with that individual's place in God's creation. For them, governing was a series of individual acts that ought to be guided and judged by the virtue of the actors. God and society had expectations for those to whom much power had been given. Scripture, custom, and history taught them how to use that power. A providential God would reward and punish the use and misuse of it—and punishment and reward flowed from God to whole nations if the governors of the people were virtuous. If they were not, the paradigm of Sodom and Gomorrah was invoked, along with examples from Greek and Roman history. Narratives of martyrdom carried the same message: obedience pleased God.

This conception of politics was caught neatly by an anecdote related by Sir Francis Bacon. He remembered, "When any great officer, ecclesiastical or civil, was to be made, the queen would inquire after the piety, integrity, learning of the man. And when she was satisfied in these qualifications, she would consider of his personage. And upon such an occasion she pleased once to say to me, 'Bacon, how can the magistrate maintain his authority when the man is despised?' "[13]

Thomas Norton, the Remembrancer of London, wrote James Hawes, the newly elected Lord Mayor of London, a letter of advice that described the virtues necessary to be chosen a magistrate under Elizabeth. As "the mediate Lieutenant of most great and mighty God," Mayor Hawes, Norton instructed, was "Blessed of God

---

[12] H. W. Saunders, ed., *The Official Papers of Sir Nathaniel Bacon of Stiffkey, Norfolk as Justice of the Peace 1580–1620*, Camden Society, 3rd ser., 26 (1915), 64–5.

[13] Francis Bacon, "Certain Apothegms of the Lord Bacon's," in *Work*, vol. 1, 123.

with sufficiency for that experience which the honor of the place requireth by reason whereof you are not subject to such need as might make a man apt to corruption or to contempt." He has "an upright mind to serve God and the Queen sincerely." He was "noted a man of good charitable disposition and a tender heart to the poor," and, Norton said, "You are not young. You have not lived obscurely. You have had long experience and been in place of knowledge and of both politic and judicial understanding." Norton describes the Privy Council and all the City's officers in similar terms, all ready to deal in matters of justice, equity, and service.[14]

This is one reason William Cecil was obsessed with genealogy as a form of history. He saw breeding as an indication of both station and virtue—and family histories could tell you much about behavior, as well as who had to listen to whom. For Cecil, who personally wrote out copies of long genealogies, government rested on genealogy, since status and birth order determined authority and the right to give orders. The working of providence was evident in the rise and falls of families and the states they ran.[15]

This certainty that birth and authority went together prompted Cecil to work with the Earl Marshal, Thomas Howard, duke of Norfolk, to strengthen and regularize the College of Arms' oversight of social status. Throughout the 1560s the Heralds systematically visited the nation, to ensure that no one was usurping the title of gentleman or esquire, undermining the natural order. Cecil seems to be behind the 1566 bill introduced in Parliament for the reformation of the Court of Chivalry, making it a court of record.[16] Conceiving governance in terms of those who have the right to govern meant that the state could not be separated from the people born to run it. Burghley read widely in the genealogies of royal families, as well as working them out for himself and having them painted on the walls of his houses, along with maps of Elizabeth's counties, foreign cities, and states.[17] This was not simply evidence of his desire to climb the social tree—although he undoubtedly did aspire for his family to rise, as their merit deserved. It was about understanding how God had arranged the world and the place of people in that arrangement.

Reading his favorite author, Cicero, reinforced this Christian tendency to see politics as the expression of individual virtue. *De officiis, Contra Verrem, De re publica*, and *De finibus bonorum et malorum* taught him that the individual had duties to the commonwealth, and that the individual could choose the path of virtue. Senecan stoicism taught the same thing, and so did the Bible. And so, of course, did the histories he read. This quest for personal virtue was summed up by his

[14] BL Add. 33,271, fols 28–31. My thanks to Michael Graves for giving me his transcription of this. See Michael A. R. Graves, *Thomas Norton the Parliament Man* (Oxford: Blackwell, 1994), 59–62 for his contextualization of the advice.

[15] Anthony Grafton, *What was History? The Art of History in Early Modern Europe* (Cambridge: Cambridge University Press, 2007), 162.

[16] Richard Cust, "Earls Marshall and the Defence of Honor in Elizabethan England," unpublished paper presented at *Rethinking Politics in Sixteenth Century England*, April 18, 2009, at the University of Warwick.

[17] James M. Sutton, *Materializing Space at an Early Modern Prodigy House: The Cecils at Theobalds, 1564–1607* (Aldershot: Ashgate, 2004), 56–70.

brother-in-law Nicholas Bacon's personal motto, *mediocria firma*, the golden mean that kept a man doing his duty well. It is probably not an accident that William Cecil often reminds you of Cato the Censor, with his stern sense of duty, virtue, and tradition. The examples of famous Greeks and Romans were freely used as templates for modeling and understanding action. Sir Thomas Smith, in fact, made the comparisons explicit, using Roman history as a foil for England.

Consequently, the governor's first question when choosing men to serve as magistrates was "Who," not "What." Candidates' social status and wealth were the deciding factors. It was presumed that status and local influence were sufficient qualifications. This did not always produce good results, but it was the system. For the Elizabethan management, however, the choice of magistrates was increasingly complicated by ideology.

One of the managerial tasks facing Elizabeth's council was coping with a hierarchical system into which religious affiliation had been injected. Could men be trusted to serve their Queen if they did not recognize her as their liege lord? The Pope, a usurping foreign power, threatened good governance by luring the governing classes from their proper allegiance. Therefore, the council tried to make ideological distinctions among the key people in local government, especially the justices of the peace. Thrice they surveyed them, and through the process we can glimpse the problems presented by formal attempts to secure sympathetic local government when there was no easy way to deny authority established by birth and money.

In 1564 the Privy Council asked the bishops to investigate the attitude of their local justices of the peace toward the settlement of religion. The result was lists that categorized local gentlemen as "favorers," "neutrals," and "non-favorers," giving us a picture of just how Catholic or Protestant the bishops believed the front line of law enforcement to be. However, the Privy Council did not act systematically against most of the men on the list. Although known to oppose the Queen's religion, many continued to serve on the local benches.

Although the Treason Act of 1562 had made it treason to refuse to take the Oath of Supremacy included in the Act of Supremacy of 1559, it was not until 1569, in the fervid atmosphere around the Northern Rebellion, that JPs were asked to take the oath, and there was an attempt to weed Catholics out of the Inns of Court.[18] However, as the case of Edmund Plowden of Berkshire illustrates, men continued to serve in many places if they gave their bond for good behavior. Plowden had been identified as a Catholic in 1564 but kept his offices; in 1569 he refused the Oath of Uniformity and was removed from the Commission of the Peace. Placed under a bond of 200 marks, his legal career went from strength to strength, especially as Under Steward of the Duchy of Lancaster. Moreover, he was not removed from the Middle Temple. In 1577 a list of the benchers of the Inn identified him as a papist, very learned, of very good living. He had the Queen as one of his clients.[19]

---

[18] 5 Eliz. I, c. 1.

[19] HPT sub Plowden, Edward. F. A. Inderwick, ed. *The Inner Temple: Its Early History as Illustrated by its Records, 1505–1603* (London: Stevens and Sons, 1896), 478. Norman Jones, *The English Reformation: Religion and Cultural Adaptation* (Oxford: Blackwell Publishing, 2002), 127–8.

Again, in the fall of 1587, during the Armada crisis, the Privy Council bade the bishops to give an account of the JPs within their dioceses. The results were instructive, though not in the sense the council wanted.[20] The system of governance did not readily permit them to weed out all Catholics, since Catholics with the right standing could hardly be excluded from the bench. It was very difficult for them to escape their way of perceiving authority as accorded by birth and position.

The bishops were clear about the problem. They could not nominate to the bench Protestants who did not have sufficient birth and status for appointment. Scory of Hereford confessed that he would like to see men like his chancellor appointed considering "there is so little choice of such as be favorable to this religion."[21] Bishop Robert Horne at Winchester thought the solution was converting the existing members of the benches and the young aristocrats before they inherited office. The young earl of Southampton and young William Lord Sands "might be now in their youth so trained in religion that hereafter when they come to their authority and rule they should not hinder the same."[22]

It appears that it was Horne's suggestion that the council chose to follow. "Once a family entered the ranks of the magisterial gentry, the central government had a very powerful incentive not to offend unnecessarily the natural rulers of the localities," says Ron Fritze, so, as justices died or retired the Queen tended to appoint younger than usual men to the commissions of the peace. It indicates, he says, that the degree to which the central government could enforce the Reformation was influenced by the extent to which the natural rulers of a given county community shared the religious inclinations of the regime.[23]

The magistracy was in a Neoplatonic universe in which honor and duty, derived from lineage and office, flowed both toward and away from the center. Magistrates had duties to their betters and their Queen, but they also had duties to their families and localities that made their responses much more a matter of self-interest than is sometimes admitted. Concepts of honor, obedience, lineage, and service certainly motivated people, but honor, and slight, was in the eyes of the beholder, just as when to serve and how enthusiastically was a calculation that related to values that were more localized than general. Honor was a "discourse tool" that could be used to justify behavior.[24] But it carried a multitude of meanings, making it hard to use.

In a society in which honor was very important, the invitation to serve was evidence of status. It conferred honor along with work. By the same token, to be skipped over or displaced was a dishonor that brought shame and embarrassment.

[20] Strype, *Annals*, vol. 3, 2, 448–76.

[21] Mary Bateson, "Collection of Original Letters from the Bishops to the Privy Council, 1564, with returns of the justices of the peace and others classified according to their religious convictions," in *Camden Miscellany*, 9, Camden Society, new ser., 53 (1895), 17.

[22] Bateson, "Collection," 54.

[23] Ronald H. Fritze and William B. Robison, "Age and Magistracy: An Ambiguous Connection? The Situation of the Justices of the Peace of Hampshire and Surrey, 1485–1570," *Lamar Journal of the Humanities*, 20 (1994), 47–8.

[24] William Palmer, "Scenes from Provincial Life: History, Honor, and Meaning in the Tudor North," *Renaissance Quarterly*, 53 (2000), 448.

On the local level, honor, an abstract concept, turned into power and responsibility. Honor demanded that one serve, but, noblesse oblige, one had to use the power given for the desired ends or it might be withdrawn. Certainly your peers would be aware of your behavior in positions of honor and might shame you.

Listen to the way in which William Parr, Marquis of Northampton, Lord Lieutenant of Northamptonshire, tried to provoke obedience to an order for a special muster in 1560, in preparation for war with Scotland and France. Writing to his deputies, Lord Zouche, Sir John Spencer, Sir Robert Lane, and Edward Mountague, he reprimanded them for failing to hold proper musters. He expatiated on how he knew their loyalty to the Queen and their country; he explained how their disobedience "toucheth me in estimation," and he urged them to consider how appreciative the Queen would be of their good service, as she was of the service of gentlemen in other shires. Of course, if they did not do good service, serving their private respects, he would rather hide their behavior from her than have her know of their dishonor. Pleading and shaming, he tried to get the command carried out.[25]

This fear of dishonor may be why the many, many commissions issued by the Crown were built of careful layers of prestige and connection. Local commissioners did most of the work, but it was done under the formal eyes of the great men of the region and the state who were also appointed. All commissions for the peace contained members who represented the local hierarchies, the regionally powerful, and the servants of the Crown.

J. S. Cockburn's edition of the assize records makes this clear. The entry for each assize begins with a list of all the members of the commission who had the right to attend. Cockburn makes a distinction in these lists between the "honorary" JPs, who were not expected to attend, and the county magistrates who were (and who were sometimes fined if they did not). It is apparent that in this sense "honorary" should be read as "men of honor" whose names lent honor and authority to those associated with them. The acts of the county magistracy are thus given greater weight by being linked to all levels of the hierarchy, giving all of them joint responsibility for the assize. When Lord Treasurer Burghley's name appeared on every commission of the peace, it was not to honor him; it was to honor those associated with him—and to give him standing to interfere. For example, at the Hertford assize of March 4, 1573, there were thirty-eight justices of the peace on the list; eighteen actually appeared. The most senior justice present was Sir Ralph Sadler. A major landowner in the county, he was also Chancellor of the Duchy of Lancaster and a member of the Privy Council. In him the interests of the county and the Crown came together. He and Justice John Southcote of the Queen's Bench (a JP in Hertfordshire as well as the presiding justice) conducted the gaol delivery.[26]

Burghley's presence on the commission of the peace in every county underscores the importance of the law as a point of leverage and interaction between the local governors and the Crown. The English mingling of all the ruling classes in the

[25] *HMC, Manuscripts of Lord Montague of Beaulieu* (1900), 9–11.
[26] H. S. Cockburn, ed., *Calendar of Assize Records: Hertfordshire Indictments Elizabeth I* (HMSO, 1975), vol. 7, 1.

commissions was a unique and important method of governance. In France, for instance, men of great birth were not expected to provide local justice, leaving that to mere men of law. When he was Lord Chancellor, Francis Bacon reminded the justices of this, remarking that commissions of oyer and terminer united the varied levels of magistracy in a singular pursuit of justice, despite the differences between them. The commission, he proclaimed, "knits government elsewhere with the government of corporations, and puts them together." This, he said, created a commonwealth so strong that you could not make a better one "with a level."[27]

This knitting together of local leaders, a product of feudal rights and Tudor management, is visible in all sorts of commissions issued by the Privy Council, as the central and the local shared responsibility. The formula that required all the commissioners, or any two or three of them, to conduct a piece of business, kept the window open for central engagement while making it clear that the locals could get on with the business at hand. At the same time, the great men who served on the Privy Council expected to take a hand in local business. After all, it was local power that prepared them for service to the Queen. It was also local power that made it possible to extend the power of the monarch into the localities. That is why it was important for Privy Council members to maintain and expand their particular areas of influence. For instance, Burghley, perhaps the most influential man in England because of his relationship to the Queen, nonetheless systematically accumulated local offices. He was steward and recorder of the town nearest his country seat in Lincolnshire, Stamford. He was also steward of King's Lynn and Yarmouth, recorder of Boston, surveyor of royal lands in Lincolnshire, keeper of Rockingham Forest and Cliffe Park, *custos rotulorum* of Lincolnshire and Northamptonshire, and steward of numerous royal estates in the area. In London he was steward, escheator, bailiff, and clerk of the manor of Westminster, where he also had a home. He became Lord Lieutenant of Lincolnshire in 1587 and of Hertfordshire and Essex in the following year.

As Wallace MacCaffrey has pointed out, he did not hold these jobs *in commendam* or *sine cure*. Burghley involved himself deeply in local business, the regulation of trade, and the provision of schools and almshouses. He arbitrated local disputes, and sat on the Commission of Sewers concerned with fen drainage. He was as important a figure in his own region as he was at court. He was, from 1559, an active chancellor of Cambridge University, steward of Trinity College lands, and steward to the bishoprics of Lichfield and Coventry, St David's, and Winchester.[28]

Burghley was not alone in playing an active role on multiple levels, bridging national and local government. We see the same pattern with most powerful people. For example, William Fleetwood, Recorder of London, was active socially and legally across a wide range of categories. A good friend of Burghley's, as well as other Privy Councillors, including the earl of Leicester, Thomas Sackville Lord Buckhurst, Ambrose Cave, Sir Ralph Sadler, Sir Francis Walsingham, and Lord

[27] Francis Bacon, "The Lord Chancellor's Speech in the Starchamber 13 Februarii 1617," <http://www.uofaweb.ualberta.ca/historyandclassics/pdfs/496-BACON-SPEECHES.pdf>. Accessed Nov. 29, 2008.
[28] ODNB *sub* William Cecil, Lord Burghley.

Cobham, as well as Archbishop Parker. He corresponded with them all, reminiscing about their discussions on such issues such as the succession and points of law, as well as history—he had access to the men at the top.[29]

And he had access to the networks of power in greater London. Fleetwood worked closely with every lord mayor and all the aldermen of the city, as well as in the surrounding shires. Himself a freeman of the Merchant Taylors, he became Recorder of London in 1571 and kept up a hectic pace. In the last week of September and the first week of October, 1575, he participated in nineteen legal events. These included the oyer and terminer for Middlesex with the mayor and other justices; Middlesex and Surrey sessions of the Court for the Conservancy of the River Thames; sessions in Southwark for sewers, bawds, and harlots and in London for ale houses; the swearing in of new sheriffs for London at the Guild Hall and again at the Exchequer; the election of a new mayor for London; quarter sessions with the justices of Surrey and with the justices for Buckinghamshire; Admiralty sessions in Southwark; and gaol delivery for Newgate prison. He reported all of this in a letter to Burghley that ended with his hope to see him, his wife and daughter Anne, and "Mr. Chancellor of the Dutchy" (Sir Ralph Sadler) socially at the end of the week.[30]

A calculation of exactly how many members of the magisterial classes Fleetwood was in contact with in those days is impossible, but it included all of the governors of London, the barons of the Exchequer, the justices of Surrey, Buckinghamshire, Southwark, and London, and a long list of others, high and low, including sewer and river commissioners along with bawds, counterfeiters, and ale vendors. A map of Fleetwood's "social grid" would show that he, like most others of the magisterial class, had a complex set of informal as well as formal connections that were not kept distinct from one another. Moreover, Fleetwood was, like most of them, a creator of law as well as a lawyer, since he was a very active member of Parliament until his death in 1594.

It was through these contacts, from the highest to the lowest, that the social knowledge of informal government passed.

Burghley understood this so well that he carefully tracked locations and relationships of the magisterial classes. He grasped that in the small world of the ruling elite most things came down to genealogy and geography—an understanding that is reflected in everything from the popular chorographies of the day to the visitations of the Heralds. His anonymous biographer asked rhetorically, "what nobleman or gentleman and their dwellings, matches and pedigrees, did he not know?" He could, claimed the biographer, describe the locale of a gentleman's home better than the gentleman himself.[31]

---

[29] J. D. Alsop, "William Fleetwood and Elizabethan Historical Scholarship," *The Sixteenth Century Journal*, 25 (1994), 155–76.

[30] CP 160/80. A full transcription was printed by Haynes and Murdin in *A Collection of State Papers, Relating to Affairs in the Reigns of King Henry VIII, King Edward VI, Queen Mary, and Queen Elizabeth…*, vol. 2: *1571–1596*. A partial transcription is at *Calendar of the Manuscripts of the Most Hon. the Marquis of Salisbury, Preserved at Hatfield House, Hertfordshire*, vol. 2: *1572–1582*, 116–17. Note that the two transcriptions disagree about the date. Haynes and Murdin say it is October 1, 1573, and HMC Salisbury puts it at October 2, 1575. Fleetwood himself dated it as the "first Sunday in October, 1575."

[31] Collins, 65–7.

These connections of people and places were multiplied by networks that ranged from patron and client to father-in-law and brother-in-law, with friendships and business relationships mixed in to varying degrees. Burghley, as a rising man, was building a dynasty, but at the same time he was building affinities, which were useful on many levels. He married his children well. His eldest son, Thomas, wedded the daughter of Lord Latimer, giving him family ties to the earls of Northumberland, Westmorland, and Rutland. His daughter Anne married Edward de Vere, seventeenth earl of Oxford. He had granted himself the wardship of young de Vere and raised the two together. It may have been politic, but the earl was beastly to his wife and a pain to his father-in-law—but their daughters were children of an earl. His other daughter, Elizabeth, married William Wentworth, eldest son of Lord Wentworth of Nettlestead. Robert Cecil married Elizabeth, daughter of William Brooke, Lord Cobham, a perfect match with another leading administrator's family.

All of this expansion of his kin network gave him opportunities to mix, mingle, and expand his acquaintanceship. His son Thomas's entry into the Percy family gave the Cecils an important tie to power in the north, and Burghley had probably hoped his marriage of Anne to the earl of Oxford would do the same in the south.

The use of these family connections, by blood or marriage, was not directly political. Like patronage, family ties were much larger than any particular instance, so that one seldom sees a "do it my way" sort of order from an esteemed relative. However, family did fit into the broader model of honor, in that membership in the right family made you honorable, and relationship to an honorable person made you worthy. "Who are his/her people?" was an important question, since it grafted a person onto an extended chain of relationship and acquaintanceship.

As an example Henry Cheke, Burghley's nephew, comes to mind. William Cecil had married Mary Cheke in 1541. She died early in 1544, but William remained connected to the Cheke family for the rest of his life. Mary's brother Sir John, once Cecil's tutor, had died in Mary's reign, leaving a son, Henry. When Henry was fifteen, in 1563, he wrote his Uncle William a letter in Greek asking for his patronage. As a result, Cecil oversaw his education at Cambridge.

Five years later, the university Senate sought to win favor with its chancellor, Cecil, by offering Henry an MA. They praised him for being like his late father, Sir John, in learning, piety, and purity of life, and justified their generosity by pointing out that they had recent precedents among the Howard and Seymour families for electing youths of twenty. They earnestly sought Cecil's approbation. Then, assuming Cecil's silence was consent, the Senate acted a week later, offering young Henry his MA and a seat in the Senate. Henry had the good sense to write his uncle William and ask his permission before taking the degree. It is clear from the ornate, italic Latin of these letters that the university thought it would please Cecil by honoring the memory of his old tutor and brother-in-law. Young Henry claimed to have nothing to do with his promotion, which is likely.[32]

Eventually, Henry was made secretary to the Council of the North. Over the years, he wrote Cecil many letters, always asking for more patronage. His uncle

[32] BL Lansd., 10/fols 157; 169; 171.

generally supported him, though never as much as Henry hoped.[33] If we look at this story one way, it is clear that family ties were important and that Cecil saw it as duty to support young Cheke, giving him an education and some patronage. If we look at it another way, we can see the Senate of Cambridge University seeking to curry favor with their chancellor by honoring his relative with a gratuitous MA. In neither case was there a direct quid pro quo, but Henry invoked his social capital and Cambridge hoped to use it to create institutional social capital.

Marriages could create important alliances and move money, so they frequently played a part in regional politics. In 1564 Sir William Cecil advised the earl of Bedford, departing for his post as governor of Berwick, "Do what you can, to make the gentlemen accord amongst themselves; and to extinguish old factions, either by some device of marrying, or by redemption of titles of land, such like incumbrances, which commonly the seeds of discord [sow]."[34]

Some of the value of a marriage had to do with the honor of improved connections, and some of it had to do with the power of the marriage bond. It could create friends where there were no friends before. As Burghley told the recusant Sir Thomas Copley, living as a religious exile in France, he was disposed "to conceive well of you because I knew you were of blood and kindred to my wife, so as your children and mine by her were to be knit in love and acquaintance by blood, and in deed as I have good cause to love my wife well, so have I always taken comfort in loving her kindred." He promised to show her relatives "all good friendship." He had not, he said, been "able to make demonstration of my good will before your departure, having no cause directly offered, yet did I at sundry times oppose my self both in Council, and otherwise, to my last L[ord] Howard of Effingham, whom I found many times sore bent against you..."[35]

William Howard, Lord Howard of Effingham, Lord Admiral and dutiful member of the Privy Council, was incensed against Copley because he jilted a Howard kinswoman in favor of Mildred Cecil's cousin, Katherine Luttrell. The land the Howards could not get by marriage they sought to get by claiming it was forfeited by Copley's exile.[36]

In this rare example we can see observance of kinship obligation at the highest level of government, turning a dispute in the council concerning the legal status of exiles into a grudge match between families. These men knew one another well, and high politics were often family politics. The other side of this story, of course, is that family relations could be a positive tool of government, since family pressure could be brought to bear on people who were dishonoring their status. People often married their children to their friends' children, for friendship formed another bond, as did the civil niceties of the small societies to which the magistracy belonged, whether they were towns, colleges, inns, guilds, or commissions of the peace. It was in these relationships that social knowledge was cemented as multiple generations interacted personally. One of the lessons they taught was that the maintenance of friendly relations made

[33] Strype, *Cheke*, 140–1. BL Lansd., 7/fol. 56; NA, SP 12/39 fol. 115; SP 12/48/fol. 52; SP 12/49 fol. 165; SP 12/69 fol. 15; SP 12/74 fol. 124.

[34] BL Harleian 6990, fol. 3v.   [35] SP 12/99 fol. 30v.

[36] Retha Warnicke, "Family and Kinship Relations at the Henrician Court," in Dale Hoak, ed., *Tudor Political Culture* (Cambridge: Cambridge University Press, 1995), 34.

honor flow and made life easier. This was well known to the authors of courtesy books, but it was seldom explained as a political skill. In 1622 John Reynolds published a translation of Eustace de Refuge's 1615 *Treatise on the Court* that made it explicit.

De Refuge, a contemporary of Robert Cecil, was a successful and highly placed ambassador and judge under Henri IV and Louis XIII, thanks to his personal skills and a very good marriage. Late in his life, de Refuge distilled what he knew about politics into his *Treatise*, which is hailed by its most recent translator as "the early modern management classic on organizational behavior."[37] In England, John Reynolds translated it, at the prompting of Sir Edward Sackville, soon to be the fourth earl of Dorset. Reynolds presented it to the future Charles I as a manual for those involved in the court "that virtue might not be robbed of her desserts, and honor by vice, but that merit and reward might still march hand in hand…"[38] The first book of the *Treatise* is dedicated to civility, which he subdivides into affability, graceful speech, and appropriate apparel. All of these are about encouraging access and trust. A courtier who speaks judiciously and pleasantly "will speedily engender a hope that they may easily have access to us, and converse with us as often as they please."[39] "Access," or "acquaintanceship," makes inferiors comfortable in opening up their thoughts, as it were, to a friend. Of course, these affable conversations must be conducted with decency and gravity, without coarse or inappropriate humor, as befits the rank and condition of the speaker and his audience.

"But as the respect and honor a great man sheweth us, is not only agreeable and pleasing to us in respect of his person: but also because his countenance and favor purchaseth us more credit in those who are present," he says, there is also a risk: "right to his disrespect and disdaine, doth not only anger us because of himself but it is insupportable in respect of the base esteem that others make of us, to see us so sleighted and neglected of him."[40] Burghley summed up this principle pithily when troubled by the lawsuits filed against him by the earl of Oxford. Reviewing the earl's "cavilations," and the response of the Queen and the court to them, he was reassured. "The greatest possession that any man can have is honor, good name, good will of many and of the best sort."[41]

Recognizing that men were very sensitive about their honor, Cecil told the earl of Bedford: "let it not appear, you use any man, with singular affection, above the rest, and yet you may use (indeed) as you see cause, men either of wisdom, or credit."[42]

De Refuge instructs in the use of jokes, flattery, and other skills of the courtier, but the point of his first book is that political success lies in skillful relations with other people. In particular, the effective courtier knows how to perform good offices for others. Favors are the "cement of human society, and the fetters and

[37] J. Chris Cooper, ed. and trans., *Eustache de Refuge, Treatise on the Court: The Early Modern Management Classic on Organizational Behaviour* (Boca Raton, FL: Orgpax Publications, 2008). Cooper does not translate the first book of the *Treatise*, focusing only on how to manage the CEO/prince.
[38] John Reynolds, trans., *A Treatise of the Court, or Instructions for Courtiers: Digested into two books. Written in French by the noble, and learned iuris-consull Monsr Denys de Refuges, Councellor of Estate, and many tymes ambassador (in foraigne parts) for ye two last French kings his masters* (London: 1617), sig. (a) v [STC (2nd edn)/7367].
[39] Reynolds, *A Treatise*, 9.   [40] Reynolds, *A Treatise*, 10.   [41] CP 160/115, dorse.
[42] BL Harleian 6990, fol. 2.

manacles" "wherewith we may enchaine and captivate others, especially at Court, where the interest and performance thereof is the...cord, that conjoins and combines so many people, one to another: yea, although for the most part, they are drawne thereunto with different and contrarie affections."[43]

He solemnly warns, however, that you should not expect direct reward for good offices. You should do good deeds without any expectation, and "take heed that he not suddenly demand of him a recompense, for fear that being discovered, to desire and crave the like, he make it apparent he did it purposely for the same end."[44]

If enchained by a favor, he says, we must seek every opportunity to repay the debt, but this is to be done carefully, since we do not want it to appear that our friend did it only to gain an advantage. The timing of the repayment is of key importance. We should be neither embarrassingly quick, nor impolitely tardy in doing it. We must seek opportunities to return it, yet we must do it without flattery or ostentation.[45] We must avoid the appearance of motives that dishonor ourselves, or our benefactors.

His *Treatise* makes plain the politesse that was practiced, or was supposed to be practiced, among people of rank as a normal negotiation of power. Recent scholarship on gift giving in honor cultures supports de Refuge's point. The archives are full of correspondence about favors sought and given, along with gifts sent and received. They were recognized as the common currency of patronage because they invoked the obligations of the honor community.[46]

Deer and other foods were the common currency of favor. When John Isham was chosen Warden of the Mercers' Company in 1567, he called on his gentle friends for help. Not being a gentleman himself, he had no deer park to draw on and no right to hunt when he gave a feast for the Company. "Having had great good will and liking of gentlemen," Isham managed to assemble thirty-three "fat and large" bucks. He put them on public display in his house and invited his friends to be impressed. They were, as his son recalled, for "it was thought, that not one man before his time nor since...had the like by a great many."[47] It was visible, and edible, evidence of his wide connection to his social betters.

In 1587 Julius Caesar, once Burghley's ward who had become the City of London's civil lawyer and was soon to be the sole judge in the Court of the Admiralty, petitioned Burghley for a deer. Caesar needed it for entertaining a company in London the following Monday.[48] Caesar's ability to call upon Burghley for such a gift, in rather groveling terms, indicates his inferior status; Burghley's willingness to give confirms his superior generosity. Both recognized that their mutual bond was confirmed and continued by the gift.[49]

Small gifts were also important currency. In 1563 the earl of Shrewsbury gave William Cecil six pasties as a token of friendship.[50]

---

[43] Reynolds, *A Treatise*, 20.   [44] Reynolds, *A Treatise*, 22.   [45] Reynolds, *A Treatise*, 26.
[46] Felicity Heal, "Food Gifts, the Household and the Politics of Exchange in Early Modern England," *Past and Present*, 199 (2008), 60–1.
[47] Thomas Isham, "The Life of John Isham," in G. D. Ramsay, ed., *John Isham Mercer and Merchant Adventurer: Two Account Books of a London Merchant in the Reign of Elizabeth I, Northamptonshire Record Society*, 21 (1962), 171.
[48] Lansd. 54/fol. 168.   [49] Heal, "Food Gifts," 41–70.
[50] Lambeth Palace Library, Talbot Papers MS.3206, fol. 441.

Of course, the most important good deeds that could be done for others were the extension of patronage by giving offices that were either in a person's grant or that the patron could get other patrons to provide. Often the provision of these appointments was, like Caesar's request for a deer, extended to recognize and maintain a relationship, rather than as a direct act of governance. Burghley recognized this when, in his letter denying the existence of a *regnum ceciliana*, he invited William Herle to consider "how and upon whom for these late years all manner of offices good and bad, spiritual and temporal have been bestowed, [to whom] the persons benefitted do belong and whom they do follow."[51] "To whom they belong" and "whom they follow" are telling phrases. All of these "courtesies" were about maintaining working relations with those below and above you, wherever you were in the hierarchy. They were conducted person to person, and they were about showing respect, deference, trust, and honor, as appropriate, in order to keep the machinery of government and self-advancement working well.

The government run by Elizabeth and Burghley can be best described as a late feudal, customary system that was gradually growing more formal. It recognized that families of power and influence should and could look after their own locales, depending on the monarch to enhance their authority, arbitrate their disputes, and organize their defense. Together with their fellow magistrates, the locally powerful worked with the Crown to keep the peace and defend the nation, when they felt like it, if they got around to it. This localization of power hobbled the monarch, because Elizabeth and her council had to motivate, mollify, and reward the appropriate powerful people. In a system with such limited coercive power, the use of the informal networks of influence was the key to the success of men like Burghley. Deference, honor, patronage, family connection, and professional acquaintance had to be used to maintain and extend the Queen's influence.

And so what was the nature of Elizabethan government: was it an authoritarian despotism? A monarchical republic? Given the way in which the Queen and council interacted with local elites, depending on honor, favor, and connection to create consensual cooperation, we can describe it as a composite state, but it is dangerous to talk of it as either a despotism or a monarchical republic. It was not despotism, because it depended upon the local leaders to enforce their common decisions. It was not a republic, in anything like the classical definition of the word, because it recognized the monarch's role and ownership of the whole. It did have shared governance, each magistrate within his degree, for common causes, which made it a common weal, bearing in mind Elyot's distinction between *res publica* and *res plebiea*. It is clear that it was a system that required management, rather than fiats, but managing had to be done with a gentle touch that evoked friendship and honor. It throve best when there was willing conformity. To Burghley and others of their generation it was obvious how to govern. They had the social knowledge to work with the magisterial classes for the common good, encouraging the disparate parts to work together.

---

[51] SP 12/181/42 fol. 155, <http://www.livesandletters.ac.uk/herle/letters/203.html>. Accessed May 30, 2014. This foliation disagrees with the manuscript, which shows this passage at SP 12/181/ fol. 160. It is in Burghley's hand.

2

Managing Virtuously

The winning of Honour is but the revealing of a man's virtue and worth without disadvantage.... Degrees of honour in subjects are, first *participes curarum* [sharers of cares], those upon whom princes do discharge the greatest weight of their affairs; their right hands, as we call them. The next are *duces belli*, great leaders; such as are princes lieutenants, and do them notable services in the wars. The third are *gratiosi*, favorites... to be solace to the sovereign, and harmless to the people. And the fourth, *negotiis pares* [those equal to the business]; such as have great places under princes, and execute their places with sufficiency. There is an honour, likewise, which may be ranked amongst the greatest... that is, of such as sacrifice themselves to death or danger for the good of their country.

Francis Bacon, 1597[1]

To modern people, who think of government in terms of centralized bureaucratic control, the weak Elizabethan state with its diffused shared power seems very odd. It is hard for us to imagine a political world in which power was decentralized, in the hands of unpaid people who assumed their duties out of a combination of ownership, birth status, and shared responsibility, and who saw the state as necessary for local liberty. Tudor people had trouble imagining any other world. The social knowledge they brought to bear on governing was shaped by custom, class, gender, education, religion, and law. Some of it was ancient, some of it was new, but what it had in common was its dispositional and practical nature; it did not require formal analysis because it was commonly accepted. It was what Pierre Bourdieu famously labeled "habitus." The Elizabethans called it "virtue."

Virtue, of course, only attaches to individuals, so the story of Elizabethan management is ultimately about personalities. Therefore, it is important to understand how Elizabethans conceived their duty and enacted their virtue. Choices, bounded by circumstance and personality, are the demonstration, or antitheses, of virtue.

The Elizabethan magistrates were mostly born in the latter half of Henry VIII's reign. Educated in the 1530s, 40s, and 50s, they were the people who ran Elizabeth's England. Bred in the world of Christian humanism, nascent Protestantism, and the royal supremacy, they were trained to live the *vita activa*, in which their virtues were embodied in their actions for the good of the common weal.

---

[1] Francis Bacon, *Essayes. Religious Meditations. Places of Perswasion & Disswasion* (1597), fols 12v; 14v [STC (2nd edn)/1137.5].

For these Elizabethans the idea of the commonwealth was powerful, and they used the common good as a touchstone for the rest of their lives. The people now sometimes classified as "monarchical republicans" were often the Edwardian "commonwealth men" under another label, continuing to think of themselves in the ways developed in their younger years. The leading civil servants were mostly Cambridge educated in the days when Sir John Cheke's version of civic humanism and Greek were fashionable. But even if they did not all attend a university, the ruling classes shared a strong consensus on the life that positions of responsibility required them to lead. They had a God-given duty to run the country under their anointed Queen.

Sir Thomas Smith sought to explain English government to his French hosts in 1564, dividing English society into four classes of men. The fourth class, proletariats (*proletarii*) or workers, he described as the "sort of men which do not rule." The other three sorts, nobles, gentlemen, and burgesses, did rule. All were represented in Parliament because they were men of substance and property, and all of them served in the magistracy: "each of these hath his part and administration in judgments, corrections of defaults, in election of offices, in appointing tributes and subsidies, and in making laws."[2]

These people took their parts noblesse oblige. Tudor magistrates ruled because of and by virtue. Virtue, for them, meant two things. First, there was the virtue of God in Christ. This divine ordering of the world, also associated with the seventh order of angels, known as powers or "virtues," made it possible for grace to overcome sin. God's power ruled, and in ruling gave power to those chosen by God to rule. As Thomas Norton's translation of Nowell's *Catechism* put it, "All things would run to ruin, and fall to nothing, unless by his virtue, and as it were by his hand, they were upholden." "The whole order of nature and changes of things...do hang upon God."[3]

Magistrates, placed in their positions by divine mandate, were expected to strive for a virtuous life pleasing to God. As it said in the biblical book of Kings, they were to heed the charge of the Lord to walk in his ways and keep his "statutes and commandments."[4]

The Almighty expected those to whom He gave authority to discipline His people, for the sins of the people would be held against those who bore authority over the *proletarii*. As Archbishop Sandys announced at Paul's Cross early in the reign, God would require the blood of the magistrates if through negligence, evil example, or want of correction those in their charge were lost.[5] Francis Darby repeated this warning in 1601, declaring that if Parliament did not curb drunkenness the Almighty would "lay his heavy hand of wrath and indignation upon this land."[6]

---

[2] Thomas Smith, *De republica Anglorum*, ed. Mary Dewar (Cambridge: Cambridge University Press, 1982), 76–7.

[3] Alexander Nowell, *A Catechisme, or First Instruction and Learning of Christian Religion. Translated out of Latine into Englishe* (1570), fol. 25v [STC (2nd edn)/1525:12].

[4] Geneva Bible, 1 Kings 2:3.

[5] J. Ayre, ed., *The Sermons of Edwin Sandys* (Cambridge: Parker Society, 1842), 265–6.

[6] BL Stowe Ms. 362, fols 84v–85.

The duty of the magistracy to God was stressed whenever Elizabethans were involved in the legal system. Assize sermons emphasized and re-emphasized it; members of Parliament invoked it; and even jury charges summarized it. Richard Crompton's 1584 edition of Fitzherbert's book on the office and authority of the justices of the peace includes a charge to a jury that defines the role of those invited by the Queen to participate in ruling the nation. The exhortation is a complete cosmology beginning with the Creation and progressing through the Fall, the unruly life in a state of nature, and the Flood, arriving at God's revelation of the Ten Commandments. After that, God set kings over men, who must obey them as God's ministers, protecting the righteous and taking due vengeance on sinners. The justices of the peace and members of the jury share in that authority, owing their duty to the Queen and to God, a sacred trust sealed with an oath on the Bible. The oath binds them, among other things, to enforce the "good laws and statutes, which we have received by the authority of the high Court of Parliament of this realm, for the common wealth of her Majesty's subjects."[7]

The right of members of Parliament to give consent for the entire realm came to them through their birth and office, a natural result of their place in the social hierarchy. It was not granted by "the people"; it came from God through the monarch. From the beginning of parliaments it had been assumed that the commoners elected to them were armed with a power of attorney (*plena potestas*) that gave them the authority to bind those who sent them. The Elizabethan political theorists Hooker, Smith, and Lambarde were in agreement that members of the Commons gave consent on behalf of those *for* whom they were sent, not *by* whom they were sent.[8] Thus, consultation with a constituency was not necessary. They spoke and voted on any issue freely, without reference to those on whose behalf they appeared. Moreover, it meant that the person representing a place need not be from that place. As Sir John Neale observed, "there was no incongruity in employing a stranger as attorney."[9]

Their votes bound the entire nation, but the entire nation was not invited to the selection of members of Parliament. The entire upper house was unelected, with each peer speaking only for himself. Not even the bishops, dividing their time between Parliament and Convocation, consulted their clergy. Their right to vote came from God, their social position, and, crudely, their power.

In the nether house the members for boroughs held their seats because of choices made according to local customs, but seldom through election. Frequently the aldermen of a borough would make the choice, or at least the nomination, presenting their choice to the common council or the freemen for ratification. Thus we cannot say that the borough representatives sitting in Parliament had been elected in the modern sense.

---

[7] "An Exhortation to the Jurye," in Anthony Fitzherbert and Richard Crompton, *L'Office et aucthoritie de justices de peace 1584*, ed. P. R. Glazebrook (London: Professional Books Ltd, 1972), sig. CCi–[CCiiij v].

[8] Vernon F. Snow, ed., *Parliament in Elizabethan England: John Hooker's Order and Usage* (New Haven: Yale University Press, 1971), 182. David Dean and I have argued this point before in *Parliaments of Elizabethan England* (Oxford: Blackwell, 1989), 2–4.

[9] J. E. Neale, *The Elizabethan House of Commons* (Harmondsworth: Penguin, 1963), 151.

The county members had been returned by the electors of their shires, but the number of men who could meet the financial qualifications for the franchise was small, and deference bade them to consent to the choices of their betters. As the Privy Council put it in 1597, "we doubt not much but the principal persons of that county will have good regard to make choice without partiality or affection..."[10] Those "principal persons" were frequently the leaders of the few dominant families, making their selection long before the electors were invited to ratify their choices. As Mark Kishlansky has demonstrated, a "free" election was one in which there was no opposition. Members of Parliament were "selected" by consensus of a community's leading men. Politics was not a place where ideologies competed; it was a place in which social standing was ratified.[11]

So magistrates, placed in authority by God's virtue, had to walk in the ways of the Lord, modeling self-control and responsibility. Accepting God's calling, they served, at least theoretically, out of duty. It was this self-control that was expressed in another usage of the word "virtue." This virtue was manifested by a life lived in conformity with the principles of morality. The virtuous governor voluntarily obeyed and enforced God's moral laws and abstained, on moral grounds, from vice. Elyot recognized this in his *Book Named the Governor*, noting that "virtue be an election annexed unto our nature, and consisting in a mean, which is determined by reason."[12]

God demanded that magistrates recognize the higher good of the community, and Elizabethan magistrates in search of a rational understanding of virtue, enforced by conscience, found it clarified in custom, in law, in the classics, and in theology. It was assumed that reason and revelation worked together to guide them. Therefore, their virtue was a compound of feudal values, in which service to one's lord was enshrined, humanistic ideas of *virtu* imbibed from extended exposure to Roman authors, and the workings of English legal culture. It assumed the natural existence of a monarch, and it envisioned members of the governing classes as a part of the same natural chain of being. People of this class could quote Romans 13:1, "Let every soul be subject unto the higher powers: for there is no power but of God: and the powers that are, are ordained of God."[13]

Members of the magisterial community knew that this passage meant not only that they should obey their monarch, but also that they, in their positions as landlords, aldermen, justices, and other roles, ought to be obeyed. God had instituted them, too. According to their places in the hierarchy, everyone served for conscience sake. Conscience required them to "Give all men therefore their duty, tribute, to whom you owe tribute: custom, to whom you owe custom; fear to whom fear: honor to whom you owe honor."[14] Magistrates of all kinds were the ministers of

[10] APC, 27, 361.

[11] Mark Kishlansky, *Parliamentary Selection: Social and Political Choice in Early Modern England* (Cambridge: Cambridge University Press, 1986), 11–12.

[12] Elyot, *Governor*, 2.

[13] Romans 13:1, quoting the Geneva Bible translation. Educated Elizabethans probably knew it better in the Latin of the Vulgate: "omnis anima potestatibus sublimioribus subdita sit non est enim potestas nisi a Deo quae autem sunt a Deo ordinatae sunt."

[14] Romans 13:5–7. Quoting the Geneva Bible translation.

God. This reason was exercised in the seat of magisterial judgment. In 1584 Richard Crompton reminded the justices reading his edition of Fitzherbert's *Handbook* that Bracton likened the seat of justice to the throne of God, and justice was exercised for God, not for men.[15]

As Sir John Cheke formulated it, "the magistrate is the ordinance of God, appointed by him with the sword of punishment...and therefore that that is done by the magistrate is done by the ordinance of God...because he hath the execution of God's office."[16] The duties that fell on people of their status were described by St Paul as requiring them to cast away the works of darkness and put on the armor of light, governing in accordance with God's law of love and the second table of the Ten Commandments. As William Cecil was wont to say, "seek first the Kingdom of Heaven," for honesty and religion "are the grounds and ends of good men's actions."[17]

The magistrates might also have been able to quote Isaiah 49:23 when thinking of the Tudor dynasty: "And kings shalbe thy nursing fathers, and queens shalbe thy nurses."[18] This appears on the frontispiece of the 1584 statute book of Corpus Christi College, Cambridge. The quotation from Isaiah topped an illustration of Elizabeth being crowned by the virtues Justice and Mercy, while supported by the virtues Fortitude and Prudence. These same virtues graced the frontispiece of the Bishops' Bible, a corrected edition sponsored by Archbishop Parker. For use by all clergy, it showed Elizabeth supported by virtues. Justice and Mercy were crowning her, with Prudence and Fortitude in support (see Fig. 2.1).[19]

In the statute book and some versions of the Bishops' Bible, a cartouche beneath the Queen reads "non me pudet Evangelii Christi virtus enim Dei est ad salutem omni credenti" ("For I am not ashamed of the Gospel of Christ: for it is the power of God unto salvation to everyone that believes.")[20] Under this is a small depiction of Archbishop of Canterbury Matthew Parker, the former Master of Corpus Christi, preaching, annexing the authority of the church to that of God's anointed Queen.

The message that rule was upheld by virtues was clear to the magistracy, although the Elizabethans were troubled by the requirement that they live virtuously and enforce virtue according to their consciences guided by reason.

The idea that God's chosen rulers had to be supported by virtue was Biblical, but the images of virtue put before the public were often classical. If Tudor people knew they had to govern virtuously, their role models for political virtue were derived from Greek and Roman sources, with their didactic historical tales.

---

[15] "As toutes mes companions del myddle Temple que sunt Iustices de peace," in Fitzherbert and Crompton, *L'Office...de justices de peace*, np.

[16] Sir John Cheke, *The Hurt of Sedicion Howe Greueous it is to a Commune Welth* (1549), sig. Aiiij [STC (2nd edn)/5109].

[17] Collins, 68–9.

[18] Isaiah 49:23, quoting the Geneva Bible. Vulgate: "Et erunt reges nutricii tui, et reginae eorum nutrices tuae."

[19] Corpus Christi College, Cambridge, MS 582, front end paper. *The Holi Bible* (London: 1569), frontispiece [STC 2nd edn)/2105].

[20] Romans 1:16.

Fig. 2.1. "Elizabeth Supported by Virtues," *The Holi Bible* (London: 1569), frontispiece [STC (2nd edn)/2105]. Early English books tract supplement interim guide/Harl.5936. British Library.

Sir Thomas Elyot had made this clear in his discussion of the education of the ruling classes in his *Book Named the Governor*. Elyot's work is the first that explicitly takes training the magistrates of England as its purpose. Elyot, who claimed to be self-educated, had extensive managerial experience in local, regional, and royal structures. It was a meditation on governing by a practitioner. As he says in the preface, he was "continually trained in some daily affairs of the public weal...almost from my childhood."[21] Born in 1490, be became a friend of Thomas More and probably an acquaintance of Erasmus. He was schooled in the Middle Temple as a lawyer, following in the footsteps of his father, who was a judge of the Common Pleas. Beginning in 1515, he spent years as a justice of the peace and was twice a sheriff. From 1510 to 1526 he was clerk to the justices of assize for the western circuit. In 1523 he became the senior clerk of the King's Council, handling the affairs of the Court of Star Chamber as well as conciliar business. When Wolsey fell, Elyot lost the council job, but he was knighted for his services in 1530. In the leisure that followed, this experienced public servant wrote *The Book Named the Governor*. Shortly after he dedicated it to Henry VIII, Elyot was sent as Henry's ambassador to the emperor Charles V. Elyot failed to advance the cause of Henry's divorce, and he fell from grace at the court. He turned to writing for the rest of his life.

Elyot was a monarchist. He dismissed Aristotle's argument for a mixed polity quickly, insisting that there would be chaos without one sovereign ruler. But rather than lingering on the education of princes, he immediately took up the discussion of the inferior governors who rule on the monarch's behalf. Elyot called the wise man who was granted authority as an inferior governor a *magistratus*. Elyot Anglicized it as "magistrate" for lack of an English word to describe these officers. "I intend," he said, to write of the magistrates' "education and virtue in manners which they have in common with princes," as well as their offices and duties.[22] Elyot, experienced as he was in government, was recognizing the decentralized nature of rule under the English monarchy.

Although he cloaked it in humanist rhetoric, Elyot's understanding of the managerial reality is immediately apparent. He wants his governors to be virtuous, but he also recognized that superiority of birth was one of the key ways in which English governors received power, and that these men had to have enough wealth to support their service. Moreover, he says, they need good manners to be good governors. And these manners are those of the gently born, since "where virtue is in a gentleman it is commonly mixed with more sufferance, more affability, and mildness, than for the most part it is in a person rural or of a very base lineage." When a person is "worshipful"—has the birth and virtues of a gentleman—the people will obey him less grudgingly. Of course, it is natural that gently born people have these manners, since their parents can afford to give them the education that creates such paragons of affable severity.[23]

The virtuous education Elyot prescribed for the magistrates-to-be was an exhaustive training in the liberal arts. Once basic fluency in Latin and Greek was achieved, elegance of expression was added by introducing the children to great

---

[21] Elyot, *Governor*, xiii.   [22] Elyot, *Governor*, 13.   [23] Elyot, *Governor*, 14.

poets. Homer should be read first, and then the *Aeneid*, since they reinforce each other. Vergil's *Bucolics* are there, too, as are Lucan, Ovid, and Hesiod, all chosen because they unite great style with tales children like. The children, "inflamed by the frequent reading of noble poets," are primed to desire personal experience of great matters and model themselves on heroes.[24]

In his *Defence of Poesie*, Sidney expounded this point. The poet's job, he said, was "feigning notable images of virtues, vices, or what else, with that delightful teaching." He knew that everyone, children and adults, preferred to learn through stories, and that great poetry could teach good behavior. "Glad they will be to hear the tales of Hercules, Achilles, Cyrus, Aeneas, and hearing them, must needs hear the right description of wisdom, value, and justice..."[25]

Music, painting, and poetry teach the young governors about harmony, a deeply political principle that they will recognize when they read Plato and Aristotle on public weals. Dancing with women taught lessons of concord and moderation, gave form to the mean between sloth and celerity, and taught a man to do things in due time and in due measure, learning "of a brawl in dancing."[26]

At about the age of fourteen Elyot's young governors are set to the real work of learning how to govern themselves and others, reading rhetoric, history, and cosmology. This learning prepares them to give counsel and to speak in assemblies. In particular, the child, at about the age of seventeen, when his reason was developed enough to bridle his "courage," would enter the most important part of the curriculum. Beginning with Aristotle's *Ethics*, the student would go on to Plato and to Cicero's *De officiis*:

> Lord God, what incomparable sweetness of words and matter shall he find in the...works of Plato and Cicero; wherein is joined gravity with delectation, excellent wisdom with divine eloquence, absolute virtue with pleasure incredible, and every place is so enforced with profitable counsel joined with honesty, that those three books be almost sufficient to make a perfect and excellent governor.[27]

The last book to come into the curriculum was the Bible. Every nobleman needed to know it, but it was to be treated as a sacred jewel. Those who failed to read it with faith might be struck dead, like the priest who touched the Ark of the Covenant.

Elyot was very clear about the importance of this curriculum for the magisterial classes. All this dancing, art, history, and language study prepared a man for the active life of governing. The man who had this training would be able to speak as well as Cicero had spoken when he prosecuted Verres.[28]

Tudor governors understood that the key tool of government was first and foremost the art of rhetoric. Magistrates had to be able to speak convincingly if they were to be effective leaders. England needed a virtuous magisterial class that had the tools requisite to leadership in a culture that was primarily oral, and which required men of standing to cooperate wisely with one another in interchanges that worked like good dancing. The purpose of their speaking was action, so they

---

[24] Elyot, *Governor*, 31–3.
[25] Philip Sidney, *The Defence of Poesie* (1595), sig. C.3; E 2 [STC (2nd edn)/904:16].
[26] Elyot, *Governor*, 77–81.   [27] Elyot, *Governor*, 39.   [28] Elyot, *Governor*, 51–6.

had to have at their fingertips the inspirational exempla provided by biblical, classical, and historical authors. An exhortation was expected to apply the weight of historical experience to the problem at hand.

Richard Rainolde, dedicating his *Foundations of Rhetoric*, explained it was the capstone of learning. "For the end of all arts and sciences, and of all noble acts and enterprises is virtue…Who so is adorned with nobility and virtue…will," with good rhetoric, "move and allure the favor and support of virtue in any other," as Cicero says, "even to love those whom we never saw, but by good fame and bruit beautified to us."[29]

Sir Thomas Wilson recalled that Sir John Cheke taught his students to imitate the Greek orator Demosthenes. The Greek was worthy because he "so familiarly applying himself to the sense and understanding of the common people," provided such a good example "that none ever was more fit to make an English man tell his tale praise worthily in any open hearing, either in parliament or in pulpit, or otherwise."[30]

The utility of this training is obvious when we look at addresses to justices, juries, special commissions, and other groups charged with governing. For example, William Lambarde's speech to a special session of the justices in Kent, called to investigate a disturbance in which rioters tried to chop down a house, is a textbook example. He lays out his "*loci communis*" in just the way Elyot describes them in *The Governor*.[31] We could cite dozens if not hundreds of speeches in the courts, to Parliament, at public celebrations, and in churches that used the tools of rhetoric, following a cursus that proceeded from ancients to moderns, and finally to the Bible.

Of course, speaking included spoken Latin, and Latin prepared students to speak English. On December 10, 1563, the court was at Windsor, hiding from the plague that was ravaging London. At dinner that day in Sir William Cecil's chamber there was a lively debate about how to educate young men in Latin, provoked by a report that students had run away from Eton to avoid the beatings. Some believed that beating was necessary to force them to learn it, while others, including Cecil, disagreed. They bantered pro and con, prompting Sir Roger Ascham, the Queen's Latin Secretary, to write a book on the question called *The Schoolmaster*.

Ascham recalled that at the time he and Elizabeth were reading Demosthenes' oration against Aeschines, in Greek, which drove home the need for leaders to speak with eloquence. It prompted him to think about how better pedagogies could produce that eloquence.[32] The result was a guide to teaching Latin well, without violence. The imparting of this learning, he said, needed no more justification than that provided by his friend Johan Sturmius in his book *De institutione principis*: the language opened up both eloquence and virtue. Here, Ascham used

[29] Richard Rainolde, *A Booke Called the Foundacion of Rhetorike…* (1563), Dedication [STC (2nd edn)/20925a.5].

[30] Thomas Wilson, trans., *The Three Orations of Demosthenes Chiefe Orator among the Grecians…against king Philip of Macedonie: most nedefull to be redde in these daungerous dayes, of all them that loue their countries libertie, and desire to take warning for their better auayle, by example of others…* (1570), Dedication [STC (2nd edn)/6578].

[31] Conyers Read, ed., *William Lambarde and Local Government: His "Ephemeris" and Twenty-nine Charges to Juries and Commissions* (Ithaca, NY: Cornell University Press, 1962), vii; 153–7.

[32] Roger Ascham, *The Scholemaster* (1570), sig. B.i–B.ii [STC (2nd edn)/832].

the example of Xenophon's book on the education of King Cyrus of Persia, the *Cyropaedia*, suggesting that English children needed to be governed to learn to self-govern. (Xenophon's idealized King Cyrus was a persistent model, a man that everyone from Cicero to Cecil saw as model general and governor.)[33]

Ascham argued that children had to learn through good precepts read in books, and by aping the virtues of their teachers and their betters. Gentlemen of the court, and schoolmasters, were living models. In his own education at St John's, Cambridge, Ascham recalled, it was the example of Sir John Cheke and Dr Redman that taught him most eloquently. Their lives "of excellency in learning, of godliness in living, of diligence in studying, of counsel in exhorting, of good order in all thing[s]" had made St John's the nursery of more learned men than the entire University of Louvain.[34]

That St John's was the nursery of learned leaders of the Elizabethan state was obvious to the men at Cecil's dinner table that evening in 1563. Many were alumni. When he formed Elizabeth's government, Cecil sought like-minded colleagues; bringing together so many Cambridge men that Winthrop Hudson once explained the Elizabethan settlement through a book entitled *The Cambridge Connection*. Hudson concluded that this small, Cambridge-educated elite, with deep ties through marriage and patronage, had, thanks to their educations, a shared vision of the state and the religion it ought to support.[35] It was this group, thought Wallace MacCaffrey, using its education, that crafted a new understanding of how royal governance worked. Their expertise, their offices, and their virtues gave them independent standing as lesser magistrates.[36]

This sort of education led these men to think and talk like Romans of the late Republic. But, of course, these men were Christians as well as classicists, often using classical rhetoric to explain a Christian system of values. Educated in virtue, it was assumed they were able to apply it.

When Matthew Hutton, Archbishop of York, wrote Burghley in 1597 about appointing a replacement for the earl of Huntingdon as Lord President of the North he expressed a common opinion:

> If the Queen could resolve on a man, her commission and instructions, and the ordinary proceeding of the Court, known to the learned counsel here, would sufficiently enable him. Lord Huntingdon was very raw when he came down, but having a resolute will to serve God and Her Majesty, grew to great experience. If the Queen choose one who fears God, and loves the present State, God will enable him.[37]

"Fears God, and loves the present state" sums up the virtue of the magistrate. The First Table of the Decalogue commanded fear of God, and, by extension, God's

---

[33] Ascham, *Scholemaster*, fol. 13. Cicero said that, as the governor of Cilicia, he had "put into practice the whole *Education of Cyrus*." Cicero, *Letters to Friends*, ed. D. R. Shackleton Bailey (Cambridge, MA: Harvard University Press, 2001), 2, no. 114 (IX.25), 3.

[34] Ascham, *Schoolmaster*, fols 20v–21.

[35] Winthrop Hudson, *The Cambridge Connection and the Elizabethan Settlement of 1559* (Durham, NC: Duke University Press, 1980).

[36] Wallace MacCaffrey, *The Shaping of the Elizabethan Regime* (Princeton, NJ: Princeton University Press, 1968), 479–83.

[37] TNA SP 12/262 fol. 120.

anointed ruler. Glossing the sixth commandment, the Geneva Bible explains that honoring your father and mother actually means that you must honor "all that have authority over us."

Much of this thinking about God and virtue had been honed in the reign of King Edward VI, a formative period of the Elizabethan magistracy.[38] Thomas Becon, chaplain to Edward Seymour, duke of Somerset and Lord Protector to Edward VI, wrote a little work entitled *The Governance of Virtue*, dedicating it to Edward's daughter, Jane Seymour. Much of the book is about fearing God and avoiding idolatry, especially papist idolatry. It expatiated on obedience, just in case the "magistrates and higher powers" were thought not to be doing right by the commonwealth. He provided a battery of scriptural references to use when tempted to disobedience, beginning with Romans 13. God, he noted, "cannot suffer his magistrates to be disobeyed, his commonweals to be disturbed, his politic or civil laws to be condemned, his godly and honest orders to be broken."[39]

The second branch of Christian virtue came in the next six commandments of the Decalogue, and they were generically sins and crimes, such as murder and robbery, covetousness and adultery, that the magistrates should avoid personally and punish corporately.

Becon justified his book on virtue first by explaining the importance of virtue in people raised to rule. The ancients, though not Christians and without fear of God, knew virtue was important. They were anxious for it

> but only unto the advancement of themselves, unto the maintenance of good politic civil and honest orders, unto the ability of ruling in a commonweal, unto the polishing of their wit, unto eloquence, unto immortality of their name enforced not both themselves to be learned and also sought all means possible to have their children brought up in good letters.

Now, said Becon, pagan virtues were reinforced by Christian piety.[40]

In 1559 Elizabeth was the dedicatee of a translation of the Lutheran jurist Johannes Ferrarius Montanus's book *Touching the good ordering of a common weal wherein as well magistrates, as private persons, be put in remembrance of their duties.* In the dedication, William Bavande, the translator, explained that, although the law tried to make her subjects "embrace justice, temperance, upright dealing, and all kinds of virtues," it never fully succeeded.[41] Therefore magistrates were needed to encourage virtue by enforcing the law.

---

[38] Catharine Davies, *A Religion of the Word: The Defence of the Reformation in the Reign of Edward VI* (Manchester: Manchester University Press, 2002), 140–68.

[39] Thomas Becon, *The Gouernaunce of Vertue teaching al faithfull Christians, howe they oughte dayly to leade their lyfe, [and] fruitefully to spend their tyme vnto the glorye of God and the health of their owne soules*, in *The Early Works of Thomas Becon*, ed. John Ayre (Cambridge: Cambridge University Press, 1843), 393–485; quoting 456.

[40] Becon, *The Gouernaunce of Vertue*, 398.

[41] William Bavande, trans., *A Woorke of Ioannes Ferrarius Montanus, touchynge the good orderynge of a common weale wherein as well magistrates, as priuate persones, bee put in remembraunce of their dueties, not as the philosophers in their vaine tradicions haue deuised, but according to the godlie institutions and sounde doctrine of christianitie* [1559] sig. Cii v [STC (2nd edn)/10831].

The magistrate who esteemed both God and the Queen by living virtuously and enforcing virtue, was himself honorable, for the result of virtue was honor. As Burghley liked to say, "Honor is the reward of virtue, but it is got with labor and held with danger."[42] Honor, says Malcom Smuts, was at the heart of the cultural system, applying especially to peers and gentlemen. They were expected to show "prowess, courage, loyalty, liberality and magnanimity, along with a fierce pride and assertiveness associated with those born to command." Ironically, although honor was expected to be inborn in men of the upper social ranks, it had, as Burghley noted, to be constantly demonstrated in actions.[43] Honor was a matter of good reputation among your peers, based on one's prudent actions. It was less derived from internal virtues than from society's judgment. It came from multiple attributes that could be mixed in many ways.[44]

The gentlemen who ran local government were very aware that lineage made one gentle, and that honorable service was expected of them and their ilk. Service was a duty, and in doing it, honor had to be maintained.[45] As Richard Cust has put it, "Honor can be said to mediate between the aspirations of the individual and the judgment of society. It therefore provides a means of exploring the values and norms of a society, and also the ways in which individuals compete to sustain or increase their status and power within that society."[46]

To make Cust's description concrete, look at the gates Dr Caius built for his college in the 1560s. New students entered the college through the Gate of Humility. While studying in the college they would pass through the Gate of Virtue every day, and finally, when they left to receive their degrees, they departed through the Gate of Honor. Students came from abasement to honor through virtue. For the magistracy, the Gate of Honor was primarily guarded by the Queen, which made honor an important managerial tool. Honoring, withholding honor, and dishonoring were forms of influence.

As Sir Francis Bacon explained it, honor was received through the Queen by performing various roles:

> The winning of Honor is but the revealing of a man's virtue and worth without disadvantage.... Degrees of honor in subjects are, first *participes curarum* [sharers of cares], those upon whom princes do discharge the greatest weight of their affairs; their right hands, as we call them. The next are *duces belli*, great leaders; such as are princes lieutenants, and do them notable services in the wars. The third are *gratiosi*, favorites; such as exceed not this scantling, to be solace to the sovereign, and harmless to the people.

---

[42] Collins, 70.

[43] R. Malcom Smuts, *Culture and Power in England, 1585–1685* (London: Macmillan, 1999), 8.

[44] Felicity Heal, "Reputation and Honour in Court and Country: Lady Elizabeth Russell and Sir Thomas Hoby," *Transactions of the Royal Historical Society*, 6th ser., 6 (1996), 161–2. Linda Pollock, "Honor, Gender, and Reconciliation in Elite Culture, 1570–1770," *Journal of British Studies*, 46, 1 (2007), 5–6.

[45] Felicity Heal and Clive Holmes, *The Gentry in England and Wales 1500–1700* (Stanford, CA: Stanford University Press, 1994), 24–33.

[46] Richard Cust, "Honour and Politics in Early Stuart England: The Case of Beaumont v. Hastings," *Past and Present*, 149 (Nov. 1995), 58–9.

And the fourth, *negotiis pares* [those equal to the business]; such as have great places under princes, and execute their places with sufficiency.[47]

The tensions created by the need to live and rule honorably by pursuing godly virtue were partially mediated by the law. The law, especially the common law, was taken to be almost a form of revelation and its enforcement was proof of magisterial virtue. In the formulation being taught by Christopher St Germain and Thomas Starkey in the 1530s, English law was made of a compound of the laws of nature, reason, custom, and what we would call statute and precedent.[48] Their students, who became the leaders of Elizabethan society, presided over the reformulation of the sources of law, making Parliament supreme. In the process the natural law and the law of God were both degraded in authority. Now Parliament had the right to provide the ultimate definition of law. This made Elizabethan legal thinking, and parliamentary activity, exciting and transformative.[49]

Across the Elizabethan era the study of law became more and more popular, and the long domination of Elizabeth's government by Sir William Cecil and Sir Nicholas Bacon, both lawyers, contributed to an increasing emphasis on the law and the importance of its enforcement by the gentlemen of the commissions of the peace, coroners, burgesses, and all the other officers who served their locales. Bringing their humanist ideals and their rhetorical training to bear on issues of governance, they evolved and promoted the understanding and use of the law.[50]

The power of legal thinking in Elizabeth's reign helped transition the culture toward a more active and powerful centralized state, but for the Elizabethans it was the safeguard that could ensure social coherence while permitting the rethinking of the place of the individual and the state spawned by the Reformation. In the radical privatization of the soul inherent in the Protestant belief that each person was her or his own priest, guided only by scripture and saved only by faith, the self is separated from the social.[51] For strict predestinarians, this was especially true, since Calvinism subjected the state to the elect. It was this that prompted William Perkins to write his *Cases of Conscience* and Richard Hooker to counter in his *Laws of Ecclesiastical Polity.*[52]

The rarified air of theology was exhilarating, but in the daily lives of the magistrates it still came down to the frame provided by the law. Those who acquired a copy of Fitzherbert's *New Book of the Justice of the Peace* first printed in 1538, or

[47] Francis Bacon, *Essayes. Religious meditations. Places of perswasion & disswasion. Seene and allowed* (1597), fols 12v; 14v [STC (2nd edn)/1137.5].

[48] DeLloyd J. Guth, "Law," in Robert Tittler and Norman Jones, eds, *A Companion to Tudor Britain* (Oxford: Blackwell Publishing, 2004), 80.

[49] G. R. Elton, "Lex Terrae Victrix: The Triumph of Parliamentary Law in the Sixteenth Century," in D. M. Dean and N. L. Jones, eds, *The Parliaments of Elizabethan England* (Oxford: Basil Blackwell, 1990), 15–36.

[50] Christopher W. Brooks, *Law, Politics and Society in Early Modern England* (Cambridge: Cambridge University Press, 2008), 59–61.

[51] For an excellent formulation of this argument see Debora Kuller Shuger, *Habits of Thought in the English Renaissance: Religion, Politics and the Dominant Culture* (Berkeley: University of California Press, 1990), 103–4. See also David Little, *Religion, Order and Law*, 2nd edn (Chicago: University of Chicago Press, 1984), 132–66.

[52] Little, *Religion, Order and Law*, 81–130.

Lambarde's *Eirenarcha* of 1579, or Crompton's much extended version of Fitzherbert entitled, in Law French, *L'office et aucthoritie de justices de peace*, first issued in 1583, were not looking for theological insights. They were engaged in the pragmatic duties of the magistracy. It was their job, as William Lambarde told a quarter session at Maidstone in 1596, to tune the organ pipes of the laws to make a delightful harmony to the commonwealth.

> The distribution of our country's laws is in great favor put into the hands of you and us, our parts and duty it is so to order and move the same that they may sound out and speak to all, not confusedly and without delight, but melodiously and so as it may be pleasing to God's will, answerable to her Majesty's desire, joyful to the hearts of others, and comfortable to our own consciences.[53]

Favored by God and the Queen by appointment to the commission of the peace, they were to rule according to their informed consciences for the good of their neighbors. The same was true for those favored with appointments as bailiffs, constables, coroners, and others charged with keeping the peace. Of course, it was doubly true for those born to rank. They were responsible, and that responsibility was expressed through their use of the law.

In a sermon on the virtues of the magistrate, delivered by Robert Pricke of Denham, Suffolk, we get a list of these virtues. Pricke describes six of them: wisdom, courage, true fear of God, true dealing, hatred of covetousness, and "That in his whole behavior he give a good example to his subjects."[54]

Wisdom is necessary, he says,

> Because it were an unworthy thing, that a body endued with light and understanding (such as the common-wealth is) should be ruled and guided by a head, blind and void of right judgment and reason.... without this virtue the magistrate cannot possibly discern between good and evil, right and wrong, lawful and unlawful. He cannot understand the positive laws of his own dominion; much less the law of God, the true ground and foundation of all good laws. He cannot exhort and encourage his subjects to that which is good, nor dissuade and exhort them from evil. Lastly he can determine nothing according to equity.[55]

The true fear of God was, says Pricke, the thing that restrained the magistrate from evil and caused him to perform his duties. Magistrates who truly fear God will do nothing to displease Him, and "practice the duties which he hath commanded. So that this excellent virtue, it is that which doeth season, and make good use of all graces wherewith the magistrate is endued."[56] He clinches this with Jehoshaphat's exhortation to the judges of Israel to be careful about what they do, for they execute the judgments of the Lord. Fearing the Lord, they will not play favorites or take bribes.[57]

[53] Conyers Read, ed., *William Lambarde and Local Government*, 125.

[54] Robert Pricke, *The Doctrine of Superioritie, and of Subiection, contained in the fift commandement of the holy law of Almightie God. Which is the fundamental ground, both of all Christian subiection: and also of like Christian government, as well in church, and common-wealth, as in very schoole and private familie* [1609], sig. C6 [STC (2nd edn)/20337].

[55] Pricke, *The Doctrine of Superioritie*, sig. C2v–3.

[56] Pricke, *The Doctrine of Superioritie*, sig. C3–4.   [57] 2 Chron. 19:6–7.

The magistrates lived in a complex network of interlocking local courts run by local gentlemen whose lives and deportment were expected to be models of Christian magisterial behavior. Their activity meant that the policies of the state were as much local creations as central, since the laws were filtered through the needs and perceptions of local officers and the communities in which they lived. Elizabethan magistrates lived in a cozy world where the insularity of the magistrates was seldom interrupted. Nonetheless, they enforced the law as they understood it and as they needed it.[58]

Of course, they and their selected representatives made the laws they enforced through parliamentary statutes. Consequently, the statute law reflected their changing values as well as making their values enforceable.

All of this is important because members of the magisterial classes had, perforce, experience with the law. Participation in local enforcement was seen as a sign of one's social status, and ambitious men sought it. Even those without ambition needed a working familiarity with it, since people of property had to be conversant in the complex web of legality that enveloped them. The Elizabethans were notoriously litigious, and many a gentleman had books like William West's *Symbolaeography which may be termed the art, description or image of instruments, extra-iudicial, as couenants, contracts, obligations, conditions, feffements, graunts, wills, &c...* on his library shelves, helping him act as his own lawyer.[59] It became popular for gentry families to send their sons to the Inns of Court for a year or two, not to make them lawyers but to make them conversant in the law.

All of this familiarity with the law meant that legal ways of thinking were widely spread and understood. The common law state of mind was common among the magistracy, with its categories influencing the ways in which people thought. But, of course, there were other sides of the law that were important both philosophically and practically. The links between human law and natural law were held to be strong, and the civil lawyers of the equity courts and the church courts operated within the logical systems of the natural law.

The need for a familiarity with the laws had been recognized late in the reign of Henry VIII when Nicholas Bacon, William Carey, and Thomas Denton coauthored a report calling for the creation of a new Inn of Court, run like a humanist academy, for educating the sons of the rich and powerful in the liberal arts and the law.[60] This education mattered because, as Bacon later said, "The law itself is but a durable and dead thing; the servitors and ministers to the law...give life thereto."[61]

What did it mean to be taught to think legally? And how did that influence governance? One of the things most striking about the common law was its emphasis

---

[58] Steven Hindle, *The State and Social Change in Early Modern England, c.1550–1640* (New York: St Martin's Press, 2000), 175.

[59] William West, *Symbolaeography which may be termed the art, description or image of instruments, extra-iudicial, as couenants, contracts, obligations, conditions, feffements, graunts, wills, &c...* [1592] [STC (2nd edn)/25267a].

[60] R. M. Fisher, "Thomas Cromwell, Humanism and Educational Reform," *Bulletin of the Institute for Historical Research*, 50 (1977), 151–63. D. S. Bland, "Henry VIII's Royal Commission on the Inns of Court," *Journal for the Society of Teachers of Law*, 10 (1969), 178–94.

[61] Quoted in W. J. Jones, *The Elizabethan Court of Chancery* (Oxford: Clarendon Press, 1967), 32.

on procedural correctness, so it certainly emphasized a hyper-awareness of due process. A simple mistake in drafting could invalidate a legal proceeding. For instance, if you drew up an information against an offender under a statute passed by the Parliament "holden" on January 23, 1559, it could be thrown out because the Parliament's opening was delayed until January 25, 1559, and so the information should have said.[62] This sort of error produced a "jeofail," an error that nullified the action unless there was legal room for the person starting it to admit to the court "I have failed" (*I'ay failly* in Law French) and get it continued.

This precision in drafting was complicated by the languages used in the courts. The pleading in common law cases was in Law French, the peculiar legal dialect inherited from the Normans, which had evolved into a tongue understood only by those who attended an Inn of Court. In the equity courts, the language of record was Latin. Latin, of course, was used in the ecclesiastical courts, so, with the exception of places like the Court of Requests and Chancery, where proceeding by English bill was permitted, familiarity with the law required learning, which set the magisterial classes somewhat apart from everyone else. It took some knowledge to understand and use a system that provided bilingual instructions like: "Le forme de certificat de recognisance de peace sur le dit briefe de cerciorare, est in tiel maner: Virtute istius brevis, ego G.S. unus custodum pacis in com. S. infrascript..." (It begins in Law French: "The form of the certificate of recognizance of peace under the said writ of certiorari, is in this manner," switching to Latin, "By virtue of this letter, I G.S., a justice of the peace in the county of S. beneath written...")[63]

The law demanded precision of language, too, a thing that played into the hands of the humanist educators. Although it is, as Sir John Baker notes, very difficult to draw direct lines between the humanistic education and the changes in English law in the sixteenth century, it is undoubtedly there. Familiarity with classical texts brought them to an historical understanding of legal texts, informed by a sense of anachronism. This was not so much evident in their pleadings as in their way of approaching legal precedent and in the rising use of "master" narrators of the English law, such as Bracton.[64]

Baker also notes that the new learning promoted a more rational approach to the law, emphasizing not only ordering of the sources, but also a more schematic approach. This combined with a higher sense of equity to create a great faith in the law than hitherto.

Besides learning, the virtues of a man of law included rectitude, patience, and mercy. These, conjoined with the proper use of authority, could provoke panegyrics like the one written upon the death of Chief Justice James Dyer. The long poem ends with an epitaph on Dyer's tomb. It celebrated this "Cato of our time," asserting that:

> From self revenge, he ever did refrain.
> And yet severe when it with Justice stood:
> A *Tullie [Cicero]* right, all for his Country's good.

---

[62] Jones, *Faith by Statute*, 81.

[63] Fitzherbert and Crompton, *L'Office... de justices de peace*, fol. 111v.

[64] John Baker, *The Oxford History of the Laws of England*, vol. 6, *1483–1558* (Oxford: Oxford University Press, 2003), 13–52.

The point of the poem was didactic, since the life of good Justice Dyer illustrated "precious virtues." "English Historiographers," says the author, "which have quiet recourse unto the Muses, are bound to eternize the memories of the good magistrates deceased (who were the instruments of our blessings, that the dead may have their right, and the living encouragement to virtue)."[65]

It was the sort of epitaph that all magistrates would have liked. To be honored for their virtuous rule was to be successful in life's fight.

The English ruling classes were directed in their governing by their concepts of virtue. In relating to their tenants, sitting on the bench, mustering their county's troops, voluntarily collecting taxes, and a myriad of other duties, they had little oversight by human authority. It was their knowledge of their places in the world, their fear of God, examples of great Greeks and Romans, legal customs, and their loyalty to God's handmaiden Elizabeth that gave them context for their lives as rulers.

The various virtues of the ruling classes were generally understood, and all Elizabethans participated in the "habitus" of virtue that held their society together. And this joint comprehension made virtue a managerial tool. Everyone valued it, and it was a standard reference point for individual behavior.

To see what it meant to live and rule virtuously, let us turn to the mental world and personality of Sir William Cecil, Lord Burghley. His conception of virtue guided his actions as Elizabeth's chief manager.

---

[65] George Whetstone, *A Remembraunce of the Precious Vertues of the Right Honourable and Reuerend Iudge, Sir Iames Dier, Knight, Lord cheefe Iustice of the Common Pleas who disseased at great Stawghton, in Huntingdon shire, the 24. of Marche, anno. 1582* [1582] [STC (2nd edn)/25345].

3

William Cecil, Lord Burghley, Manager

I shall speak like an Italian idiot...and this I say with the testimony of a good conscience, which mind I gather not of any other philosophy, but of his precepts that hath commanded me to love mine enemies, for therein only is the difference, betwixt a Christian and a gentile....

For when all the glory and wit, when all the wealth and delight of this world is passed, we must come before the judge, that will exact this rule of us...I thank God, I do submit all my concepts and thoughts as mere folly, to the wisdom and piety of the Gospel. You may say it is strange to see a secretary of estate that is an artificer of practices and consuls to fall thus low into divinity. Well so simple I am what so ever the world may judge of me for the place and therein percase I do deceive the world.

> Principal Secretary Sir William Cecil, writing to Sir Thomas Smith,
> Ambassador in Paris, January 11, 1563[1]

Policy is born from a conceptualization of the world and of experience. The ideas one has about what is good and preferable are ideological in nature, but they are delimited by the contexts in which decisions are taken, and defined by the customary assumptions of society. Before we can start talking about particular circumstances in Elizabeth's state, it is good to sort out how Elizabeth's primary manager, William Cecil, Lord Burghley, saw himself, his context, and his duty.[2] How did he understand magisterial virtue? How did his ideology define his choices? If he wished to rule virtuously in the service of his Queen, what did that mean to him in practice? Clearly, his personality influenced his leadership style, and his values were stamped on the managerial system he directed.

William Cecil was born and educated among royal servants and the magisterial classes. His maternal grandfather, William Heckington, had died in 1508, but he came of that class. He was wealthy, with land and houses in and around Bourne, Lincolnshire. He left his daughter Alice the home in which William Cecil was born. William's paternal grandfather, David Cecil, was Yeoman of the Guard to Henry VII, becoming Sergeant-of-arms to Henry VIII and serving as Sheriff of

---

[1] BL Lansd. 102/fol. 55.

[2] I will refer to William Cecil as Cecil from the time of his birth until his elevation to the peerage in 1571 as Lord Burghley. After that, he will be "Burghley." The common practice of referring to his son Robert as "Cecil" in the 1590s is not being used here. Instead, when I mean Robert Cecil I will name him as such.

Northamptonshire and Justice of the Peace for Rutland. His father, Richard, was Yeoman of the Wardrobe to Henry VIII. As Stephen Alford so nicely expressed it, "the Cecils served."[3]

Coming up to St John's, Cambridge in 1535 at the age of fourteen, William was converted to evangelical Christianity as a student, while acquiring a deep love and familiarity with the classics in both Latin and Greek. From Cambridge he went to Grays Inn, in 1541, to study law, although he never took a law degree.

Born in 1520 or 1521, by the time William was twenty-one he was a member of Parliament and married. By his twenty-third year he was the Recorder of Boston; by his twenty-sixth he was the *custos breviorum*. Moving in the circle around Queen Catherine Parr, he came to the notice of Edward Seymour, duke of Somerset and rose as Seymour rose, achieving the position of Principal Secretary and member of the Privy Council in September, 1550. It was an astonishing achievement for a young man of thirty.

Rising so rapidly in the Edwardian regime, he was involved, sometimes intimately, with the plans of the regime's leaders and intellectuals. His political apprenticeship occurred at a stratospheric level, and made for him a world of connections. Handling the correspondence of the Privy Council, he was in a position to know and to be known. He was learning the managerial techniques of the Tudor state, and thinking about its problems, by his late twenties. At the same time, he was participating in the intellectual culture of the Edwardian "commonwealth men," Protestant intellectuals who believed in social reforms.

Cecil fell from grace when Edward died in July 1553. Although he was implicated in the succession plot of Jane Grey, he never seems to have been convinced of its legality. At least, that is what he told Queen Mary, and he seemingly took an active part in putting Mary on the throne. He submitted to Mary in a carefully crafted apologia. Stephen Alford, who details his activities in the month or so it took from Edward's changing of the succession to Cecil's submission to Mary, suggested Cecil had purged his archives of any evidence that would tell a different story. However, Cecil's story, and it sounds true to the man, was that he had acted according to his conscience, and his conscience had brought him to a place of safety. His conscience, he said, had been influenced by Chief Justice Montague's insistence that only Parliament could alter the succession. The episode had taught Cecil that legitimacy was everything and only Parliament could provide that legitimacy.[4]

Although he lost his high office under Mary, he conformed religiously and remained involved with government and active in life at court.[5] We catch glimpses of him in the royal presence at odd moments, as when Dr Caius presented his petition to Queen Mary to re-found Gonville Hall in Cambridge as Gonville and Caius in June of 1557.[6] He was even sent to escort Cardinal Pole from

[3] Stephen Alford, *Burghley: William Cecil at the Court of Elizabeth I* (New Haven: Yale University Press, 2008), 3–6.

[4] Alford, *Burghley*, 63.   [5] Alford, *Burghley*, 69–80.

[6] John Venn, ed., *Biographical History of Gonville and Caius College, 1349–1897* (Cambridge: Cambridge University Press, 1901), vol. 3, 37. Venn transcribes Caius's letter describing the presentation, with Cecil present.

France to England. The two bookish men became friends, and the cardinal appointed him High Steward of his estate in Wimbledon. Pole left him a silver inkstand in his will.[7]

However, there is evidence that he worked to support the Protestant cause while conforming, and he certainly remained close to Princess Elizabeth. Perhaps he was seeking some middle ground for his beliefs, since he supported the printing of Protestant books during Mary's years, allowing a secret press to function on his Lincolnshire property.[8] Certainly, Cecil knew people who had gone into exile, like his father-in-law, and some, like his tutor and brother-in-law Sir John Cheke, who had recanted under pressure, but Cecil had stayed home and worked his way back into service.

Cecil had become a Nicodemite, like most of his fellow councilors, and like his future queen, Elizabeth.[9] That meant that he dissimulated his religious beliefs. Having tasted the fear of execution, he worked hard to convince Mary that he was just following orders. However, to be a Nicodemite was seen by the ardent Protestants as betraying God. As Cecil's friend Bishop John Hooper said, "Nicodemes, that can speak of Christ in the night, or to their friends, but openly they will confess nothing with the mouth, nor do anything outwardly, for fear of the world, that should sound to God's glory. And these men be assured they shall have their reward, that Christ will deny them before his father which is in heaven."[10] The translator of Johann Wigand's *De neutralibus et mediis* termed these people "jacks of both sides." They were men who "craftily cloak and dissemble religion," pretending to be Catholic or gospeller as needs be, "to walk ... in the middle and most safe way."[11]

Those godly Edwardians like Cecil had found themselves wanting. They invented excuses, and were forced to reconsider their relationship to God and the Crown. Nonetheless, when Elizabeth came to the throne on November 17, 1558 her first act was to appoint Cecil her Principal Secretary.

From late November 1558 until his death in August 1598, Cecil was the most powerful and important manager of Elizabeth's England. First as Principal Secretary of the Privy Council and then as Lord Treasurer Burghley, he oversaw the daily operation of the royal government.

During his lifetime he was often seen as having overwhelming, and sometimes sinister, influence over Elizabeth. Gabriel Harvey, a younger contemporary rhetorician, referred to him as the Nestor of his time—a wise counselor possessed of "sweet

[7] Thomas Mayer, ed., *Correspondence of Reginald Pole* (Aldershot: Ashgate, 2004), vol. 3, 571.

[8] Elizabeth Evenden, "The Michael Wood Mystery: William Cecil and the Lincolnshire Printing of John Day," *Sixteenth Century Journal*, 35, 2 (2004), 383–94.

[9] M. A. Overell, "Vergerio's Anti-Nicodemite Propaganda and England, 1547–1558," *The Journal of Ecclesiastical History*, 51 (2000), 296–318.

[10] John Hooper, "Homily in Time of Pestilence," in *The Later Writings of John Hooper*, ed. Charles Nevinson, (Cambridge: Parker Society, 1852), 356.

[11] Johann Wigand, *De neutralibus et mediis: Grossly Englished, Jacke of both Sides. A godly and necessary Catholic admonition, touching those that be neuters, holding by no certain religion or doctrine ... to stay and stablish Gods elect in the true Catholic faith against this present wicked world*, trans. Anon. (London, 1562), sig. B.i [STC (2nd edn)/25612]. For further on this see Norman Jones, *The Birth of the Elizabethan Age: England in the 1560s* (Oxford: Blackwell, 1993), 18–20.

words," a "clear-voiced orator," whose voice "flows sweeter than honey."[12] Others saw him as the power behind the throne to such an extent that at least one attempt to assassinate him was foiled, and he was accused, with his son Robert, of creating a *Regnum Cecilianum*. Richard Vertigen, in a Catholic libel, said he was "the primum mobile in every action without distinction...to him her Majesty is accountant of her resolutions ..."[13]

From the very beginning of the reign, people noticed his authority over the Queen's government in operational affairs. When, in 1563, Elizabeth began issuing proclamations regulating wages all over the country, place by place, a part of his larger economic agenda, it was "much cried out upon" by men who knew "Mr. Cecil was all the doer of that matter," a "cruel and extreme man."[14]

Modern historians have shared two views of Burghley's role in Elizabeth's government. He was either *the power behind the throne*, the brains of the operation, or he was simply following orders. Alan Smith wrote a book entitled *William Cecil: The Power behind Elizabeth* in which he said "this very unexciting little man" controlled Elizabeth because "In her heart she knew he was her master."[15] Stephen Alford's 2008 biography of Burghley makes a similar case, but more subtly, while David Loades has argued that Elizabeth was careful never to surrender her power to him.[16]

Recent historiography has raised the question of "monarchical republicanism," with Burghley suspected of playing some part in envisioning a sort of constitutional monarchy that kept the royal woman in her place. Patrick Collinson's seminal article in which he coined the "monarchical republic" pondered Cecil's actions in thinking about a regency council, but he also noticed how nervous Cecil was about doing any such thing. This raises the issue of how much Burghley thought of himself as living in a "monarchical republic," versus how much he conceived of his role as managing a late feudal state. As Alan Cromartie has remarked, this "republicanizing way of talking" has to be offset by the "growing imaginative purchase of the idea of English monarchy," a process to which Burghley was integral.[17]

In short, everyone then and now recognized him as a key figure in Elizabeth's government, but their understanding of how he played that role is often contradictory. His biographers have, not unreasonably, focused on him as a man of policy. Conyers Read's exhaustive two-volume life of Burghley scarcely noted that he was anything more than a policy machine. He devotes little time to Cecil's many years of service in the law courts.[18] Stephen Alford, while rightly putting a human face on the policy

[12] Virginia Stern, *Gabriel Harvey: His Life, Marginalia and Library* (Oxford: Clarendon Press, 1979), 152.

[13] "Certain True Notes upon the Actions of the Lord Burghley," Bacon, *Works*, vol. 6, 198.

[14] TNA SP 12/19 fol. 84v.

[15] Alan Gordon Smith, *William Cecil: The Power behind Elizabeth* (New York: Haskell House Publishers Ltd, 1971), 48.

[16] Alford, *Burghley*. David Loades, *Elizabeth I* (London: Hambledon and London, 2003), 181–3.

[17] Patrick Collinson, "The Monarchical Republic of Queen Elizabeth I," in Patrick Collinson, *Elizabethan Essays* (London: Hambledon Press, 1994), 31–58. Alan Cromartie, *The Constitutional Revolution: An Essay on the History of England, 1450–1642* (Cambridge: Cambridge University Press, 2006), 89.

[18] Conyers Read, *Mr Secretary Cecil and Queen Elizabeth* (London: Jonathan Cape, 1955). Conyers Read, *Lord Burghley and Queen Elizabeth* (London: Jonathan Cape, 1960).

wonk, does not wrestle with how this man actually ran Elizabeth's government. But if we are to understand Elizabeth's government, we have to understand him, for he did manage, day-to-day, the Elizabethan state. His richly illuminated patent making him Lord Burghley visually and legally summarizing his status (Fig. 3.1).

The big issues—Mary, Queen of Scots, the Armada, and the religious settlement—required Her Majesty's attention as well as Burghley's, but the daily operation

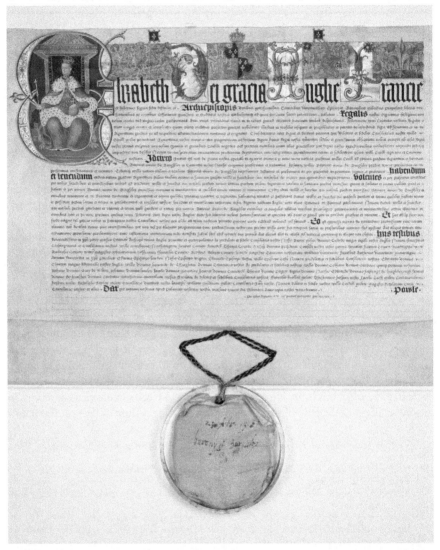

Fig. 3.1. Illuminated letters patent creating William Cecil as Lord Burghley, 1571, Burghley House, MUN 18518. My thanks to Jon Culverhouse, Curator at Burghley House, for the use of this illustration.

demanded Burghley's sole attention. If we follow his archive day by day, we can see him at work, followed by his clerks, busily annotating, dictating, writing, attending courts and meetings, taking counsel, and making decisions. Operational decision-making was his job, and he did it thoughtfully and methodically, bringing to bear his own particular values and processes.

His conception of problems, his reasoning processes, his consultative style, and his decision-making were rooted in his instinctual social knowledge of his society and his adherence to its values. Certain generalities are obvious. As he approached governing, he brought to bear his humanistic training, his religious values, his belief in hierarchy, and his commitment to the rule of law.

Cecil was a son of the early Reformation, arriving in Cambridge when the Reformation Parliament was still in session and Henry VIII was busy explaining why he was the Supreme Head of the Church in England. He was a fresher when Chancellor Thomas Cromwell stopped the teaching of canon law in the university and ordered the reading of the scriptures. It was a time of evangelical excitement. As Burghley wrote about his time at Cambridge and his Christian faith, he came

> to have knowledge of the Gospel of our Savior Jesus Christ, the knowledge whereof began about that time to be more clearly revealed here in England then it had been many years before, being thereby taught that there was no other means of salvation of my soul but by the passion death and resurrection of Christ Jesus, the son of God (in whom, as I ought, so I do) put my whole confidence and trust, and do desire that assurance of his holy spirit to have grace during this frail life, to continue in the assurance and to have a desire to obey his will and commandments in living religiously and devoutly as far forth as the infirmity of my flesh will suffer.[19]

Cecil has been characterized as a hottish Protestant, but when we separate the defense of the realm from his theological preference we see a slightly different sort of Protestant. He was a rather old-fashioned one who valued religious performance, without showing any of the behavior of the more Gospel-minded. He prayed in Latin on his knees—the funeral monument he designed for himself in 1562 shows him, in full armor, kneeling before an open book, while his wife and children are also praying from books—and he was punctilious about attending prayers, but he was too practical to make a good religious ideologue.[20] He certainly hated the Pope, but, like his mistress, he took a latitudinarian approach to much of the religious controversy of the day. He seems to have actually read his Catholic opponents like Bellarmine, if William Whitaker is to be believed, and he certainly took the position that obedience to the Queen was more important than theological niceties.

What was his theology? Clearly he was a Protestant, but his vision of living religiously and devoutly is hard to catch. In 1547 Cecil wrote the preface to Queen Catherine Parr's book *The Lamentations of a Sinner*. In it he argued for another sort of education. Queen Catherine, Henry VIII's widow, he wrote, "refusing the world wherein she was lost, to obtain heaven wherein she may be saved," forsook ignorance

---

[19] TNA PROB/11/92, fols 241v–242.   [20] CP, CPM II 14.

"to come to knowledge, whereby she may see." She abandoned superstition to embrace true religion. The reader, Cecil argued, would be encouraged by Catherine's humble example to become a member of Christ: "which is all things in all: no folly to forget the wisdom of the world, to learn the simplicity of the gospel: at the last, no displeasantness to submit... to the school of the cross, the learning of the crucifix, the book of our redemption, the very absolute library of God's mercy and wisdom.... I would thee warned that profit may ensue."[21]

But he was only about twenty-six when he wrote that, and he had a great deal of religious experience yet to come. By the end of Edward's reign he had been intimately involved in creating Edwardian Protestantism.

He had conformed under Mary, rather than face the persecution that came to many of his old friends and colleagues. He has been described as a Calvinist, but he probably agreed that the doctrine of double predestination was too dangerous for public discussion. As some of the returning Protestants told Elizabeth in 1559, "it was best that such articles be passed over in silence" lest they provoke disobedience.[22] Until the end of his life, his theological preference took a back seat to his conviction that he served God by serving the Queen. His disputes with predestinarians were more about her fear of pushing people into opposition than theological preference.

He was deeply attracted to Stoic philosophy. This, too, goes back to his student days in Cambridge when tutors introduced him to Cicero and Seneca, as well as to Erasmus and other modern reformers. His most important teacher, John Cheke, was dedicated to the proper study of Greek as a way to achieve a pure understanding of the Gospels.[23] Cheke deeply influenced Cecil, for, as Sir Thomas Smith observed, "Sir John Cheeke... was your brother-in-law, your dear friend, your good admonisher, and teacher in your younger years, to take that way of virtue, the fruit whereof you do feel and taste to your great joy at this day."[24] Cheke's educational ideals were based on those of Isocrates and Demosthenes, men who believed in the *vita activa*, and on Roman virtue as found in Cicero. Roger Ascham, another of his students, summed them up when he commented that Cheke thought Plato, Aristotle, and Cicero were the "handmaids" of the Word of God, directing us toward truth.[25]

Understanding the Word of God with the help of Plato, Aristotle, and Cicero was what young William Cecil was trained to do, and it showed throughout his life. He followed God with Stoic virtue, and he thought using the tools of formal academic analysis.

---

[21] William Cecil, "The Preface," Catharine Parr, *The Lamentacion of a Sinner ...* (1548). No pagination [STC (2nd edn)/4828].

[22] CCCC, 121, p. 147.

[23] Winthrop Hudson, *The Cambridge Connection and the Elizabethan Settlement of 1559* (Durham, NC: Duke University Press, 1980), 54.

[24] Thomas Wilson, *The Three Orations of Demosthenes* (1570) [STC (2nd edn)/6578], dedication.

[25] Roger Ascham, *The Whole Works of Roger Ascham*, ed. Dr Giles (London, 1865), vol. 2, 45. "Verbi Dei cognitionem Platonis Aristotelis Ciceronisque lectione quasi ministra et ancilla comitatam et eum finem mihi esse propositum ad quem reliquum vitas meae cursum Dei voluntate intendam atque dirigam Verum."

It also placed him in the same theological school as Peter Martyr and Martin Bucer, the two refugee professors who spent much of Edward's reign in England, and whose theology recognized the authority of kings and magistrates without accepting the Pope.[26]

Cheke's evangelical theology and his dominance of Cambridge led to the invitation to Martin Bucer to come from Strassburg to the university in 1549. By then Cecil was working for the Privy Council, but Bucer, and his fellow immigrant Peter Martyr at Oxford, electrified evangelical circles. Bucer's great book *De regno Christi* is a manifesto of the church active in the world, catching the theology that men like Cecil found so empowering. It may not be an accident that among the books in Burghley's office at his death was Peter Martyr's *Commonplaces*. Martyr, who had taught at Oxford and who was a close friend of many of Cecil's close friends, expounded the Ten Commandments under headings like "of bondage and Christian freedom," "of justification," and "of Law." The section on law took an interesting turn into Cicero's *Tusculan Disputations* and Aristotle's *Nichomachean Ethics* for an explanation of why law and moral philosophy are the same thing and how philosophy could be used for expounding as well as obeying the law.[27] Since human law was based on divine law, as understood through philosophy, students steeped in this theology believed in the need to interpret God's law and man's law rationally. That might explain why Cecil and his Cambridge friends rose to such high places in the state. Cheke's students knew that service to the commonwealth was required by God and by reason.

Thus, Cecil's education deeply imbued him with scholastic rationality, with stoical skepticism, and with a Protestantism that saw a link between God's will and the Queen's authority. His approach to governing was humanistic and rational, with a sad skepticism that his fellows sometimes took for coldness in religion. His deep belief in rational analysis is visible in the dozens of personal memos he wrote to himself, and as preparation for speeches, analyzing problems *in utramque partem.*

Arguing in this way, he was forced to recognize the pros and cons within each argument, and it had important implications. The method was about establishing conditional truth, determined by setting forth arguments that incorporated positions from either side and weighing which was more probably true.[28] It was such a key part of rhetorical training that Cicero described it as a system of philosophy that "gives birth to fluency in speaking." Using commonplaces, it sought to foresee and respond to all points of view.[29] It was the perfect tool for a man of Cecil's profession and disposition.

[26] Torrance Kirby, "Peter Martyr Vermigli's Political Theology and the Elizabethan Church," in Polly Ha and Patrick Collinson, eds, *The Reception of the Continental Reformation in Britain* (Oxford: Oxford University Press, 2010), 83–106.

[27] Pietro Martire Vermigli, *The Common Places of the Most Famous and Renowmed* [sic] *Diuine Doctor Peter Martyr* ... (London: 1583) [STC (2nd edn)/24669].

[28] Ann Vasaly, *Representations: Images of the World in Ciceronian Oratory* (Berkeley: University of California Press, 1993), 187–8.

[29] Cicero tells Brutus that of all the philosophies none is a better preparation for speaking in the Senate ("in senatu sententiam diceret") than that which teaches this style of argument. M. Tullius Cicero, *Paradoxa stoicorum ad M. Brutum*, ed. J. G. Baiter and C. L. Kayser, paras 1–2. <http://www.perseus. tufts.edu/hopper/text?doc=Perseus%3Atext%3A2007.01.0045%3Asection%3D1>. Accessed June 9, 2014.

In these memoranda we find him carefully rehearsing policy on paper by listing propositions, reasons, and proofs, for and against, according to the rhetorical *cursus* he was taught by teachers like Sir Thomas Wilson and by the masters of classical oratory like Cicero.[30]

Through these propositions that he debated with himself we can get a sense of his values, of his goals, and, ultimately, of the nature of his mind and how it was stocked. The evidence on the paper is of a deeply thoughtful man who applied his learning to the problems he had before him, using all the tools of his extensive reading, his religious value system, and his concepts of political virtue and justice to serve the common weal. He had learned from Cicero that fortitude and toil is selfish and devoid of justice if it is used for private ends rather than for the common good.[31] Or, to put it in Cecil's own words, "Good princes ought first to prefer the service of God and his Church, and next of the Commonwealth, before their own pleasure and profit."[32] As he told the earl of Bedford:

> serve uprightly and truly, and to do therein as you can, and then may you be bold of praise; And, if you miss of that, yet, of no dishonor; for nothing, indeed, is honorable, but well-doing: the Weal of your country (I mean, the quietness of such, as you have authority to govern) is your mark, shoot thereat, guiding your purpose with the fear of God, and so shall you gain the love of God and man.[33]

Certainly the weal of his country was the duty uppermost on his mind. Perhaps that is why he thought so carefully about political issues. Serving God and country required care.

This attitude encapsulated the beliefs of many of the young men that would become the pillars of the Elizabethan establishment. For them, the service owed to God took precedence, but for many that service was more or less identical to serving their Queen. One of Burghley's apothegms held that you could not speak ill of princes, as the Lord's anointed, but you should pray for them.[34]

His last written advice to his son, just before his death, summed up a key part of his personal philosophy: "Serve God by serving of your Queen for all other service is indeed bondage to the Devil."[35] Serving God and serving the Queen may have seemed a contradiction to many of his contemporaries. You cannot imagine John Knox or even Archbishop Grindal equating the service of the two. Yet Burghley managed it.

In his personal religious life he was exact, and methodically legal. His anonymous biographer describes him living a highly ordered religious life: "His piety and great devotion (the foundation of all his actions) was such as he never failed to serve his God, before he served his country; for he most precisely duly observed his exercise of prayer, morning and evening, all the time he was Secretary, never failing to be at the chapel in the Queen's house every morning." Even in old age and sickness,

---

[30] Stephen Alford, *The Early Elizabethan Polity: William Cecil and the British Succession Crisis, 1558–1569* (Cambridge: Cambridge University Press, 1998), 16–23.

[31] Cicero, *De officiis*, trans. Walter Miller (Cambridge, MA: Harvard University Press, 2001), I, xix, 65.

[32] Collins, 70.   [33] BL Harleian 6990, fol. 1.   [34] Collins, 68.

[35] Read, *Burghley*, 547.

unable to attend chapel, "he used every morning and evening to have cushion by his bedside, where he prayed daily on his knees, without fail, what haste or business soever he had..."[36] Burghley is described as never missing a sermon, and as one who, as master of the house, ensured that his servants did not, either. They were expected to attend morning and evening prayer, and to hear a sermon in the chapel every Sunday.

Writing to his old friend and tutor, Sir Thomas Smith, in 1563, Cecil expressed his Christian view of his duty. He told Ambassador Smith: "I do submit all my concepts and thoughts as mere folly, to the wisdom and piety of the Gospel. You may say it is strange to see a secretary of estate that is an artificer of practices and consuls to fall thus low into divinity. Well so simple I am what so ever the world may judge of me for the place and therein percase I do deceive the world."

He had an intense sense of the irony of a man in his position attempting to live by the wisdom of the Gospel:

> I know the place which I hold hath been of years not long passed, adjudged a shop for cunning men, and yet surely I think, the opinion commonly conceived thereof, that be worse than the persons depraved. Some cause I have so to think, that knowing before Almighty God, my disposition to deal with all men plainly, and indeed my inability, or as I may say of myself my dullness to invent crafts, yet do I not escape evil judgment, desirous to avoid as much as I may that opinion, and where I cannot content with patience and testimony of my own conscience to endure.

When all was said and done, he wrote, his conscience had to be guided by "His precept that hath commanded me to love mine enemies, for therein only is the difference, betwixt a Christian and a gentile."[37]

Certainly his self-image as a Christian statesman was not one shared by the entire world, but it is interesting that he thought of himself that way. Guided by his conscience, deeply learned in theology, he sought to understand his duty intellectually. So Burghley's approach to the Bible was scholarly, and he clearly saw it as something to be understood intellectually via the original languages. His, and his wife Mildred's, deep learning in Greek undoubtedly contributed to this approach to the Word of God.

Hugh Broughton rehearsed a conversation with the Lord Treasurer about theology in his dedication to Burghley of his book on the proper identity of Melchisedek, the Old Testament priest. Broughton, England's most prominent Hebraist, was critical of translations, such as the Geneva Bible and the Bishops' Bible, that rendered the Old Testament from the Greek rather than the Hebrew. The dedication of the book to Burghley, Broughton said, was prompted by a three-hour discussion they once had. Broughton had been summoned from Cambridge to the court to consult with Burghley about the Greek translation of the Old Testament known as the Septuagint.

The Lord Treasurer had a series of learned questions about why the Greek was used by scholars in preference to the Hebrew ("Wasn't it," Burghley asked, "right to use the Greek, since the Apostles had used it?"), about certain points of translation,

---

[36] Collins, 56.   [37] BL Lansd. 102, fol. 55.

and a range of other issues. "I could not faster run then through any part of mine own studies," said Broughton, "then you pursued in demands for the chief matter. Your shortness in propounding questions, readiness in conceiving a full answer, diligence in trying Scriptures, dexterity in replying upon color of doubt, quickness in trying what confidence I had in mine assertions: and lastly, singular gentleness of encouraging my studies, with entreaties to repair often to you" encouraged him to go on with his research.[38]

It is clear from much of what he wrote that be believed in the great chain of being within the family, and in society. Master of the Court of Wards from 1561, he was, in a way, the official guardian of the purity of the aristocratic classes, but many suspected he was not one himself. He worked hard to prove that he was worthy of his status, and that his children deserved to marry up the social ladder. At the same time, his awareness of rank influenced the way he thought about government. For him it was closer to a family firm than a structure, and he certainly ran it that way, paying careful attention to who was related to whom and who lived where.

In about 1589 he composed a curious memorandum which he entitled "Counsellors of Blood and Allegiance." In it he schematically worked out all the ways the current members of the Privy Council were related to one another. Demonstrating that Sir Francis Walsingham was the father-in-law of the nephew of the earl of Leicester and so on, he graphically illustrated that England was a family business dominated by a complex set of intermarriages.[39]

His own place within this family business was nebulous, so he required a genealogy that would justify his authority. Over the years he worked out multiple versions of the history of the Welsh "Sitsill" family, proving he was related to the Herberts, the Vaughans, and other important families, all the way back to the Norman Conquest. Did he know these genealogies were semi-fictions? I doubt he could admit it, since he was proving to himself that his position was legitimate. Wherever he came from, it became true that his family was related, through his children's marriages, to great families.

Burghley understood the importance of birth and honor so well that he carefully tracked the locations and the relationships of the magisterial classes. He grasped that in the small world of the ruling elite most things came down to genealogy and geography—an understanding that is reflected in everything from the popular chorographies of the day to the visitations of the Heralds. His anonymous biographer asked rhetorically, "what nobleman or gentleman and their dwellings, matches and pedigrees, did he not know?" He could, said the biographer, describe the locale of a gentleman's home better than the gentleman himself. He continues, "He took great pains and delight in pedigrees, wherein he had great knowledge, and wrote whole books of them with his own hand, which greatly augmented his knowledge both abroad and at home."[40] We find confirmation of this throughout his papers, with pedigrees for the Neville, Talbot, Wentworth, Dacre, Touchet,

---

[38] Hugh Broughton, *A Treatise of Melchisedek Prouing him to be Sem, the father of all the sonnes of Heber, the fyrst king, and all kinges glory: by the generall consent of his owne sonnes, by the continuall iudgement of ages, and by plentifull argumentes of scripture* (1591), Epistle Dedicatory. [STC (2nd edn)/3890].
[39] BL Lansd. 109/fol. 200.   [40] Collins, *Life*, 65–7.

Vaughan, Fleetwood, Carew, Cutts, Fitzwalter, Wingfield, Grey, Perrot, and other families, often in Burghley's holograph.[41]

This custom he had of understanding people by placing them within their kin groups was, perhaps, related to the Court of Wards, but there is evidence of a deeper meaning. For instance, when Sir Thomas Egerton was a candidate for Attorney General, Burghley worked out the genealogical associations of Thomas's father, Sir Richard, in his pocket diary, suggesting that birth and social status were considered by Burghley to be pertinent to office holding.[42]

However, he enjoyed genealogy as a deep study, going far beyond the recent past. He once wrote out the genealogies of the kings of France on the back of a piece of scrap paper, beginning with the Merovingians.[43]

Another indication of his interest in genealogy, history, and the Bible is the large and complex "collectanea" of the rulers of Jerusalem he drafted (see Fig. 3.2). Extending over fifteen folios, it is a comparative genealogy and timeline of the kings of Judea, beginning with David, and going on to trace the Maccabeans, the Assyrians, the Persians, the Egyptians, the Romans, and the members of the Sanhedrin. More than a set of family trees, it contains a running historical commentary, adding notes such as the one that says in the thirty-fifth year of Herod's reign Christ was born, and in the same year Herod murdered 40,000 innocents.[44]

Another, nastier, example of his genealogical knowledge, his belief in social hierarchy, and his querulous old age, comes from a letter written by Sir John Hollis. Hollis had failed to turn up for a Star Chamber case against him, and Burghley had denounced him from the bench in a way that, Hollis complained to him, "sorted ill with the dignity and gravity" of Burghley's character and besmirched the judgment seat. The Lord Treasurer,

> not satisfied to commit me for being absent, to imprison and punish my tenants for erecting some few buildings (according to the general error) contrary to the proclamation, it pleased you also to lay me open as a most miserable wretch, a covetous cormorant, an unworthy and noisome member to the common-wealth. Your Lordship then digged into my ancestor's grave, and pulling him from his threescore and ten years' rest, pronounced him an abominable usurer, a merchant of broken paper, so hateful and contemptible a creature that the players acted him before the King with great applause.

Hollis, however, knew how to hit back in a way that he knew would hurt Burghley's pride. If he was to question Hollis's gentle pedigree, said Sir John, Burghley ought to consider how "many others from innkeepers, butchers, and other mechanical occupations" have risen "to be sole governors of great commonwealths. These many answer with Iphicrates, 'Let them who are noble from the beginning reprove others' unnobleness.'"[45] Using the Athenian shoemaker and general to humble

---

[41] Entering "pedigree" into the search engine of the State Papers Online produces a list of some fifty entries in Burghley's papers, which represent only those documents identified as pedigrees by the calendars.

[42] BL Royal App 67, fols 1–3.   [43] CP 141/33.   [44] TNA SP 12/255 fols 116–30.

[45] HEH 267 contains the entire letter. HMC Salisbury VIII, 270 leaves off the salutation and a bit at the end.

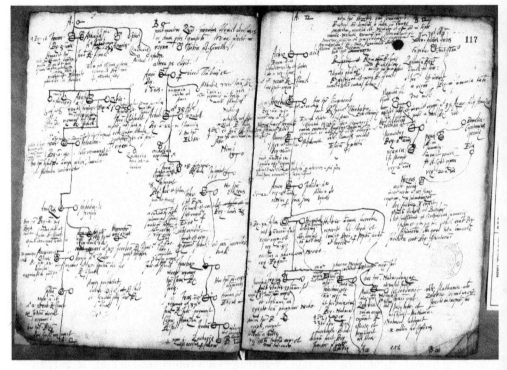

Fig. 3.2. A leaf of the collectanea of the rulers of Jerusalem, in Lord Burghley's hand, TNA SP 12/255 fols 116v–117.

Burghley must have given Hollis malicious glee. His letter was endorsed by Burghley's clerk "A saucy letter."

Hollis's letter hurt him on two levels. Obviously, it impugned the social status of his family. But it also suggested that Burghley was not virtuous in doing his duty. Virtue he considered to be essential in all the Queen's servants, and especially so in the nobility. "I have often heard him in his speech," says his biographer, "greatly reverence and extol nobility, holding it most precious as that reward of virtue, and virtue in nobility could neither be sufficiently esteemed nor rewarded."[46] Of course, virtue accounted for his own rise into the nobility, and it allowed him to praise the nobility while urging them to virtue. He walked a fine line!

Reinforcing his humanistic education, his religion, and his belief in hierarchy, there was his legal education. He was a lawyer and a judge, and he was deeply interested in legal structures and processes. His training at Gray's Inn had shaped him, and his career kept him engaged in the law. We know that as a young Principal Secretary to King Edward's Privy Council, Sir William had intended to write "An order of the policy and officers of the realm, their order and duties"

---

[46] Collins, 46.

and a book "setting forth of Bracton, the lawyer, that he might be seen and read of all men."[47]

That Cecil had aspired, in his thirties, to do what his friend Sir Thomas Smith later did in *De republica Anglorum*, and that he was interested in making Bracton's foundational legal ideas easily available is revealing. It helps us understand a great deal about his administrative values. At their core was Bracton's certainty that the king has no equal. As Bracton said in chapter 2 of *De legibus Angliae*:

> The king has no equal within his realm, nor *a fortiori* a superior, because he would then be subject to those subjected to him. The king must not be under man but under God and under the law, because law makes the king, for there is no *rex* where will rules rather than *lex*. Since he is the vicar of God, and that he ought to be under the law, appears clearly in the analogy of Jesus Christ, whose vicegerent on earth he is.[48]

This assertion had been used to justify Henry VIII's authority over the church, and it appears in 1558 in one of the briefs Cecil received about the possible restoration of Protestantism in the weeks in the run up to the Parliament of 1559.[49] For Burghley it may have boiled down to serving God by serving the Queen, but it also embodied an entire state of mind about religion, the state, and his place in both. His place was to make the Queen's rule, within law, effective in the service of God. God had appointed Elizabeth as His vicar in England, and England's prosperity depended upon Cecil's ability to ensure that her law was carried out. He was not there to influence theology.

Carrying out the law was not a theoretical question for Burghley. He spent his entire career enacting and enforcing it. He sat in Parliament sporadically in the reigns of Henry VIII, Edward VI, and Mary, and then in either the Commons or the Lords, in every Elizabethan Parliament in his lifetime. Burghley held legal office as recorder or *custos rotulorum*, as a high steward, as Chancellor of the Order of the Garter, and as Solicitor General. In 1561 he became the Master of the Court of Wards and began presiding over his own court. In 1572 he became Lord Treasurer and sat in the Court of the Exchequer. As a Privy Councilor he sat in the Court of Star Chamber.[50]

In Star Chamber Cecil even delivered what became a dictum, recorded by Justice Dyer: "Fides magna adhibenda est testibus presentibus quam testimoniis eorum absentium" ("More trust is to be placed in witnesses who are present than in the evidence of those who are absent"). Applied in a trial in Star Chamber concerning a forged will, Cecil and his colleagues held that forging to confirm a nuncupative will did not fall under the Act against Perjury of 1563.[51] This dictum helps explain why his legal activities are not more noticed. They occurred in venues in which individual legal voices were buried in the common voice. (One is reminded of

---

[47] John Strype, *The Life of John Cheke* (Oxford: Clarendon Press, 1821), 101, note.

[48] Bracton, *De legibus et consuetudinibus Angliae* (Bracton on the Laws and Customs of England). Bracton Online, http://bracton.law.harvard.edu. Accessed Feb. 8, 2011.

[49] TNA SP 12/1 fol. 159.

[50] Star Chamber attendance registers, HEH, EL 2653.

[51] J. H. Baker, ed., *Reports from the Lost Notebooks of Sir James Dyer* (London: Selden Society, 1994), vol. 1, 168; 189.

Burghley's nephew, Sir Francis Bacon's, observation that "It is generally better to deal by speech than by letter.... To deal in person is good when a man's face breeds regard, as commonly with inferiors.")[52]

References to his legal activity crop up throughout the *English Reports* for the period. Coke, for instance, tells how, in the dispute over the right of Lord De La Warre to sit in the House of Lords, the case was referred to Lord Burghley, who heard it personally in his chambers in Whitehall. In consultation with the justices, Burghley concluded that the right of a peer to sit was not affected by the corruption in blood of his ancestor.[53] Other judges remarked on the case in which a lawyer tried to argue that a decision rendered by the earl of Leicester and Sir William Cecil was wrong because *humanum est errare*.[54]

Constantly concerned about the larger implications of legal decisions, Burghley paid careful attention to them. His anonymous biographer relates:

> He was so careful, in administration of justice, as, many times, he favored the subject in the causes of the prince; as, when one Mr. Throgmorton had a case in the Exchequer, which was hardly recovered for the Queen upon a nice point, he would not suffer the judgment to be entered, but with condition, to enter the reasons; and that it was a case of the Queen's prerogative, and not of law.[55]

Although none of the accounts of the case mentions his presence at either the first or second trial of Sir Moyle Finch vs. Throckmorton in 1591, it is clear that he had followed this very complex case with care. In brief, one Thomas Throckmorton had been late with his rent owed to the Crown and was ejected on the motion of Sir Moyle Finch, years after he missed his payment. Some judges argued that, in law, the lease had been voided by the late payment; others held that in conscience it should not be treated as void.[56] The case was argued at Sergeants Inn. Opinions were so divided that only when Justice Manwood died, changing the number of votes, was there a resolution of the issue, which went against Throckmorton and in favor of the Queen's right to make the lease in reversion if the tenant seised failed to pay on time.[57] Burghley's refusal to enroll the decision without a note of protest

---

[52] Francis Bacon, *Essayes. Religious Meditations. Places of Perswasion & Disswasion. Seene and Allowed* (1597), fols 12v; 14v [STC (2nd edn)/1137.5].

[53] De La Warre's Case 11 CO. Rep. 1 b. in ER, 77, 1145.

[54] Baker, ed., *Dyer*, vol. 1, 188.   [55] Collins, 54.

[56] Susan Cogan, "Catholic Gentry, Family Networks and Patronage in the English Midlands, *c.*1570–1630" (University of Colorado, unpublished PhD dissertation, 2012), 236, n. 40. Cogan explains, citing WRO CR1998/Box 53: "In 1588 Sir Moyle Finch acquired the reversion of Ravenstone and immediately attempted to seize the manor on the grounds that in 1564 the annual rent payment was tardy. Throckmorton explained that the rent, which was paid by his father Robert, was delayed by a negligent servant but that a 'Quietus Est and full discharge thereof made,' after which the Throckmortons had continued to enjoy the land and pay annual rent for 22 years until in 1588/9 Finch launched a series of lawsuits in attempt to claim the manor. Throckmorton argued that since the queen held the reversion of Ravenstone at the time of the default she would have been the rightful claimant of reversion. Since the queen had determined not to reclaim it and instead issued a *Quietus Est* and allowed the Throckmortons over two decades of subsequent use and possession, the family rightfully possessed the manor."

[57] Quoting Sir Moyle Finch vers Throckmorton (1688) Moo KB 291 in *English Reports*, 72, 587. See also Sir Moyle Finch against Throckmorton (1653) Cro Eliz 221 in *English Reports*, 78, 477.

gives us a sense of his grasp of the larger impact of the decision on society, as well as his authority.

But we should not forget how much of his governing was tied to legal problems, and to problems for which he sought a legal answer, from excess of apparel to witchcraft to rape. His virtue demanded he use all of his skills, authority, and values in solving real world problems.

Thanks to his many memoranda *sub utramque partem* we can see how all the elements of his training and beliefs came together in his mind as he sought to solve issues of governance.

His "problem sets" about the regulation of usury in 1571 and about defense of the realm in 1569 make good examples because we can see him applying religious values, historical and legal precedents, friendly consultations, and legal understandings to questions of policy.

The economic problems of the 1560s were a constant concern to Cecil and the Privy Council, and his extensive notes on the question of usury legislation let us into his ideology and his approach to theology. In particular, the economic distress provoked discussions of bankruptcy, usury, poor relief, and the role of wealth in the commonwealth, discussions that led to proposals for legislation in the Parliaments of 1562/3, 1566, and 1571. Cecil, in considering these problems, covered seventeen folios with arguments that knit them together under the rubric of usury. These folios, covered with his unmistakable long, thin pen strokes, are undated and unpaginated but they were almost certainly written in late April 1571.[58]

Although the issues were clearly political and economic, for Cecil they were to be answered first legally. He locates usury within the matrix of God's law, nature's law, and man's law.

Recalling that natural law is a form of revelation, Cecil laid out a series of questions to be analyzed, happily shifting back and forth between English, Latin, and Greek:

1. Whether it be against nature or not?
2. Whether it be forbidden by God's word or no?
3. Whether it be a judicial or moral law?
4. Whether, if it be wholly forbidden or but where it is used with the poor?
5. Whether, if it be not unlawful by God's law, yet it be convenient to prohibit it by man's law?
6. Whether in making a law for it, it be convenient to prohibit it generally and to provide for particular cases that may chance, or to leave them to the construction of the Chancery?[59]

The answer to whether usury is against nature was sought first in scripture. The etymology of "usury" was traced from the Latin into the Greek and from the Greek

[58] BL Lansd., 101/#24 and #26. Because these are unpaginated and are clearly part of the same exercise, I have considered them together.
[59] BL Lansd., 101, 26, fol. 120.

into the Hebrew, causing him to conclude that the Old Testament passages that forbade usury were based on a Hebrew word meaning "to bite," *neshek*, which he translated back into Latin as *morsus*. This definition, in keeping with the latest Christian translations of the Hebrew word, opened the possibility that usury only occurred when "biting" was felt. This argument, however, did not entirely convince him, for, as he remarks elsewhere in his jottings, "it is no argument *ab etymologia ad rem*, for etymologies comprehend not always the sense of a word." A thing is more to be understood in its action than in its origins. Nonetheless, he appended three Latin legal definitions of usury.

The process and content of his analysis is interesting because it tells us not only how he thought, but who he read. He, like all the authorities on the subject, quotes Exodus, Leviticus, Deuteronomy, Nehemiah, Psalms, and Ezekiel, concluding that the case for permitting it outright was weak. But were the Old Testament prohibitions moral or judicial? Did they apply at all times and places, or only in particular circumstances that could be invoked by the judges? He called Chrysostom, Augustine, and Pope Gregory the Great as witnesses on this issue, adding the Fathers of the Church to the teachings of the Bible.

Here his friend Sir Nicholas Throckmorton, whom he consulted in the matter, pointed out a distinction between conscience and action: "Nothing external is evil *nisi quatemus interna actio animi accedit*," so intent must be taken into account. If the lending at interest is not done with an evil conscience, it is not sin. This leads him into analysis of the human conscience, sin, and the law. He begins with a *syllogismus conscientiae* from Gratian: Nothing evil should be done, ergo this evil thing should not be done.

But Cecil was not entirely convinced that Gratian's glossing of St Paul, "'*omne, quod non est ex fide,' id est omne, quod contra conscientiam fit, 'peccatum est,'*" was right.[60] Cecil knew that there were, by his count, at least six situations in which errors of conscience can occur, leading to wrong actions, though endorsed by good consciences. Besides, human law cannot take conscience into consideration. It must deal in actions. Even if it is not sin in God's sight, men may punish it, for the human law takes man as the measure of all things. So is usury a secular offense rather than *malum in se*, evil in itself and always forbidden?

This led him to consider the secular effects of usury and whether they needed to be controlled, turning the argument into a consideration of the causes and treatment of poverty, bankruptcy, and other social effects of usury, as well as the utility of lending capital at interest to support widows, orphans, and students.

As we attempt to follow Cecil's logic across all these bits of paper, written in multiple languages and containing scraps of conversations had with his learned friends, we can see that he is trying to understand whether God has created an absolute ban on usury, or if its regulation is a matter of conscience, public morality, and social impact. It appears, in the end, that all of this careful thinking brought him to the conclusion that Christ "medleth not with contracts, but with justice of

---

[60] Aemilius Friedberg, ed., *Decretum magistri Gratiani* (Graz: 1959), vol. 1, 1226–7.

contracts." This focus on justice rather than form puts it in alignment with the moderate reformers who stressed intention over action, heart over head.

What does this teach us about how he conceived governance and his role in it? His duty to God and God's relation to the state? We can see that he has a well-developed theory of the two swords, but that he is carefully separating morality that affects public affairs—the second table of the Ten Commandments—from morality that affects God's honor—the first table of the Ten Commandments. Justice is a public good; loving your neighbor has a public dimension; and not everything needs regulation.[61]

In his internal debate on usury we can see his humanism, his religious values, his legal conceptualization, and his concern for good governance all brought to play on an issue. In his memo on defense of the realm in 1569, we can see these, as well as a deep streak of pragmatism.

His way of thinking about England's international context can be found in the 1569 "Short memorial of the state of the realm," written in his own hand, perhaps as a draft of a speech. Like the usury argument, it is laid out schematically, arranged according to "persons" and "matters," for, as he says, the perils "are many, great and imminent. Great in respect of the persons and matters."[62]

The "persons" are Queen Elizabeth, "herself as patient," and the Pope, and the kings of France and Spain and the Queen of Scots as "instrument, whereby the matters shall be attempted against" Elizabeth.

The analysis of the "matters" follows, each beginning with a statement of the goals of Elizabeth's enemies, followed by bulleted analyses of how their goals might be achieved, and then bulleted reasons England might be vulnerable to their efforts. Next appears a discussion of the current political situations in France, Flanders, and Scotland that showed a detailed knowledge of the French religious wars and internal Scottish politics.

After several pages of analysis of the threats, concluding with thoughts on how the larger situation of the kingdom is impacted by the particulars, he considers how to deal with them. "Wherefore," he says, and proceeds by a series of "therefore" and "then followeth" statements, with bulleted points and sub points to determine possible actions. In the end he wrote another memo, which he endorsed "Extract of the book of the state of the realm," which summarized the memo "of remedies against the conspiration [sic] of the Pope and the two monarchies." It lists twenty-three numbered action points.

Several are diplomatic, with ambassadors delivering messages to the kings involved, calling for a defensive league of Protestant princes.

Some are practical, calling for internal tightening of the ramshackle system of church and state. Defects in religion were to be remedied by visitations in all

---

[61] For more detailed analyses, see Norman Jones, *God and the Moneylenders: Usury and Law in Early Modern England* (Oxford: Basil Blackwell, 1989), 34–43, and "William Cecil and the Making of Economic Policy in the 1560s," in *The Commonwealth of Tudor England*, ed. P. Fideler and T. Mayer (London: Routledge, 1992), 169–93.

[62] CP 157/2.

dioceses, hunts for seditious books, and "all means used to advance religion in the realm" as a way of resisting the Pope's evil intent.

Some address what he calls the decay of civil policy, outlining reform of the Council of Wales, and a "renewal" of the book of justices of the peace. Both the reform of the Council of Wales and the reworking of the *Liber pacis* were undertaken, with a clear eye on local politics, in 1569. The third goal was larger—the reform of the lawyers of the realm, who should be "reduced to the obedience and execution of the laws." He and Bacon tried to reform the lawyers, but they could not convince Parliament.

Nine items were declared to stop the decay of the martial state of the realm, including breeding better horses, fortifying Berwick, ensuring adequate provisions of powder, shot, and armor, and putting the Navy in readiness with "captains named for the seas."[63] This was clearly based on his knowledge of the musters and the situation in Berwick and in the Navy.

Last was a set of economic considerations, using trade to pressure France and Spain while insulating English merchants from their retaliation. More trade to Muscovy, Hamburg, and Eastland was to be encouraged, while trade to Flanders was to be stopped and goods coming from Spain subjected to "a good view." Over the next few years much of this would be acted upon.

This meditation is fascinating because it demonstrates what a systematic, holistic thinker he was. Once again we can see the rhetorical *cursus* laid out, point by sub point. We can see his broad reading in history brought to bear, and we can see how he developed a response to the building threat by thinking about it from multiple aspects. Although he does lapse into the language of providential smiting at one point, he clearly sees that his analyses should lead to actions which can change the foreseen outcomes of these religious tensions. The fact that he then acted on some of them underscores the relation between analysis, policy, and actually governing.

Of course, the document may have been an outline for a speech, for his speeches were notable for their qualities. Henry Peacham, writing in the early 1620s, suggested that Burghley was one of the greatest orators of his age, admired for "public speeches in the Parliament house and Star Chamber: for nothing draws our attention more than good matter, eloquently digested, and uttered with a graceful, clear, and distinct pronunciation."[64]

The way in which he conceived interconnected issues is important to notice, and so is the way he understood the limitations of his own system and sought to fix them. Although he clearly thought of England as a Protestant state, he was no ideologue when it came to thinking through how to protect it. He was methodical about this, as he was about everything. As he once observed to the Privy Council: "All counselors by their contrarieties are best esteemed whereby perfect choice may follow, so, in matters of moment, propounded in consultation, the best and soundest resolutions are taken, by comparing commodities with inconveniencies."[65] All

---

[63] CP 157/8.

[64] Henry Peacham, *The Compleat Gentleman* (1622), 44 [STC (2nd edn)/19502].

[65] Yale, Beinecke Library, Osborn Shelves Fb 6, "Certain Replies and objections answered, by William Lord Burleigh, at the Councell Table."

of his formal thinking helps us understand how he conceived his role, his beliefs about human nature, his value system, and his self-conception as a gentleman and a servant of the Crown.

His vision of himself is, naturally, complicated and hard to discover. However, patterns appear in the hundreds of thousands of words he wrote that allow us to estimate not only how he saw his place, but also how his self-understanding changed over time. His education and early experiences were formative, but so were his experiences in office and in the ever-shifting world of politics and religion.

Among his key personal values were rationality, curiosity, stoic self-control, and loyalty. The testimony of those who knew him, and of his literary remains, suggests that he lived a highly ordered life and valued those who did likewise.

This personal approach to leadership and management made him calm, thoughtful, and calculating. It reflected the Ciceronian ideal of virtuous leadership he so valued. Henry Peacham tells us that Burghley "to his dying day, would always carry…about him, either in his bosom or pocket," a volume of Cicero, "being sufficient (as one said of Aristotle's *Rhetoriques*) to make both a scholar and an honest man."[66]

This phlegmatic temperament was one of his key leadership tools. He is reported as being imperturbable. Cicero taught that a statesman should have a tranquility that allowed him to lead a dignified and self-consistent life. He must be free from disturbing emotions, "not only from desire and fear, but also from excessive pain and pleasure, and from anger, so that we may enjoy that calm of soul and freedom from care which bring both moral stability and dignity of character."[67] Cecil practiced this.

But the lessons of the classics were not always positive. After all, Cicero lived in a revolutionary age, and, although he was in some ways a defender of the late Republic, he was also part of its decline. Perhaps Burghley loved him for his language and his stoic moderation, but found in Cicero support for his fear of faction. Cicero's age didactically taught that imperial order was to be preferred over the political chaos inhabited by Cicero and Caesar.

When Cecil thought about the decline of states, he was probably inclined to the view of Livy, who asked readers of his history of Rome to note the life and morals of the community, and the qualities of the men who led the Republic to victory. As their morals decayed Rome decayed, until the Republic could bear neither its diseases nor its remedies.[68] That diseased age, of course, was Cicero's age, an age when the Roman Republic, having endured the wars between the *optimates* and the *populares*, the revolts of the Gracchi, the Social Wars, the two triumvirates, the Catiline conspiracy, and other increasingly desperate events, finally found peace under the emperor Augustus, father of the *pax romanorum*, the man who preserved the great Roman empire. Even Cicero's death, when he was ripped from his sedan chair and beheaded by the supporters of Mark Antony, underscored the political

---

[66] Peacham, *Gentleman*, 44.   [67] Cicero, *De officiis*, I, xx, 69.

[68] Livy, *History of Rome*, Bk 1, Preface, at http://etext.virginia.edu/etcbin/toccer-new2?id=Liv1His. sgm&images=images/modeng&data=/texts/english/modeng/parsed&tag=public&part=front. Accessed Feb. 12, 2012.

point that republican disorder murdered the state. Perhaps Elizabethan statesmen knew from Roman history what Ronald Syme took from it when he wrote the *Roman Revolution*: popular factions can only be controlled through power, and Augustus had to take control to save Rome.[69]

One of the lessons Cecil must have learned from the history of Cicero's times was the danger of faction. But he did not need the ancients to teach him that lesson, since he could learn equally well from his own times. One of the notable things about the Elizabethan political world, compared to earlier in the dynasty, was the ostensible absence of faction—but this was not an accident. Burghley and the Queen understood its dangers and harnessed the very causes of faction in the interest of national preservation. When Burghley read Cicero's letters, or thought about the Catiline conspiracy, he must have heard the echoes of the Tudor world he knew well. After all, he himself had seen several rebellions and participated in court putsches.

His contemporary biographer, who had worked with him for twenty years, observed that when divisions in council and trouble abroad caused factions and fear, Burghley's "temper and wise foresight ever qualified and reconciled" divisions and prevented fear. In fact, one of Burghley's apothegms was that division in counsel was dangerous, "if not a subversion of the state."[70]

This, too, was a lesson taught by Cecil's favorite author. Cicero's *Epistolae familiares* were packed with the faction fights of the late Roman Republic. According to Webbe, who published a translation of Cicero's letters in 1620, Burghley, "a grave and powerful Magistrate, of weightiest employments, about a great Monarch...made these letters his glass, his rule, his Oracle, and ordinary pocket-book: an honor justly due unto the Prince of Eloquence."[71]

Apparently, he was never excited, which made avoiding faction easier. He did not have a fan's passions. He received foreign intelligence daily, and "not so few as 20 or 30 other letters" in a day, filled with news good and bad. His biographer reports he spoke temperately of the good news and kept the ill news to himself, often commenting that the enemy "shall do no more than God will suffer them."[72]

In 1564 he explained his calm rationality by suggesting one should strive for virtue while learning from life:

> Things growing, which daily, from time to time, do increase; whose example, if a man would follow, he should as his body groweth in age, so his wit with knowledge, his conditions with virtue should amend; and as we do live we grow towards death, by moments of time; so should we grow towards heaven, by multiplying of virtues, and good gifts.[73]

In sum, William Cecil strove to be the sort of virtuous Christian humanist leader described in the books and sermons that informed the ruling classes about their

[69] Ronald Syme, *The Roman Revolution* (Oxford: Oxford University Press, 1939).

[70] Collins, 69.

[71] "To the Reader," *The Familiar Epistles of M. T. Cicero Englished*, trans. J. Webbe (1620) [STC (2nd edn)/5305].

[72] Collins, 30.   [73] BL Harleian 6990, fol. 1.

duties and how to perform them. He actively pursued and acted upon his virtues, and he built a bureaucratic machine to help him.

Burghley's "daily growing" was informed by experience and knowledge, and active management made gathering knowledge necessary. He had to do complex calculations of cause, effect, cost, and supply, constantly looking at Elizabethan governance from different angles, using historical context and current knowledge as tools.

His problem is reminiscent of Jeremy Bentham's design for a panopticon, a prison in which a single warden could see every prisoner. Bentham was giving architectural form to the trick Burghley had to perform mentally. Of course, he could not see every actor, but every decision required inspection from multiple points of view. The problem had to be identified, the preferred solutions considered, the actors examined, their status inspected, their motives calculated, the law calibrated, the mechanisms of communication explored, the money counted, the moral and social preferences totted up, the Queen's opinion weighed, and the most up-to-date knowledge brought to bear. When he had done all that, his value system helped him decide what to do. After a while, some of it became automatic, the sort of thing he could do easily and instantly, but for some issues and in some circumstances, effective leadership required continual and repetitive care.

Part of what he did so easily is hard for us to assess because it is hidden within the values of his political culture. The instinctive social knowledge that came from life in his world is not available to us, so what made sense then may be hard to grasp now. We can see how he prepared to do the job, and the values underlying it, only through his carefully built information retrieval system.

The cabinets full of documents that his clerks managed, many of them in his hand or annotated by him, became the brain of the Elizabethan state. They were organized roughly in the format in which the Calendars of State Papers Domestic and Foreign were arranged in the nineteenth century. We can see this from the list of manuscript books in his office when he died. Some of these were finding aids, some were reference works. The manuscripts included:

1. Large book of the musters of England 1591
2. Book of Treaties with foreign Princes
3. Book of maps of Ireland in large
4. Description of the state of the duchy of Lancaster with the lands, officers and fees
5. Book of Parliament Men anno R 39
6. Book of Justices of the peace
7. Summary of the treaty of peace between her majesty and the king of Spain in anno 88
8. Commonplaces of my M[aster's] collection
9. Notes of alliances of princes
10. Articles of the earl of Essex for defense of the realm against an invasion with the lords answer thereto

11. Journal of my Mr. Negotiations in France
12. Style and Titles of princes
13. Book of Latin letters
14. Book of Ireland under Sir William Russell
15. Book of Ireland Lo: Burgh lls justices
16. Book of Scotland Border
17. Book of Low Countries and Germany
18. Book of France and Brittany
19. Book of France of later matters
20. Collections of things past by my L. Treasurer
21. Calendar of Sir Francis Walsingham's papers
22. Book of maps of Ireland in colors
23. Book written by a reconciled Papist
24. Discourses of the Low Countries, France, and Germany
25. Collection of Scottish matters
26. Collection of ordinances and valuation of money
27. Prayer for the Queen going to the Parliament
28. Coat and Arms of the Cecils[74]

These manuscript books of reference suggest his passion for information necessary to the state. His clerks and he needed to find the documents in their archive, his "books" were his own "calendar of state papers." The collection let them address grandees properly and provided needed historical precedents and insights. It was primitive, but without it no real central influence could be exerted.

The "Calendar of Sir Francis Walsingham's Papers" kept among Burghley's manuscripts gives us another glimpse into managerial organization. The books and papers at Walsingham's home and at court were organized like Burghley's, though with some different headings, such as "navy, havens, and sea causes" and "Religion and Matters Ecclesiastical" kept in boxes. The "Table Book" (or "Tables of Matters") register shows "matters concerning" Ireland, Scotland, France, Guernsey and Jersey, Flanders, Poland, Spain, Portugal, the Hanse, Denmark, Muscovy, and other places, suggesting a geographical filing system. The manuscript books listed include books of "Home Matters," "Treaties," and a "Register of Intercourses."[75]

The inventory of Burghley's office included printed books, too, and they throw further light on his managerial tools and values. At first, the printed books on his desk seem odd. That he owned a printed copy of Hugo Grotius's work is not a surprise, until we realize that Grotius was only about seventeen when he wrote the collection of poetry on Burghley's shelf. The presence of poetry is as shocking as the

---

[74] TNA SP 12/268 fol. 65.   [75] BL Stowe, 162.

youth of Grotius—Burghley was not known to care for poetry—until we find that it is a dramatic dialogue between Philip II, Henri IV, the Pope, and Elizabeth I. Grotius gives Elizabeth an eloquent speech denouncing the Pope, saying, "Did you think me a fool?...that you dared to say I was prepared to lend an ear" to his demands that she bend her royal knee to his wooden idols and muttered prayers in heathenish tongues. Asking her to do it is as pointless as harnessing wolves or plowing sand. "My purpose is fixed," he has her say, "to keep faith with my allies and honor treaties."[76] Designed to influence the English court, perhaps it did. Certainly, it was propaganda of which Burghley needed to be aware.

Burghley's work as an orator is reflected in some books, such as *Polyanthea: Hoc est, opus suavissimis floribus celebriorum sententiarum tam graecarum quam latinarum*...of Domenico Nani Mirabelli. An alphabetical list of topics, it provides Greek and Latin tags, like Isocrates' observation "Anima civitatis civilibus legibus continetur" ("The soul of a civilization is contained in its laws"). Francoise de Belleforest's collection of great oratory had the same utility. His two volumes contained speeches by Thucydides, Tacitus, Sallust, Caesar, and many, many others, along with modern models such as Machiavelli, Petro Bembo, and Silvius Aeneas Piccolomini. There was also a handy catalog of wise sayings of state in French.[77]

So he needed information he could access, and he needed the didactic tools of an orator. He also needed orientation in space and time. He never visited much of the land he ran for Elizabeth, just as she had not. He had seen part of the north, since he had traveled twice to Scotland as an invader, in 1547 and 1560, but he had never seen Cornwall, Wales, Ireland, or most of the rest of the realm. Geographical ignorance presented a problem that could not be easily solved, except by trusting people who had local knowledge.

However, Burghley tried to know. He needed, and loved, maps. Lawrence Nowell, antiquarian and tutor to the earl of Oxford, in Burghley's house, proclaimed Cecil's love of maps when he proposed to him a national mapping project.[78] This resulted in the Nowell–Burghley Atlas, bound in limp vellum for ease of transport, containing maps of England, Wales, Ireland, and part of Scotland. Burghley annotated it with his itineraries in 1564–70. It had a sketch of Burghley himself on the cover, and he had annotated it with lists of distances.[79] R. A. Skelton says, "Time and again we find him collating and annotating, and even drawing, maps to analyse a situation or work out policies and instruction. In any business conditioned by geography, it is clear that he had the habit of thinking in a cartographic idiom..." Moreover, he had an exceptional sense of geography, which "was evidently fed upon an acute visual perception and memory and on exceptional facility in constructing in his mind's eye a picture of terrain whether on strategic or tactical scales from the

---

[76] Hugieani Grotii Carmina, TNA SP 12/268 fol. 65. E. H. Bodkin, "The Minor Poetry of Hugo Grotius," *Transactions of the Grotius Society*, 13 (1927), 97.

[77] Francois de Belleforest, *Harangues militaires, et concions de princes, capitaines, ambassadeurs, et autres manians tant la guerre que les affaires d'Estat*...(Geneva, 1595). http://www.e-rara.ch/gep_g/content/titleinfo/976657. Accessed Aug. 17, 2013.

[78] BL Lansd. 6 fol.135.   [79] BL Add. 62540, fols 3, 4v, 5.

study of appropriate documents, supplemented by his correspondence and (for his own country) personal observation."[80]

His office had several sets of maps in both manuscript and print. Some were the annotated versions, but he also annotated them himself. And he also owned chorographies of the regions of the land (Fig. 3.3). Camden's *Britannia* was in his office, along with Abraham Ortelius's *Theatrum orbis terrarium*, and John Norden's recently published *Description of Hertfordshire*.[81] Perhaps the Ortelius was the hand-colored 1570 edition, which he signed on the title page. In 1584 the backs of the maps were annotated with military intelligence. The map of France, for instance, had notes on the garrisons of the port towns (Fig. 3.4).[82]

He supplemented the maps he could get with other kinds of intelligence. His correspondence with Sir Henry Norris, the ambassador in Paris in 1567, displays his attempts to minimize his ignorance. He asks Norris to "send me a note of the names of the charts that are thought newest, and of the author of their setting forth, and the places where they be printed, I may chance to trouble you with craving of some." Then he requests "the names of the chiefest nobility of France, and with whom they be married; adding thereto any other thing that may belong to the knowledge of their lineage and degrees, as you shall think meet."[83] Clearly, he was applying to France his own social mapping models he used to keep the nobility of England straight in his head.

Of course, the ambassador's job was to gather intelligence while representing the Queen, so it was essential that ambassadors kept up a steady flow of information back to the court. Cecil defined it this way, telling Norris that Elizabeth liked his "advertisements" to her "which she wisheth you to continue. She alloweth your discretion, in writing apart to me, in matters containing trouble and business, and to her of advice."[84] He had written much the same letter to Sir Thomas Smith when he was ambassador in Paris, noting that he could not answer all of Smith's private letters, since he had to write the Queen's letters first, so the ambassadors did not get as good as they gave.[85]

Besides the press of royal business, other things slowed communications. All that writing took time, and, as he told Smith, there were only twenty-four hours in a day. The post was often slow and confused, too. Cecil himself frequently told the ambassador that his responses were slowed by illnesses that prevented writing, by business of all sorts, and by lack of messengers. The fact that he had to follow the court, which was frequently in motion, meant that messengers from the ambassador had a hard time finding him.[86]

---

[80] R. A. Skelton, "The Maps of a Tudor Statesman," in R. A. Skelton and John Summerson, *A Description of Maps and Architectural Drawings in the Collections made by William Cecil First Baron Burghley now at Hatfield House* (Oxford: The Roxburghe Club, 1971), 3–4. My thanks to Susan Cogan for this reference.

[81] SP 12/268 fol. 65. Alford, *Burghley*, 147; 236.

[82] Stamford, Burghley House, BKS 16611.

[83] *Cabala, sive, Scrinia sacra mysteries of state and government* (1663), 141.

[84] *Cabala*, 135.   [85] BL Lansd. 102, fol. 48.   [86] BL Lansd. 102, fol.141.

Fig. 3.3. Printed map of Devon, dated 1575, with marginal notes by Lord Burghley relating to the defense of the county, BL Royal 18 D.III fols 11v–12.

Apparently, when Cecil was with the Queen, she shared Ambassador Norris's letters with him, but when he was not, he was out of the information loop. At one point he told Norris that because it was term time, he had to be in London, remarking,

> I have not had the commodity to see your advertisements; nevertheless, you shall do well to continue your accustomed manner of advertising her Majesty as fully as you can, for in these troublesome times, the accidents being so diversely reported as they are, it is meet that her Majesty should be largely advertised, and because it may be that your letters may come in this term time while I am at London, I pray let me have some repetition of your advises in such letters you shall write to me.[87]

Adding to the confusion was the use of ciphers, which needed to be translated before secret information could be gleaned. Cecil, as Principal Secretary, had the ciphers, but if he was not at court there was a problem. Being ill in the summer of 1568, unable to attend the Queen, he explained to Norris that letters from the embassy

---

[87] BL Lansd. 102, fol. 143.

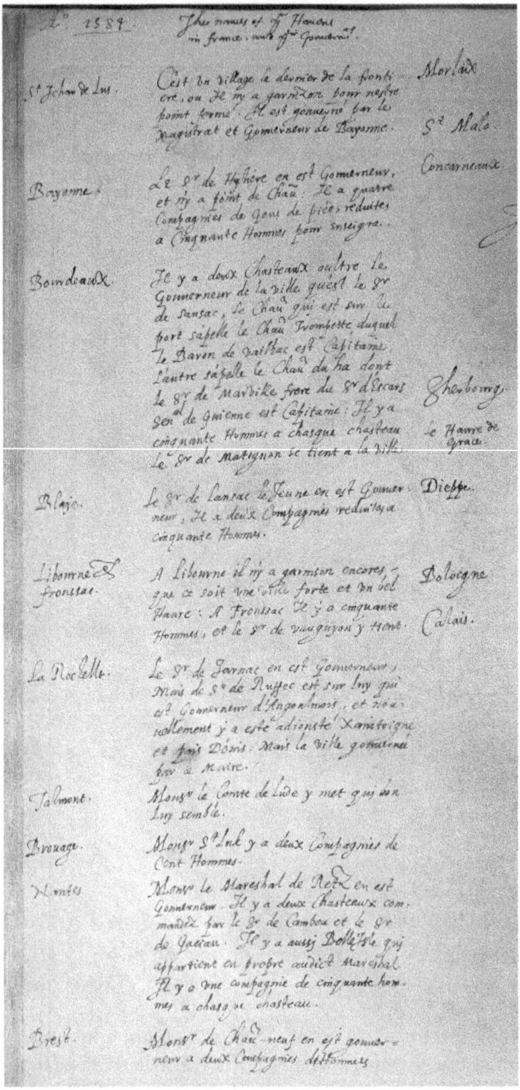

A° 1584. The names of ye Havens in France with their Governours.

St John de Luz. C'est un village le dernier de la frontiere, ou il n'y a garnison pour n'estre point fermé. Il est gouverné par le magistrat et Gouverneur de Bayonne.

Bayonne. Le Sr de Hylhiere en est Gouverneur, et n'y a point de Chasteau. Il a quatre Compagnies de gens de pied, reduites a Cinquante Hommes pour enseigne.

Bourdeaux. Il y a deux Chasteaux oultre le Gouverneur de la ville qu'est le Sr de Sansac, le Chasteau qui est sur le port s'apelle le Chasteau Trompette duquel le Baron de Vaillac est Capitaine; l'autre s'apelle le Chasteau du Ha dont le Sr de Mardike frere du Sr d'Escars Senal de Guienne est Capitaine. Il y a cinquante Hommes a chasque chasteau. Le Sr de Matignon se tient a la ville.

Blaye. Le Sr de Lansac le Jeune en est Gouverneur, il a deux Compagnies reduites a cinquante Hommes.

Libourne & Fronsac. A Libourne il n'y a garnison encores, que ce soit une ville forte et un bel Havre: A Fronsac il y a cinquante Hommes, et le Sr de Vauguyon y tient.

La Rochelle. Le Sr de Jarnac en est Gouverneur, Mais le Sr de Ruffec est sur luy qui est Gouverneur d'Angoulmois, et nouvellement y a este adiouste Xaintoigne et pais d'Onis. Mais la ville gouvernee par le Maire.

Talmont. Monsr le Comte de Lude y met qui bon luy semble.

Brouage. Monsr St Luc y a deux Compagnies de Cent Hommes.

Nantes. Monsr le Mareschal de Retz en est Gouverneur. Il y a deux Chasteaux commandez par le Sr de Cambou et le Sr de Gascan. Il y a aussi Belle Isle qui appartient en propre audict Mareschal. Il y a une compagnie de cinquante hommes a chasque chasteau.

Brest. Monsr de Chasteauneuf en est gouverneur a deux Compagnies de Hommes

Morlaix
St Malo
Concarneaux
Cherbourg
Le Havre de Grace
Dieppe
Boloigne
Calais

Fig. 3.4. "Anno 1584 The names of the Havens in France and their Governours," Abraham Ortelius, *Theatrum orbis terrarum* (1570). Burghley House, BKS 16611, leaf 9. My thanks to Jon Culverhouse, Curator at Burghley House, for the use of this illustration.

had gone to him, and then had to be sent on, deciphered, to other members of the council.[88] Naturally, this delayed the responses.

Communication with Norris was difficult, even though it was of the highest importance. Communication within the realm was complicated, too. For instance,

[88] BL Lansd. 102, fol. 150.

in 1584 a messenger for the Exchequer submitted his travel expenses for riding "with all diligent haste" to deliver a letter from Burghley to Francis Cotton in Portsmouth. Arriving there, the messenger learned Cotton had gone to Chichester, so he had to turn his horse toward Sussex. It took him six days of riding from the time he left Westminster with the letter until he returned with Cotton's answer. All that travel cost 20s., a not insignificant amount.[89] This sort of confusion and delay must have occurred frequently.

Getting someone to carry a message, especially an important one, was difficult. The Auditor in Ireland wrote Burghley that "not trusting every messenger" the Master of the Rolls had "requested me by some friend of mine" to deliver a letter to him.[90]

So he could only "see" what others wrote to him, when and if their letters arrived. And letters did not always arrive.

Elizabethan managers did their best to maintain communication with informants from all over. They collected the news reports (*avissi*) printed abroad, and they had networks of correspondents charged with supplementing their knowledge of foreign affairs. Burghley was willing to pay for good information, but not "the common advises of the occurents abroad," which could be had from any merchant.[91]

Recently a small industry has sprung up around Elizabethan espionage. Stephen Alford has studied the archive of Robert Beale, Clerk of the Privy Council, and John Cooper has added a carefully scholarly voice to the study of Walsingham's intelligence network.[92] Concentrating on foreign threats, and often preoccupied with the activities of English exiles and Mary, Queen of Scots, the network had agents in the major cities of Europe.

When Walsingham was dying in May, 1590, he gave Burghley his papers on diplomacy, including his "book of secret intelligences." Through it Burghley was informed of the names of Walsingham's foreign agents and their pay. As usual, Burghley wrote them down on one of his lists, and proceeded to ask whether he was getting his money's worth. He trimmed the list, reducing the cost, but he, like Walsingham, continued to use "intelligencers" to gather information in foreign countries.[93]

Alford and Cooper have tried to reconstruct the way secret information was acquired and handled. Ciphers were used, and over the course of the reign they became more and more sophisticated. Very few people had access to the ciphers, or could see the information that was being gathered, but as it came in, it was added to what the ambassadors, the *avissi*, and oral sources were supplying.

In the archives we catch glimpses of the way information was received. But for every letter there are hundreds of oral conversations that are beyond recovery. The information nodes of royal management included several places where the leading people congregated, shared information, and debated strategies. These "intelligences" that now move along the dotted lines of informal organizational charts via email,

---

[89] HEH, HM 1418.   [90] TNA SP 63/110 fol. 3.   [91] *Cabala*, 140–1.
[92] John Cooper, *The Queen's Agent: Francis Walsingham at the Court of Elizabeth I* (London: Faber and Faber, 2011). Stephen Alford, *The Watchers: A Secret History of the Reign of Elizabeth I* (London: Penguin, 2013).
[93] Alford, *Watchers*, 264–6.

telephones, and other media, then mostly occurred face to face. Thus it was important for the leading managers to meet and work together all the time.

The court was a great ear, sucking in gossip and information from all over, and at many levels of access. Parliaments, too, when they met, functioned as another way of connecting and informing. The assize courts, with their justices and other officials riding out from London to meet with the justice of the peace and other county notables, were a major place of two-way communication. Concentrating this oral news, and collating it with other sources of information, the clerks and their bosses prepared it to be used in meetings of the Privy Council, and when briefing the Queen.

We can glimpse this in Burghley's retelling of events to ambassadors. He once described to Norris the scene at a dinner attended by the French ambassador, Norfolk, Arundel, and Leicester, the Lord Chamberlain, and himself, in 1569. He and the ambassador "entered more privately" into a discussion of Norris's situation in Paris, where, the French ambassador said, Norris was disliked for his support of French rebels. Cecil replied in defense, and they had a civil discussion before going in to dine.[94]

Many of the same men who met in the council attended the Star Chamber sessions, where they commingled with the justices of the main courts. They served together on commissions, they were appointed to the occasional Court of Delegates to hear appeals, and many had bouge of court, frequently dining together there.

Spend enough time in Burghley's archive and you will come to see the management of the Elizabethan state as a three-dimensional game of chess. He was constantly calculating and recalculating the positions and likely moves of kings, queens, bishops, knights, and pawns. He needed to know a great deal about individuals, places, states, and history to move his pieces effectively. How you behaved toward all those people was molded by Christian values and ancient traditions, both inherited and learned from the classics, and the most recent policy and information.

Looking over Burghley's life, we can see that he was a man of deep commitment and highly structured habits. He believed he occupied a place granted him by providence, and with duties to match his blessings. He believed in God's hierarchy, and therefore put service to the Queen first, while showing deference due to others of high degree. He conceived of himself as a man of Christian virtue. In this careful, methodical life of unrelenting managerial work he achieved his highest goal—he kept Elizabeth on the throne to do God's will. His piety required it.

And so who made the policy? Elizabeth or Burghley? We can see from his records that he certainly thought deeply about governing, and that he understood his place in government. He very carefully observed the appointed roles of the Queen and himself, while maximizing the mechanics of government at his command. He and Elizabeth agreed on his role, and he soberly performed it the best he could. The reward for his devotion to duty was a life of toil in the Queen's service.

[94] *Cabala*, 165.

The toil he performed for Elizabeth for thirty-nine years was complex. He stood, like a conductor, before a group of diverse players, attempting to keep them all playing the Queen's tune for the good of the commonwealth. How he kept them working can be seen in his approaches to particular managerial assignments he undertook as he attempted to keep the varied drivers of the Elizabethan state pulling in the same general directions.

4

Managing Locally

> For how can law be enforced if they are too slothful to creep out their doors to any court, sessions or assizes, for the due administration thereof, except they be drawn thereto by some matters of their own, nor cannot endure to have their ears troubled with hearing of controversies of their neighbors for the good appeasing of the same, or how can the uncarefull man that maketh no account of any of the common causes of his country, but respecteth only his private matters and commodity become a diligent searcher out, follower and corrector of felons, murderers, and such like enemies of the common weal?

> Lord Keeper Bacon, in his speech at the closing of Parliament, 1559[1]

All this theory about virtue was only as good as the men who ruled, and they were not all saints. They had their own interests, friends, families, and attitudes that shaped their relationship to the Queen. For them, government was useful primarily as a way of making life in their region of influence livable. They had a vested interest in enforcing some laws, as long as their own passions and interests were not offended. They had an interest in creating new laws, if they served their needs. Given their large independence, Burghley, Elizabeth, and the other councilors had to ensure the cooperation of the magisterial classes to make a nation of semi-autonomous "countries" work together for the common good. It could be tricky.

In September 1587 Edward Fleetwood, the godly minister at Wigan in Lancashire, wrote a hasty letter to Lord Burghley, warning him that Henry Stanley, fourth Earl of Derby, was on his way to court to complain about Burghley's attempt to reform the Commission of the Peace in the earl's territory. As the likelihood of war with Spain was increasing, the Privy Council, seeking to ensure that justices of the peace would enforce the laws against Catholics, had surveyed the bishops asking for the names of men who could not be trusted to defend the national religion. Consequently, Burghley had removed a few and provoked the furor that was descending on him from Lancashire.

Fleetwood had preached the assize sermon at Wigan, trying his best to stir the justices and juries to favor the godly cause, as instructed by Burghley and the Ecclesiastical High Commission. The minister reported,

> I thought good...to lay forth...in the pulpit to their faces that...concerning the corrupt state of the whole country [county], that every guilty conscience of them

---

[1] Hartley, *Proceedings*, vol. 1, 50.

might gather up that which was due unto it.... Whereof it pleased my Lords the Judges to take so good notice, that they delievered the chief points thereof after to the juries in charge, and the same also more specially recommended to the Justice of Peace to be in their continual services regarded. All which so nearly touched the guilty consciences of the disinterested sort, that they began, for the residue of the assizes, to pluck down their high looks, and sought better to pacify their discontented minds, and to brook their emulated friends than before they seemed to do.[2]

That Rev. Fleetwood was needed to stir up the guilty consciences of the magistrates to do their duty is indicative of a key problem in Elizabethan government. The center had very poor control over the periphery, depending on the consciences of the powerful gentlemen in the locales to see to it that the law was enforced. The problem in Wigan was that Derby, a leading player in the region and a good Protestant, was very unhappy with the way Burghley was meddling in local affairs. Derby was so perturbed he went to court to complain in person.

That his complaint would be taken seriously was certain, since the Privy Council had very little authority in Lancashire without the help of the earls of Derby. Sir Francis Leake, writing of the third earl, warned Cecil in 1569, "all the keys of Lancashire... presently hang at the earl of Derby's old girdle." The council had to hope for Derby's allegiance.[3] Both the third and fourth earls sat in Elizabeth's Privy Council, a concession to the council's weakness in the shire, and recognition of the continuing power of the Stanley family.

In regions where there was one dominant family, or in which the dominant families were too Catholic to fill the country benches, competitions emerged. Old families were being pushed out, and ascending families were pushing in, often in competition with other emerging local leaders. Cathryn Enis has shown that in Warwickshire, where the mostly Catholic Throckmortons, Catesbys, and Ardens were in decline, the Dudley family and the Hatton family were jockeying for local power. This is visible in competition for appointments to the Warwickshire commission of the peace, where their clients appear on the commissions for various years. Enis argues that, in fact, the clients of Lord Chancellor Hatton were intentionally being placed on the commissions to counteract the rising power of the Dudleys. Exploring the dense tangle of kinships and connections in the county and in the court, she shows how, in the wake of the 1569 revolt, the commission expanded in numbers and the traditional families were pushed out, making way for the Dudleys and their clients. However, by the mid-1570s the gentry not favored by the Dudleys began to push back, with men—like Edward Arden, an enemy of Robert Dudley—coming on. Arden's execution in 1583 was attributed to this animosity. Moreover, these anti-Dudley men tended to be anti-Puritan as well. Mostly connected to the legal establishment, men such as Justice Sir James Dyer were less willing to do Leicester's bidding. In this case, the politics at court,

---

[2] BL Cotton Titus B/II fol. 239. Edward Fleetwood waged a lively fight against the lax religion of men on the commission of the peace in Lancashire. See David Sinclair, *The History of Wigan* (Wigan: Wall, 1882), vol. 1, 156–62.

[3] B. W. Quintrell, "Government in Perspective: Lancashire and the Privy Council, 1570–1640," *Transactions of the Historic Society of Lancashire & Cheshire*, 131 (1982 for 1981), 43.

and the religious disputes in the nation, were being played out within the Warwickshire commission of the peace. It is a classic example of the way in which the local and national intermingled.[4]

The Tudor form of government inherited by Elizabeth was a set of interlocking chains of local and regional authorities that tangled and crossed all the way to the royal court. Many governing entities, such as leet courts, were independent or semi-independent authorities that belonged to landlords as parts of their demesnes. Many of these landlords were members of aristocratic families who literally owned and controlled whole regions. Others belonged to oligarchs, most often urban aldermen. Yet others belonged to the great ecclesiastical foundations, such as cathedrals, or bishoprics. Some were controlled by institutions such as Cambridge and Oxford universities, self-governing entities within self-governing cities, enjoying separate parliamentary seats. The greatest property owner of them all was the Queen, whose sheriffs collected royal rents in all the shires.

The thing that gave the monarchy real power over all these putative servants was the law and the reciprocal services it provided to the nation in common. Recognizing the power of the local landlords and oligarchs, the royal law was enforced through various officers with royal commissions. The most obvious of these were the justices of the peace, panels of locally influential people who were expected to ensure that the royal peace was kept in their localities.

The justices of the peace were appointed by commission under the great seal to perform a number of functions. At the heart of their duties were three charges. First, they were to maintain the peace and enforce statutes, proclamations, and ordinances. Second, they were to enquire into felonies and misdemeanors committed in their county and to force those indicted to appear for trial. The third was that two or more of them, sitting together, could hear and determine the charges against those indicted. To be eligible to serve, a man had to be worth at least £20 a year, unless he was a lawyer. Because of the need for men trained in law there was an exception allowed for them, and it was common for one of the lawyers to be appointed by the Lord Keeper to serve as the *custos rotulorum* (keeper of the rolls) of the county's commission of the peace. The commission was also served by a clerk of the peace who drew up the legal processes and recorded deeds. The justices of the peace were the cutting edge of the Queen's law in the locales.[5]

The justices of the peace were backed up by the judges of the royal courts in Westminster who, riding out three times a year to the localities to hold assize courts, met with the locally powerful and the justices, to try offenders against the Crown's law. They conducted "gaol delivery," trying those imprisoned by local authorities according to common law. These trials were held with the aid of juries of local people, of sufficient wealth to be eligible to be jurors, who determined the guilt or innocence of the parties charged.

---

[4] Cathryn Enis, "The Dudleys, Sir Christopher Hatton and the Justices of Elizabethan Warwickshire," *Midland History* 39, 1 (2014), 1–35.

[5] J. H. Baker, *The Oxford History of the Laws of England* (Oxford: Oxford University Press, 2003), vol. 6, 265–71.

These assize trials were major points of interaction between the powerful and the influential. The judges were feted with banquets, and the great and the good were preached at by important clergy. The judges updated the justices on new laws and emphasized their duties, the whole event reinforcing the links in the chains that bound locales to the court and various elites to one another.

In time of war the Queen had to depend on all these gentlemen to perform the services owed by men of their stations and offices. Her expectation that they would ensure justice and defense was often disappointed, and local elites sometimes stood together against the Queen's demands.

A fine example of this comes from the early 1580s, when the Privy Council set out to create a trained band of soldiers in Yorkshire, under the command of Henry Hastings, earl of Huntingdon, and the Lord President of the North. On May 20, 1584 they wrote ordering the levying of 10,000 foot soldiers and 400 horsemen in the county of York. The letter, received a week later, shows what the privy councilors knew about local matters in Yorkshire. The troops were to be

> committed to the several and principal charge of your lordship yourself, and to our very good lords the earls of Rutland and Cumberland, and to the Lord Darcy as persons of the best degrees having houses and places of residence in the county, and so most fit to have the general charge of the power of the county, wherein we do not forget the Lord Scrope and the Lord Euers were for the former respects also very meet for this service by that the Lord Scrope is to attend his charge at Carlisle and the Lord Euers is by her Majesty ordered to have the charge of the power of the bishopric [of Durham]…

Relying on great landlords to command the force, they advised about the organization of the band in units led by the lesser gentry: "And that under all these generals the numbers may be particularly committed to the leading of knights and gentlemen able to lead some 300—some 200—and some 100," noting that raising 10,000 would not be hard since there were 42,000 men certified on the muster rolls submitted by these gentlemen.

The order ended with another, sharper, demand: "advertise us, how soon you can proceed to the execution of your commission for the execution of the statute for fortifying of the frontiers, for Her Majesty is therein so earnest to have speed used, as she blameth us greatly, for that the same hath not been executed since the making of the statute, being a matter of so great importance, and the time so long past whereupon we have promised her…"[6]

Clearly, Huntingdon's "Loving Friends" on the Privy Council were utterly dependent on the willingness of the regional gentry to carry out their order. Unfortunately for them, the Yorkshire men were not enthused.

Two months after receiving the order, Huntingdon wrote the Privy Council the bad news:

> the country is altogether unable to array and furnish so great a number of footmen, especially for that there is not in the whole country armor and weapon sufficient in any

---

[6] HEH, HM 30881, fols 1v–3.

good manner to furnish a far less number. And what a heavy burden it would be for them to provide the armor wanting with ready money, your Lordships can well consider, and the former charges which the country hath not long since sustained in sundry services both towards Ireland and Scotland as hitherto they have not forgotten it.

As for the 400 horsemen, they can only raise 300 in the whole country. Nonetheless, he promised that the shortage will be "supplied by the good wills and forward dispositions of the noble men and gentlemen in this country, upon whom in truth the whole burden of the same is like to light."[7]

Faced with this polite refusal, Secretary Walsingham drew up a set of responses he recommended to the Privy Council. The greatest concessions were that the number of footmen was reduced to 6,000, the information on the "livings" (incomes) of the tenants were no longer requested, and, although it was desired that gentlemen lead all these troops, their lack of experience might require that people experienced in war be recruited. But Huntingdon did not win on all points. It was made clear that the expense of raising, arming, and maintaining this force would be borne by him and his associates in Yorkshire. This was communicated to Huntingdon with a comment by the Queen, who, he was informed, "notwithstanding such excuses, as are by them of the county pretended of former services towards Ireland and Scotland, had thought and yet thinks that the said shire was and is able to have furnished a greater number." Nevertheless, not meaning to grieve her subjects, she reduced the levy to 8,000 or "if that cannot in your Lordship's opinion conveniently be done" to 6,000 men.[8]

By early September 1584, the Lord President was ready to act, ordering the mustering and view of the footmen of the county and the raising of 400 light horsemen. But the demand for horsemen was met with howls of complaint from the gentlemen. The responsibility for paying for a light horseman was placed on those whose property was of a certain value. Since their properties were notoriously undervalued, and their rents constantly rising, the gentlemen of Yorkshire pleaded that they were poor and over taxed. They simply could not pay for more than 300 light horsemen.

It was in August 1585, more than a year after the first request for mustering the troops had been issued, that the Privy Council wrote to Huntingdon ordering him to proceed to the mustering and training of 6,000 footmen and 400 horsemen. In response, Huntingdon wrote to Lord Burghley a letter of explanation in which he pointed out that the musters recently taken had confirmed the impossibility of finding 400 horse. The problem was the poverty of the gentry. There were not enough gentlemen able to pay for an entire light horseman individually and, although it might be possible to create syndicates to finance horses, he did not think that was a good idea.

Burghley, taking this intervention from his old friend in good part, communicated it to the Privy Council, prompting another letter to Huntingdon. The council, on August 19, noting that the season had been unseasonably bad, agreed that he need not continue with the training of the footmen until the spring, when he was to see to it that all was in order. As for the horses, they were sure "far greater number would (and ought to be found according to the statute, and the clause of apparel answerable to the

⁷ HEH, HM 30881, fol. 3v.   ⁸ HEH, HM 30881, fols 3v–5.

finding of horses) wherefore we think the proportion not so great but that the county may yield the same to be had always in readiness for the necessary defense thereof…" Consequently, he was to look again for sufficient supply of war horses.[9]

Next year, 1586, the negotiations continued. By now they were becoming more pointed, and the Privy Council had raised the request for horsemen to 800. Huntingdon recounted to the council his negotiations with the Yorkshire gentry over who was to supply what. Raising the money for the needed equipment was a problem, and, despite a council order to purchase weapons, shot, and powder in London, he did not act. Much of this was connected to the issue of how to pay for things. The council acidly told the Lord Lieutenant: "for if so necessary a cause tending to the defense and benefit of themselves, and the whole realm they will so obstinately and precisely do nothing but what is required by the letter of the law, it may happen that the observation of other laws will be required of them, which will touch their purses more deeply than this thing doth."[10] When men were sent to the musters, the money to support them was supposed to be brought with them. Constables may have collected it, but it was not necessarily forwarded, as we see from a letter from Edward Strange to the JPs in 1588, demanding that the constables be forced to turn over the money so they could buy armor.[11]

Huntingdon, in turn, sent a sharp letter to the justices of the peace. Those of the Quorum were each expected to provide two horsemen armed with petronells (carbines), and those not of the Quorum were to provide one. But most importantly, they were to ignore the rate book in assessing military costs on their neighbors. Once again, the responsibility was pushed out to the local gentlemen. Huntingdon left it to the justices of the peace, saying "withdraw yourselves together according to your several divisions, and upon conference among yourselves set down such as you shall think fit to impose this charge upon, which if you shall not be able to perform upon this first meeting, then I would require you to agree among yourselves of a day and place of meeting again…" He added, "you are not in this service for the levying and furnishing of these men to have any regard to the subsidy book," noting that the book did not contain lots of people who could afford to contribute.[12]

By the summer of 1588 the council was still demanding and Huntingdon was still negotiating the raising of the troops. On May 24, with the Spanish Armada at sea, he ordered all the bands to exercise. They did not know how to use their guns, and he wanted them drilled with live fire, but only half charges to save powder and match. Each man was to be paid 6d a day for his diet, and the diet, with the powder and match, were to be paid for "by some equal and indifferent assessment to be made by the Justices" on every township.[13] Each township was to raise the money and send its head constable to deliver it. Collecting it was not easy. In the same way, the Privy Council ordered the aldermen of Hull to send as many ships as were "convenient," furnished with as much food, powder, and shot as they could "on a sudden" obtain.[14]

---

[9] HEH, HM 30881, fols 10v–11v.   [10] HEH, HM 30881, fol. 19v.
[11] HEH EL 6290; HEH EL 6284–9.   [12] HEH, HM 30881, fols 21v–24.
[13] HEH, HM 30881, fols 80v–81.   [14] HEH, HM 30881, fols 118–118v.

In the second week of August 1588 Huntingdon wrote Secretary Walsingham with the news that a Spanish ship had arrived in the Firth of Murray, and the Scottish borderers were ready to march with the Spanish into England. Consequently, he broke up the assize at Newcastle that had brought all the leading men together, sending the gentlemen home to their usual defensive stations against the Scots. Meanwhile, he summoned the trained bands he had so much difficulty in raising and preparing.[15]

This letter crossed one from the Privy Council, written August 20, containing instructions about what troops to station where in preparation for meeting the Spanish. Men were ordered to York, Tynemouth, and Hartlepool, and various ships were dispatched. By the time these instructions arrived, however, Huntingdon had already made his own arrangements, so this bossy order from the court was too late. The Privy Council was working from poor, outdated information at best. Recognizing the impositions made on the gentry in the "north parts," Burghley scrawled in the margin of the draft order "Letters thanks gents. of B.," underscoring the need to make them feel appreciated.[16]

On August 22, 1588 Huntington upbraided the gentlemen of Durham for their coldness in paying for the weapons needed to defend themselves against the Spanish, while offering a compromise that anything they gave would not be entered in the subsidy book, ensuring them that paying this tax would not become a fixed part of their duties.[17]

The story of Yorkshire's inglorious contribution to the defeat of the Spanish invasion is edifying because it makes clear how dependent the central state was on the local gentlemen, and how much regional defense was a regional matter. The Privy Council was reduced to fuming, cajoling, and compromising; the Lord Lieutenant was reduced to negotiating with the justices of the peace, and the justices, when they were willing, were reluctant to force their truculent neighbors to admit their wealth or do their duty.

This story could be repeated endlessly across Elizabeth's reign, in many contexts. The openings and closings of Parliament usually contained a demand that the justices carry out the laws made by their representatives. Speaking in the Queen's name, the Lord Keeper explained the system this way in 1571. Her Majesty, having approved the laws and published them,

> yet ceases not there but granteth out her commission into every of her shires to men which are, or should be, of the greatest consideration within the limits of their charge, which for the better executing of them are sworn to see the execution of her laws to them committed within the limits of their commission. And yet besides all this, by her Majesty's commandment a number of these justices are yearly once at the least called into her Highness' Star Chamber and there in her Highness' name exhorted, admonished and commanded to see to the due execution of their charges.[18]

Although admonished, exhorted, and commanded, the justices of the peace were not always very attentive, enthusiastic, talented, or open to orders that might affect

---

[15] HEH, HM 30881, fols 120–120v.   [16] TNA SP 59/26 fol. 118.
[17] HEH, HM 30881; there is no pagination in the latter part of this letter book.
[18] Hartley, *Proceedings*, vol. 1, 191.

their interests. Like the reluctant gentlemen of Yorkshire, they sometimes preferred to ignore or negotiate an order rather than enforcing it.

Perhaps the greatest surprise is that many of them did try to enforce the laws they were handed. We have already seen the popularity of handbooks for justices of the peace, and there were certainly some very diligent gentlemen and aldermen who worked hard to maintain the peace in their communities. Clearly, their understanding of their duties, and their sense of virtue, led them to do what they could for the common weal and their Queen. However, orders from the center were often ill fitted to local situations, so even men with the best of intentions had a hard time fully carrying them all out.

Penry Williams recognized the nature of this system of government when he commented, "The strength of Tudor government lay in a skilful combination of the formal and the informal, the official and the personal."[19]

This mix of the personal and impersonal meant that attention had to be paid to the virtue of the magistrates. If they, as individuals, could not be depended upon to act properly in relation to their duties, the state was in trouble. Exam questions at Oxford voiced the puzzle of what goodness and reliability looked like in the magistracy. *Bonus civis est vir bonus?* Is a good citizen a good man? *Expedit reipublicae ut magistratus sint quaestuosi?* Is it good for the commonwealth if magistrates are greedy? What was the right balance between self-interest and the interest of the community?[20] William Cecil put it bluntly: honesty and religion are the grounds and ends of good men's actions, without which they will never prosper. Answering the Oxford questions, he held that an honest man's word was better than a bad man's bond, and that "private gain is the perverting of justice, and pestilence of a commonwealth."[21]

From the beginning of Elizabeth's reign, Cecil sought to improve the quality of the commissions of the peace. Multiple holograph drafts attest to his attention to core administrative values. He wanted an honest, disinterested magistracy. No one, the Queen ordered in Cecil's own hand in 1561, should be appointed to the commission who was a retainer or servant of any other person.[22] As time went on, he sought again and again to gather information about the justices' trustworthiness, frequently turning to the bishops for advice about things he could not ask the justices themselves. In general, he wished to know whether justices of the peace were sound in religion, and if their wives or servants were recusants; if their fathers were in the commission (unless the fathers were elderly or otherwise unable to come to sessions); and if they lived in the county or were nonresident more than ninety days a year. Did those living in the county attend quarter sessions or gaol delivery? Were they "common attorneys," or were they ecclesiastical persons of less rank than an archdeacon or chancellor? (These might attend, Burghley adds in a notation, if they pay £20 a year in subsidy.) In short, could they be trusted with places of authority as men whose virtues, wealth, and lack of compromising entanglements would keep them honest and active?[23]

---

[19] Penry Williams, *The Tudor Regime* (Oxford: Clarendon Press, 1979), 462.

[20] John M. Fletcher, ed., *Registrum annualium Collegii Mertonensis, 1567–1603* (Oxford: Clarendon Press for the Oxford Historical Society, 1976), 304, 338.

[21] Collins, 69–70.   [22] TNA SP 12/17 fols 100–1.   [23] BL Lansd. 53, fol. 166.

In 1572, the Lord Treasurer drafted a memo that proves both his concern about the qualities of the men who did the work of local government, and that his 1561 efforts had failed. He thought that if the lords of the council and the judges, when attending courts and assizes, would note down the names of those who took excessive fees and send them to the Queen, some reform might happen. At the same time he called for the Privy Council to review "commissions of the peace in all shires" "and the unmeet persons removed, and their rooms supplied, with more trusty and honorable persons," and that "good and faithful men be appointed sheriffs." The personal qualities of good governors were those of a boy scout: honest, fair, trustworthy, faithful, honorable. Moreover, by 1572 he had added the desire that they were "not condemners or deriders of the orders of religion established by Act of Parliament."[24]

Lord Keeper Bacon noted the characteristics of poor magistrates, who only attended court to look after their own interests. Impatient with their neighbors, they will not listen carefully to them. They were not interested in the "common causes" of their country, searching out felons and correcting enemies of the commonweal.

Contrarily, good magistrates do not mislead juries, acquit people for gain, indict people for malice's sake, interfere at inquests, or commit champetry and maintenance (sharing the proceeds of law suits). These acts are the true enemies of justice and must not be committed by anyone who has an office of justice to execute. It was a "monstrous disguising" to have a justice who committed these crimes, offering injury and wrong rather than the help he was sworn to provide. Such a man sows strife instead of appeasing "brabblings" (obstinate quibbling) and controversies. "If you cannot reform [these justices] for their greatness, you ought here to complain [to Parliament] of their evilness."[25]

Such paragons of justice were not easy to find, especially since appointment to the commissions of the peace was an honor much sought after by gentlemen for themselves, and by patrons for their clients. The Queen's need to have religiously correct, legally supportive justices of the peace was often thwarted by powerful people who fought to get themselves and their friends appointed, and who took umbrage if they were removed from the commissions.

Elizabeth, Cecil, and Bacon all recognized this from the beginning of the reign. Bacon's denunciation of the "bad justices" in his closing speech to the Parliament of 1559 summarized the problem. He asked what good it did to make good laws to weed out evil in the commonwealth, if the laws were not to be enforced. Good enforcement preserved the Queen's peace, ensured justice "between subject and subject," and prevented religious strife. The assembled leaders of magisterial society were being reminded of their duties when they went home.

Unfortunately, it was obvious that lectures about the evils of those who suborned justice were not enough. At the opening of the Parliament of 1563, Bacon returned to the same theme, announcing one of the Queen's initiatives for that session. Good religious discipline was one goal, but another was ending the lack of

[24] BL Lansd. 104, fols 27–27v. This documented is not dated, but 1572, the date estimated by the *Calendar*, seems right.

[25] Hartley, *Proceedings*, vol. 1, 50.

good governance because of the "fearfulness, slothfulness or corruption of temporal officers that ought to see to the due execution of them":

> ... therefore I have thought oft with myself what might be the best remedy, if not to make all laws perfectly executed (for that I can hardly hope of), yet to make them in much better case then [sic] now they be. And when I had all thought, I could find no more helps but this. The first, by having great care in the choice of these officers that have the execution of laws committed unto them. The second, by making sharp laws to do as much as may be for the banishing of sloth, corruption and fear from them. A third way there is which I mean to open to you, and nevertheless to leave it to your judgments. This it is: there would be throughout the realm a triennial or biennial visitation in this nature made of all the temporal officers and ministers that by virtue of the office have in charge to see to the execution of laws.

He proposed that the Queen, every two or three years, create a commission to review the behavior of those charged with enforcing the law, empowered to punish those who had failed in their duties, demonstrated corrupt intent, and otherwise were poor magistrates. They were to be sharply punished.[26]

Thus charged, the Parliament of 1563 passed an important law that had the effect of uniting the magistracy more closely with the Queen. Entitled "An Act for the punishment of such persons as shall procure or commit any willful perjury," it sought to prevent some of the offenses listed by Bacon. It increased the penalty for perjury, suborning jurors, bribing witnesses, and committing other offenses against justice in any of the Queen's courts of record from £10 to £40, with the alternative of imprisonment and mutilation. Interestingly, it was a proviso added to this Act that may have had the most effect. It protected the power of the Court of Star Chamber and of the Council of the North and the Council of the Marches of Wales, assuring their "absolute power" to punish perjury.[27]

Whereas more local courts really could not escape the power of regional grandees, it was harder to influence members of the Star Chamber, who were members of the Privy Council (often grandees themselves) and judges of the central courts. This prompted a turn to conciliar government in places where local justice was hard to get. As J. G. Bellamy pointed out, "The greater volume of conciliar justice in the 16th century can thus be considered to have enhanced governmental authority." Before the Act, less than 6 percent of Star Chamber cases involved perjury. By 1602, 17 percent of Star Chamber's business was connected to perjury.[28]

[26] Hartley, *Proceedings*, vol. 1, 83.

[27] 5 Eliz. I, c. 9. This Act was clearly a Crown-sponsored measure, closely related to Bacon's instructions at the opening of Parliament. However, it was not, as G. R. Elton thought, linked to a document known as "Considerations delivered to the Parliament, 1559." Section 18 of that document does propose punishment of juries by attaint, "as it was at common law before the statute." But the document is misdated. It actually belongs to 1584–5, as internal evidence proves. Thus it calls for a return to the pre-1563 status quo. See G. R. Elton, *The Parliament of England, 1559–1581* (Cambridge: Cambridge University Press, 1989), 72. Elton was working from the printed version of the document in R. H. Tawney and E. Power, eds., *Tudor Economic Documents* (London: Longmans, 1963), vol. 1, 325–30. It is an inaccurate copy of CP 152/96.

[28] J. G. Bellamy, *Bastard Feudalism and the Law* (Portland, OR: Areopagitica Press, 1989), 142–4. M. D. Gordon, "The Perjury Statute of 1563: A Case History of Confusion," *Proceedings of the American Philosophical Society*, 126, 6 (1980), 438–54. M. D. Gordon, "The Invention of a Common Law Crime: Perjury in the Elizabethan Courts," *American Journal of Legal History*, 24 (1980), 145–70.

By creating a way to resist the corrupting power of local influence the statute made central government useful to many, but it did nothing to change the Queen's dependence on the local gentlemen. William Tyldesley, a justice from Buckinghamshire and a good Protestant commonwealth man, wrote a lament about lax enforcement to his cousin, Sir William Cecil, in 1561. Tyldesley summed up the situation with the popular proverb *Omnia venalia Roma*—everything is for sale in Rome.[29] He undoubtedly would have agreed with Hugh Latimer, who in Edward's reign glossed the proverb, saying "everything is for money at Rome and Rome is come home to our own doors. If they buy they must needs sell for it is wittily spoken *Vendere jure potest, emerat ille prius* He may lawfully sell it if he bought it before."[30]

But Tyldesley was explicit about the problem. For him it was not theoretical; his colleagues on the bench were the problem. Reviewing the poor enforcement of the penal statutes, he observed, "I do see no man earnestly bent to put laws in execution, but every man letteth slip and pass forth. So that for my part, I do look for no less but subversion of the realm, which must needs follow, for all things worketh to that end."[31]

So his colleagues were willing to look the other way, to license their friends to sell wine, to allow suppressed ale houses to be restored, and to profit from regrators and forestallers. But that was if they were at home to do their duties. In his corner of Buckinghamshire and the surrounding counties the laws are not enforced because:

> Sir Henry Nevell has not been at home of all this summer, nor yet like to be, and that Mr. Weldone and Mr. Ward be at the court, and that Mr. Norris is sick. And of Mr. Holrye being alone etc. And for Middlesex our neighbors, I do think they had no letters [from the Council], or else if they had, then surely I think that, coming unto Sir Roger Chomeley, they be utterly forgotten in the bag of his coat, and so nothing done there ...[32]

If they came together, they might be disinclined to enforce the law because they blamed Cecil's unnecessary meddling for the burden of enforcement. They name you behind your back, he told Secretary Cecil, "to be a cruel and an extreme man." This was in the context of the setting of laborers' wages, a national effort at the time, which was clearly not enthusiastically embraced by the employing classes.[33]

So the Privy Council had to find men who, by its lights, could be trusted to do the job and to do it honestly. This may be why the lists of the justices of the peace were changeable. Good management required careful selection and attention to the details about status, community, and ideology. Allison Wall's study of the justices shows the commissions of the peace to be unstable bodies which changed frequently as the Crown sought energetic local support and the local powers sought to extend and ensure their influence. As she says, "Above all, we cannot assume that

---

[29] TNA SP 12/19 fo. 85. This document as printed in R. H. Tawney and E. Power, eds. *Tudor Economic Documents* (London: Longmans, 1963), I, 330–4, is condensed and inaccurate. Tawney and Power printed as a separate document the schedule of wages Tyldesley sent from Buckinghamshire, when it is clearly associated with his letter.

[30] Hugh Latimer, *Seven Sermons before Edward VI*. Edward Arber, ed. (London: 1824), I, 165.

[31] TNA SP 12/19 fo. 84v.   [32] TNA SP 12/19 fol. 85.   [33] TNA SP 12/19 fol. 84v.

the ruling order in a county was stable." Attempts to control the selection of just-ices were frustrated by competing interests at court and in the counties. Interests of the state were often at odds with the demands of local patronage networks, undermined by men and women of influence who sought to use, or refused to use, the law for their own ends. Burghley, she observes, "tried constantly to secure suitable hard working justices, but, even so, JPs dismissed after his enquiries often returned to the bench."[34]

Their return to the bench may have been because they were part of the local power structure and could not be left off, even if their abuses were well known. The Games family of Brecon, for instance, were a long-established gentry family that provided three Elizabethan MPs, nine sheriffs, and justices on every commission of the peace for the county. But they were constantly disturbing the proper adminis-tration of justice. They were reported for coming armed to the assize and threat-ened the clerk in 1579. Riotous behavior in the late 1580s and early 90s led them into a Star Chamber case. At one point, John Games tried to get his cousin the sheriff to select a jury of Games family members and their retainers to try John's servant on a murder charge. The council ordered the local justices of the peace to make them behave, but there was no response.[35]

In Warwickshire the competition between the Dudley family and the rising Sir Christopher Hatton impacted appointments to the commission of the peace. Although both sides were Protestant, their client networks ensured that some gentry families continued to serve, while the Catholic side of the Throckmorton family was shut out of Warwickshire service by the Dudleys because they were allied with Hatton. Cathryn Enis has shown that when Hatton joined the Privy Council in 1577, he began to insert his own people into the commission, including known Catholics, prompting Leicester to complain to Burghley that the papists were merrier in the county than they had been since Queen Mary's time.[36]

Obviously, the Elizabethan state was dependent on the cooperation of local mag-nates, who practiced "self-government at the King's command." As Steve Hindle has noted, the vast majority of magistrates served not because they belonged to the monarch's affinity, although in theory they did, but because the monarchs recog-nized that the localities could not be governed without them, or men like them.[37]

So the state had to be managed through the traditional tools of patronage, cooption, coercion, intimidation, and joint interest provided by the late feudal structure of its system. However, Elizabethans introduced new considerations into this trad-ition of local government. Cutting across all of the older methods of conducting local rule was the beginnings of an "ideologized" political system that worried about the religious identity of its functionaries. Religious conformity was added to

[34] Alison Wall, "'The Greatest Disgrace': The Making and Unmaking of JPs in Elizabethan and Jacobean England," *English Historical Review*, 119, 481 (2004), 332.

[35] Pamela Redwood, "The Games Family versus the Borough of Brecon, 1589–1606," *Brycheiniog*, 25 (1992–3), 67–78.

[36] Enis, "Dudleys, Hatton and the Justices," 4–5.

[37] Steve Hindle, "County Government in England," in Robert Tittler and Norman Jones, eds., *A Companion to Tudor Britain* (Oxford: Blackwell Publishers, 2004), 99, 102.

the virtues that prepared them to function as justices. Religious correctness had emerged as a qualification for the magistracy in the thought of the Edwardian commonwealth men, and in Elizabeth's time the need for the justices to support the religious settlement was an ongoing concern.

William Cecil kept meticulous records about local gentlemen, managing the selection of justices of the peace, annotating them, and inserting names. His insertions came at transition points—the opening of the reign in the early 1560s, the rebellion in the north in 1569, the Armada crisis in the 1580s—that required special attention to the nature and religious allegiances of the men who served on the commissions of the peace across the realm.

For instance, in the North Riding of Yorkshire only two of eight named as "unfavorable" by the Archbishop of York in 1564 were removed, even though some of them were later to lead the 1569 rebellion. At the heart of the matter was the shortage of potential magistrates. A memo concerning the vacant chancellorship of the Duchy of Lancaster in 1568 puts it succinctly: "The Chancellor nominateth the sheriffs and justices of peace in that county palatine and there be not at this instant many that are known to be of good religion and sufficient living to supply those places."[38]

Cecil and his fellow councilors had their hands tied by the interconnected nature of local life and its impact on local government. For all his care, however, few seem to have been removed because of their religious affiliation. Susan Cogan's exploration of recusant families in the Midlands led her to conclude that there were many reasons for men being removed from the bench, and religion was only one of them. Many continued to serve in county offices if they were reliable, and county leaders maintained diverse client bases in order to make counties governable. Although the increased administration of the oath of supremacy from 1569 on forced some out of government, it did not force all Catholics out.[39]

What one believed was less important in this voluntary system than to whom one was related or who one had for a patron or client. The bishops, in their letters to the council, were explicit about this, telling us what was really on the council's mind as it searched for ideologically dangerous justices.

Moreover, the patronage needs of members of the council itself often protected men whose religious opinions were suspect. In Warwickshire Lord Chancellor Hatton had a tendency to appoint conservatives, even Catholics, from his client base, in competition with the Dudleys who were excluding them. These tensions could even force the expansion of the size of a county's commission, to make room for more clients, including some known recusants. The political necessity of stability required that room be made for members of both affinities.[40]

This helps account for why very little happened as a result of these surveys. John Gleason, in his study of the Elizabethan and early Jacobean justices, notes that the impact on the commissions of the peace was muted. Although some papists were

---

[38] TNA SP 12/46 fol. 143.

[39] Susan Cogan, "Catholic Gentry, Family Networks and Patronage in the English Midlands, c.1570–1630" (University of Colorado, unpublished PhD dissertation, 2012), 156–9.

[40] Enis, "Dudleys, Hatton and the Justices," 18–21.

eliminated at those times, none of the purges seems to have been really thorough. A formal and outward conformity sufficed. A loyal bench was desired, but the influences that narrowed the choice of JPs to the leaders of the county were so strong that considerable aberration had to be tolerated.

The first generation of Elizabethan bishops, full of the same zeal that had produced their abortive attempts to create a new discipline for their new church, took the council's 1564 request to evaluate the religious sympathies of justices seriously. As John Scory of Hereford said, the council's commitment had "for the present driven away fearfulness of offending any person." However, it soon became apparent just who he was willing to offend. Hereford's list begins with John Scudamore of Holme Lacy. Sheriff of Herefordshire four times, he had been on the commissions of the peace for Herefordshire and Gloucestershire since 1528. He was a JP for Worcestershire from 1532 until 1559, for Oxford in 1540, and for Salisbury in 1554. He was the receiver of the diocese of Hereford, and he sat on the court of augmentations for four western counties from 1536 until its abolition in 1554. He helped dissolve the chantries, too. A member of the Council of the Marches of Wales since 1553, he became the Custos Rotulorum of Herefordshire about 1561, as well as High Steward of Archenfield in 1564. He was a knight of the shire for Hereford in the Reformation Parliament. Further complicating the removal of a man of Scudamore's local weight and importance were his connections to the powerful Croft family. His grandson, another John, was the ward of the powerful Sir James Croft. Sir James was a rising star in Elizabeth's court in the 1560s, becoming Controller of the Household in 1570, and using his considerable patronage power in Herefordshire to great effect.

Not surprisingly, as a senior member of one of Herefordshire's three leading families, John Scudamore retained all of his offices until his death in 1571. He did take the oath of supremacy, but he was, by his will, exactly what John Scory thought he was, a Catholic.[41]

Another denounced by Scory was Thomas Havard of Hereford. Scory said the justice was "by common fame…a daily drunkard, a receiver and maintainer of the enemies of religion, a maintainer of superstition and namely of abrogated holy days. He useth to pray upon a Latin primer full of superstitions. His wife and maidens use beads and to be short he is a mortal enemy to Christian religion."

But what else was Thomas Havard? He had been sheriff of Hereford, sheriff of Brecon, mayor of Hereford four times, justice of the peace for Hereford since 1538, escheator of Herefordshire and the Marches, and a member of Parliament six times. He continued to be a justice until 1569, when he refused to take the oath of supremacy during the next survey of justices. He died, still an alderman of Hereford, in 1571, aged seventy-five.[42]

---

[41] HPT, Bindoff, ed., sub SCUDAMORE, (SKYDMORE), John (by 1503–71), of Holm Lacy, Herefs. At <http://www.historyofparliamentonline.org/volume/1509-1558/member/scudamore-%28skydmore%29-john-1503-71>. Accessed July 30, 2014.

[42] HPT, Bindoff, ed. Sub HAVARD, Thomas (1495/96–1570/71), of Hereford. At <http://www.historyofparliamentonline.org/volume/1509-1558/member/havard-thomas-149596-157071>. Accessed July 30, 2014.

In their places, who was to be appointed? Scory's suggestions underline the hard problem he faced. In place of men of established authority and rank, he had to suggest people like the chancellor of his diocese, considering "there is so little choice of such as be favorable to this religion."

The bishops were urging the removal of some of the most senior and experienced men in their dioceses. Robert Horne at Winchester was very direct about the problem. There was a dearth of "favorers" on the current commission. On the bright side, there were a number of men on the commission who "might be moved to favor religion"; and the young earl of Southampton and young William Lord Sands "might be now in their youth so trained in religion that hereafter when they come to their authority and rule they should not hinder the same." Although this shortage was serious, he was also concerned about the constables, bailiffs, and members of grand juries for inquests. They, he argued, should also be tested for religion.

The problem of who could serve on commissions for the peace was especially interesting because some bishops were forced to recommend retention of men who did not support the religious regime, accepting that there were no men of estimation to govern. The more local knowledge the Privy Council had, the more difficult it was to improve the county benches.[43]

Of course, there were many reasons for men to be removed from the commission of the peace, besides religion. The 1587 report for Devon and Cornwall recommended removal of justices of the peace described in these ways: "furious and inconsiderate"; "made gain from his office"; "a pouler and piller of the people"; "in times past a great papist now in the other extreme, a server of time, extreme covetous, corrupt and a great maintainer of factions"; "old fornicator, corrupt and ignorant"; "very infamous, corrupt fraudulent and accounted a papist"; and "envious, proud and corrupt, inconsiderate and furious maintainer of factions in the country," among other faults. None of them was just a papist.[44]

The jobs the justices of the peace undertook were not all ideological. They had to be even-tempered, considerate, and willing to work hard. Neither a Catholic nor a Protestant was happy to get an order like the one sent by Chancellor Bromley to the justices of Norfolk ordering them to oversee the speedy repair of a lane called Christmas Lane, near Metfield in Suffolk. This sort of work was not ideological, requiring nothing more than a willingness to devote time to making the constables do their jobs.[45]

Justices of the peace were the first line of enforcement, control, and justice. As Richard Crompton put it in the preface to his 1584 edition of Antony Fitzherbert's *L'Office et aucthoritie de justices de peace*, they were *fundamentum civitatum*, bearing in their locales the authority of the monarch, whose oath mirrored their own.[46] The JPs were, as a group, wealthy, well educated, ambitious, and "more than the

---

[43] J. H. Gleason, *The Justices of the Peace in England, 1558 to 1640* (Oxford: Clarendon Press, 1969), 71–2.

[44] BL Lansd. 53/fols 170–170v.

[45] HMC, *Report on the Manuscripts of the Family of Gawdy* (1885), 18.

[46] Sir Anthony Fitzherbert and Richard Crompton, *L'Office et aucthoritie de justice de peace, 1584* (London: Professional Books, 1972), Epistola.

mere creatures of the royal administration; in brief, they were the leaders of their counties."[47] As Mark Goldie has observed, the "Crown's capacity to exert its will depended upon the cooperation of county magistrates and village constables."[48] The commission of the peace set the magistracy apart and gave them authority, but it was also a badge of recognition of their standing. This same standing meant that they were frequently involved in other governmental activities. In any given Elizabethan Parliament more than a third of the sitting members were also justices of the peace; most justices of the peace were muster masters; many were aldermen and commissioners of sewers—the list of overlapping duties is complex and long. Thus, the men who enforced the law were intimately concerned in making the law—a rational and useful connection that co-opted them into enforcement.[49]

This, in turn, allows us to better understand the ways in which they were treated, whether they were categorized as "favorer," "not favorer," or "indifferent" to Protestant religion by their bishops. Whatever they thought, their local positions, marital connections, and economic power had to be a part of the equation.

The influence that local magnates could exert in getting their clients chosen to serve on the bench (or as sheriff) was well understood by the Privy Council and by Burghley in particular. The patronage of honor was part of it, but part of it was the management of affairs that required communication between all the players. That is why the bench in every county had a mix of the nationally great, especially local nobility, bishops, and members of the Privy Council, along with the locally powerful, those who aspired to greatness, and those fated to inherit titled greatness.

A justice of the peace was appointed by the monarch under the Great Seal, so the lord keeper was responsible for the commissions of the peace. The appointments were made upon the suggestion of others such as courtiers, lords lieutenant, other justices of the peace, justices of assize, friends, influential people, and even the monarch. There were always significant numbers of titled dignitaries among the justices, especially in those areas in the north and west where local influence was more in the hands of the nobility. Gleason tells us that in 1562 three fifths of the bishops were justices. Likewise, most secular lords and baronets served, so that all commissions included lay peers as well as a bishop.

Sitting on the top of all local commissions of the peace after 1572 was Lord Treasurer Burghley who, the royal justices in Westminster agreed, was a sort of super justice of the peace. He, ex officio, was a justice of the peace everywhere in the realm. Lawyers were careful to note, however, that he could not, unlike local justices, order imprisonment without cause.[50]

There was no set way of selecting JPs, and in many cases the position seemed almost hereditary, reflecting the standing of important families. Besides the obvious peers, baronets, and bishops, many chosen must have been known to the lord

[47] Gleason, *Justices*, 96.

[48] Mark Goldie, "The Unacknowledged Republic: Office Holding in Early Modern England," in Tim Harris, ed., *The Politics of the Excluded, c.1500–1850* (Basingstoke: Palgrave, 2001), 154.

[49] P. W. Hasler, ed., *The House of Commons, 1558–1603* (London: HMSO, 1981), vol. 1, 58.

[50] "John Hynde's Case, 1576," in John Baker, ed., *The Lost Notebooks of Sir James Dyer* (Selden Society, 1994), vol. 2, 355.

keeper. Common memberships in colleges and Inns of Court, family ties, marriage, membership in Parliament, neighborly connections, and other things threw them together. It appears that this was especially true of members of the Inns of Court. Of course, those with these connections used them to obtain appointments, and patronage clearly played a role in securing selection as a justice of the peace.[51]

All of this meant that if the commissions of the peace were to play their role effectively, their composition had to be attended to with care. This William Cecil did. In January 1559 he carefully annotated the Book of the Peace. Again, in November or December 1561 a list of JPs bears his alterations.[52] In two *Libri pacis* in the Lansdowne manuscripts he has marked the lists with a series of crosses, squares, circles, and triangles. Beside these, he made notes about their places of residence, the names of the fathers or brothers of the wives of the JPs, and subsidy assessments. "O" apparently meant that they were approved, while a triangle indicated disapprobation. Noting the assessed value of each person, he was seeking to ensure that they were worth the legal minimum to serve as justices of the peace.[53]

He also rearranged and annotated the lists. First, he went through them as prepared, making corrections. In some places he added names. Discovering that the justices for the bishopric of Durham had been left off altogether, he wrote all the Durham commissioners in himself. Then, noting he had the order of precedence wrong in Durham, he crossed out Sir George Bowes's name, put Lord Euers in his place, and then put Sir George in his proper place. In other instances he rearranged the lists in order to get their social precedence right, so that in Derby's list he inserted Sir Edward Seymour's name, having moved it up the list to place it ahead of Sir John Pollard, not behind it as originally written.[54] In many places he added names. He put two names in at the end of the Staffordshire commission. One, Thomas Trentham, was not appointed at the time, but he did become Sheriff in 1571.[55]

Working, perhaps, from the first list, Cecil prepared another list in his own hand of the members of the commissions according to their social rank, beginning with members of the Privy Council, and following with nobility, the bishops, and the deans.[56] Having done that, he prepared yet another of JPs by county. Written in his distinctive hand, it is tightly packed and much interlined with insertions.[57] The next list, this time in a secretary's hand, has his further corrections. Notably, in the list for Northamptonshire he has struck out the earl of Bedford and inserted in his place of precedence the Bishop of Peterborough and himself, Sir William Cecil. At the end of the list he adds another five names, including that of his eldest son, Thomas Cecil. These Cecil additions recognized his family's prominence in the county thanks to their seat at Burghley House.[58]

What we learn from the exercise is the kind of care Cecil took to know who was on the commissions and to understand who might be on the commissions. It is also striking that he left it to the commissioners themselves to enforce the oath of

[51] Hasler, *Commons*, vol. 1, 56–60. Wall, "The Greatest Disgrace," 313.
[52] Gleason, *Justices*, 61.   [53] TNA SP 12/59/fols 14, 15.
[54] TNA SP 12/59/fol. 90v.   [55] TNA SP 12/59/fol. 92v.
[56] TNA SP 12/59/fol. 95. HPT, sub Thomas Trentham.
[57] TNA SP 12/59/fol. 95v.   [58] TNA SP 12/59/fol. 96.

supremacy. The mechanisms of local government put them in the odd position of enforcing the rule on themselves.

This sometimes led to ironic results. In Hereford, John Scudamore of Kenchurch, a cousin of John Scudamore of Holme Lacy, also a justice of the peace, wrote a letter to the bench, refusing to take the oath of supremacy. Nonetheless, he was summoned to sit and, when the oath was offered, Scudamore earnestly expressed his refusal and referred them to his letter, "which letter afterwards, with some difficult, he redelivered, requiring us to set our hands to it, that it should not be altered. In reasoning and laboring with him to conform himself to subscribe as others had done, it fell out by his own confession, that he never took the oath when he was sheriff of this county."[59]

Still a sitting member of the Hereford bench, he and his colleagues crafted a solution to the problem. He had made his refusal clear, but not taking it did not automatically remove him; he was on the bench when oaths were being taken. "For as much as your honors did not express your meaning unto us to deal with such recusants, we are much perplexed," wrote his fellow justices to the Privy Council, before, at Scudamore's own suggestion, placing him in the custody of the sheriff. He was not, at that time, removed from the commission, and he subscribed shortly thereafter.[60]

Edmund Plowden, an eminent lawyer who had been denounced as a Catholic by his bishop in 1564, was confronted in 1569 with a demand that he take the oath. Extemporizing, he refused to sign until he had read the Act. He then expressed a concern about the "generality" of the law, and refused to sign. He hoped his refusal would not be interpreted as resistance to Elizabeth, to whom he swore love and obedience, but his conscience prevented him from subscribing. As required by the Act, he was made to give bond for his good behavior and he continued with his legal practice.[61]

As the Spanish fleet gathered at Cadiz for the invasion of England in 1587 the Privy Council again fell back on the bishops for advice about the JPs. This time the council asked very interesting questions about the connections of the justices under survey. They wanted to know who should be put on the current commissions, who should be left out, what fathers had sons in commission, and who was not worth at least £20 in land.[62] The bishops understood the questions to be about much more than just religion. They took it upon themselves to comment on the qualities and connections of serving justices and possible justices.

Sometimes their concerns were about religion, or, more frequently, their kinfolks' religion. Walter Baskerville in Hereford had a recusant wife, as well as the further disqualification of being dead. Humphrey Baskerville was "not thought well

---

[59] TNA SP 12/60 fol. 63.

[60] TNA SP 12/60/fol. 6. HPT, Bindoff, ed. Sub SCUDAMORE, (SKYDMORE), John (by 1503–71), of Holm Lacy, Herefs. http://www.historyofparliamentonline.org/volume/1509-1558/member/scudamore-%28skydmore%29-john-1503-71. Accessed July 30, 2014.

[61] TNA SP 12/60 fols 130–130v; 135. HPT, Bindoff, ed. Sub PLOWDEN, Edmund (1519/20–85), of the Middle Temple, London; Plowden, Salop; Shiplake, Oxon. and Burghfield, Berks. At <http://www.historyofparliamentonline.org/volume/1509-1558/member/plowden-edmund-151920-85>. Accessed July 30, 2014.

[62] Strype, *Annals*, vol. 3, 2, 453–4.

affected in religion," but he was also noted for incontinency, his great age, and his inability to work.[63] The Bishop of Worcester glossed his report with an observation that complicated the picture. Some left out of the commission had recusant wives. He could not accuse the men of the same and, other than being suspected of recusancy, they were notable "for wisdom, livelihood, reputation and discrete government, of the best and meetest men that were in that association." He also noted further virtues and vices in the men listed. Edward Blunt, esquire, had been left out of the commission. Although his wife was a recusant, the bishop noted that she was "Lord of Aburgavenies daughter," and that Blunt himself was not inferior in wisdom to anyone on the commission. On the other hand, John Russell, who was on the commission, was commended for forwardness in religion "but not so for discretion."[64]

In Bath and Wells more of the men on the commission were sound, as were those that had been removed, with the singular exception of John Sidnam. His wife was recusant; his eldest son's wife was a recusant, and suspected to have been married at a Mass. His mother and father were described as "lady-matins folks," while one of his beloved brothers was a seminarian at Rheims. Moreover, his wife's father, though not a recusant, was backward in religion, "and so is all his alliance; and more countenanced by his place."[65]

Archbishop Sandys of York was outspoken in his opinion of former and sitting justices. Of the sitting he had low expectations. Take the West Riding, for example. Robert Lee he characterized as a "notable open adulterer," who would not be reformed and who used his authority to work private displeasure and serve other men's turns. Peter Stanley was noted to be a great fornicator of small wisdom and less skill, being "ever at commandment without further respect," willing to go both ways. Thomas Wentworth was "a very senseless blockhead; ever wronging, and wronging his poor neighbors," being a regrator and forestaller. James Tither was a sour papist, ready to hinder any matter touching papists. Worse, he depended upon Sir Thomas Fairfax to make good his evil causes. He was full of contention. George Woodruff had an obstinate recusant wife. "Such men as have such wives are thought very unfit to serve in these time." The last member, Brian Stapleton, was a great papist, just like his eldest son. "He liveth at London and keepeth company with Sir Robert Stapleton. He keepeth no house, having no wife."[66]

Sandys told Burghley that in his report he chose not to deal with knights, even though some were of the "baddest sorts," unfit to govern, being so out of order themselves. The egos involved made things difficult, since if anyone was brought into the commission, everyone else of similar standing thought they should be in too.

Sandys was ducking some of the hard issues, but he was reflecting a reality that Cecil understood perfectly well. Even in times of national crisis social standing and connection were managerial considerations. In short, social status was a key to service, as much as skill as a leader.

Occasionally the attempts to ensure that justices were appropriate to the job backfired. The case of the multiple Richard Shelleys is an example that reveals the

---

[63] Strype, *Annals*, vol. 3, 2, 454.   [64] Strype, *Annals*, vol. 3, 2, 456–8.
[65] Strype, *Annals*, vol. 3, 2, 462.   [66] Strype, *Annals*, vol. 3, 2, 464–5.

complexities faced by the Privy Council. There were at least three men named Richard Shelley, all were based in Sussex and Kent, and they seem to have all been related. One, Sir Richard Shelley, was a star diplomat for Queen Mary. In response to the Elizabethan settlement of religion he went into the employ of Philip II of Spain, and spent the rest of his life in the Mediterranean. A devout and unyielding Catholic, he was also an "intelligencer" for Burghley and Walsingham, which earned him an invitation to come home from Venice that he never used.[67] Other than his religious scruple, he was described to Burghley in glowing terms: "The chief nobles [of Venice] wonder at him for his learning and good life...we have need of such men as he, for experience and time have learned him to be a good commonweal man."[68]

Richard Shelley of Worminghurst in Kent, and William Shelley, Sir Richard's nephew, were noted for being obstinate papists. In 1586 William was condemned to death for treason, but reprieved thanks to the Venetian Sir Richard's interventions with Burghley and Elizabeth.

The third Richard Shelley, from Lewes in Sussex, suffered from association with all the Catholic Shelleys. The Privy Council, unsurprisingly, included his name in a list of men to be removed from the commission of the peace in Sussex because he was unsound in religion. But he was not unsound in religion. This mistake prompted the council to write him a personal letter admitting they had made a mistake, "and that it hath been no small disgrace" to be put off the commission. They tried to demonstrate their good opinion of him by restoring him and, "quenching all bruits and evil opinions" caused by his removal, promoting him to the Quorum.

Honor restored, he went on to be used on several commissions against recusants, including his kin. The council reassured him "that in any thing wherein his credit and reputation is to be maintained, he shall always find their Lordships ready" to support him.[69]

There were other commissions on which gentlemen could serve, too. In particular, the commissioners of sewers had important authority in their neighborhoods, presiding over drains and streams. A statute of Henry VIII allowed six or more of these commissioners to hold enquiry by jury into damages, to assess rates for drainage and repairs, to impose punishments, and to hear and determine suits connected to their responsibilities.[70] These standing commissions had a similar composition to the commissions of the peace, with the same social strata represented. For the River Lea, which empties into the Thames in London, the commissioners for sewers were very important people, including, in 1587, Lord Chancellor Hatton, Attorney General Popham, the earl of Leicester, the earl of Rutland, Lord Burghley, a number of London aldermen, and other well-known men.[71] These commissions were often important in settling local disputes, carrying out duties that only lightly concerned drainage.

Choosing these commissioners was a process like choosing justices of the peace, especially since the two groups overlapped. Once again, Burghley was involved. The Bishop of Durham, for instance, wrote to him that "this winter, sundry gentle

---

[67] HPT sub Sir Richard Shelley.   [68] TNA SP 99/1 fol. 7.   [69] TNA PC 2/12 fol. 133.
[70] 23 Hen. VIII, c. 5.   [71] BL Lansd. 53/fol. 169.

and simple have been with me for renewing the commission of sewers, but I thought first to acquaint your lordship therewith, that the commissioners may be named by your lordship."[72]

Although it began with the gentry, enforcement of the laws hardly stopped with them. Beneath them were the local constables, petty constables, and presentment juries, local men who were expected to carry out orders from the justices of the peace. In many instances, it was they who had to navigate the difficult shoals between distant laws and local personalities. As Keith Wrightson observed, "the very complexity of relationships within small communities made it exceedingly difficult to judge the behavior of an individual without bringing into play a host of personal considerations." These personal considerations were very important—so important that presentment juries, charged with identifying people under suspicion, seldom presented anyone until, in the 1590s, they were given lists of specific questions to address.

The independence of the constables and juries mirrored the concerns of the justices of the peace, in that they were not likely to act enthusiastically unless action would preserve harmony among neighbors. As Wrightson says, it was not a national condition of social harmony that was sought, but more a "negative absence of disruptive conflict locally."[73]

Wrightson's formulation gets to the heart of the task facing Elizabethan government: Preventing disruptive conflict, while securing cooperation on the national level. The Crown's job was to keep the peace and defend the realm. The tools at its disposal were blunt, and depended upon gentlemen whose personal interests and eccentricities had to be allowed in exchange for their work and their money. This meant that the primary job of William Cecil, Lord Burghley and the other members of the Privy Council was to maintain the flexible personal ties that kept everyone cooperating in the interest of the common weal.

If we examine how parliamentary representation worked we get another angle on the intertwining dance of values, favor, and service played out between patrons and clients.

Several studies have looked at the relationship between patrons and Parliament, and all of them agree that parliamentary representation had little to do with the reasons a person was sent to Westminster. In his examination of the operation of the clientage network of Robert, earl of Leicester and his brother Ambrose, earl of Warwick, in the Parliaments of 1559, 1563, 1566, 1571, 1572, and 1584, Simon Adams found little evidence that a client's role in Parliament was directly influenced by his patron. Although some of the Dudley clients initiated important debates on the succession and Mary, Queen of Scots, nothing indicates that their participation in Parliament was in any way a concerted action on behalf of their patrons. Adams concludes that his look at the Dudley connection leads to a whiggish proposition: "Active Elizabethan parliamentarians were active because they

[72] TNA SP 12/256 fol. 182v.

[73] Keith Wrightson, "Two Concepts of Order: Justices, Constables and Jurymen in Seventeenth-century England," in John Brewer and John Styles, eds, *An Ungovernable People: The English and their Law in the Seventeenth and Eighteenth Centuries* (London: Hutchinson, 1980), 21–46.

wanted to be, not because they were the instruments of faction of the men-of-business of the Council."

Being the client of a magnate did not mean giving your vote in accord with his wishes, but it did free one to speak with greater impunity. Leicester, says Adams, created a "climate of benevolent tolerance towards Parliament-men (similar to his tolerance towards Puritan agitators) which encouraged them to express their views without fear of the consequences. If things could (and did) get out of hand, that was in the nature of a free Parliament, not the product of factional politics."[74]

Jim Alsop reached a similar conclusion by looking at exchequer officials who sat in Parliament. In a scathing analysis of the History of Parliament Trust's biographies of members of Parliament, in which shadowy if not fictitious patronage connections were used as a *deus ex machina* whenever evidence was lacking, Alsop exploded the Nealean idea that connection or office holding could directly account for either the presence or behavior of exchequer personnel in the Commons. Exchequer officials who had seats tended to have them for the same reason they were exchequer officials. Both their offices and their seats were expressions of patronage on the part of their patrons.[75]

The good will of their patrons did not require them to support the parliamentary objectives of their patrons—if they had objectives. Nor did the fact that they held government office cause them to advance the council's policies or protect vested interests. Of the forty-five exchequer officials who sat in Elizabethan parliaments twenty-two left traces in the records of the Commons, but few can be tied to the promotion of the interests of the exchequer. In a few cases there was a connection, but even then those connections are so rare that it cannot be argued that a man was sent to Parliament in order to influence legislation touching the exchequer.

Like Adams, Alsop deduces that the exchequer men in Parliament did not use their seats to promote the interests of either their patrons or their offices. "By all appearances," he writes, "selection and performance were essentially personal—established by the individual and not by the common office-holding experience.... We possess no reason to believe its officials constituted a parliamentary interest group."[76]

Clientage was a complicated thing. You could be a client of several at once, and, at the same time, be a patron. Sir Julius Caesar's stellar career in the law benefited from a number of patrons stretching back to his father's time. Lord Treasurer Winchester was patron to Cesare Adelmare, Julius's father, and probably brought him into the orbit of William Cecil. Adelmare addressed Cecil as "dominus et patronus," and Cecil acted the part. When Adelmare died, it appears that Cecil took the wardship of the boy and raised him in his household. At some point the aspiring lawyer met Judge of the Admiralty David Lewes, who saw to it he was

[74] Simon Adams, "The Dudley Clientele and the House of Commons, 1559–1584," in N. Jones and D. Dean, eds, *Interest Groups and Legislation in Elizabethan Parliaments: Essays Presented to Sir Geoffrey Elton, Parliamentary History* 8, 2 (1989), 233.

[75] J. D. Alsop, "Exchequer Office-Holders in the House of Commons, 1559–1601," in Jones and Dean, eds, *Interest Groups and Legislation*, 242–53.

[76] Alsop, "Exchequer Office-Holders," 268.

properly educated in the law in Paris. Caesar was given parliamentary seats by
Charles Howard, Lord Howard of Effingham, Lord High Admiral of England.

Eventually, he inherited David Lewes's position in the Court of Admiralty and,
with Sir Francis Walsingham's help, he became a bencher in the Inner Temple.
Under James I he became Chancellor of the Exchequer and married, as his last
wife, the niece of Sir Francis Bacon.[77]

We know all of this because of the trail of letters by which these patrons performed their work. And yet there is no evidence that they expected much in return.
They saw talent and they supported it. They needed people like Julius in their
hand-picked managerial cadre.

Managing local cooperation in England was easier because of the homogeneity
of the upper classes and the way they identified with the monarchy. They shared
rule in a way that was unusual in early modern Europe because Elizabeth and
Burghley had built up working ties with them. As Janet Dickinson has said, the
troubled Elizabethan rule in Ireland underscores Elizabeth's success in England.
In Ireland, the mighty earls of Desmond, Kildare, Ormond, and Clanricarde were
needed to rule the land, but their power also had to be restrained. Lacking an Irish
equivalent of the Wars of the Roses to put them in their places, Elizabeth alien-
ated the rulers of Ireland, Old English as well as Gaelic, provoking the Nine Years
War that began in 1594 with the earl of Tyrone's revolt. Dickinson observes, "the
failure of Elizabeth's government to co-operate with the Irish nobility highlights
the extent to which co-operation rather than conflict characterized the English
nobility's relationship with the Crown."[78]

Of course, those ties were a two-way negotiation. They encouraged cooperation
with the English magistracy by being responsive to their concerns. Consultative
government required it.

Local magistrates knew the realities of life in their neighborhoods, which is one of
the reasons managing them could be difficult. Their experiences did not necessarily
match with the expectations of the Queen and council. But this meant that the
Queen and council, in order to maintain their support and loyalty, had to be attentive to their needs, helping them to solutions and protecting their interests. They
often had mutual interests, even if both sides sometimes chaffed at the process.

When Elizabeth came to the throne, the nation had a complex set of economic
and social problems that had become worse and worse in the 1550s. The economic
crisis sparked by the loss of the wool staple at Calais, the crop failures, the epidemics,
the inflation, the costs of war: all contributed to popular demand for something to
be done. The people Elizabeth brought in to run her business recognized this, and
some, like Sir Thomas Smith and Sir Thomas Gresham, had spent a great deal
of time thinking about how to solve the problems. But many of the solutions the
Elizabethan regime sought to impose came up from the local magistracy. Local experience provided models and prods for social and economic legislation.

---

[77] Norman Jones, "David Lewis, the Founding Principal of Jesus College," *The Record* (2009), 41–2.

[78] Janet Dickinson, "Nobility and Gentry," in Susan Doran and Norman Jones, eds, *The Elizabethan World* (London: Routledge, 2011), 298.

One example of a national effort prompted by local needs is the Statute of Artificers, the law that set the agenda for labor management for centuries to come. Since the 1540s problems with under- and unemployed people had been roiling local governments. Towns, cities, and other governments had attempted local fixes, trying to control wage inflation, limit competition through controlling apprenticeships, and get the vagrants off the streets. Early in Edward's reign, Sir Thomas Smith wrote a memorandum to Cecil, which took the title *The Discourse of the Commonweal*, analyzing the issues and arguing for governmental remedies.

Certainly Cecil, Smith, and others of the Elizabethan regime brought all this thinking with them into the government, and began acting on it with things like the re-coinage. But we can see in Parliament and in other places growing pressure from local rulers for a national structure that would govern wages and apprenticeships. Members of Parliament, members of the council, the assize judges, the clergy—everyone was groping for a way to fix problems that were larger than any particular parish or county. In this case, it appears that the council was following rather than leading.

The tool available to the council for dealing with wages was a statute of 1514 that declared wage rates. Using that, it tried to get the justices to enforce the rates. Naturally, that blew up on them. Inflation made those rates impossibly low. As the preamble observes, the wages in the old statutes "are...too small and not answerable to this time, respecting the advancement of prices." Consequently, says the Act, it was time to digest all the old laws into a single Act that would banish idleness, advance husbandry, and pay proper wages to the laborers.[79]

The Act as passed turned into a macédoine of regulations on laborers and apprentices, working hours, misbehaving masters, punishments for justices who did not set wages, powers to force people to work in the harvest, financial penalties for paying too much, restrictions on labor mobility between shires, and a host of other things. Thirty-one named trades made it into the statute. But at its heart was a clause empowering the justices of the peace of every shire, riding, and liberty, along with mayors and bailiffs, to set wages annually. Recognizing that different places had different circumstances, the Act directed them to consult with "grave persons" about plenty and scarcity and other factors that affected what an appropriate wage was for that place. Engrossed on parchment, these would be proclaimed and enforced. They were subject to alteration as needed, but the clause gave local magistrates a national framework in which to regulate wages.[80]

The history of the Act of Artificers has been the subject of lively debate, since it is so complex, but it is clear that it was responding to pressures for a common framework to control wages and labor arising from experiments all over the country.[81] Tyldesley's letter to Cecil helps us see why. The justices in Buckinghamshire thought he was a cruel man for trying to enforce a national standard; giving the

---

[79] 5 Eliz. I, c. 4.1.   [80] 5 Eliz. I, c. 4.11.

[81] Donald Woodward, "The Background to the Statute of Artificers: The Genesis of Labour Policy, 1558–63," *The Economic History Review*, new ser., 33, 1 (1980), 32–44.

local justices the authority to set wages in their localities matched their needs and inclinations much better.[82]

On the particular level, the Queen had to be willing to respond to petitions for changes that would help local interests. In Mary's reign the Vintners' Company began a campaign to repeal an Edwardian statute governing the wine trade and asking for new letters of incorporation. They tried again in 1559, and again in the Parliament of 1566. Writing to Elizabeth and Leicester they complained that the company's liberties were being damaged because not all wine sellers were under one government. Mayors could grant wine-selling licenses without the permission of the vintners, and the Queen began fixing the prices. In short, they wanted their monopoly back.

Secretary Cecil investigated their petition, exploring the repeal's effect on the customs revenue, the navy, and what good repeal would do for the commonwealth. To help his investigation, the company gave Mildred Cecil £40 in canvas and napkins, and they gave the earl of Leicester two tuns (roughly 1980 liters or 500 US gallons) of wine. The result was the introduction of a bill in the House of Commons in 1566, which, though it passed, was then rescinded. The vintners' lobbying had included a drunken lunch for the members before the vote, and when the members came back the following Monday, they reversed themselves. Although they failed in parliament, the Queen issued letters patent exempting them from the statute.[83]

This sort of self-interested communication was an essential part of governance then and now, and it required Burghley and his colleagues to listen, and to provide enough support and justice that they were perceived as having the power to solve problems. It was what the central authority could do for the local, protecting its interests and ensuring its success. Steve Hindle has shown that it was these local forces, pushing for the protection and use of central authority, that helped strengthen the Crown in the early modern period. Depending on magistrates, jurors, and other local men to enforce the law, Elizabeth and Burghley enjoyed their support as the guarantors of stability and prosperity.[84]

What can we learn from these investigations into the powerful about how Cecil and his colleagues sought to manage local government? First, we see how hard it was to influence local rule. Powerful and well-connected men were not easily kept from governing, so thought had to be given to their malleability. Moreover, no matter what their religious persuasion, their personal standing in their communities was paramount, so compromise with their consciences had to be sought. Their bonds of kinship and connection had to be taken into account whenever the Privy Council sought to manage local government. If they chose the wrong people, or offended someone, they might lose much of their influence. Consequently, continuous dialogue was very important.

  [82] TNA SP 12/19 fol. 84v.

  [83] Norman Jones, *Birth of the Elizabethan Age England in the* 1560s (Oxford: Blackwell, 1989), 244–5.

  [84] Steven Hindle, *The State and Social Change in Early Modern England, c. 1550–1640* (New York: St Martin's Press, 2000).

Second, it is astonishing how much Cecil seemed to know about the local governors. Naturally, he knew his home counties best, but the notes in his hand we find scattered across these documents suggests a first-hand grasp of who was who and where they stood in the social hierarchy. Managing England meant using the system that the ruling classes understood, while tweaking it to make it more effective. The Elizabethan leaders improved conciliar government, and therefore royal power, but their managerial efforts were also hampered and constrained by the system they inherited. In a world in which honor, duty, and conscience had precedent, managing the ruling classes was a bit like herding cats. That said, however, the cats cooperated because they benefited from royal government. Initiatives often rose from the bottom up, demanding national solutions to what might have been dismissed as local problems.

5

Managing Through Perception

> Therefore at the last, being desperate...they are fallen into another crooked
> course of malicious persecuting the happy estate of this country and government
> by choosing out of certain shameless, spiteful, and furious brains having a trade
> in penning infamous libels, not only in the English, but also in Latin and
> other strange languages. And by these means they have lately caused certain
> seditious books and libels to be compiled and printed in divers languages,
> wherein their final intention appeareth to be blasphemy and as it were to
> accurse their native country...bending their malice most specially against
> two, who be certainly known to have been always most studiously and
> faithfully careful of her majesty's...virtuous government...by this her majesty's
> declaration it be known that the said books and libels be...condemned to be
> the works of despisers of God's true religion, of obstinate traitors...
>
> Proclamation ordering the destruction of seditious
books, September 28, 1573[1]

Elizabethan governance required keeping people's minds focused on the
common good, and managing that focus was a haphazard art. Certainly, it
demanded a great deal of patience, finesse, and backscratching to maintain
consensus. Elizabeth's state had to appear to be working effectively in the
common interest—the emperor must appear to be clothed. Therefore, Elizabeth
and her managers tried influencing the impressions people had of the Queen
and her regime. Burghley was deeply interested in shaping public perceptions
by carefully managing news and information. He was very concerned about
making sure the regime's message was clear and believable, never appearing to
be weak or unreasonable. He understood this so well that we might say he was
managing the "public sphere."[2]

This management of perception was positive, in the sense that the Privy Council
was proactive in delivering its preferred interpretations. But it was also negative, in
the sense that messages conflicting with those of the regime were actively blocked
by censorship, restrictions on the sale of books, and the outlawing of rumors.

---

[1] H&L, vol. 2, 377–8.

[2] Peter Lake and Steven Pincus have posited what they identify as the "post-Reformation public
sphere," a distinct precursor to that of the Civil War era. If we look at Burghley's mediation of information, it is clear that he would have agreed about the existence of a "public sphere," in which issues
of political economy were debated, in manuscript and print. Peter Lake and Steve Pincus, "Rethinking
the Public Sphere in Early Modern England," *Journal of British Studies*, 45, 2 (2006), 270–92.

Propaganda and censorship in Elizabeth's reign waxed and waned between the low horizon of Machiavellian propaganda and censorship and the astral plain of extravagant praise for Gloriana.

Cyndia Clegg, surveying the ground, suggests that very little that could be called propaganda was aimed at Elizabeth's subjects. Formal propaganda addressed international audiences and was delivered in Latin.[3]

English was used to tell the Queen's official version of events to the public, using internal messages aimed at the powerful people that ran the country. John Cooper observes that because the Tudor monarchy remained remarkably dependent on the consent of its local governors, it invested heavily in regal display and efforts to secure voluntary obedience.[4] This meant mobilizing all means of communication, including pulpits, presses, proclamations, progresses, and even executions.

Messages for "home" and "abroad" were generally under Burghley's direction. He commissioned, edited, and even wrote them.

We can see this from the very first days of the reign, as the Elizabethan settlement of religion was making its troubled way through Parliament. When it appeared that the Acts for religious supremacy and uniformity would fail, a disputation was held at Westminster between Catholic and Protestant divines. It ended with the Catholics declared contumacious and arrested, removing enough Catholic votes from the Lords to make re-establishing Protestantism in England possible. On March 31, 1559, the day after the disputation ended, a "Declaration of the proceedings of a conference begun at Westminster, concerning certain articles of religion; and the breaking up of the said conference by default and contempt of certain bishops, parties of the said conference" was drafted, double spaced to make room for interlineations. It explained what had happened, providing a rationale for arresting the stubborn disputants. It was not a story that could be published without careful editing, and the drafts show William Cecil making extensive revisions between the lines before it was fair copied and given to the Privy Council to sign. It was then published.[5] From the very first, Cecil was anxious to make Catholics appear to be uncooperative subjects.

Year after year he drafted declarations for the Queen to deliver, addressing sensitive issues. A good example is the Queen's statement announcing her reasons for giving aid to the Low Countries against the king of Spain in 1585, justifying what would become a long war. It starts as a straightforward statement of the issues, but

[3] Cyndia Clegg, "Censorship and Propaganda," in Susan Doran and Norman Jones, eds, *The Elizabethan World* (Oxford: Routledge, 2011), 179.

[4] J. P. D. Cooper, *Propaganda and the Tudor State: Political Culture in the Westcountry* (Oxford: Clarendon Press, 2003), 210–13.

[5] Norman Jones, *Faith by Statute: Parliament and the Settlement of Religion, 1559* (London: Royal Historical Society, 1982), 123–8. TNA SP 12/3/fols 166–73. *The Declaracyon of the Procedynge of a Conference, begon at Westminster the last of Marche, 1559 concerning certaine articles of religion and the breaking vp of the sayde conference by default and contempt of certayne bysshops, parties of the sayd conference* (London, 1559). The STC dates this as "1560?" but it makes no sense for them to have waited for a year to print it. I suspect it was printed within hours of the signature of the draft by the Privy Council, probably under a signet letter sent to Jugge and Cawood, the Queen's printers. [STC (2nd edn)/25286.]

Burghley's hand is all over the draft. He added context and precedent drawn from historical research. Reassuring his readers in an insertion, he scribbled:

> the proof whereof by examples past is to be seen and read in the ancient histories of divers alterations and expulsions of the lords and ladies of the counties of Brabant Flanders Holland and Zeeland, by the states and people of the countries and by such expulsions, came Philip the duke of Burgundy to his title, for which the king of Spain interest is derived, but the further disquisition hereof we leave to the view of the monuments and records of the countries.[6]

Burghley was clearly developing a historical and theological justification for the intervention. Elizabeth, in Burghley's version, had only the best intentions. Burghley's interlineations in the draft are shown in italics with brackets around those coming from the first version and double brackets around those from the second version. Elizabeth is intent on

> aiding them in this their great calamities and miseries [*and imminent danger*], and until the countries are delivered of such strange forms as do now oppress them, and recover their ancient lawful liberties, and manner of government which are the very only true end of all our actions [*now intended without any purpose to make war, towards the King of Spain but to procure peace in all parts*] howsoever malicious tongues may utter their cankered counsels [[*at this day the world aboundeth with such blasphemous reports in writings and libels, as in no age the Devil hath more abounded with notable spirits replenished with all wickedness. But therefore we leave the revenge to God*]] to the contrary, but thereof we make no answer [*leaving the revenge to God the searcher of hearts hoping that he beholding* [[*the sincerity of*]] *our heart*] will perchance give success to our intentions, whereby [[*a Christian*]] peace may ensue to his honor, and comfort to all them that love peace truly, and will seek it sincerely.[7]

Clearly, he was anxious that this declaration have the right impact on its hearers and readers.

The battle for the minds of Elizabethan elites was fought in an international arena on terms set by the European context of the Reformation and by geopolitics. Burghley paid careful attention to both, in positive and negative forms. He frequently commissioned scholars to respond to foreign books, and sought to prohibit the printing, importing, and selling of seditious books.

Burghley himself had been a censor during the reign of Edward VI, appointed, along with other members of the Privy Council, to review English books. By late in Edward's reign either the King or six of his privy councilors had to give permission for publication. As Stephen Alford says, it is hard to see how this worked in reality, but it shows that Cecil had early experience with seditious books.[8]

---

[6] BL Lansd. 94/fols 47–51v. The quotation is of Burghley's marginal note, inserted on fol. 49. The insertion was incorporated in the next version, BL Lansd. 94/fols 78–82v.

[7] BL Lansd. 94 fols 51–51v; 81v. The Lansdowne catalog dates the first from 1575 and the second from 1585, but they are both clearly 1585.

[8] Stephen Alford, *Kingship and Politics in the Reign of Edward VI* (Cambridge: Cambridge University Press, 2008), 173.

Burghley liked reading history and theology, and discussing it with learned men, so he kept abreast of religious dispute literature and sought to influence the debates. He had a pragmatic view of the uses of learning. A *sola scriptura* Protestant and an *ad fontes* humanist, he believed in historical truth. This led him to read widely, making abstracts of his reading, and to use it to inform his messages. Debating with Sir Thomas Tresham over Tresham's Catholicism, he sent him a reading list. Their correspondence shows them discussing the first five councils of the Church, and Tresham reported that, having read the ecclesiastical history Burghley recommended, they had much in common—expect for their interpretation of scripture.[9]

Burghley saw history as a warning against factionalism and a corrective to religious utopianism, a study that provided a perspective on the divisive topics of his day. Certainly a Protestant, he nonetheless had the irenic skepticism of someone whose historical studies had made the world more grey than black and white. Consequently, he not only read history, he commissioned it as a form of apologetic to influence public perception.

When Robert Bellarmine's *Controversies* was printed in 1586, Burghley conversationally approached the Regius Professor of Divinity in Cambridge, William Whitaker, and asked him for his opinion on the new work. Bellarmine had based it on an historical argument for the truths of Catholicism, and Whitaker reviewed it with appreciation. Then he wrote a refutation, which he dedicated to Burghley. In its preface, Whitaker recalled his discussion with the Lord Treasurer. "I," he said, "allowed Bellarmine the merit of dealing less dishonestly with the testimonies of the fathers than is customary with others, and of not captiously or maliciously perverting the state of the question; a fault, which I found, had particularly disgusted you in certain writers." Asserting that religious dispute should avoid craftiness in the pursuit of truth, Whitaker acknowledged that, while Catholics erred grossly in this respect, "our own party stood not so wholly clear of the fault, as became the investigators of truths so sacred; which proportion as they are more heavenly in their nature, and concern us more nearly, should be searched into and handled with much the more sincerity."[10]

Whitaker's reminiscences of Burghley's disgust with those people who treated high matters with sleight of hand meant that the Lord Treasurer at least appreciated an argument from evidence, even if it reached unacceptable conclusions. His own analytical style makes that clear. Burghley was concerned that the truth had to be simply clad to be convincing.

But that did not mean that his public messages were without spin. It appears that one of the things Burghley did in the hectic days leading to the conviction of the duke of Norfolk for treason in the Ridolfi plot was to publish a short, anonymous, pamphlet entitled *Salutem in Christo: Good Men and Evil Delite in Contrarities*. Stating that good men will be "well satisfied" to know the truth about the duke of Norfolk, it lays out the case against him. It makes a series of assertions—each

---

[9] CP 162/70.
[10] William Whitaker, *A Disputation on Holy Scripture: Against the Papists, Especially Bellarmine and Stapleton* (Cambridge: Parker Society, 1849), 8.

beginning "it is well known"—and then provides the facts of the case against Mary of Scotland and the duke. It names names and gives dates. It ends by saying "I" know this is true because "this present day" the Lord Mayor and Council of London were called before the Privy Council in the Star Chamber, and told the same.[11] Published on the day of the public announcement of Norfolk's treason, it was printed in four different editions. It is a classic Burghley move designed to sway public opinion with a reasoned, timely, historicized spin that made the Queen's case.

Perhaps he was sensitive because the arrest of Norfolk had led to a plot to assassinate Cecil himself, as an enemy of all noble men. Thrice would-be assassins had waited for him in his garden, and there were plots to shoot him as he sat in his study window, or when he was returning from court.[12]

In response to *Salutem in Christo*, an anonymous author, believed to be John Leslie, Bishop of the Scottish see of Ross and a supporter of Mary, published a *Treatise of Treasons*. It was a long book exonerating Mary and Norfolk. In its preface, it claims that the return of Protestantism to England was a plot, orchestrated by Cecil and Sir Nicholas Bacon, to seize power in England. It takes the story of the Trojan horse and uses it as an extended metaphor for how Burghley, aka "Sinon,"[13] and his mates convinced Elizabeth, aka "Priam," to admit heresy into England, aka "Troy." There is even a poem that makes the allegory and its origins clear, "Allusio ad praesentem Angliae conditionem, ex. Aeneid. Lib. 2," adding a Virgilian gloss to his Homeric comparison.[14]

The *Treatise* makes a point-by-point refutation of *Salutem in Christo*, defending Ross's own reputation, exonerating Elizabeth of everything but weak ignorance, and blaming everything on her evil ministers, in particular Burghley, whose plot against the rightful succession includes killing Queen Mary of Scotland and the duke of Norfolk.[15]

Burghley and Bacon had misled the kingdom, Ross argued, denying the inheritance of Mary, and reducing England to a "Machiavellian" state. The *Treatise* angered Burghley, prompting him to demand that Sir Francis Walsingham, ambassador in Paris, find out who wrote it: "he vomits his choler and despite chiefly against me and my Lord Keeper by nick names," wrote Burghley. "God amend his spirit or else confound his malice. And for my part if I have any such malicious or malignant spirit, God presently consume my body to ashes, and my soul to perpetual torment in Hell." He demanded that the queen mother of France find and punish the author and printer.[16]

---

[11] *Salutem in Christo: Good Men and Evil Delite in Contrarities* (1571) [STC (2nd edn)/11506].

[12] CP 5/61.

[13] Sinon was the Greek deserter who convinced the Trojans to admit the wooden horse into their city.

[14] My reconstruction of the events around this publication is prompted by Peter Milward, *Religious Controversies of the Elizabethan Age: A Survey of Printed Sources* (Lincoln, NE: University of Nebraska Press, 1977), 108–9.

[15] John Leslie, *A Treatise of Treasons against Q. Elizabeth, and the Croune of England diuided into two partes: whereof, the first parte answereth certaine treasons pretended, that neuer were intended: and the second, discoureth greater treasons committed, that are by few perceiued: as more largely appeareth in the page folowing* (1571), np [STC (2nd edn)/7601].

[16] BL Harleian 260/fol. 405.

Preparing to limit the damage, Burghley carefully wrote an abstract of the contents of the *Treatise*, including refutations and asides, which ran for many pages.[17] He also sent the book around to his friends and advisers, ensuring they had the right responses. Archbishop Parker got it, with a letter complaining that he and Bacon were "bitten with a viperous generation of traitors, papists, and I fear of some domestic hidden scorpion." Parker counseled patience. A reply would simply stir things up, whereas he could rest on his clear conscience. "Conscia mens recti mendacia ridet etc.," he reminded him, slightly mangling Ovid. But his meaning was clear: the mind conscious of its rectitude laughs at lying rumors.[18] Certainly Burghley wanted everyone to know the accusations were lies!

Agreeing with Parker's advice, he did not write a book in response. Instead, he wrote a proclamation against incitement to treason, ordering the destruction of seditious books, especially those attacking Her Majesty's two ministers who have "most studiously and faithfully" watched over her estate. No traitorous malice was allowed against them, who employed all their "cares, travails, diligence, and watching, with manifest loss and hindrance of their own health." Burghley, of course, drafted it with Bacon's help.[19]

From beginning to end, we can see Burghley trying to manage the fallout from the arrest of the duke of Norfolk, laying the "certain" facts before the public and defending the Queen's, Bacon's, and his own reputation with a nationally distributed proclamation.

Public communication through proclamations was a well-established Tudor technique. Cecil and his colleagues were versed in the method of reaching the public with statements from the Queen printed in official black letter type. Proclamations fell roughly into the categories of those prohibiting things, those mandating things, those declaring things, and those explaining things.[20] In his study of Marian and Elizabethan proclamations, Fred Youngs noted that proclamations were used for economic management, social management, and religious management. Sir Geoffrey Elton divided them into three generic types, declaratory, prerogative, and statutory, depending on their purpose and origin.[21] Elton and Youngs agreed that the use of proclamations was idiosyncratic by reign, with those of Elizabeth becoming much longer and more informative than earlier ones. However, Elizabeth's did not preach theology, which Mary's did.[22]

The Elizabethan proclamations were instructional. Proclaimed at market crosses and in other central places, they were oral communication as much as written, reaching the literate and illiterate. But, more importantly, the proclamations, and the letters to the magistrates that accompanied them, delivered the Queen's message

---

[17] TNA SP 53/11/fols 40ff. (there is no clear pagination).

[18] *Parker Correspondence*, 444–5. The quote echoes Ovid, *Fasti*, 4.311: *Conscia mens recti famae mendacia ridet*.

[19] H&L, vol. 2, 376–9. The draft, with Burghley's corrections, is at TNA SP 53/11 fols 38–9. Bacon's comments are at TNA SP 12/92 fol. 66; CP 159/109.

[20] Frederic A. Youngs, Jr, *The Proclamations of the Tudor Queens* (Cambridge: Cambridge University Press, 1976), 17.

[21] G. R. Elton, "Government by Edict?" *Historical Journal*, 8 (1965), 269.

[22] Youngs, *Proclamations*, 15; 184–7.

across the realm. Their drafting and enforcement was managed by the Privy Council, while their distribution was ensured by the Chancery. All justices got them; town councils entered them into their minute books. Depending upon the issue, supplemental instructions were issued to those charged with enforcement. Around the proclamations there was a constellation of further communications concerning issues of central concern, often with local nuances. Sometimes dispensations from orders were granted by the council, and sometimes proof of action taken was demanded.[23]

Their range was great, and they demonstrate the management of the public perception of Elizabeth. Even graphic representations of the Queen were controlled. A 1563 proclamation was issued prohibiting the drawing, painting, engraving, or portraying of Elizabeth. An official portrait was to be issued, and the "deformed" portraits were to be removed "until they may be reformed which are reformable."[24] The council would continue attempts to control images of the Queen throughout the reign.[25]

They also used proclamations to control religious controversy, explaining actions taken and denouncing treasonous theology. For the most part, proclamations having to do with religion were about protecting the Queen's honor (and that of her councilors) and supplementing the statute law in times when it was deemed necessary. They were always about teaching the public the "right" position, and about ensuring obedience. The ones that supplemented statutes were often precursors to another form of communication, public trials and executions.

We can see this interplay between proclamations, statutes, and printed propaganda around the arrest and execution of Edmund Campion, the first Jesuit executed for treason. We begin with a proclamation on January 10, 1581 ordering the return from the continent of all seminarians, and the arrest of all Jesuits in the realm. Issued in the heat of the furor caused by Campion's "Brag," it confronted a basic problem. Few in England knew what a Jesuit was, how one was made, or what one looked like. Thus the proclamation had to explain about the seminaries (English colleges) for Catholic missionaries established in Rome and elsewhere. Some who had attended them "carry the name of Jesuits," trained by the Pope to corrupt the simpler sorts of English people and disturb the kingdom. All parents, guardians, and kin with children overseas without a license were ordered to inform their bishop and call them home. Anyone who seemed to match the description of an evil Jesuit or seminarian should be reported to a public officer, lest they be accused of being maintainers and abettors of traitors.[26] It was designed to establish in the popular mind an association of treason with Catholic missionaries.

After Campion and two seminary priests were "justly, lawfully, publicly, and orderly indicted, arraigned, condemned, and executed" for treason, another proclamation was issued on April 1, 1582. Repeating much of the information about what a Jesuit was, reminding people of the previous proclamation against them,

---

[23] Youngs, *Proclamations*, 45–8.   [24] H&L, vol. 2, 240–1.
[25] H&L, vol. 2, 240, n. 1.   [26] H&L, vol. 2, 481–4.

and recalling their duty to report them, it explained why they were traitors. The Queen made it known "to her good and faithful subjects...whereby they may not be abused nor inveigled by these...wicked, false, and dangerous traitors and seducers" the connection between them and the rebellion in Ireland. The proclamation then set out a definition of treason—luring people to disobedience and rebellion—that was later incorporated into statute law.[27]

Burghley edited the draft of the 1581 proclamation, and the definition of treason may have been his.[28] Certainly, it was the definition he later defended in his 1583 book *The Execution of Justice in England*.[29] First published in English, it was immediately translated into Latin and French for continental audiences (and perhaps the Queen's subjects in Ireland and the Channel Isles who knew no English). All of these efforts were aimed at public education. Loyal subjects needed to identify and report these threats to the Queen's godly government.[30]

This national system of public proclamations was used for "economic management for the public interest," "economic management for private interest," and "social management," much more than for religious management.[31] What management meant in this context was the identification of a problem, assertions about the cause of the problem, and the announcement of a solution. Sometimes actions were required of authorities, but sometimes it was enough to denounce the evil, or to state a policy.

In a state that assumed good government was about virtuous action, the problems of the community were generally associated with people whose lack of virtue hurt their neighbors. A random example is the proclamation of November 28, 1576, "Postponing Licenses to Buy Wool Fells." Listening to the "lamentable" complaint from the clothiers and their employees because of the shortage and high price of wool, the council moved to help them. It admitted that murrain had caused sheep to die in large numbers, but it also identified a moral failing at the heart of the problem. Licenses had been granted for the purchase of wool, "upon reasonable consideration," to individuals who, "through their insatiable greediness...without any regard had to the great mischief that thereby groweth to the commonwealth," had engrossed great quantities of it. This was contrary to the Queen's intention in issuing the licenses, and these greedy people were buying "yearly greater quantity of wool than they ought to do." Thus, the

---

[27] H&L, vol. 2, 488–90. 27 Eliz. I, c 2.   [28] TNA SP 12/152 fols 4–8v.

[29] William Cecil, *The Execution of Justice in England for Maintenaunce of Publique and Christian Peace, against certeine stirrers of sedition, and adherents to the traytors and enemies of the realme, without any persecution of them for questions of religion, as is falsely reported and published by the fautors and fosterers of their treason. Xvii. Decemb. 1583* (London: 1583) [STC (2nd edn/4902].

[30] Conyers Read, *Lord Burghley and Queen Elizabeth* (London: Jonathan Cape, 1960), 244–55. Stephen Alford, *Burghley: William Cecil at the Court of Elizabeth I* (New Haven: Yale University Press, 2008), 241–51. Robert Kingdon, ed., *The Execution of Justice in England by William Cecil and A True, Sincere, and Modest Defense of English Catholics by William Allen* (Ithaca, NY: Cornell University Press, 1965), xiii–xxxvii.

[31] Youngs, *Proclamations*, 103–35, 136–55, 156–74.

clothiers are deprived of a ready supply and their employees thrown out of work, "to the decay of divers good towns."[32]

Translated, the problem was that the people with these licenses, called "wool drivers," were purchasing wool on futures. Traveling from shire to shire and sheep master to sheep master, they were advancing money on wool to be delivered at shearing time. They were especially active in the winter, between Christmas and Candlemas. At that time of the year, the money from the previous spring's sale of wool was running out, and Christmas and Candlemas were traditional dates when debts came due. At that time, the wool drivers could buy the next shearing at a low price from penurious farmers. This meant that the other clothiers found less to be bought during the spring shearing.[33]

What was to be done about this greed? It was ordered, on pain of imprisonment during the Queen's pleasure, that no one with one of the special licenses should buy wool in England and Wales before the Feast of All Saints next ensuing (November 1, 1577). Moreover, anyone with such a license was ordered to register it in the Court of Exchequer, "whereby her majesty may be informed of the contents" and order taken against further damage. Justices of the peace, mayors, and other officers were charged with enforcing the order and empowered to commit offenders to ward, where they would await knowledge of the Queen's pleasure in their cases.

The Queen and council were well aware, however, that the licensed brokers were not the only people in the market for wool, in competition with the clothiers. The members of the Company of Merchant Staplers had a monopoly on wool exports, and they, too, were buying it and sending it abroad. In fact, they were paying premium prices for the fine nape wool from the necks of sheep, so the wool drivers held that back for the Staplers, who paid more and exported it to the looms of the Spanish Netherlands, where the revolt had dried up the supply of Spanish wool.[34]

Rather than being mysterious greedy strangers roaming the pastures, the Staplers were a powerful London company, so the proclamation did not accuse them of evil intentions. But it did ask them to stop exports until the end of February next, a rule that may not have had much effect, since the annual wool pack was shipped in March.

Checking on the situation, in June 1577 the council asked clothiers from Chester to Newbury, Wiltshire to Suffolk, about the causes of the wool shortage. In response, they repeatedly blamed the licensees. Sometimes they also blamed the Staplers. There was almost universal agreement that the greed of the licensed wool drivers was the problem.[35]

---

[32] H&L, vol. 2, 414–15. Unknown to everyone, perhaps, was the fact that wool production was falling. Wool prices had been in decline since the 1550s, and many farmers were shifting to cereal crops, away from sheep. Joan Thirsk, *The Agrarian History of England and Wales, 1500–1640* (Cambridge: Cambridge University Press, 1967), 638. Oddly, the proclamation never mentions "wool fells," the unshorn skins of dead sheep. It applies to all wool.

[33] "An answer to certain articles against the late proclamation concerning wool," BL Lansd. 28 fol. 61.

[34] BL Lansd. 28/fol. 62.   [35] For examples see TNA SP 12/114, fols 44, 48, 59, 61.

Meanwhile, the council wrote to the justices of the peace, ordering them to extract bonds from known brokers and engrossers—they named names—ensuring that they would not buy more wool than they and their apprentices could use in a year. They were, in Tudor parlance, bound for good behavior. Their greed had to be mitigated.[36]

The use of moral opprobrium and shame was a normal part of Tudor social control, and the main delivery system for lessons in virtue was the pulpit. In sermons and homilies read to congregations, Elizabethans were told what to do and what not to do, discouraged from anything that might hurt the commonwealth. Of course, God's honor was the most important thing for them to remember, but other lessons were pronounced there, too. With people forced to attend church, and with the Protestant obsession with sermons, it behooved the Queen to ensure that the right lessons about citizenship were being taught there.

Obedience was the most important lesson, and the proclamation announcing the religious injunctions of 1559 that put the Elizabethan settlement into operation laid out the church's duty. Every person having cure of souls was to use their wit, knowledge, and learning to declare, quarterly, that "the Queen's power within her realms and dominions is the highest power under God, to whom all men within the same realms and dominions, by God's laws, owe most loyalty and obedience." They were to preach, or read a homily, and they were to provide the Bible and Erasmus's *Paraphrases* for all to read, "whereby they may the better know their duties to God, to their sovereign lady the Queen, and their neighbor, ever gently and charitably exhorting them...that in the reading thereof no man to reason or contend but quietly to hear the reader." Preachers were to be licensed, and the royal injunctions were to be read quarterly so everyone would know the duties of the clergy. The injunctions laid out the duties of clergy and laity, defining the qualities of school teachers, and stating the necessity of catechizing the youth. They also forbade the use of contentious words, like "papist," "schismatic," or "sacramentary."[37]

This was followed by the proclamation "Appointing Homilies to be Read in Churches." These homilies had been written in the time of King Edward VI and expanded in 1562, ensuring that everyone heard the right doctrine and learned the right morals.[38] In response to the revolt in 1569, another homily was added, against willful rebellion. This one, a sermon in six parts, pounded home the godly duty of obedience to magistrates, identifying rebellious subjects with Lucifer who fell from Heaven to the pit and bottom of Hell.

The sixth part of the sermon ended with this moral: "In God's word princes must learn how to obey God, and to govern men: in God's word subjects must learn obedience, both to God and the princes." "Now, good people, let us pray," it says, reciting a prayer of thanksgiving for the suppression of the late rebellion. Awakening the people from their careless security, the miseries following the

---

[36] A. Hassell Smith, *The Papers of Nathaniel Bacon of Stiffkey*, vol. 1, *1556–1577, Norfolk Record Society* (1978–9), 258–9.

[37] H&L, vol. 2, 117–32.   [38] H&L, vol. 2, 132–3.

rebellion "scourged some of the seditious persons with terrible executions, justly inflicted for their disobedience to thee, and to thy servant, their sovereign."[39] Clearly, the good people were meant to understand what disobedience led to, and to agree with the condign punishment meted out by Elizabeth's provost marshal to the rebels.

Control of the pulpits, and the messages they delivered, was a major managerial concern throughout the reign. The Queen, however, had weak influence, since advowsons were often impropriated, putting the right to appoint clergy into private hands, and towns, guilds, colleges, and other organizations often hired their own preachers. This made the licensing of preachers by the bishops important, especially in those places that had major pulpits with large audiences, such as Paul's Cross in London.[40] Certainly, in the 1560s it is clear that Cecil himself was approving preachers for Paul's Cross, in coordination with Archbishop Parker.[41] Parker worked with his bishops to ensure that no preacher was licensed who would disturb the religious peace, and the Ecclesiastical High Commission instructed bishops not to license men who might disturb "godly quiet, repose and concord."[42]

The subject matter addressed in Paul's Cross sermons was frequently determined in consultation with Cecil and the council. In October 1562, after the Queen nearly died of smallpox, the council ordered Paul's Cross to be used to publicize her recovery, stopping "vain bruits" about her health being heard in London.[43] That same month, Bishop Grindal of London, preparing to preach at Paul's Cross on the apostasy of the king of Navarre, wrote Cecil asking "If there be any other matter which you wish to be uttered there [Paul's Cross] for the present state, I would be pleased to know it in time, if your leisure serve."[44]

Naturally, the pulpits were used to celebrate moments of national rejoicing, such as the anniversary of Elizabeth's accession, November 17.[45] When George Gifford, vicar of Maldon, Essex and author of *A Dialogue between a Papist and a Protestant*, spoke at the Cross in 1591, he expatiated on unity and concord, the gift of the Queen's good government, and how papists were attempting to set brother against brother. He urged his hearers to submit themselves to their pastors. "The virtue itself which is here commended is that same which St. Paul doth so earnestly exhort and persuade all Christian men unto, to keep the unity of spirit in the bond of peace."[46]

---

[39] *Certain Sermons or Homilies Appointed to be Read in Churches in the Time of Queen Elizabeth of Famous Memory* (London: SPCK, 1846), 587–642. The quotations come from 640 and 641.

[40] Mary Morrissey, *Politics and the Paul's Cross Sermons, 1558–1642* (Oxford: Oxford University Press, 2011), deals at length with the importance of sermons at Paul's Cross as political tools that needed to be controlled.

[41] *Parker Correspondence*, 260–1.   [42] *Parker Correspondence*, 242, 382.

[43] Millar MacLure, *Register of Sermons Preached at Paul's Cross,1534–1642*, revised and edited by Peter Pauls and Jackson Campbell Boswell (Ottawa: Dovehouse Editions, 1989), 46.

[44] William Nicholson, ed., *The Remains of Edmund Grindal* (Cambridge: Parker Society, 1843), 253.

[45] Morrissey, *Paul's Cross*, 130–59.

[46] *A Sermon Preached at Pauls Cross... by M. George Giffard...*(London: 1591), sig. A. 3v [STC (2nd edn)/11862.3].

No major public events occurred without sermons. Assize sermons were preached wherever royal justices went on their rounds, stiffening the resolve of the gentlemen of the bench and the jury. Sermons opened Parliament, too. In 1571 Bishop Sandes of London lectured the Queen and Parliament on the text "fear God and serve him in truth," showing how, reported Thomas Hooker, "religion is chiefly to be sought in virtue and truth," without which the Queen could not govern.[47]

Hortatory and thanksgiving sermons were frequently joined by exhortations to repentance in the face of God's chastisement through plague and other troubles. They may have been ordered by authorities, but they may also have been preached because it was obvious to all that decayed virtue led to divine punishment.

Of course, sermons were part of the propaganda war against the papists, Brownists, and other religious enemies. It is impossible to separate church from state in these performances, but many were clearly prompted and supported by the political leadership, refuting attacks on the authority of church and state. John Jewel's famous "Challenge Sermon" is a fine example of this. Preached at Paul's Cross on November 26, 1559 and repeated again at court the next March, it challenged the Catholics to justify their church using the scriptures and the writings of the church fathers. It set off round after round of confutations and refutations, disproofs of reproofs, and other polemics in sermons and in print. Jewel's sermon was expanded to become the *Apology for the Church of England*, printed in Latin and then translated into English by Anne Bacon, Sir Nicholas Bacon's wife and William Cecil's sister-in-law. Distributed widely, it provided grounding for future responses to Catholics, in print and in sermons. It also stimulated an outpouring of Catholic responses, running to twenty-nine publications.[48]

Jewel was very clear about what he was doing in these sermons and publications. Making the historical case for the English church, he compared himself and his fellows to early Christians who were wrongly accused of coming together "either to kill the magistrates or to subvert the commonwealth" when they met for the Eucharist. His point to his readers was that English Protestants were no threat to established order:

> Truly, we neither put off the yoke of obedience from us; neither do we disorder realms; neither do we set up or pull down kings; nor translate governments; nor give our kings poison to drink; nor yet hold to them our feet to be kissed; nor, opprobriously triumphing over them, leap into their necks with our feet. This rather is our profession; this is our doctrine: that every soul…ought to be subject to kings and magistrates.…Our common teaching also is, that we ought so to obey princes as men sent of God; and that whoso withstandeth them, withstandeth God's ordinance.[49]

Teaching obedience and virtue was a primary role of the church, not cynically, as a mere manipulation of power, but with deep conviction that Elizabeth's state was

---

[47] Hartley, vol. 1, 243. [48] Milward, *Religious Controversies*, 1–8.

[49] John Jewel, *The Apology of the Church of England* (London: Cassell, 1888), <http://anglicanhistory.org/jewel/apology/04.html>. Accessed Dec. 31, 2013.

God's creation. The pulpits were one of the easiest and fastest ways of responding to crises, spreading news, and teaching virtue.

The goal, managerially, was to reform and control public virtue, ensuring God was pleased and obeyed. Set forms of public prayer were used to the same end. In March 1585 Dr William Parry was executed for plotting to kill the Queen. Having worked as a spy on the continent for Burghley, he was actually a double agent. A member of Parliament, and a secret Catholic, he spoke against the bill denouncing Jesuits and seminary priests, and was denounced by a fellow conspirator for plotting with Cardinal Como to murder Elizabeth. The spinning of this sensational case was necessary. An official, though anonymous, publication was printed detailing the evidence against Parry. Its long title serves as a guide to its contents: *A True and Plaine Declaration of the Horrible Treasons, practised by William Parry the traitor, against the Queenes maiestie. The maner of his arraignment, conuiction and execution, together with the copies of sundry letters of his and others, tending to diuers purposes, for the proofes of his treasons. Also an addition not impertinent thereunto, containing a short collection of his birth, education and course of life. Moreouer, a fewe obseruations gathered of his owne wordes and wrytings, for the farther manifestation of his most disloyal, deuilish and desperate purpose.* The case against him was made in enthusiastic hyperbole and chilling detail. A man of "mean and base" parentage, his insolent nature led him into treason, which was detailed over fifty-three pages. Appended to these were three prayers.[50]

One, the longest, was to be used at court and in Parliament. Praying for all kings, princes, countries, and peoples who profess the Gospel, but especially for Elizabeth, the petitioners thanked God for saving her. Then they asked God to confound and overthrow her enemies and cast them into the pit they had dug. "Discomfort them, discomfort them, Lord," they recited. Confessing their unworthiness, they sought God's help in reforming and repenting.

A second prayer was for all "loving subjects" to use. It did not contain a confession of sin like the one for the court and Parliament. It declared that God's children prostrated themselves before Him with praise and thanksgiving for the delivery of Elizabeth from "the hands of strange children" attempting bloody and most barbarous treason. These unnatural disobedient subjects had sought to shed her blood to "the great disquiet of the church and utter discomfort of our souls." But all is well, "her soul is delivered and we are escaped," and they thank God and ask Him to continue his loving kindness toward the Queen.

A third prayer was for members of Parliament only. It asks God to recognize their special role, thanking Him for allowing them to taste his "sweet holy spirit" and for the "liberty granted unto us at this time to make our meeting together." They prayed for "good minds to conceive, free liberty to speak, and on all sides a ready and quiet consent to such wholesome laws" as declare them to be His people.[51]

---

[50] *A true and plaine declaration of the horrible treasons, practised by William Parry the traitor* ... [STC (2nd edn)/19342a].
[51] Strype, *Annals*, vol. 3, 2, 330–3.

These kinds of public prayers and popular publications were expected to shape public perception of events, and carried within them instructions about the behavior of virtuous citizens. The same messages were delivered orally, so great leaders had to be effective speakers.

Burghley and Bacon were considered by contemporaries to be model rhetoricians, which was high praise in an age that set great store by oral performance. As Fulke Greville, poet, parliamentarian, and civil servant, summed up the importance of eloquent speech:

> For the true Art of Eloquence indeed
> Is not this craft of words, but forms of speech,
> Such as from living wisdoms do proceed,
> Whose ends are not to flatter, or beseech,
> Insinuate, or persuade, but to declare
> What things in Nature good, or evil are.[52]

In a Petrarchan manner, the quality of the speech was tied to the quality of the man, and so men were carefully trained to use the rhetorical *cursus* set out by the greats such as Quintilian.

Burghley is a good example of this civic humanist preparation. His oral style, like his written style, analyzed *in utramque partem*, expressing both the positive and negative positions, anticipating his opponents' objections. His was a formal, orderly process, summing up his arguments with an apt Latin tag that he expected his interlocutors to understand. His learning was evident to all when he made classical quotations his own. It made him a powerful public speaker in an age that valued a proper rhetorical technique in which truth was buttressed by ancient authorities.

Much of what we do know about Burghley's skill in rhetoric comes from his editing. He was a fierce editor. Hundreds of drafts have his spiky writing on them. Parliamentary bills, royal orders, instructions to diplomats, letters, and important speeches—he compulsively edited them all. He was constantly trying to get the message right for the audience.

Sometimes, rather than edit them, he wrote them himself. The most striking instance of this is a draft of a speech to be delivered by the Speaker of the House of Commons to the Queen at the closing of Parliament. There is no date on it—internal evidence suggests 1571, since the Speaker apologizes for the Common's behavior and assures her that the members were happy to shut up when ordered to—and the whole document is in William Cecil's hand. He wrote the draft, and then he went back and made revisions. To my knowledge, there is no surviving account of this speech, but Cecil would not have delivered it himself. Presumably his draft was handed to the Speaker, Christopher Wray, in 1571. Wray's lackluster performance as Speaker in that Parliament might well have prompted Cecil to intervene, putting the appropriate words into his mouth.

[52] Fulke Greville, *Humane Learning*, 110, as quoted in Kenneth J. E. Graham, *The Performance of Conviction: Plainness and Rhetoric in the Early English Renaissance* (Ithaca, NY: Cornell University Press, 1994), 115.

Cecil makes the Speaker admit that some of what had gone on in the House had "miscontented" the Queen. However, he proclaimed their loyalty, demonstrating how Parliament should behave toward the Queen:

> I can assure your majesty, that in this assembly wherein I was always present, there was never found in any speech private or public an argument or token of any person that showed any intention to be offensive to your Majesty. And for proof hereof when it pleased your majesty to direct me to declare your pleasure to the Common house in what sort you would they should stay any further proceedings in debating of the manner of reformation of such things as they thought might be reformed in the Church, I found them all generally and particularly ready to obey your majesty as having by Gods ordinance a supreme authority for the purpose ...

And so they surrendered care of the church to her, asking her to continue "to see such abuses as are crept into the Church by the negligence of the ministers may be speedily reformed to the honor of Almighty God, and to your own immortal praise, and comfort of your subjects."

The Speaker petitioned the Queen's assent to the bills passed by the two houses, using the "authority which you have like to God Almighty who, as he giveth life ... to all his creatures great and small, so your Majesty shall give life and continuance, to the fruits of our consultations, without which your royal assent, [by your own breath,] the same shall become without life and sense, [vain] and our labors therein lost ..."[53] It was Cecil's formula, and a powerful organic mixed metaphor.

Lord Keeper Bacon, said by George Puttenham to be the most eloquent man England ever bred, answered this ghostwritten speech in the Queen's name.[54] He made it clear that she appreciated those who behaved themselves modestly and dutifully, and would not forget those who, in their audacious, arrogant folly challenged her prerogative. Bacon was responding to the groveling done by the Speaker, making it clear that Her Majesty was not amused, but would not hold the badness of a few against the obedience of the greater part of the two houses. The weightier part of the Queen's speech demanded their dutiful execution of the laws they made.[55]

Rhetoric of this sort was an essential working tool of leaders. Burghley and Bacon were better at it than many, which gave them gravitas as leaders of the state and legal community. But it was important because the spoken word was as powerful as the printed word in the managerial world in which they lived. Hearing was easier than reading for most of the Queen's subjects. The interplay between proclaimed information, declared information, preached information, speeches, and print was obvious to Elizabethan managers, who used all the forms to define

---

[53] BL Lansd. 104 fol. 150–3v. His interlineations are in brackets.

[54] Robert Tittler, *Nicholas Bacon: The Making of a Tudor Statesman* (London: Jonathan Cape, 1976), 64–5.

[55] Hartley, vol. 1, 185–93.

how people understood events, to outline virtuous actions, and to enforce ideals of obedience.

In a system with weak controls, it was essential to get the story right, to convince magistrates to act as the Queen needed them to act. It was also necessary to convince the public that in obeying the Queen's magistrates they were obeying God. Alternative narratives were a danger to the Queen's peace and to the kingdom's prosperity.

6

Managing Up and Managing Down

The place of a secretary is dreadful if he serve not a constant prince, for he that liveth by trust, ought to serve truly, so, he that liveth at mercy, had need be careful in choice of his master . . . the first day of his duty is the first day of his misery, for, if he be not worthy of trust, he is less worthy of life. And a suspicion of a secretary is both a trial, a condemnation, and a judgment.

Sir Robert Cecil[1]

The Queen was the font of power for Burghley and all other royal officials. She imbued them with authority, and she could remove it with a remark or a gesture. Her refusal to see an official or a courtier could severely undermine his authority, his influence, and his prospects.

Elizabeth understood this and used it to her advantage. One of her mottoes was "Video et Taceo": "I see and I remain silent." In the rhetoric of leadership the all-knowing eye that said little, saw much, and sometimes acted was a powerful tool. She seldom personally communicated with her servants in writing, preferring to do it verbally, with them on their knees before her.

The ritual of the court was designed to reinforce her power and magnificence, and to keep her subjects in their places. We get glimpses of how this worked in practice, even though the lack of writing from the Queen makes it hard to penetrate her silence.

Elizabeth was not an easy sovereign to work for. Strong willed and strongly conservative, especially when it came to her personal powers, she was happy to berate those with whom she disagreed. Burghley and his colleagues had to learn to mollify her, to convince her, and to obey when there was no other choice. She took council individually from her councilors, rather than from the Privy Council, which kept them divided and competitive. Sometimes, as in the aftermath of the Anjou match, each one was required to write his opinion to her, making it hard for them to have a united front. Over time, as Wallace MacCaffrey says, her councilors, a remarkably stable group, "had to live with the basic rhythms of the royal personality." Her unwillingness to act until forced to, her vacillations even then, and her unpredictable temper taught them to be careful. Any of her decisions could be reversed at her whim.[2]

As Elizabeth supposedly told the earl of Leicester, her greatest favorite, "God's death, my lord, I have wished you well, but my favor is not locked up for you that others shall not partake thereof, for I have many servants unto whom I have and

---

[1] New Haven, Yale University, Beinecke Library, Osborn Shelves Fb 6, fols 376–7.
[2] Wallace MacCaffrey, *Elizabeth I* (London: Edward Arnold, 1993), 360–1.

will at my pleasure bequeath my favors and likewise resume the same"; "I will have here but one mistress and no master." When Robert Naunton recalled this story in the 1630s, he was making the point that Elizabeth "ruled much by faction and parties, which she herself both made, upheld, and weakened as her judgment advised."[3] In short, she managed her managers, each according to their station. She was deeply aware of their powers and precedence, an order enacted in formal moments like the processions of the Knights of the Garter (see Fig. 6.1).

When you worked for Elizabeth, you understood who was in charge. At the same time, her councilors needed her to make decisions that could direct their actions. Her unwillingness to give firm orders left them frustrated and unsure. If they acted without knowing her will, or if their actions misfired, they could become the uncomfortable objects of one of her rages.

Fig. 6.1. *Procession of the Knights of the Garter* (Henry Hastings, 3rd earl of Huntingdon; Walter Devereux, 1st earl of Essex; William Cecil, 1st Baron Burghley; Arthur Grey, 14th Baron Grey of Wilton; Edward Stanley, 3rd earl of Derby; Henry Herbert, 2nd earl of Pembroke; Charles Howard, 1st earl of Nottingham; generic Knight of the Garter), after Marcus Gheeraerts the Elder. Photograph of engraving (1576), 16 1/8 in × 21 3/4 in (410 mm × 553 mm). Reference Collection. NPG D31857. National Portrait Gallery, London.

[3] Naunton, 41.

Her anger was probably something the councilors, courtiers, and ladies in waiting came to expect. Most of them suffered periods of exile from court, until her disapproval cooled. The young women who served her often married secretly because Elizabeth never approved, and when the Queen learned they had married her anger was epic, and the ladies' exiles from her favor sometimes lasted forever. Even Burghley was subjected to this treatment after the execution of Mary, Queen of Scots. He was punished for convincing Elizabeth to do something she did not want to do, but which her council believed must be done.

The story of how the council orchestrated the pressure on Elizabeth to get her to sign the order for Mary's execution is well known. As is the famous refusal of Amias Paulet, her jailer, to conveniently murder Mary, at Elizabeth's request: "God forbid that I should make so foul a shipwreck of my conscience or leave so great a blot to my poor posterity to shed blood without law or warrant."[4]

In the aftermath, Elizabeth was angry with all involved. Secretary Davison was permanently exiled from court, and Burghley was, justly, blamed for persuading her to kill her cousin. It is the language he used when he tried to get back into favor that is interesting here. All his authority came from her favor, and he was desperate to re-establish his access to her. As her anger with him grew, he reasoned it was because he was not able to speak with her: "I conceive," he wrote her, that her ire

> increaseth by reason your Majesty hath not heard me as you have heard others, whom your Majesty hath admitted to your presence. Which through my lameness and infirmity being not able to come near your presence is only denied me. And yet such is my desire to appear before your Gracious Majesty, as I am most willing, to endure any pain to be carried to some place, yea to be laid upon the floor near your Majesty's feet, there to endure your Majesty's pleasure, hoping by God's goodness, who knoweth best my thoughts past and present to be so reverent to your Majesty and careful of your favor, that I shall find some drops of your mercy, to quench my sorrowful panting heart.[5]

Long before he wrote his groveling letters begging to be allowed back into her presence, he articulated to Edmund Grindal the importance of abasement for smoothing relations with his Queen. In 1577, Archbishop Grindal made the grievous error of assuming that he, as Primate of All England, could lecture the Queen on what should be done with the church she governed. Refusing to obey her order to suppress prophesying, clerical study groups that she thought encouraged Protestant radicals, he wrote her a "book" of 6,000 words to that effect and awaited her response. Meanwhile, his friends at court, Burghley and Leicester, sought to protect him from the Queen's temper. They thought she would cool off, and Burghley tried to keep Grindal away from court until it was safe. But it was never safe.

In May 1577 Grindal was sequestered and placed under house arrest in Lambeth Palace. He had appeared before the Privy Council and refused to retract his stubborn resistance to Elizabeth, who intended to remove him from office.

---

[4] Conyers Read, *Lord Burghley and Queen Elizabeth* (London: Jonathan Cape, 1960), 367.
[5] BL Lansd. 115, fol. 89. Holograph draft.

At the end of November, Burghley sent his good friend the Dean of Westminster to Grindal with a letter explaining how to mollify the Queen's anger. The archbishop had been ordered to either confess his fault to the Queen, or to accept deprivation. Here is how Burghley scripted Grindal's confession of guilt: First, he was to admit that the Queen had acted on counsel from the bishops and judges of the realm, who warned her that the "prophesyings" were "inconvenient" and so her order was justified.

> And herein to use good speeches of her Majesty, as a prince that in all her particular doings hath showed her wisdom, in doing nothing without good cause to move her thereto. And therefore they were to be greatly condemned that would in any wise seek to find fault with her Majesty. And in this point, the Archbishop should do well to use the more lowly speech, as in good reason he may do without offence of his conscience.

Second, he had to admit that he was disobedient to the Queen's "supreme authority ecclesiastical" and that she had acted justly toward him. Moreover, he was to agree that the nature of his offense required her to force his public declaration of his error. Burghley urged him to expatiate on her justice, and on his reprehensible disobedience. In doing this, Grindal could, in order to protect his own conscience,

> use a more general speech to acknowledge his fault and to crave pardon, for what purposes his grace may say that he is very sorry that he hath in this sort offended her Majesty, as he is charged, and that he requireth her Majesty to pardon him ... and not to interpret his doings to have been with any meaning to offend her Majesty, but considering he now seeth upon what considerations her Majesty did proceed he is very sorry that he hath herein offended her Majesty, and so conclude with all humble request of pardon and firm promises of obedience to her Majesty as far forth as in all duty he is bound.[6]

This recognition of Elizabeth's grace, wisdom, legality, and authority was designed to blunt her anger and allow his restitution as archbishop. The council hoped to prevent a larger scandal.

Throughout the crisis, the council worked to keep Elizabeth from doing something they believed she would regret. Sir Thomas Wilson, the principal secretary of the Privy Council at the time, shows us how they were trying to manage her peremptory anger. He told Burghley the Queen was still "much offended" by Grindal,

> and disliketh our doings for dealing with him so at large, whom her highness would see deprived for his contempt committed. But I answered that a deprivation of an Archbishop cannot be done so soon, and if that course be taken, he would ask the benefit of the law and pray counsel to his assistance, whereby the matter would grow bigger [?] before it be decided. I ... trust upon your coming, her Majesty will be otherwise advised, and take that course which is more safe, more easy, and as honorable as the other, which is, his resignation.[7]

---

[6] BL Lansd. 103/fols 14–15v.   [7] TNA SP 12/122 fol. 24.

But Grindal did not follow Burghley's script. He became a prisoner of conscience, even though he was not deprived.[8]

Grindal's experience was extreme because he refused to give in to the Queen's imperious order. Most people crumpled before her, and her privy councilors were used to being used as her whipping boys.

Yet Elizabeth also knew how to mollify. Archbishop Parker, writing to Lady Anne Bacon, suggested her husband, the Lord Keeper, could take lessons from the Queen about how to be imperious without losing loyalty. Parker said that he was unabashed to speak to his Queen what his conscience and heart required, but that meant he sometimes felt her displeasure: "…this other day," he said, "I was well chidden at my prince's hand." "And yet her highness being never so much incensed to be offended with me, the next day, coming by Lambeth bridge…and I according to duty," meeting her, "she gave me her very good looks and spoke secretly in mine ear, that she must needs countenance mine authority before the people to the credit of my service …"[9]

Lord Thomas Scrope of Bolton had a warming experience of her personality. Just appointed to his father's office of Lord Warden of the Western Marches, he was unable to answer the Queen's questions on all points, and he had relatives who had incurred her anger. However, his "grief was quickly razed by her acceptance." Having tasted her grace and learned her virtues, he said, he would endeavor to deface his faults.[10]

Although they were often touched by her anger, they also received Elizabeth's affection. They responded to her petting, spending fortunes to prove their appreciation of her attentions. She teased them with pet names. The earl of Leicester was her "Eyes," Principal Secretary Walsingham was her "Moor," Lord Chancellor Hatton was her "Sheep," and Burghley was her "Spirit." The short Sir Robert Cecil was her "Elf." She kept them around, too, even though they all suffered the occasional chill of temporary banishment from her radiance. So, although they had to keep flattering her, she had their loyalty.[11]

Often her servants were caught in nearly impossible binds between powerful forces with contrary agendas. Burghley himself told the earl of Essex that Elizabeth had expressed her "high displeasure" to the Lord Treasurer "with words of indignity [and] reproach," calling him a "miscreant and a coward" for believing that Essex should not profit from Spanish prisoners he had taken. When Burghley argued that they should hear the earl first, she "increased her ireful speeches that the Treasurer either for fear or favor regarded the Earl more than herself." Then he received a letter from his sister-in-law, Lady Russell, informing him Essex was accusing him of the same, in reverse. He characterized himself as caught like Odysseus, between Scylla and Charybdis: "my misfortune is to fall into both. The danger of the one doth not

---

[8] The blow-by-blow account of this drama is provided in Patrick Collinson, *Archbishop Grindal, 1519–1583: The Struggle for a Reformed Church* (Berkeley: UCLA Press, 1979), 233–65.

[9] Gemma Allen, ed., *The Letters of Lady Anne Bacon, Camden Society*, 5th ser., 44 (2014), 63.

[10] TNA SP 15/32 fol. 136.

[11] MacCaffrey, *Elizabeth I*, 361–2. Steven W. May, *Queen Elizabeth I: Selected Works* (New York: Washington Square Press, 2004), 228.

free me from the other." "My cases were miserable, if against you both I had not comfort by God through a good conscience..."[12]

Burghley, in this case, was in trouble for having supported a position contrary to the Queen's. He wanted to reason with her, but she would have none of it. In order to prevent that from happening too often, Burghley and his colleagues glossed the information they provided the Queen, and played information brokers between her and other powerful folk. They had to ensure that the Queen was never surprised, but they also strove to deliver their messages in ways that would lead to the outcomes they preferred.

For example, look at the role of councilors and the Queen in negotiating the conflicts between the Talbot and Stanhope families.

George Talbot, earl of Shrewsbury, died in early November, 1590. His son and heir, Gilbert, immediately sent word of his father's death by his servant, Thomas Kitson, to Lord Burghley. Kitson rode all night, and, after a delay caused by a shortage of post horses, arrived at Burghley's London house at 5 a.m. As soon as Burghley's chamber door was open, his servant, Mr Maynard, delivered the news. Having read the letter, Burghley sent for his daughter-in-law and "by her did presently advertise her Majesty." Elizabeth, thus informed, was able to express to Gilbert's neighbor John Stanhope, a gentleman of the privy chamber, what a loss George Talbot's death was to her, "both for his liking and fidelity to herself and her estate." Later that night she used the same words again, and she, and the Lord Chamberlain, praised the qualities of Gilbert as the new earl of Shrewsbury.[13] Stanhope dutifully relayed this information to Shrewsbury. Burghley had done his job, making sure the Queen was informed, so she could play her part in condoling and in praising.

The correspondence between Gilbert Talbot and John Stanhope occurred not long before a dispute between the earl and John Stanhope's brother, Sir Thomas, broke out over the weir on the River Trent that Sir Thomas had built to run his flour mills. This battle demonstrates the ways in which councilors managed disputes. In these situations, they had to assess who had influence with the Queen, what the Queen wanted and was likely to do, and how to ameliorate the situation while maintaining the cooperation of the powerful disputants, their relatives, and friends.[14]

According to Shrewsbury, it began when Stanhope insulted Shrewsbury's honor with proud, false, "unmeet" words, damaging his credit. Offended, he asked various friends close to the throne to get the Queen to "right" him. Stanhope, he believed, thought his influence at court was such that no matter what indignity he offered to the earl, it would be tolerated. He begged them to get Elizabeth to "perform her most gracious words in that behalf, and not suffer my poor honor and reputation (which above my life I desire may be preserved to do her service and

[12] Thomas Birch, ed., *Memoirs of the Reign of Queen Elizabeth from the Year 1581 until her Death...from the original papers of his Intimate Friend, Anthony Bacon...* (London: 1754), 146–7.

[13] G. Dyfnallt Owen, ed., *Calendar of the Manuscripts of the...Marquess of Bath ...*, vol. 5, *Talbot, Dudley and Devereux Papers, 1533–1659, Historical Manuscript Commission*, 58 (1980), 102, 100–1.

[14] This dispute was explored in detail by Wallace T. MacCaffrey, "Talbot and Stanhope: An Episode in Elizabethan Politics," *Bulletin of the Institute of Historical Research*, 33, 87 (1960), 73–85.

honor) to be thus wounded." The earl assured them that he could not continue to serve the Queen with such disgrace upon his name.

Shrewsbury wrote to Elizabeth, including signed certificates testifying that Stanhope had called him a liar. His witnesses declared Stanhope preferred lies to truth, and that he had said Shrewsbury was "no Lieutenant," implying he was unworthy of becoming the Lord Lieutenant in the county in succession to his father, George.

This dispute could not be ignored: although Shrewsbury was querulous and feckless, he was powerful in Derbyshire and Nottinghamshire, and he had to be treated with the respect and honor due to an earl.

Burghley took Shrewsbury's complaints to the Queen. He and Vice-Chamberlain Heneage had read them, and Burghley laid them before Her Majesty, who, he said, thought Shrewsbury justified, if they were true. But she pointedly observed that the witnesses were all Shrewsbury's own men. Sir Thomas Stanhope was to be sent for, if he could travel. Furthermore, the Queen, Burghley reports, had heard from Stanhope's friends that Shrewsbury had called him a knave. The well-informed Queen already knew of the disorderly proceedings, and that names have been subscribed to Shrewsbury's petition against the weir by people who knew nothing of the matter. Shrewsbury, Burghley warned him darkly, had better be ready to explain this.

Vice-Chamberlain Sir Thomas Heneage also wrote to Shrewsbury about the meeting with Elizabeth. He speaks of himself as the one who read the letters to the Queen. When she "misliked" the matter, he made a speech to her, showing Shrewsbury's value to her and to the realm, the justice of his cause, and his loyalty. Where Burghley sternly warned the earl to be prepared to answer, Heneage urged him not to show, in letter or message, that he doubted the Queen's will to protect his honor, "out of her princely nature and justice."

As the two councilors told the story of the meeting with the Queen, we can see different styles of self-representation, each taking credit, but one warning of her distrust of the story and the other claiming to have won the Queen over, while telling the hothead to shut up.[15] In both cases, they tried to manage the earl's relationship with the Queen.

The information available to Elizabeth was key to her decision-making, and having the Queen's ear made all the difference. Shrewsbury, who soon found himself being investigated for suborning witnesses, as Burghley had warned, blamed it on Sir Michael Stanhope, "so near to her Majesty as that he may fill her ears."

Naturally, Elizabeth and Burghley knew that Shrewsbury was notably difficult. His battles with his father, and with his stepmother, Bess of Hardwick, would have been common gossip. Shrewsbury kept things stirred up in his corner of the country. So Stanhope probably had more influence with the Queen than Shrewsbury could muster, but Shrewsbury did his best to poison Elizabeth against Stanhope through Burghley and others at court.

[15] HMC Bath V, 105.

On the other hand, Burghley and his colleagues also knew that Sir Thomas Stanhope had bad relations with many of his neighbors, and the Star Chamber and the Privy Council had intervened in his fights with John Zouche, Henry Sacheverel, and John Molyneux. In the late 1570s Stanhope had been imprisoned in the Fleet by the council for his misbehavior.[16]

Notwithstanding, Sir Thomas was an important local official, often used by Burghley when there were commissions against Catholics, which might explain the rumor Shrewsbury eagerly reported. He said Sir Thomas advised another of Shrewsbury's enemies that there was an easy way to be quit of the earl. "Let him tell the Queen," he said, "that the Earl of Shrewsbury is a papist, and then see who can get it out of her head."[17]

Shrewsbury told all this to Burghley, presumably as a countermine. He then wrote a very similar letter to Sir Thomas Heneage, to ensure that his friends at court could help block Stanhope, and perhaps cut off Michael Stanhope before he further poisoned the Queen against him.[18]

As the feud went on, it escalated. Shrewsbury eventually sent armed men and a crew to divert the River Trent at Shelford, Nottinghamshire, so Stanhope's mills lost power.[19] The countess of Shrewsbury sent Sir Thomas a message informing him he was a reprobate, and his son John was a rascal.[20]

In the meantime, there was a concerted effort by the Privy Council to damp the quarrel. It took the form of some honest truth telling. Formally, it came in a letter to the sheriff and justices of Nottinghamshire expressing concern that the abuses against Shrewsbury and Stanhope "are very odious and some of them most intolerable, tending to defamation and to breed troubles, division and quarrels which already is kindled too far in that county." They ordered the commission of the peace to examine anyone suspected in the matter, under oath.[21]

Privately, the council members took another tack. Lord Howard of Effingham, Lord Buckhurst, and Sir Thomas Heneage wrote to Shrewsbury collectively and individually, advising him to drop his vendetta against Stanhope. Their joint letter warned him that Sir Thomas was "a gentleman of such credit and strengthened with that special favor from her Majesty which his near friends possess at Court." Therefore, if Shrewsbury pursued his attack, he would "be deprived of the great and honorable hopes of serving her Majesty, which your birth and desires would in short time have brought upon you."[22] He would be dishonored if he lost the Queen's trust.

Buckhurst expatiated in his private letter. Moving Shrewsbury to some "friendly end," he explained how things worked at court. He assured him that "the continual presence of these two [Stanhope] brethren in court, with the near place they have with her Majesty, and which is above all the rest, the special favor which her Highness doth bear to them, will always prevail in so great advantage against you, as it will not be

[16] HPT, Hasler, ed. Sub STANHOPE, Sir Thomas (*c*.1540–96), of Shelford, Notts. At http://www.historyofparliamentonline.org/volume/1558-1603/member/stanhope-sir-thomas-1540-96. Accessed July 30, 2014.

[17] HMC Bath V, 108.   [18] HMC Bath V, 109.   [19] CP 169/70.

[20] HMC Bath V, 119.   [21] TNA PC 2/20 fol. 287.   [22] HMC Bath V, 110.

possible, neither for you nor your friends to carry this cause …" Because the Queen favored them, and because most men's eyes were fixed on her example, the Stanhopes were "mightily friended and favored" in the Privy Council. "They shall never want," he wrote, "means and matter enough prively here in Court to wound you, being one of the great dangers and infelicities of this place, that even the meanest may do us more hurt than peradventure the greatest can do us good."

Shrewsbury, he observed, hurt himself by not being at court, and by making trouble in his own country. It is "policy" he said, not to increase the power and countenance of people like Shrewsbury "when in the country you dwell in you will needs enter in a war with your inferiors there." When a great man turned on his inferiors, "we think it justice, equity and wisdom to take care that the weaker part be not put down by the mightier."

Buckhurst urged Shrewsbury to knit a fast knot of friendship with Stanhope, for mutual profit and the happiness of their friends, to the earl's honor, strength, and benefit, earning him the love of so many gentlemen of worth, wealth, and wisdom.[23]

Lord Howard of Effingham took up the same themes, warning Shrewsbury that the dispute might prevent the Queen from calling him to "that place that many of your ancestors possessed." Her Majesty, he said, had due respect for him as an earl, but—and this was important—those who have their kin and friend near the monarch find favor with the prince. Thus "meaner" people may benefit more than those born to rank. "What would our adversaries put in her Majesty's ears if we, your poor friends here, had refused the means we took" to defend him—but their defense of him prompts some to say they are nourishing unkindness rather than seeking resolution.

He assured Shrewsbury that they had written to Sir Thomas in the same vein, in their roles as brokers. Both men were threatened with dishonor, both were told their behavior was bad for the realm, and both were encouraged to make up. Shrewsbury would have none of it. "I cannot," he wrote to Howard of Effingham, "have Sir Thomas Stanhope's misusing of me smothered or shuffled up."[24]

Although the councilors insisted they were loving friends of the parties, they were well aware of the dispute's potential for violence and misrule. Their next step was to call on the commission for sewers to adjudicate the use of the weir on the river, but that, too, failed. Shrewsbury complained of intimidated justices who would not do their jobs, and he demanded that a new sheriff be appointed for Nottinghamshire to ensure justice.[25]

As they feared, Shrewsbury raised the stakes when the writs were issued for a parliamentary election in January 1593. Burghley, who was ill, made the effort to write Shrewsbury about the rumors they were hearing about his intention to attend the Nottinghamshire election with "some great extraordinary company" to ensure that his brother-in-law, Sir Charles Cavendish, was elected a knight of the shire. "Your Lordship would use your honorable wisdom and accustomed temperance to stay all quarrels that may be dangerous to the breach of the peace," Burghley wrote, attempting to ensure that the election was proper. He was also moved to write

[23] HMC Bath V, 110–11.   [24] HMC Bath V, 113.   [25] HMC Bath V, 113, 115.

because he had heard of "querrelous brabbles" between Sir Thomas's son-in-law and one of Shrewsbury's dependents. In a postscript he added, "Your Lordship answers at your commandment, but not to wrestle at this time." All of this was wrapped in assurances of the love he bore the earl, but the meaning was clear: no trouble.[26]

Unfortunately, the rumors were true, and Shrewsbury intruded his nominee as the knight of the shire for Nottinghamshire, defeating Sir Thomas and his party, the supporters of the earl of Rutland. Rutland was a minor at the time, and his influence over the county, as well as his ability to support his clients, was weak. It was into this opening that Shrewsbury threw himself, causing continuing trouble in the area. Writing to Burghley, Shrewsbury presented the election chaos as the fault of Sir Thomas Stanhope, whose armed followers had seized the shire hall, forcing the election to move to the castle.[27] Duels, the defacing of arms, and other "brabbles" continued.

Meanwhile, the dance of deference and "friendship" went on. The riot at the weir in Shelford was to be heard in the Star Chamber in May of 1594, and Shrewsbury happened to drop by Burghley's house beforehand. Playing on the old man's tenderest spots, he afterward wrote a chatty letter about Burghley's four grandchildren, admiring his building project and offering some decorating advice. After this softening up, he asked his help in the Star Chamber, hoping Burghley "according to law and equity will pronounce your sentence therein." Expressing his affection, he prayed God to grant Burghley perfect health "to live so see more years than any of your kindred."[28]

In the end, the Privy Council did what Shrewsbury had been warned would happen. It informed the justices of Nottinghamshire that it was Her Majesty's pleasure Sir Thomas was to be allowed to repair and enjoy his weir. Importantly, they were ordered to drop the charges of riot that had been brought against Sir Thomas and his servants for defending the weir, and told to look for the people who had tried to burn it.[29] It was a thorough victory for Stanhope, even if it did not do much to pacify the troubles between the families.

Wallace MacCaffrey summed up this complex feud by observing that the Queen and Burghley were prepared to overlook some casual violence, but eventually Shrewsbury "felt the heavy, though sometimes slow-moving, hand of government."[30] Ultimately, it was as the council told the earl—intimate access to the court overcame his regional greatness. The Queen's preferences, who had access to her, the power of local magnates, family ties, friendships, local economic interests and loyalties, and even religious identities were in play as the council managed conflict in that "far country" of Nottinghamshire. Likewise the parties in the dispute used their network of connections to influence the outcomes. Everyone was managing up or down.

---

[26] HMC Bath V, 116–17.   [27] Lambeth Palace Library, Talbot Papers MS.3200, fol. 164.
[28] HMC Bath V, 124–5.   [29] TNA PC 2/20 fol. 529.
[30] MacCaffrey, "Talbot and Stanhope," 85.

This, of course, was the natural managerial condition in Elizabeth's state, and it helps account for the Tudor enthusiasm for arbitration. Although we are used to thinking of the importance of the common law to Tudor rulers, the legal system of Tudor England was inefficient and expensive. The number of cases that actually reached resolution in the courts was tiny. Most were settled or abandoned before trial. Because going to law was clumsy and expensive, it was common across the many forms of law practiced in the realm to use arbitration as a quick and easy way to resolve disputes.[31]

Commonly, mediation and arbitration required resort to "friends amicably intervening," people who could be counted on to help resolve the dispute out of their good will toward the parties. They were not paid, and their interventions could be informal or formal. As in the Shrewsbury/Stanhope dispute, there was a great deal of room for loving friends to mediate before a more formal arbitration occurred—but they might both be happening at the same time, as various tracks were taken to the same end. A law suit might start the process, but in a well-ordered community, the intervention of friends was much more effective in ending a dispute than was a court order.

Mediation is generally confused with patron/client relations, since clients did turn to their patrons when they needed mediation in a suit; they needed someone who knew someone. One of the sorts of favors that could be sued for was dispute resolution. If one could get the help of a person greater than the disputants, pressure for settlement could be brought to bear. This was something the local magnates knew well, and it was used to keep their "countries" quiet. If that failed, of course, it moved higher up the chain, perhaps as far as the Queen, without any formalities.

The querulous Talbot family gives us an example of mediation at a very high level. Gilbert's father, George, had a long-running, bitter dispute with his wife and her son. The countess, Elizabeth née Hardwick, had married him as her fourth husband. Their relationship was very bad, and made worse by her sons by her Cavendish husband. By 1584 they were living apart and indulging in bitter acrimony. It was a marriage all the Queen's horses and men could hardly put back together again. But she, the Lord Treasurer, the Lord Chancellor, the earl of Leicester, and Secretary Walsingham tried. They met with the parties, negotiated, and got nowhere. Finally, the Queen completed the mediation with an order designed to settle the squabbles. She had hoped, she told them, to see the unkindness between them "by our mediation brought to some good end and accord, both in respect of the place we hold, which requireth at our hand that we should not suffer in our realm two persons of your degree and quality, to live in such a kind of divided sort, as also for the special care we have of yourself."[32]

Burghley, like other great men, got frequent requests for mediations. It is unclear if they were handled like other petitions—presumably, it mattered how well he

---

[31] John Baker, *Oxford History of the Laws of England*, vol. 6, *1483–1558* (Oxford: Oxford University Press, 2003), 331–4. Derek Roebuck, *Mediation and Arbitration in the Middle Ages. England, 1154–1558* (Oxford: Holo Books, the Arbitration Press, 2013), 400.
[32] TNA SP 12/207 fols 12, 21.

knew you and who you were—but it was assumed that he could be a present help in a time of need. Later in the reign we see Sir Robert Cecil and the earl of Essex playing a similar role in mediations, though they seem to have been more willing to take them on than Burghley.

Arbitrations were more formal, and therefore more visible. William More of Loseley, whose papers survive in Surrey, was an active justice who was involved in several arbitrations. Often, these were directed from a court to local justices, with instructions that they find a solution without further legal recourse. Sometimes the cases were sent from the highest level. Burghley gave them a dispute concerning foreign glassmakers in Sussex and the construction of a glasshouse. He wanted it resolved because the Queen was anxious to encourage the art of glass-making in the realm.[33] More and his colleagues worked on it for six years, but never found a solution the parties would accept.[34]

Even small cases were handled through arbitration. In Beeld in Brecknock a dispute over a house in 1580 led to both parties giving their bond for £10 to accept the decision of their arbitrators. The men nominated to resolve the case were "not to depart out of the town" until they reached an agreement.[35]

Seeking resolution through arbitration was common, and generally successful, since it was a well-established practice, but sometimes local arbitration was not possible—often because of the unequal power between parties. And, sometimes, people who had agreed to arbitration refused to perform their duties. Up until Elizabeth's reign, it was common for Star Chamber to issue a writ, *dedimus potestatum ad audiendum et finaliter determinandum*, granting the power to hear and decide disputes to local gentlemen like William More. The use of the writ declined, but the concerns for maintaining local justice and calm did not. The court of the Star Chamber, which embodied the Queen sitting judicially, was composed of the members of the Privy Council and the judges of the central courts. The court and the council met in the same room, with a red rug covering the table when the Privy Council was sitting, and a green rug on it when the court of Star Chamber was meeting. As the Star Chamber became a more exclusively criminal court, the Privy Council continued to nominate people to hear and resolve disputes.[36]

Arbitration was not always the answer, but it was another way in which service could be done, through officially recognized "loving friendship" for those both below and above.

It was important that the powerful had their social standing and honor recognized properly, in the proper order, carried the right armorial bearings, and were allowed the appropriate funeral hatchments. All of this was overseen by the earl marshal and his High Court of Chivalry. Disputes over precedence and arms had

[33] More Molyneux Family of Loseley Park, Historical Correspondence, vol. 8, 1564–1628, 6729/10/34. Surrey History Centre, <http://www.nationalarchives.gov.uk/a2a/records.aspx?cat=176-6729&cid=10-46#10-46>. Accessed March 12, 2009.

[34] More Molyneux Family of Loseley Park, Historical Correspondence, vol. 8, <http://www.nationalarchives.gov.uk/a2a/records.aspx?cat=176-6729&cid=-1#-1>. Accessed July 30, 2010.

[35] TNA WALE 30/51/16.

[36] J. A. Guy, *The Court of Star Chamber and its Records to the Reign of Elizabeth I*, Public Record Office Handbooks no. 21 (London: HMSO, 1985), 47–9.

to be handled at the very highest level, and with great political dexterity, if the great families were to be kept from quarreling. Not surprisingly, Cecil, from the time he became Elizabeth's right-hand man, was involved in smoothing out the prickly spines of social rank.

The earl marshal's Court of Chivalry technically used civil law, but in the Elizabethan period it appears that the earl marshal did not always follow the ancient course of his own court, intervening personally, and pouring oil on troubled waters with the help of commissioners as needed. The complexity of the problems he, and the heralds, faced in sorting out pedigrees were enormous. A 1590 letter from the dowager countess Russell, Burghley's sister-in-law, underscores this.

Written to Burghley, who was one of the commissioners in the case (and who rendered an opinion in his own hand), the redoubtable dowager countess begged her brother-in-law to establish the rights of her daughters to use the arms and estate of the earl of Bedford. Her late husband, John Russell, had been heir to the earl of Bedford, but died in 1584, before inheriting from the earl, who died in 1585. Nonetheless, her daughters had "the whole arms" of Bedford as heirs general of the earl of Bedford. This, she urged, gave them precedence over the son and heir of her husband's younger brother, the present earl, and she wanted his arms changed so it was clear that the girls were in the first line of descent. It would establish them as proper heirs of the earl, so that the law, which "favors the heirs male more than the heirs general," would not deprive them of their right to a third of their grandfather's estate. Her daughters, she said, were wards of the Queen, which proved they were the earl's heirs.

Her claims were rejected in 1593, but she believed the judges had conflicts of interest in the case. At one point she demanded that Burghley arrange for the Queen herself to question each judge individually, rather than allowing some to overawe the rest.

As usual, Burghley did his homework on the case, sorting out the estate. It may have been an act of family piety, but he was master of the wards, so his nieces were his to manage, and his opinion weighed heavily. A "declaration" of the earl of Bedford's lands and rents due to the Queen was endorsed by Burghley, in his own hand, with a summary of the revenues by county.[37]

Mediating disputes over obscure coats of arms was part of the job of ensuring peace between powerful people. The ability to work out the disputes in court meant blood need not be spilled. And the authority to resolve these quarrels made the royal government useful giving Burghley and his colleagues another point of influence.

William Cecil and his colleagues worked within an elaborate informal system of trust, cooperation for mutual interest, and coercion. All of these were acted out in terms of deference and noblesse oblige, the exchange of favors and kinship obligations, formal and informal kinds of pressure. These were the soup in which government swam, and all calculations of interest took them into account. In a system in

---

[37] CP 146/62.

which there was very little hard power, the maintenance and extension of connections of mutual self-interest was essential.

A consequence of this reality was a continual negotiation between the parties who held the disparate powers that ruled the nation. Even in times of intense national crisis, these negotiations had to be respected, since the resolution of crises was dependent upon the willingness of the powers to work together.

This need to keep the powerful cooperating together extended to the men who sat on the Queen's council. Tied together by frequent proximity, shared duties, overlapping offices, education, and family, as well as their common necessity to please the Queen, they had to step carefully with one another.

A graphic example is a letter of apology written by William Cecil to his brother-in-law, Lord Keeper Nicholas Bacon. They had had a "sharp afternoon," apparently speaking words they regretted. They had been so angry with each other that Cecil wrote him a note of apology immediately after the meeting, fearing that a face-to-face apology might lead to more argument. Cecil expressed his grief and admitted that it was his own fault. When Bacon disagreed with him, "I persuaded myself I had with good will, and duty merited to my power." But he assured Bacon that his affection toward him was not impaired, "For I meant never, nor will mean, but well humbly and friendly towards you and yours and nothing shall trouble me more, than if it should appear to others, that I have not your good will..."

Bacon responded in kind: "The rules of friendship I trust to keep soundly, as you are apple of mine eye in the uttermost of troubles..." Both men agreed that this letter, with Bacon's response written on it, should be burned, but Cecil had it filed like everything else that passed through his office.[38]

Keeping upward communication open with the Queen and between peers was essential, but all Elizabethans of the ruling classes had to manage down, too. They all had long trains of clients who depended on them to use their power and influence to help them. In some cases these relationships were ancient and structured, like the duties of tenants to their landlords. Other clientage relationships were much more nuanced, and a good manager extended his clientage when he could, his power increasing as his connections grew. Proof of his standing was his ability as a fixer, solving problems, procuring jobs, arranging marriages, and doing other necessary things for "his" people. Of course, the power to fix was also the power to refuse to fix, leaving the patron in control in negative as well as positive ways.

The Elizabethan regime faced its most critical moment of internal dissent when the northern earls revolted in 1569. As we have seen, Cecil and his colleagues sensed something like it was coming, since he was already thinking about ad hoc defensive associations. Those associations recognized their dependence on the lords and gentlemen to muster and lead their men in the suppression of the rebels. On the other hand, the rebels' power derived from exactly the same place. When earls of Westmorland and Northumberland called their tenants to their standards they came. Perhaps they wanted to restore the old church and expel the heretical Queen, but that was not the summons. Their lords had called them, and those who came, came

---

[38] BL Lansd. 94/fol. 195.

as their fathers and grandfathers had come. Duty to their lords was expressed in service, defined by Mervyn James as "with horse and armor under the lord's officer."[39]

For the men summoned to muster in defense of the Queen, it was the local leaders who obeyed, or did not, and who led their local contingents. Strikingly, after the Northern Rebellion had been suppressed Cecil drafted a thankyou note for the Queen to send to certain gentlemen of Northumberland. She had heard of their good and faithful service from the lord warden, the governor of Berwick, and the earl of Sussex. She expressed her appreciation and asked for their continued fidelity.[40] Elizabeth recognized this in a remarkable letter of thanks written to the gentlemen of the north who brought their tenants to the fight, choosing service to her over service to their earl.

These loyal subjects were commanded by Thomas, earl of Sussex. In the mopping up after the fighting, the Queen ordered Sussex to exact royal revenge. In each town and hundred a certain percentage of men were to be executed, in accord with the number who mustered against her. Sussex was told to do this with care, however, since she did not wish to offend the landowners whose power she needed to continue her rule.

Sussex and Cecil knew that there was a calculus in the executions. Killing the wrong traitors might offend people who were powerful and loyal. The Queen knew it too, and when Sussex sent out the "fearful" order for decimation to Sir George Bowes, the provost marshal, noting how many were to be hanged in each town and village, there was a special note. By the Queen's special command, he was to hang hundreds of men, but no one that had a freehold or was deemed to be wealthy.[41]

The decimations were done without trial; a percentage of the population in each place was rounded up and summarily executed. The gentry, however, were granted trials, and they were carefully put into their social grids as their cases were considered.

Meanwhile, the forfeited goods of traitors were used to strengthen the regime in the north. The gentlemen who fought for Elizabeth quickly rushed to claim a share of the spoils, and Elizabeth and Cecil handed out the forfeited property and pardons with clear intent. As Krista Kesselring has observed, "the benefit the crown sought was political as much as financial, and made in accordance with the cultural codes of patronage and lordship upon which early modern order relied. Exchanges of value shaped the resolution of the rising: outward shows of deference for reprieves from the gallows; money for pardons; loyalty for land."[42]

Another important consideration, at all times, was keeping intact the patronage power of the men who had led the defense of the Queen.

In June 1570 the commander in the north, the earl of Sussex, wrote Cecil about one John Gower, asking that his life be spared, although he had been found guilty

---

[39] Mervyn James, "The Concept of Order and the Northern Rising," in Mervyn James, *Society, Politics and Culture: Studies in Early Modern England* (Cambridge: Cambridge University Press, 1986), 289.

[40] CP 157/140.   [41] TNA SP 15/18 fol. 203.

[42] K. J. Kesselring, *The Northern Rebellion of 1569: Faith, Politics, and Protest in Elizabethan England* (London: Palgrave Macmillan, 2007), 131–40.

of rebellion and sentenced to hang. Sussex laid out a set of personal connections that were, he believed, sufficient reason for Elizabeth to grant him the life of Gower. Cecil was to explain to Her Majesty that Gower is a young man, and not a part of the conspiracy, a small fry who could repent. Second, "that he is son to Serjeant Wray's sister whom I think Her Majesty favors, and I would gladly further." (Serjeant Wray, a Yorkshire man and legal star who would become Speaker of the Parliament of 1571, had just been made justice of the York assize, and would soon be a justice of the Queen's bench. The Queen did favor him.) Lastly, Sussex's secretary, John Cottrell, was engaged to marry Gower's mother, "who reposes her whole trust in me for saving her son's life." So, to please his secretary's future wife, he asked for John Gower, convicted traitor, to be spared.[43]

A few months later, he wrote Cecil again about the case, which had become more complicated. Gower's lands had been granted by Elizabeth to her groom of the privy chamber, Sir John Stanhope.[44] Sussex promised to hold Stanhope harmless, since, if Gower did not die, Stanhope could not enjoy his new property.

It took until October, but Gower was spared.[45] It is notable that Sussex was able to prevent the execution through the months that led to the pardon. And it is ironic that John Gower, though young, turned out to be the traitor he was convicted of being. He, and Thomas Wray, another relative of Justice Wray, went on to more plots against their queen. William Wharton filed a bill with the Council of the North in 1574, reporting that Gower was "lurking in corners" supported by Wray.[46] Gower fled to France and later was ordained a Catholic priest in Rome. He confirmed the story of how he had rebelled, lost his lands, and had been pardoned by Elizabeth at the behest of his relatives when under examination by French authorities in 1582.[47]

This powerful act of patronage was achieved by Sussex approaching Cecil in the posture of a supplicant, demonstrating his respect for him and placing himself in a position of clientage to the principal secretary, even though the earl was one of the most powerful men in the court. Master Secretary could do him the favor of intervening with the Queen at a time when Sussex was not at court, securing the boon and putting Sussex in Cecil's debt. At the same time, however, Cecil understood the need to keep a man of Sussex's importance mollified.

Little dramas of social status and mutual bows of recognition were constantly being performed. The gift of a stag or two for a dinner, a rich New Year's gift, a letter courteously offering information, the placement of a relative's or client's child, the shortening of a legal suit, the offer of some timber, the exchange of books—all maintained the lines of communication that crossed all sorts of social, legal, and religious boundaries.

Literary and antiquarian work provided clients with the opportunity to advertise publicly the honor and esteem of their patrons. In 1584 Thomas Palmer offered to dedicate a book to Burghley, if Burghley would arrange for his release from Aylesbury jail.[48]

---

[43] TNA SP 15/19 fol. 28.   [44] TNA SP 12/75 fols 58–58v.   [45] TNA SP 15/19 fol. 41.
[46] TNA SP 15/23, fols 109–10.   [47] TNA SP 15/19 fol. 41. TNA SP 78/7 fol. 92.
[48] BL Lansd. 43, fol. 104.

Susan Cogan's work on the Catholic gentry of the Midlands demonstrates that they, despite their recusancy, still dwelt within the sheltering system of patronage and clientage. It helped them, and it helped the Queen, who needed the Throckmortons, Treshams, Brudnells, and other great families to rule their localities. "Patron–client relationships," she reports, "helped Catholics to remain integrated into the corpus of elites, both as clients to more powerful patrons and as patrons themselves."[49] Sir Edmund Brudenell summed it up in the motto carved over his mantle at Deene Park: *Amicus Fidelis Protexio Fortis* (a faithful friend is a strong bulwark).[50]

Of course, those managing up and those managing down had more at stake than the maintenance of good friendship. As loving as they may have felt, this was about securing and maintaining social capital that could be called on when needed.

Francis Alford's inability to find a patron demonstrates his neglect of his patrons' desires and the reluctance of patrons to accept a client who was unpredictable and prone to cause political embarrassment.

Alford was a quintessential Parliament man, sitting in the House every session from 1563 until 1586. A civil lawyer, he was well connected. His cousin was Lord Buckhurst, and his brother Roger was a valued servant of William Cecil. But he never found a good patron. He himself blamed it on his outspoken defense of unpopular causes in Parliament, but it was also because his wife was a known Catholic who was caught holding Mass in their home. He was suspected of supporting Mary, Queen of Scots, both because of his speeches calling for moderation in her cause, and because he had suspicious connections in France. Writing to an unidentified person, probably his cousin, Lord Buckhurst, he explained how he was blighted. He had petitioned the Queen for a favor, but "I found her highness possessed of two opinions of me, the one that I was a papist and the other that I had intermeddled in some actions for the Scottish Queen: For the first Mr Do[ctor] Awb[rey] having delivered his own knowledge, referred the report thereof to your Lordship and the Lord Treasurer." "What the Lord Burghley will do said she I know not." Reminded that the questions about his participation in the debate over Mary, Queen of Scots had been cleared up, she remembered another reason to distrust him. Reportedly, he had made contacts with the English Catholic exiles in Paris. Although he had been cleared of that before the council, "She caused him [Awbrey] to deliver to Mr Harbert my petition as not fully satisfied for my religion."[51]

A distinct quid pro quo was unnecessary in a patronage system. Avoiding suspicion required people to maintain their honor and credit in ways approved by their patrons. A client owed his patron good, reliable services if he wished to receive them from his patron. In a venal system in which jobs were property, a patron like Burghley needed good clients to staff his bureaucracy.

---

[49] Susan Cogan, "Catholic Gentry, Family Networks and Patronage in the English Midlands, c.1570–1630" (University of Colorado, unpublished PhD dissertation, 2012), 225.

[50] Joan Wake, *The Brudenells of Deene* (London: Cassell, 1953), 64.

[51] London, Inner Temple Library, Petyt Ms. 538/10 fol. 64v.

We can see this in a letter written by Michael Hickes to Thomas Skinner. Apparently, Skinner had approached Hickes, on Burghley's behalf, about becoming one of the clerks of the Privy Council. Hickes answered with a sort of disenabling speech, claiming his handwriting was poor and his command of French weak. But, he wrote, "if it be so that this motion do proceed from my lord himself...then I would his Lordship did understand that I am most willing and ready to be commanded by his Lordship both where and in what kind of service soever it shall please him to appoint me." This was because he acknowledged himself bound to Burghley, both "in respect of my duty being his Lordship's servant," as also in equity and common reason "having received through his honorable favor further benefit, than my own attendance hath deserved."[52]

Sir Michael Hickes went on to be patronage secretary to Lord Burghley, so he knew the political purpose of patronage. It also made him a power broker in his own right, as well as a talent scout. Because Burghley had so much access to various kinds of patronage, Hickes had a great deal of influence. Just as the Privy Council tried to influence the Queen, Hickes tried to influence Burghley in the distribution of the favors in his gift, or in the gift of his friends.

Alan Smith's biography of Hickes expatiates on the sorts of people who approached Burghley through Hickes, and on the nature of their suits. They came from all classes and places, and even included men who knew Burghley personally and saw him frequently. But it was clearly important to include Hickes in the conversation, since he could remind the Lord Treasurer of their suits.

Most who wanted Hickes's mediation wrote directly to him, but about a third used letters of introduction. Other patrons would write letters drawing on their own templates, with formulas something like this one written by the earl of Huntingdon to Hickes in 1590: "This bearer, William Bowden, having a suit to your Lord where with as he informs me, he hath heretofore made you acquainted, is to desire the continuance of your good care to further the same....I humbly require you to show your good help and favor for which I doubt not you shall find him very thankful ..."[53]

Many suitors indicated that they had verbal approval for their suits from the Queen or from Burghley, but they still required Hickes's help. This could become very complicated, as various suitors vied for favors, and Burghley tried to balance between them. In 1591 the earl of Huntingdon wrote a letter to Hickes explaining that he had spoken to Robert Cecil asking him to approach his father about granting a Mrs Lee the wardship of her son. Robert promised he would, especially since the earl of Essex had also petitioned him on behalf of Mrs Lee. Meanwhile, Sir Thomas Gerrard had approached Burghley directly and was told he could have the Lee wardship if Huntingdon would agree. Huntingdon wanted Hickes to know that he did agree to give the ward to Gerrard—probably because only Hickes could make it happen.[54]

---

[52] BL Lansd. 107, fol. 166.   [53] BL Lansd. 63 fol. 197.
[54] BL Lansd. 68 fol. 29. Alan G. R. Smith, *Servant to the Cecils: The Life of Sir Michael Hickes* (London: Jonathan Cape, 1977), 56–8.

Making things happen was what a patron was supposed to do, and good govern-ance and being a good patron often marched together. The complex tale of the Garblership of London illustrates how getting public office and being helped by your patron could be the same thing.

The story begins with Philip Gunter, a London merchant who traded with William and Mildred Cecil.[55] Gunter was connected to Mildred through his activ-ities around Romford, Kent, her hometown. Selling sugar candies and bells for apparel, Gunter became a client of Cecil's. As he recalled, Cecil had given him a horse, so he was, he told him, "ever yours to use and my Lady's in that I can, and your children to the utter most of my power."[56]

In 1575 Gunter turned to Burghley for help. His son-in-law, George Southacke, a Merchant Tailor of London, was trading out of Flushing in the Low Countries. For some reason he had been defrauded of £1,800 (or £1,600, depending on the source) by the Flemings, and he was in dire straits. He had eight children under the age of nine, and Southacke's wife and children were being supported by Gunter, who turned to his patron for help in collecting the debt. Burghley responded to Gunter's pleas "to stand his [Southacke's] good Lord in taking of such further order in his behalf as he may be restored to his own for he hath no other way for his comfort but only by your Lordship's good means ..." He appointed a commission to investigate the case, which duly reported back.[57]

Unfortunately for Southacke, the Flemings were not under Burghley's jurisdic-tion, and letters to Secretary Davison show that appeals to the prince of Orange for justice went unanswered. Burghley and other lords were clearly doing what could be done, but Orange had not been moved by early 1578.[58]

At this point Burghley began seeking other ways to aid Gunter's son-in-law. An office that yielded an income, or could be traded or sold, would do nicely. On October 10, 1581 word reached him that Blase Saunders, the current Garbler of Spices and Drugs for London, had died and the office was open. Burghley quickly wrote the Lord Mayor of London asking him not to appoint anyone, since he intended to be a suitor for the office for a friend of his.[59]

Blase Saunders was indeed dead. His will was proved on October 13.[60] How-ever, the office of the Garbler of Spices and Drugs, charged with removing the impurities from them before they were marketed, was not simply in the gift of the mayor and aldermen of London. They soon found themselves caught in the middle of a patronage war. Blase Saunders's wife was a cousin of Sir Francis Walsingham, and she claimed to have inherited the office as part of her estate. It had been granted her husband for a term of years, and the years were not expired. On

[55] E. A. Fry, ed., *Inquisitions Post Mortem Relating to the City of London Returned into the Court of Chancery* (London: London and Middlesex Archaeological Society, 1980), vol. 3, 58–9.

[56] Washington, D.C., Folger Shakespeare Library, L.b.194. BL Lansd. 33, fol. 189.

[57] CP 202/127. CP 160/90.   [58] TNA SP 83/4 fol. 38; SP 83/5 fol. 35v.

[59] W. H. Overall and H. C. Overall, eds, "Offices and Officers," *Analytical Index to the Series of Records Known as the Remembrancia, 1579–1664*, British History Online, <http://www.british-history.ac.uk/report.aspx?compid=59959>, vol. 1, 279.

[60] TNA PROB 11/63, fol. 271.

October 11, Principal Secretary Walsingham wrote the lord mayor and aldermen asking to be informed of any attempt to wrest it from her.[61]

With Burghley and Walsingham in competition, the Queen weighed in. In a signet letter, she told the mayor that she wanted the lease of the garblership transferred to George Southacke for twenty-one years, under the same terms as Saunders had it.[62] We can suspect that Burghley was behind the Queen's letter, but Her Majesty had obviously let her will be known in the matter. Shortly after, letters arrived from other members of the council to the same effect, and Walsingham proposed a compromise.[63]

Southacke was granted the office. But it was not the office Burghley and Walsingham and widow Saunders thought it was. When Solicitor General Thomas Egerton investigated Southacke's claim to the office a decade later, he found that what Southacke had been granted for thirty years on October 29, 1581 was the Garblership of Spices and Drugs for the whole realm *except London* and its liberties. In exchange for £58 a year paid to the Treasury, Southacke had the power of "trying, making clean, packing, bagging, tasting, dividing, searching, separating, marking, sealing and making known of the good from the bad, of all manner of spices, drugs, fruits, seeds, woad, goods, wares, and merchandise, with liberty to search all such spices etc., as well by land as by water, in any houses, ships or places." George Southacke, therefore, had received an office—although he was complaining to Burghley that the port towns would not let him search ships and houses freely without warrant by 1591.[64]

This national garblership had been gifted to the City of London by Sir James Croft, who had acquired it from Johanne White, the widow of the patentee, Anthony White. Croft deeded it to the City in 1580, and it was in the grant of the lord mayor and the commonality. Saunders, whose death had started the competition, had held the office of Garbler of Spices for London, not the national one granted to Southacke—but since both offices were in the gift of the mayor, confusion was natural.[65]

This story ended happily. Burghley succeeded in getting an office for the client of his client. Walsingham was able to show himself as a defender of the rights of his cousin. The lord mayor was able to respond to the Queen's order.

The story of garbled grants of the garblerships indicates the complex nature of a management system in which power was extended and acquired through personal relationships. Access to someone who had power was necessary if you wanted some of it allocated. Managing up was necessary, if a patron was also managing down. He had to get and give gifts in order to ensure the support of his clients. This made even the most powerful people into groveling beggars at times, since the maintenance of the patron/client relationship demanded humble deference from clients, and the poles could be reversed, depending on the issue. But there was a reward.

[61] Overall and Overall, *Remembrancia*, vol. 1, 280.
[62] Overall and Overall, *Remembrancia*, vol. 1, 281.
[63] Overall and Overall, *Remembrancia*, vol. 1, 282.
[64] BL Lansd. 68, fol. 35.   [65] BL Lansd. 68, fol. 35.

Deference was designed to trigger a Pavlovian response in patrons. Everyone who expected to succeed had to play the game.

It was a world in which the commonwealth was served by friendships used as conduits of offices and opportunities. An informal system, it connected all sorts of people and could be used as checks and balances that did not require the complexity of law. The fact that the whole system depended upon its participants acting out the virtues of good patrons and grateful clients made it a tool of governance. Pleasing your "friends" was a good way of controlling behavior and getting things done without money directly changing hands.

Importantly, the management of patron/client relationships was not management for particular ends. It was management for the maintenance of community peace. The leaders of Elizabeth's state had to work together at least well enough to keep society running. That is why supporters of factions, fractious noblemen, gentlemen who recused themselves from religious duty, and other offenders were a problem. The ruling classes had to work together in order to rule. If they did not, chaos and even civil war might follow.

As used by Elizabeth, this system kept power in her hands because she was its source of all favor, and she did not give it away: she lent it, or rented it, out. That is why managing the fiscal side of her government was hard to do.

7

Managing Money

[Elizabeth] had as great care to preserve the revenues of the crown as a mother could have for her children . . . And yet to prove this cometh not of any natural disposition of sparing, it is manifest that she hath given to sundry persons either for reward of service to the realm some reasonable portions of lands out of the ancient revenues, the states wherein the parties have but to themselves and their heirs male of their bodies, to revert to the crown for lack of sons that for the land should serve the Crown.

Lord Treasurer Burghley, 1595[1]

THE EXCHEQUER

Governments and people run on money, and the collections and disbursement of money was a big part of Burghley's job as Lord Treasurer and Master of the Court of Wards. Collecting it, spending it, granting it, and withholding it were at the heart of his duties. These were not straightforward acts, however, since the means of collection and disbursement were primarily indirect, controlled by people who owned their jobs or who had them because of their pre-existing power, tying them to patron/client interactions. Nor was it easy to predict costs and organize payment, since the accounting systems at his disposal were clumsy and imprecise at best.

The revenues of Elizabeth's government were poorly defined, difficult to col-lect, and unpredictable. The Queen was expected to pay for normal expenses out of her regular revenues passing through the Exchequer, most notably the cus-toms taxes of tonnage and poundage and income from her rents, fees, and fines, all of which fluctuated. Worse, from a managerial point of view, collecting and accounting for them was very difficult, since they were open to corruption, under-reporting, and misappropriation, so the Lord Treasurer had only a vague idea of what was available.

Another, even less predictable, source of Elizabeth's revenue was feudal in origin. As the liege lord of all her subjects, she technically owned all the property granted to her vassals for their use. Anyone who owed knight service to her was using prop-erty that belonged to the Crown. This generated revenues, such as entry fines paid when someone took the usufruct of royal lands, and, most importantly, it gave her

---

[1] TNA SP 12/255 fols 157v–158.

the right of wardship over minor heirs. She could control a minor's lands until the boy reached his majority at twenty-one, or the girl married. During their minorities, the Queen collected the revenues from their properties while seeing to it they were cared for. In practice, Elizabeth granted or sold the use of her wards' lands to third parties, who paid for them in multiples of their estimated annual yield. Sometimes mothers or other kin received the grant, but the children and their lands mostly went to people willing to pay enough for the privilege, betting a few years' purchase price on the longevity and marriageability of the child. The oversight of minors and their estates was managed by the Court of Wards and Liveries, and, beginning in 1561, William Cecil was the Master of that court. This gave him huge patronage power, as well as placing the future of many aristocratic families into his hands. He, as Master of the Wards, retained management of estates in his hands unless he sold them.

To these semi-feudal revenues were added another source of funds, clerical taxation. The clergy had been paying voluntary subsidies to the king for hundreds of years. It began at a time when the church owned so much property that it had to support the efforts of the kings, since bishops, cathedrals, abbeys, monasteries, and other property owners could not personally serve in the way a man who owed knight service could come to the king's aid.

This ancient practice continued after the Reformation, but now the bishops were expected to act as agents of the Crown in collecting the clerical subsidy. Convocations, the assemblies of bishops and clergy that formally governed the province of Canterbury and the province of York, voted these subsidies. Added to these were the first fruits and tenths, the entry fines owed to the Crown by men who received ecclesiastical promotions. Thus there was an annual tax—the tenth—and an entry fine, first fruits, amounting to the first year's income of the diocese or benefice— and an occasional tax, the subsidy.

The bishops were the collectors of these taxes and, in the mid-Tudor period, they were personally liable for all of these debts to the Exchequer. Moreover, if a bishop died or was removed his successor assumed his debt to the Crown. This meant that the religious enthusiasm of regimes was blunted by their own desire to make the church pay what was owed. For instance, when Nicholas Ridley, Bishop of London, was deprived and burned for heresy in Mary's reign, his successor, Edmund Bonner, was held liable for Ridley's debt to the Crown. When Bonner was deprived and replaced by Edmund Grindal in 1559, Grindal was held liable for the debts of Ridley and Bonner. Grindal got relief through a law suit, but the Exchequer was not anxious to abandon the debt. A similar problem occurred in the very poor diocese of Norwich. Too rapid a turnover of bishops meant that first fruits still owed by one bishop were added to the new first fruits owed by the next bishop, impoverishing the diocese.

Queen Mary had returned the first fruits to the church. The Elizabethan settlement reversed that return, once more giving the Queen access to the church's regular revenues. The Act explained that these monies had been wrongly given back to the church, decaying the Crown, causing Parliament to feel "at the bottom of our hearts great sorrow and heaviness, as subjects careful for their natural and liege Sovereign Lady." They gave Elizabeth all the first fruits, tenths, rents, and parsonages impropriate that Mary had given away, and empowered the Exchequer to survey the church's possessions.[2]

These, combined with royal right to exchange land with vacant sees, and the clerical subsidies, gave Elizabeth an important and lucrative control over the church. Across the length of the reign, as inflation reduced the lay subsidy, the clerical subsidies were increased and, thanks to changing ecclesiastical personnel, church properties were more frequently reappraised. What Elizabeth and Burghley did not feel they could ask of the laity, they regularly asked of the clergy.

The clergy were not always reluctant to pay, since they understood better than most that their jobs and lives were dependent on the continued reign of Godly Elizabeth. If she fell, her church fell with her. Thus at least once, in 1587, the convocation of Canterbury voted an extra, voluntary, "contribution or benevolence unto her highness person only" for defense of their Queen.[3]

Each time Parliament and convocation met, convocation voted a subsidy, which was then ratified and turned into statute by Parliament. Legally, this made the tax on the clergy the law of the land, enforceable in the Exchequer. It appears that these taxes were already negotiated before the convocation of Canterbury met, passing both the convocation and Parliament with little discussion. Once the convocation of Canterbury had acted, a copy of its subsidy act was sent to the convocation of the province of York. In appropriate places the name Canterbury was struck out, York was inserted, and an identical subsidy was ratified.[4]

As a taxing entity, the church was much easier for the state to work with than the secular leaders. Elizabeth's bishops, on this issue at least, had no quibble about collecting it, and, because the church was well organized, it had less trouble in overseeing the payments.[5] Their willingness to pay led to a warm exchange between Burghley and Elizabeth in early 1585. When he dismissed the clerical contribution as "mites," Elizabeth replied "I esteem more of their mites, than of your pounds, for that they come of themselves not moved, but you [the temporality] tarry till you be urged thereunto."[6]

As Elizabeth was implying, the least perfect source of revenue for the Crown were subsidies granted by the temporality. Voted by Parliament, they were an important but only occasional tax, in the form of fifteenths and tenths. They were property taxes based on an unreformed rate book, which, as the intense inflation of the century grew ever greater, produced less and less buying power. Worse, it was very hard to collect these taxes, which were, at least in theory, only granted for national emergencies, not for day-to-day governmental operations. As the Act of 1566 expresses the formula, the tax was to subsidize the "great extraordinary charges sustained in the defense of your Majesty's dominions." But these Acts often

[2] 1 Eliz. I, c. 4.   [3] TNA SP 12/199 fol. 118.

[4] Patrick Carter, "Parliament, Convocation and the Granting of Clerical Supply in Early Modern England," *Parliamentary History*, 19 (2000), 18.

[5] Sybil M. Jack, "English Bishops as Tax Collectors in the Sixteenth Century," *Parergon*, 14, 1 (1996), 129–63.

[6] TNA SP 12/176/1 fol. 216.

had political strings attached, as in 1566 when Parliament said it was willing to pay because Elizabeth had promised to marry and establish the succession.[7]

Collecting was done by men appointed by the members of Parliament themselves, and the collectors had to give bonds for the projected yield of the subsidy, making collecting a very unpopular job. Worse, the men commissioned to collect it were to summon representatives of all the political divisions in their charge. These representatives, on pain of 40s fine for non-appearance, were, under oath, to value the property of their neighbors. If a commissioner for the subsidy died, his heirs and executors were liable to complete the collection.

Once the assessments had been made, high collectors were appointed by the commissions to receive the money. Bonded to ensure that they paid to the Exchequer what was collected, they could call on the constables to gather the money, paying each constable 2d in the pound for the service.

But of course there were all sorts of complications. Where people lived, who owned what, and what political influence was brought to bear influenced how the taxes were defined. For instance, in the 1566 subsidy the parish of St Martin in Stamford Baron was singled out in the statute to be rated and taxed as if it was a part of the town of Stamford, across the River Welland in Lincolnshire. Technically, Stamford Baron was part of Northamptonshire. It is hard to know why this provision was inserted in the Act, but who inserted it is more certain. The baron of Stamford Baron was Sir William Cecil, and he would be buried in St Martin's church at the end of his days.[8] There were many other, more general exemptions too.

Subsidy acts, therefore, were inefficient. They were intermittent, hard to collect, and especially hard to increase because they depended on the good will and hard work of the magisterial classes. The Queen needed subsidies, but they always came with a political cost.[9]

Subsidies, clerical taxes, fees, fines, and beneficences joined tonnage and poundage and other duties, fees, rents, and fines flowing through the Exchequer. Beginning in September 1572, William Cecil, created Lord Burghley in 1571, added it to his duties, officially overseeing the Exchequer as Lord Treasurer of England until his death in 1598.[10] Unofficially, he had already had broad experience with the Exchequer in the reign of Edward VI and again during Lord Treasurer Winchester's nonage. In 1563 he, Lord Keeper Bacon, and the earl of Pembroke were appointed to administer the Exchequer of the Receipt because of Winchester's ill health.[11]

The Exchequer of the Receipt was one of two "sides." It was devoted to the collection of royal revenues and payment of royal debts; the other "side" functioned

[7] 8 Eliz. I, c. 18.1.   [8] 8 Eliz. I, c. 18.25.

[9] David Dean, *Law-Making and Society in Late Elizabethan England: The Parliament of England, 1584–1601* (Cambridge: Cambridge University Press, 1996), 34–51. G. R. Elton, *The Parliament of England, 1559–1581* (Cambridge: Cambridge University Press, 1986), 151–74.

[10] W. H. Bryson, *The Equity Side of the Exchequer: Its Jurisdiction, Administration, Procedures and Records* (Cambridge: Cambridge University Press, 1975), 171.

[11] CP 153/101.

as a court of equity. Burghley played an active role in both, sitting as Chief Baron of the Exchequer as well as managing the Exchequer of the Receipt.

Presiding over collection, he also presided over disbursement. The office of the Lord Treasurer was both judicial and fiscal, but most of all, as Treasurer and Master of the Wards, Burghley was in a position after 1572 to use both systems as a part of his managerial tool chest. Of course, he had to raise money—a task that became harder and harder as the reign wore on and war and inflation ate its value—but he was also able to use it as a system for distributing and gaining favor and clientage, as well as a way of rewarding those who in a modern age would have been salaried bureaucrats—including himself.

Uniting in himself the management of the Queen's property and her incidental revenues, Burghley's influence overlapped with networks of other powerful people. He had a strong voice in how money was gathered and spent, and his fiscal biases matched well with Elizabeth's stinginess. They seemed to agree on money, a good thing in all alliances, and Burghley operated with the financial caution the Queen liked.

Burghley had a philosophy about money and how it should be used. In his apothegms, he observed, "A realm can never be rich, that hath not intercourse and trade of merchandise with other nations." He noted, however, that "Private gain is the perverting of justice, and pestilence of a Commonwealth," and that "All things of this world are but in estimation; for a little to him that thinketh it enough is great riches."[12]

His distrust of thriftlessness was manifest, too. He said that he "seldom saw goods ill gotten, but were quickly ill spent." Moreover, "the unthrifty looseness of youth in this age was the parents faults, who made them men seven years too soon, having but children's judgment."[13]

As for how money was acquired, Burghley put the community's good before the individual's profit. "Riches," he often observed, "were God's blessings to such as use them well, and his curse to such as did not." "No man," he said, "can get riches of himself alone, but by means of another."[14]

Conservative in instinct, he did not have much faith in economic innovation. Christian that he was, he knew that men are, by nature, greedy, grasping caterpillars that the commonweal must control if it is to prosper.

When it came to his philosophy on royal revenue, he was not inclined to build surpluses. He had a "sharp eye upon the farmers of the customs," for, as Burghley "used to say," "he never cared to see the treasury swell like a disordered spleen, when the other parts of the commonwealth were in consumption." Aware that too zealous an effort to collect revenue would damage Elizabeth's standing in the eyes of her people (was he thinking of Empson and Dudley, executed by Henry VIII for their successful taxation policies in the reign of Henry VII?), it became a common expression with him "that nothing could be for the advantage of the prince, which

---

[12] Collins, 70. [13] Collins, 71. [14] Collins, 70–1.

makes any way against his reputation." Consequently, he was reluctant to raise rents or put out old tenants.[15]

In his own life, he followed a course of righteous thrift. His contemporary biographer was careful to explain that he was not miserly or greedy. He gathered and spent as his station required, but it was all done temperately.[16] His vastly expensive processional houses would have, in Burghley's mind, been required by his station. He knew that to rule one had to act like a ruler—the emperor could not go abroad in a frieze coat and still be recognized as emperor.

As Principal Secretary to the Privy Council under Northumberland, his experience of Crown finance made a lasting impression. Heavy borrowing at home and abroad, the devaluation of the coinage, the wastage of Crown lands, the costs of defense, and other problems came across his desk. His memoranda from the early 1550s demonstrate how desperate the mismatch between revenue and expenses was. Between February and August of 1553 the Crown owed more than £235,000. It only had £14,000 on hand. Cecil's list of possible sources of money included borrowing £30,000 from the Merchant Adventurers on their cloths "already shipped" for two or three months; calling in the church plate; sale of Crown lands; and borrowing cloth from the clothiers in exchange for chantry lands. He also proposed reducing the superfluous costs of the courts and procuring the recovery of forfeitures under the penal laws.[17] The situation was desperate in Edward's time, and when he became Lord Treasurer he managed Elizabeth's revenues much more carefully, preventing a recurrence of the troubles of earlier times. He avoided debt, and he tried to keep the Queen's expenses within the Queen's revenues.

Consequently, he, like his queen, was very unwilling to spend or borrow. A study of the Crown's borrowing in the 1560s, 1570s, and 1580s demonstrates his fiscal management style. Elizabeth had inherited both Queen Mary's debts and her Lord Treasurer, the marquis of Winchester. Therefore, before Burghley became Lord Treasurer in July 1572, the Queen regularly borrowed money in Antwerp, following the tradition of Mary and Edward. This source of money was unreliable in the later 1560s, disrupted by trade embargoes, and it cost high rates of interest. Consequently, Sir Thomas Gresham, who arranged the loans there, urged Elizabeth to find a domestic source of credit, perhaps by legalizing usury. The usury law was modified in 1571, making room for a domestic source of money, but Burghley, finally in control of the Treasury, preferred not to borrow domestically or abroad.[18]

Instead, he managed the Queen's resources with care and rigor, maximizing the predictable side of her income, and trying to make the unpredictable easier to calculate and collect. In 1595 he wrote a long document entitled, by someone else, "A meditation on the state of England." Frederick Dietz called it an apologia for Burghley's career, because it summed up his long efforts on behalf of the Queen.[19]

---

[15] Collins, 79, 54.   [16] Collins, 43.   [17] TNA SP 10/15 fol. 31.

[18] Norman Jones, *God and the Moneylenders: Usury and Law in Early Modern England* (Oxford: Basil Blackwell, 1989), 47–65.

[19] Frederick C. Dietz, *English Public Finance, 1485–1641*, vol. 2, *1558–1641* (London: Frank Cass & Co., 1964), 85.

He began the "meditation" by musing on the fact that England was "more happy and favored than any" state in Christendom because Elizabeth was its queen. When she came to the throne, he noted, the realm was in terrible shape, thanks to Queen Mary, and it was threatened by Mary of Scotland, too. Over the years, Elizabeth had escaped many perils, far exceeding the accomplishments of her father and royal siblings, and earned the love of her people. He muses much on foreign affairs, religion, and the plots against the Queen, but the document delivers a clear, proud message about how Elizabeth and Burghley had kept government as cheap as possible in order to earn the love of her subjects.

The accomplishments he chose to highlight reflected the attitudes exemplified in his maxims about money. He believed the nation was happy because it was taxed as little as possible, and its economy had benefited from good government and good management.

Elizabeth's first economic achievement on coming to the throne was to reform the devalued currency.[20] England's coinage had been serially debased by Henry VIII, Edward VI, and Mary. By debasing the coins, they made it harder and harder for English merchants to buy abroad. This, it was believed, was the source of the rapid inflation, a concept summed up in the economic law, named for Sir Thomas Gresham, that bad, debased money drives out good money. Gresham chaired the committee tasked by Elizabeth with devising the fiscal therapy. The result was a plan for a revalued, stable, coinage.[21]

Cecil, writing on behalf of the Queen, drafted a "Summary of Certain Reasons," explaining the rationale for recoinage. A thoroughly monetarist document, it explained inflation as caused by debased coins, since all products of the earth would otherwise have stable prices. Moreover, bad coins force English people to import more than export. He held that the realm cannot be rich if its coins are poor, clinching his point with a quote from Cato.[22] The proclamation was carefully edited and improved by Cecil, in whose own hand we find the declaration that England is like "them that being sick receive a medicine, and in the taking feel some bitterness, but yet thereby recover health and strength, and save their lives."[23] The conclusion of the proclamation is also in his writing, adding that "her most honorable good meaning shalbe embraced of all her good loving subjects and every person with good will yield to bear a small burden for a time to avoid a perpetual oppression not only of themselves and their posterity but also of the whole commonwealth."[24]

Although the recoinage did not end the inflation, which was pan-European, it did help stabilize the English economy, and Elizabeth never devalued her currency. Of this, Burghley was clearly proud.

[20] TNA SP 12, 255/fol. 153.
[21] Norman Jones, *The Birth of the Elizabethan Age* (Oxford: Blackwell, 1989), 229–36.
[22] Collins, 15. The author, or Burghley, somewhat mangles Cato, *De agricultura*, 2.7, "Patrem familias vendacem, non emacem esse oportet."
[23] TNA SP 12/13 fol. 115.
[24] TNA SP 12/13 fols 105v, 107. This proclamation was printed, but it is not in H&L. The printed version is at TNA SP 12/13 fols 109–117v.

In his 1595 list of the good things Elizabeth has done for the nation, there are a number of moments when the Queen reduced the costs to communities, sparing the locals by spreading the burden of defense. Portsmouth and Berwick became national defense concerns rather than local; the cost of creating trained bands of militia was now partially borne by the Queen, like the cost of the increasing number of ships in the royal navy and the 10,000 mariners that staffed them.[25] Of course, her spending for defense paid off, he claimed, and the king of Spain and others had learned to fear her. She had more power than other kings because she had such wealth. "But to satisfy curious heads that although they know this to be true, yet are inquisitive by what means she doth thus possess so much riches, there are many particular means used...to perform the same."[26]

First, he said, Elizabeth was parsimonious with her money, only spending to maintain the honor of her estate, to defend the realm, and to relieve oppressed neighbors. This saving was a major cause of her riches.

Secondly, careful with what was received, Elizabeth and Burghley were also careful to receive more where they could. They reformed the customs by ending the practice that let customs officers either keep the money they collected or neglect its collection. One of the first things Burghley did when he became Lord Treasurer in 1572 was to investigate the practices of the officers of the customs house in London with an eye to improving the Queen's income. He asked Peter Osborne, the Treasurer's remembrancer, to propose needed reforms. Osborne made it clear that he knew the officers of the customs were corrupt, and suggested ways to check their avarice. He urged that the rate books be updated frequently, taking inflation into account, and that the officers be required to "keep the house daily in person, and take no entries but there," making their records available for inspection. Burghley, Osborne urged, should personally call them to come before him, the "chiefest to have their books true and to make them go straight for as much as is presented therein."[27] This, Burghley claimed thirty-three years later, increased her income by a "large yearly sum."[28]

Although Elizabeth had received subsidies from Parliament for defense, she had changed the way the subsidies were collected. She stopped the burdensome process of using assessors who required oaths or impaneled juries to establish the taxable value of men's property. Instead, she invited people to contribute voluntarily. Not surprisingly, this reduced the yield, but it paid political dividends for, as Burghley observed, "the subsidies as they were collected did also increase her power."[29]

This seems an odd observation, coming in a discussion of how the Queen got her riches, but it does tell us about how Burghley perceived taxation. It was better, he was suggesting, to have willing taxpayers than to have thorough tax collection.

---

[25] TNA SP 12/255 fol. 153v.   [26] TNA SP 12/255 fol. 157v.
[27] BL Lansd. 14/fol. 114.   [28] TNA SP 12/255 fol. 157v.
[29] TNA SP 12/255 fol. 157v. I have not identified how this was done, since it was an administrative action rather than a parliamentary action. I suspect that it refers to instances where men, in exchange for contributions to defense, were guaranteed that the wealth that supported their contributions would not be entered into the rate book.

This was putting a positive gloss on the problem that bedeviled him, the inability to get full collection of the taxes owed.

Over the years, the yield on the subsidies had decreased to such an extent that Parliament had to vote double subsidies in order to approximate the buying power of a single subsidy in the old days. But the system was not to be reformed. It has been thought that perhaps it was the greed of the privy councilors that prevented a revaluation of the property, but Burghley's argument here makes this seem like policy. The Queen benefited by not forcing people to declare the true value of their taxable property.[30]

Interestingly, a third example of her virtuous parsimony was that she called few parliaments, the source of extra revenues.[31] They were, he observed, unpopular because of the costs that had to be borne by shires and boroughs sending representatives. Therefore, she only called them when the nation was in crisis.

Robert Tittler confirms this dislike of parliamentary expense, since parliaments were too infrequent, too expensive, and too unpredictable to be effective as a political tool. Surveying the ways in which England's nearly 700 towns, both enfranchised and unenfranchised, used Parliament, he found that only 8 to 10 percent of them gained anything for themselves alone from Parliament during the sixteenth century. Fewer than 10 percent even brought bills to Parliament in that period. Those that did bring bills "found the process costly, prone to delays even of several years, and ultimately disappointing almost exactly half the time."[32]

Towns were frequently reluctant to send members to Parliament because the cost of supporting them in Westminster was so great. Travel expenses, per diem, and even reimbursement for lost business income during the sitting made having representation a luxury that many Elizabethan towns could ill afford. As Neale noticed many years ago, it was not uncommon for a town to choose its representatives on the basis of the member's or patron's willingness to pay the town's parliamentary costs. When the bishop of Winchester secured a Southampton seat for a client in 1572 he informed the town that his nominee could "do that city and country such service... as is required... and also will ease you of such trouble and charge as usually you have been at in that behalf; so that therein you shall further yourselves and also pleasure me..." So concerned were some towns, like Grimsby, about the cost of parliamentary representation that they required a bond of the patron guaranteeing payment of their expenses before granting him the use of their seat. For many towns it was less important that they be represented by someone who knew their interests, than that they avoid the expense of being represented.[33]

If Parliament did not provide towns with valuable political access, their willingness to be represented by outsiders presented to them by patrons is more understandable.

[30] Roger Schofield, "Taxation and the Political Limits of the Tudor State," in Claire Cross, David Loades, and J. J. Scarisbrick, eds, *Law and Government under the Tudors* (Cambridge: Cambridge University Press, 1988), 255.

[31] TNA SP 12/255 fol. 148v.

[32] Robert Tittler, "Elizabethan Towns and the 'Points of Contact': Parliament," *Parliamentary History*, 8, 2 (1989), 279–80.

[33] J. E. Neale, *The Elizabethan House of Commons* (Harmondsworth: Penguin, 1963), 148–9.

In the ten parliaments of the reign only 24.1 percent of burgesses were residents of the boroughs for which they sat. In short, very few towns took representation in Parliament seriously enough to obey the law requiring that boroughs be represented by residents of the borough.[34]

One might conclude from this that towns did not care about being represented in Parliament, but they did—although not for reasons directly attached to Parliament. Securing a parliamentary franchise was a mark of distinction for a town, helping the "newly emergent, highly mobile and largely mercantile urban leadership" secure prestige in the county and creating deference in their fellow townsmen. Having a listening ear in Parliament was useful, too. But perhaps the franchise's greatest value lay in its use in regional patronage networks. Parliamentary seats bestowed on non-residents could secure for a town good lordship elsewhere. A voice in Parliament was less important than a friend at court, and that friendship could be cemented by letting a patron choose the town's representatives.[35] However, there were other ways of ensuring the same patronage, and at a lesser cost. Such a connection was another form of mutual influence.

The Queen and Burghley clearly understood the burden of Parliament, as well as its uses, and they were careful not to overuse it. In a similar vein, Elizabeth was careful, Burghley insisted, not to oppress the people with purveyance and pre-emption of supplies. The ancient system of purveyance that allowed royal officers to take food, fodder, and transport for support of the monarch, at fixed prices below the market rate, was hated and much abused. Consequently, Elizabeth instituted cash payments by localities in lieu of purveyance. The people were, as Burghley said, "comforted being discharged of cruel purveyors."[36]

Although they may have been freed from cruel purveyors, the people who compounded were not off the hook. In an age of rapid inflation, Burghley understood the damage an outright surrender of the authority to take goods at current prices might do to royal revenues. He refused to release the Queen's subjects from the obligation to furnish commodities, but he was anxious to substitute a system in which farmers and manufacturers could contract to supply provisions at fixed prices. This assured he could get the goods at prices the Queen could afford.[37]

A first effort at this was the statute entitled "An Act of an Assignment of Certain Sums of Money to Defray the Charges of the Queen's Majesty's Household" passed in 1563. It declared that the prices of victuals and other things were inflating rapidly, so that the cost of the household "doth exceed the proportions and the expenses of any her noble progenitors...as the records of...the Exchequer" made plain. It set up a schedule of payments based on various revenue sources that were to be collected by the Lord Treasurer and transferred to the cofferer of the household. The sums to be collected were not to exceed the very precise number of £40,027/4/2½.[38] (This mathematical precision underscores Burghley's liking for data. Calculating

[34] HPT, vol. 1, 58.   [35] Tittler, "Towns," 283.   [36] TNA SP 12/255 fol. 158.

[37] A. Woodworth, "Purveyance for the Royal Household in the Reign of Queen Elizabeth," *Transactions of the American Philosophical Society*, new ser., 35, 1 (1945), 4.

[38] 5 Eliz. I, c. 32.

costs down to the halfpenny was an astonishing feat—or a mad fiction—in records kept in Roman numerals.) Interestingly, though establishing a schedule of money to be raised from various sorts of levies—the Receiver General of Kent, for instance, was to pay £2,200 from the Queen's possessions, manors, lands, tenements, and hereditaments—the Act's stated preference was that the Treasurer should assign other revenues "in default of levying the sums." In short, it was better to assign expected income than disburse cash from the Exchequer.

Compounding for purveyance was another step on this same path, and after Burghley became Treasurer the pace quickened. By 1580 fifteen shires were compounding. Then, in 1589, in the face of a parliamentary outcry against purveyance, the Queen created a commission for household causes empowered to reform purveyance. As a result, the rest of the shires were brought into a national system.

Like most things in Tudor government, compounding for purveyance required a great deal of work by local officers. The justices of the peace were charged with acquiring the supplies required, sending them to the court, and collecting the payments for the composition from their communities. It required planning and effort by the justices, so it must have been in their personal interests to make it work.[39]

As with purveyance, Elizabeth and Burghley knew the value of the Crown's rights in property and very carefully hoarded them. Rather than selling or granting land outright, as her royal predecessors had done, Elizabeth was reluctant to part with it. As Burghley says, even though Elizabeth had no children, she

> had as great care to preserve the revenues of the crown as a mother could have for her children; which princely care she professeth to hold for the preservation of the crown as a mother of her natural country and people...And yet to prove this cometh not of any natural disposition of sparing, it is manifest that she hath given to sundry persons either for reward of service to the realm some reasonable portions of lands out of the ancient revenues, the states wherein the parties have but to themselves and their heirs male of their bodies to revert to the crown for lack of sons that for the land should serve the Crown.[40]

As he suggests here, it was not in the Queen's interest to lose her revenues from feudal dues by granting this land in socage tenure.

Ultimately, Burghley's work at the Treasury shows how a government that depended upon the voluntary cooperation of the great and the good was hamstrung. People did not want to pay their taxes; they did not want to assess their neighbors; and they used every trick they knew to avoid taxation, including refusing to do their duty. Of course, they were happy if the burden was moved to someone else, as in the case of the provisioning of the garrison at Berwick and the navy in Portsmouth, or when counties were allowed to compound for purveyance, making cash payments rather than having their crops and livestock taken for the Queen's use.[41]

---

[39] Woodworth, "Purveyance," 5.   [40] TNA SP 12/255 fols 157v–158.
[41] TNA SP 255/fol. 158.

There were other problems with getting and spending faced by Burghley. Taxes and duties paid leaked away from the Queen because those charged with collecting were often stealing it, taking bribes to reduce the bill, and speculating with the Queen's money. In a world in which most jobs were lifetime possessions, it was almost impossible to sack a customs officer or an Exchequer clerk. These people lived on their fees and they had little to fear from the Crown. Often, their perquisites included the right to use the Crown's money from the time it was collected until it was called in on the affixed day. Moreover, since they were charged with watching the hen house, who would know if a hen went missing? Peter Osborne's recommendation to Burghley that customs houses have gates to prevent the disappearance of the wares within, and that the customs officers' records not be allowed to be taken out of the customs house, suggests that customs officers and merchants commonly colluded.[42]

Ironically, locking the customs house gate did not guarantee that all of the Queen's revenues from import duties would be collected. In line with the view that it was more important to have happy subjects than full collection, various groups were granted exemptions from taxes. For instance, persons of status were allowed to import wines free of duty. A list, signed by the Queen, was made of all those ranks and persons who were given this privilege. Archbishops, bishops, provosts, deans, nobility of all ranks, members of the Privy Council, the Lord Mayor and the Sheriff of London, a long list of knights and officeholders, and the Queen's household were enumerated. Certain duchesses, countesses, and ladies, such as Burghley's sister-in-law, Lady Hoby, were named. Any gentlewoman or lady, being widowed, who was of good reputation for hospitality, and who was not listed, could apply for an allowance, too, provided the total quantity allowed did not exceed the huge volume of 1,000 tuns of wine yearly—a tun was roughly 954 liters or 250 US gallons.[43]

In a similar instance, Elizabeth exempted the merchants of Chester from paying duty on Gascon wines imported through their port, and, by extension, their widows too. Decreed in 1568, Burghley was still enforcing this exemption in 1598.[44]

The thirst of this large class of people—probably a significant percentage of the wine-affording nation—must have reduced the customs revenue significantly, but, since the wine customs were farmed, the Queen lost nothing by being generous. She farmed the wine import duties to private individuals who guaranteed her income, regardless of the market. These exemptions shrank the farmers' income, but they did not change the Queen's revenues.

The wine farm was so lucrative that the farmers may not have minded the exceptions too much. In a letter to Sir Nicholas Throckmorton, Edward Tremaine, the Deputy Butler of Devonshire, tried to estimate the value of the wine farm there. Tremaine reported that it was hard to calculate the value of the farm, because it depended on how it was handled. In the past, Tremaine said, he did not take wine

[42] BL Lansd. 14/fol. 114.   [43] TNA SP 15/20 fols 223–4.

[44] Frederick J. Furnivall, ed., *Child-Marriages, Divorces, and Ratifications, &c. in the Diocese of Chester, A.D. 1561–6* (London: 1897), 166.

from a ship, "unless to serve myself or a friend," instead compounding with the merchant for a cash fee, "and never crossed any favor that he could find at the other officers' hands at the Customs house." Delicate management made a good profit, Tremaine insisted, even after the Exchequer was paid:

> Working after this sort, I made him [Anthony Throckmorton, owner of the wine farm in Devon] in money (above my £20 and pipe of wine yearly), the first year £120*l.*, when £30 might satisfy the Exchequer. The next year above £200, when £60 would have paid the Exchequer. The third year about £80, the Exchequer near about £30. These years past all has arisen upon sack, more claret having been brought in this year than in the three former ones. I offer to use it for you as you shall instruct, and out of what is made, you shall be fully answered and paid at Easter and Michaelmas.[45]

Farms on royal customs were large and lucrative, but they were not always a certain investment for the farmer since political changes put them at risk. When the trade with the Low Countries was stayed by Elizabeth in the mid-1560s, the owner of a customs farm in London informed Leicester that he had lost £627/2/2½ from the value of his farm because merchants were smuggling rather than risking the fines that would be levied if their goods came through the port. Worse, privateers under letters of marque from the prince of Orange had made the Thames mouth too risky, so shipments of valuable spices were being diverted to Bristol and Southampton.[46] It was too bad for the farmer, but he still owed the Queen his annual payment.

A more common sort of revenue measure was the "fee farm," a lease—often a very long one—on royal property. Under its terms the Queen reserved an annual rent of some significant portion of the presumed annual yield of the property. Often it was a quarter or more of the book value of the annual revenue. In return, the lessor owed no feudal dues or other rents. Because of the monastic dissolutions, the Crown owned thousands of parcels of property that were given out in fee farm. They were often very small parcels, and this was a good way to make them yield an income without any investment. There are hundreds of petitions for grants of fee farm in the records of Elizabeth's reign, most of them enticingly promising a good yield to the Queen. They were especially common in Ireland, judging by the petitions.

Naturally, these pleas for grants were often requested as rewards for service. Sir Henry Sidney, the Lord Deputy of Ireland, recapitulating his service and his relationship to the Queen, wrote asking Cecil for favors. Suffering from the stone that killed his father, while doing a thankless job, he likened himself to Pietro Strozzi, the Florentine general defeated in 1554 when his brother did not send reinforcements, Sidney self-righteously begged for support. Of course he needed troops, but he also wanted preferment for his clients in the Irish church. And he wanted a fee farm of all the abbey lands in Connacht. They had been worthless to Her Majesty, he said, and if he had the fee farm, he would pay her 300 marks a

---

[45] TNA SP 15/12 fols 132–132v. The "pipe" of wine, also known as a butt, was half a tun, approximately 480 liters.
[46] HMC Bath vol. 5, 169.

year. He would maintain the property for nothing, and build a walled town and a bridge at his own charge. If she refused him, she would lose 700 marks a year.[47]

Granting away offices and revenues was a necessary tool of Crown management. These so-called venal offices were distributed upon the assumption that the office holders would have an interest in collecting the money due, and would be better at it than a royal servant could be. A variant on fee farming, it was a means of indirect taxation.[48] Douglas Allen has argued that the outright sale of public office had a strong incentive effect, attracting people who believed they could make money from the office, and making the Crown extra money in a competitive market. Of course, buying offices was not what most people wanted. They wanted offices as free grants, receiving them as the fruits of the patronage system. That maximized the benefit to both the patron and the client, but not necessarily to the state. Allen dubiously portrays the early modern state as a rational actor in its use of these grants and sales of venal office, maximizing its revenues.[49] Burghley knew he was not maximizing revenues; he was simplifying collection.

Venal offices were the product of the late feudal management system, which guaranteed loyalty through maintenance. Those who owed service to their patron were also owed service by their underlings, so it was easier to grant an office and its revenue to a person than build a bureaucracy. The grantee was to guarantee provision of the services of the office, organizing and staffing it himself. Thus the Queen did not have to manage their work. She depended upon the office holder to ensure it was done. This was the common European practice. The contemporary Spanish Jesuit and economic philosopher Luis de Molina drew a distinction between *ministri regis*, ministers of the monarch, who were supported by royal gifts, and the *ministri publici*, ministers of the public, who acted in the interest of the public. The *ministri publici* lived from the proceeds of their offices. These ministers were allowed to set their own "just salary," which was an effective way of rewarding them in a time of rapid inflation.[50] Of course, in England this distinction was even more problematic because many officials were expected to live "of their own" and do the work of governing without any income at all. The system only worked because all the players recognized that office was the mark of respect that brought honor to the holder, and that those who held offices could be expected, at least in theory, to act virtuously. Of course, these office holders expected gifts from grateful petitioners, so some jobs were very lucrative.

All of this meant that the Queen's actual revenue was, if left to its normal course, very uncertain. Burghley could not radically change the system—perhaps he did not want to, since its very flexibility made the Queen popular without requiring a paid bureaucracy—but he, like Lord Treasurer Winchester before him, sought to bolster collection and stabilize cash flow. Winchester had reformed the customs

---

[47] TNA SP 63/20 fol.89.

[48] Douglas Allen, *The Institutional Revolution: Measurement and the Economic Emergence of the Modern World* (Chicago: University of Chicago Press, 2011), 12–13.

[49] Allen, *Institutional Revolution*, 14–16.

[50] Robert Descimon, "Power Elites and the Prince: The State as Enterprise," in Wolfgang Reinhard, ed., *Power Elites and State Building* (Oxford: Clarendon Press, 1996), 112–13.

books under Mary, insisting that the mechanisms for collection were effective. Secretary Cecil disagreed with this analysis, and when he replaced Winchester as Lord Treasurer, Lord Burghley began a new funding scheme. He regularized the collection of revenue by using tax farmers who guaranteed a return of a fixed amount and were allowed to keep the rest. He also used "promoters and informers" to find the Crown's debtors, essentially privatizing the penal side of the Exchequer. These men undertook to enforce the laws that produced royal revenue in exchange for a share of the fines collected.[51]

In the calendars of the patent rolls we find indications of how he was using the Exchequer and Wards to reward the principal officers of the state. In fact, most of Elizabeth's servants were rewarded with grants of offices and rights to revenue that never required the Exchequer to disperse a shilling. The patent rolls opened year after year with grants to Sir James Croft, in fee farm or fee simple, of various concealed lands, tithes, and other property. In each grant it was stated that they were "for the services of Sir James Crofte, controller of the Household, queen's servant, privy councilor, and at his suit." This use of the income of the Wards and Liveries, and the incorporated Augmentations, was in direct keeping with the requirements of 5 Eliz. c. 32, which had preferred the direct assignment of revenues over the collection of cash to pay the household officers. Thanks to the Act, the Controller of the Household was given £10,000 a year from the Court of Wards. Croft then granted them to others, creating a cash flow. In fact, he may have increased the revenue, since many of those he passed on were grants to search for "concealed lands," ecclesiastical properties that had escaped discovery by the royal commissioners.[52] If such lands were found, the Queen profited.

Anthony Bennett, one of the Queen's footmen, was granted, for life, the office of keeper of the jail and castle at York, with the herbage (pasturage), precinct, and other appurtenances. Bennett had to wait until the current owner of the office, Peter or Piers Pennant, gentleman usher to the Queen, died, before he could enjoy the grant. But Bennett had the assurance that it would come to him.[53] Thus the income of the office moved in reversion from Pennant to Bennett. It is unlikely that either of them spent time at York. Pennant was unable to attend to legal issues pertaining to the patent, "by reason of his continual attendance about the service of her Majesties person." Despite their absences, they were allowed to collect the income arising from their northern office.[54]

Close servants of the Queen, Pennant and Bennett escaped a reservation of income for the Crown, but most grants required yearly return to the Exchequer. For instance, William Gower was allowed, "by the advice of William Cecil, baron of Burghley, treasurer, and Sir Walter Mildmay, chancellor of the Exchequer," the

---

[51] H. E. Bell, *An Introduction to the History and Records of the Court of Wards and Liveries* (Cambridge: Cambridge University Press, 1953), 50–1.

[52] *Calendar of Patent Rolls 27 Elizabeth I (1584–1585), C 66/1254–1270*, ed. Louise J. Wilkinson, List and Index Society, vol. 293 (2002), items 1–9. *Calendar of Patent Rolls 27 Elizabeth I (1585–1586), C 66/1271–1285*, ed. Simon R. Neal, List and Index Society, vol. 294 (2002), 1129–34.

[53] *Calendar of Patent Rolls 27 Elizabeth I (1584–1585), C 66/1254–1270*, item 426.

[54] PC 2/12 fol. 167.

"perquisites, profits and issues of all courts leet and waifs and strays and reliefs, with all wastes and commons" of three manors in Hampshire and one in Wiltshire. These monastic properties were not valued in the lease, but Gower was expected to pay £17/14/– annually for their use.[55]

The formula, saying the grant was made by the advice of Cecil and Mildmay, is repeated hundreds of times through the patent rolls, and each of them is the fruit of petitions and clientage. Getting someone to convince the leaders of the Exchequer to "advise" an action was hard, and it gave them great patronage power. However, once the grant was made they lost much of their influence.

This clearly bothered Burghley, but his only defense was care in what was agreed to. Something granted away without proper research could not be recovered. This led him to pay attention to how the values of grants were determined. He was concerned that grants of concealed lands could be made on information filed by informers, rather than found by commissioners, and so he held up grants and insisted on better process.

Therefore, he issued rules to be followed for auditors, establishing the nature of the lands about to be granted; he insisted that separate grants be made for each county; and he ordered that the names of the sitting tenants on the lands always be listed—even though some did not want their names in the documents. Moreover, the auditors were to consider what might be lost to the Queen through the grant, such as wood.[56] Elizabeth, when the master of requests offered a "book" of these grants to be signed, once commented "that her subjects had been highly wronged by grants of that nature, but since my Lord Treasurer hath taken bond for their well usage he shall bear the blame."[57] No wonder Burghley was being careful!

The system required Burghley and Elizabeth to grant offices and incomes in a venal way, without strict attention to a fiscal bottom line, so they operated through a bureaucracy that was recruited venally. It made reform very difficult. The system was subjected to accidents of mortality and subsequent inheritance of authority, or the appearance of new men who had different interests and skills. Worse, the ability of the officers to resist change was powerful, and long-running feuds might impede bureaucratic efficiency.

Take for instance, the problems in the Mint. When Burghley took over as Treasurer in 1572, he established a farm of the Mint. The Queen granted it to John Lonison, the Master Worker of the Mint, but it fell to the new Lord Treasurer to negotiate the terms. Lonison complained that the fees possible in the current system were so "stretched" between the Moneyer, Richard Martin, and himself that he could not profit unless a new agreement was reached. He and Burghley argued back and forth, establishing what he would pay the Queen on each step of the minting.[58] They reached a settlement, and a patent was issued for Lonison to farm the Mint on April 18, 1572.[59]

[55] *Calendar of Patent Rolls 27 Elizabeth I (1585–1586), C 66/1271–1285*, item 225.
[56] HEH EL 1538. HEH EL 1522.   [57] HEH EL 1404.
[58] TNA SP 12/85 fols 166, 168, 177, 178, 182.
[59] BL Lansd. 14/fol. 15. TNA SP 12/86/fol. 37.

Shortly thereafter, trouble began. Lonison was accused by his colleagues of fraudulent practices, lowering the quality of the gold and silver coins stamped there.[60] An investigation was launched, and a group of privy councilors looked into the accounts. They did find that there were problems, concluding that Mr Martin, the whistleblower who brought Lonison's fraud to their attention, was not acting out of any interest but the Queen's. However, they still confronted the problem of what to do with Lonison. Their findings tell us about how hard it was to manage men who owned their offices.

First, there was the issue of what his rights under the patent were: "Because that in his answer it seems that he took it that his indenture gave him power to proceed in the course he hath done," they held, "and that the prosecution of the suit [against the other officers] in the same hath been very chargeable unto him," the commissioners recommended to the Queen that she forgive him "for all those things rising in question." This would end the controversy.

Second, Lonison had done things not in the Queen's interest, so his indenture was to be cancelled, depriving him of valuable property. However, since he owned the office of Master of the Mint, there had to be recompense. They wrote: "Nevertheless because Lonison shall not be dismissed without sufficient recompense for his service and interest," the commissioners recommended "that he have a pension of three hundred pounds by the year, during his life to be paid out of the coinage or (that wanting) then out of her Majesty's receipt and one hundred pounds by the year after his decease, unto his wife during her life out the coinage."[61]

Signed by Lord Keeper Bacon, Lord Treasurer Burghley, the earl of Sussex, the earl of Leicester, Christopher Hatton, and Principle Secretary Walsingham, the top men in English government, it underscores the problems created by venal offices. An owner of an office could abuse it, but he still owned it and had to be recompensed if he lost his property. On the other hand, there was the matter of his fraud. After he died, Lonison's estate was calculated to owe the Queen £1,939/2/2/– "as in his time he impaired the monies of weight and fineness under their just standard."[62] So Elizabeth had to buy out his patent, and then sue his estate for what he had stolen.

If the Mint was a bad dream, the Exchequer was a nightmare. There the strife in the 1580s and 90s was characterized by Geoffrey Elton as "the War in the Receipt."[63] The origins of this "war" go back to the reign of Mary, and the administration of Lord Treasurer Winchester. An attempt to restore the "ancient course of the Receipt," led by Winchester and his confederates in their own interest, had partially succeeded, but it foundered in the late 1560s. In this system, Winchester managed the case revenues of the Crown by taking charge of the Lower Exchequer and running huge sums through it. Between 1559 and 1566 £1,171,050/–/– passed

---

[60] TNA SP 12/90 fol.144.   [61] HEH EL 2219.   [62] BL Lansd. 26/fol. 29.
[63] G. R. Elton, "The Elizabethan Exchequer: War in the Receipt," *Studies in Tudor and Stuart Politics and Government Papers and Reviews, 1946–1972*, vol. 1, *Tudor Politics Tudor Government* (Cambridge: Cambridge University Press, 1974), 355–88.

through the hands of the Teller, Richard Stonley. It was 52 percent of all the money flowing into the Exchequer of Receipt.[64]

This cash flow created opportunities for Stonley, who became Teller in 1554 and owned the job until 1597. Stonley would finally lose his office for speculating with the Crown's money, but he was not the only speculator.[65] Five of the six tellers who held office from 1567 to 1571 defaulted on their accounts, costing the Queen over £44,000. Stonley had invested in land; others speculated in wine or on financial exchanges. Another of Winchester's servants, Nicholas Hare, fled to Paris as a recusant, having first sold his office to Chidiock Wardour.[66] When Burghley became Lord Treasurer in March 1572, the Exchequer was a leaking sieve.

In the Parliament of 1571, the Lords started a bill that became the Act to make tellers, receivers, treasurers, and other officers of various units of government liable for the payment of their debts. The "Anonymous" diarist of that Parliament noted it was aimed at preventing them from converting the Queen's money to their private use. He inferred it was caused by the Lord Deputy of Ireland Sir Henry Sidney's treasurer, who defaulted on £3,000.[67] In fact, the diarist's report underestimated the size of the problem. Thomas Jenyson, sent to conduct an audit in Ireland, found such disorder that he recommended stopping all payments on Irish claims until the audit could be completed.[68] Sir William Fitzwilliam, the new Lord Justice of Ireland (and Mildred Cecil's first cousin) concurred, and begged for a new treasurer.[69] Burghley carefully noted it all in one of his "memorials," listing things needful to be done in Ireland, most of which were about righting the fiscal condition of the kingdom, including finding a new auditor and a new treasurer.[70] Obviously, this bill in Parliament grew out of the frustration over the peculation that was adding to Ireland's woes.

When the bill reached the Commons, it contained a provision that made a default of more than £300 for over six months a felony, but that was gone by the time it became a statute. There had been an attempt to broaden the bill to include purveyors, too, but that had been stopped with a constitutional argument about the Queen's prerogative.[71]

---

[64] Christopher Coleman, "Artifice or Accident? The Re-organisation of the Exchequer of Receipt, c.1554–1572," in C. Coleman and D. Starkey, eds, *Revolution Reassessed* (Oxford: Oxford University Press, 1986), 186–7.

[65] HPT, Hasler, ed. Sub STONELEY, Richard (*c.*1520–1600). When he was investigated in 1597 Stonley entered in his diary: "This day after morning prayer I kept home at my books preparing to answer all persons…especially my L Treasurer who searcheth answers by my doing in my office as reason for his own discharge who hath other secretly to pray after him, yet a man good natured and in thend [sic] showeth much friendship to the honest minded." But Stonley still lost his job. Folger MS V.a.460, II, fol. 58. <http://luna.folger.edu/luna/servlet/detail/FOLGERCM1-6-6-650371-144194 ?qvq=w4s:/what/England%20and%20Wales.%20Exchequer%20--%20Manuscripts./Diaries%20 of%20Richard%20Stonley/Diaries%20of%20Richard%20Stonley%20[manuscript],%20 1581-1598.;sort:Call_Number,Author,CD_Title,Imprint;lc:FOLGERCM1-6-6,BINDINGS-1-1 &mi=169&trs=299&cic=FOLGERCM1-6-6,BINDINGS-1-1&widgetType=detail&nsip=1>. Accessed Jan. 20, 2014.

[66] Coleman, "Re-organisation," 190–1.   [67] Hartley, vol. 1, 218.

[68] TNA SP 63/32 fol. 28.   [69] TNA SP 63/32 fols 36–36v.

[70] TNA SP 63/32 fol. 152.   [71] Hartley, vol. 1, 224. 13 Eliz. c. 4.

Around the time he was worrying about the Irish Exchequer, a number of Westminster Exchequer officials died, including Lord Treasurer Winchester. When Burghley succeeded him as Lord Treasurer in 1572, he had the chance to appoint several new men in the Exchequer—creating a split between the men of the "old Treasurer" and Burghley's "new" men. This was partially driven by the new Lord Treasurer's dislike of how Winchester had run the Exchequer. He, and Treasurer Sir Walter Mildmay, began rearranging what they could. Winchester had resisted farming the customs; Burghley liked it. But at the heart of the matter were the historic customs of the Exchequer. Burghley did not like the "ancient course" restored by Winchester. Instead, he preferred the "constitution of Henry VII."

Burghley made one obvious, and seemingly necessary, change. He set up a central depository treasury in the new offices of the Exchequer in Westminster. As a result, the Queen kept money on hand. By the summer of 1585 she had £270,000, up from £102,000 in 1573. These cash reserves allowed her to quit foreign borrowing and the sale of Crown lands.[72]

One of the features of a managerial regime that depended on venal offices was the temptation—and the need—to keep power in the hands of the managers by carefully selecting who got the offices. Normally, this meant that clients—those serviceable to a patron—were first in line, but occasionally the pitch for a venal office backfired on the would-be client.

In the fall of 1575 the Queen issued a patent granting Lord Burghley the office of "broker" in England. He could appoint people to broker currency, and, in exchange, he agreed to pay Elizabeth £30 a year. The office was granted to him because, it said, giving him the sole power was in the best interest of the commonwealth, which was bedeviled by too many abusive brokers. He got the office because of concerns about the export of English bullion that had been raised by Thomas Ferrers (probably a London merchant) about how foreigners were evading the laws concerning export of coins and bullion. Ferrers had petitioned the Privy Council for a patent to enforce the old laws, and he had guaranteed to produce £4,000 of new revenue annually. The council interviewed Ferrers and then, thinking this was a good idea, gave the patent to the Lord Treasurer himself.[73] The gift to Burghley probably had to do with the fact that the person who could appoint brokers had the right to oversee and pay customs officers for enforcing the laws, which was the Lord Treasurer's purview, but it was a rich gift—potentially a fine way to reward a royal servant whose actual pay was meager, given the estate he was expected to keep.

In a sense, the broker is a good metaphor for how Burghley was forced to manage the collection and spending of money. As his memo of 1595 suggests, the maintenance of good will of the tax collectors and payers took precedence over the efficient collection of money. Moreover, because the official taxes were uncertain and poorly collected, the Crown traditionally found it more efficient to deputize collection to

---

[72] Coleman, "Re-Organisation," 194–5.
[73] TNA SP 12/75 fol. 98. TNA SP 12/105 fols 146–7. TNA SP 15/24 fols 129–129v. *Calendar of Patent Rolls, Elizabeth I*, vol. 7, *1575–1578*, item 7, 2. H&L, vol. 2, 408.

farmers and to venal office holders. In return it got a predictable income without the costs and efforts of collection. Burghley did what he could to improve the revenue, but deputizing was a better option in a world short on the facilities for collection and accounting. Giving away the revenue to offices, even in reversion, gave him a patronage tool without the complexities of paying salaries.

We can see why he preferred deputizing farmers. In some cases he had to oversee the Queen's property himself, which was a complicated affair. When Thomas Lord Paget was found guilty of treason in the Babington plot, his estates were seized and Burghley found himself in charge of an iron forge. He issued a commission to value Paget's property, but in the meantime Richard Bagot, the Sheriff, was in correspondence with Burghley about the income and expenses of the forges. Typically, Burghley's letters to Bagot are full of details about things like the purchase of wood for the smithies. Burghley edited what his secretary had written, and added personal notes (see Fig. 7.1).[74] It was a time-consuming business.

Consequently, the Elizabethan state ran without directly collecting much of its possible revenue. Not, perhaps, efficiently, but it was in the interest of many people to ensure that their property in fees, collections, offices, and other gifts from the Crown remained secure by supporting the Queen.

In a system that depended on honor, virtue, self-interest, and hopes of reward to get the powerful to cooperate, Burghley believed private profit would encourage the enforcement of the rules that generated revenue. But many gentlemen found there was no profit in service. It often cost them dearly to serve the Queen.

To be honored with an invitation to royal service was a quick road to disaster for many recipients. Sir Anthony Mildmay, son of Sir Walter Mildmay of the Privy Council, was used for diplomatic missions in the late 1570s and again in the late 1590s. His wife, Grace, complained bitterly that they nearly bankrupted him. And yet he did undertake them, as did many people asked to see that the Queen's will was done.

Responding to the Queen's order to become ambassador at Paris, Mildmay wrote to Robert Cecil with dismay:

> the smallness of my revenue insufficient to maintain the countenance of her Majesty's ambassador; my debts being of no small value, yet to be answered only from thence, my lands being so entailed as thereby I cannot be helped though necessity should enforce it: my father's will as yet unexecuted, whereby I am hitherto defrauded of his goodness towards me and thereby also the more disabled to perform any service of great expense....I will be ready in an instant to fulfil her commandment, reputing myself most happy if with the expense of my small substance and the hazard of my life I may do her any agreeable service.[75]

Of course, his plea fell on deaf ears, and off he went.

This is why it was essential that the gentlemen "pricked" for service had sufficient wealth to afford their duties. They were expected to spend it in service. In

---

[74] Folger Shakespeare Library Digital Image Collection, L.a.309. <http://luna.folger.edu/luna/servlet/view/search?q=Call_Number=%22L.a.309%22&sort=Call_Number,Author,CD_Title,Imprint>. Accessed Oct. 26, 2014.
[75] CP 42/42.

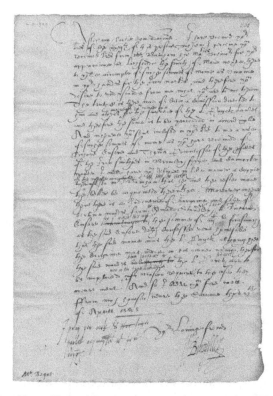

Fig. 7.1. Lord Burghley to Richard Bagot, concerning the ironworks of Thomas Lord Paget, with his corrections and postscript. Folger Shakespeare Library, Bagot Family Papers, L.a.309. http://luna.folger.edu/luna/servlet/detail/FOLGERCM1-6-6-375549-132158:To-Richard-Bagot--London-?sort=Call_Number%2CAuthor%2CD_Title%2CImprint&qvq=q:Call_Number%3D%22L.a.309%22;sort:Call_Number%2CAuthor%2CCD_Title%2CImprint;lc:FOLGERCM1-6-6,BINDINGS-1-1&mi=0&trs=4#.

towns this sometimes resulted in men refusing to accept an office, since it was ruinously expensive to pay for the feasts and festivities required of them, as well as the running costs of their new offices.

Those serving the Queen could request reimbursement, but this was not an easy matter, and hardly to be expected. When Sir Henry Norris was serving as ambassador at Paris, Secretary Cecil turned down many of his requests. His logic was clear, up to a point. "I never did, nor could allow" extraordinary expenses, "and yet I wish them paid, being laid out in the service of her Majesty." Norris was stuck with paying these costs himself.[76]

Men might go years without receiving the arrearages owed them by the Queen. In the summer of 1575 Thomas Jenyson, the Auditor in Dublin, complained that the Exchequer was not paying its bills. Some of the judges, he said, were

[76] *Cabala*, 142.

three or four years behind on their pay. Patentees had not received their fees, annuities were not paid, and the money owed for victuals was not forthcoming. He estimated that the amount owed was at least the equivalent of a year's income for Ireland.[77]

To be fair, the Queen often did not receive her arrearages either, but that must have been of small consolation to her creditors. As Jenyson observed two years later, "Arrearages now sperate will in a few years grow desperate if they be not severely called for."[78] Of course, he then proposed a commission be granted to himself to collect the money, but his accounting for the costs of the Lord Deputy of Ireland made it clear that the expenses were much more than could be afforded—and yet the office holders were expected to keep government running.

The agents of the Privy Council, like the councilors themselves, served without pay, but they could ask for repayment. One of the problems, however, was the official costs allocated for services were often years out of inflationary date. Even the clerks of the Privy Council had to petition for increases to their allowed costs "sundry times."[79] Their fees did rise, but Burghley tried to keep a lid on them, just as he tried to control the household expenses, by drawing up schedules of permitted fees so he could tell people like poor Norris whether he could be paid.[80] With their fees often unpaid or in arrears, it was no wonder that the preferred system was granting the income from properties and leaving it up to the recipient to collect it.

Men were expected to serve, gambling for reward. Rory Rapple has documented the ways in which military service was hoped to lead to financial reward, but seldom did. Captains, often younger sons deprived of prospects by primogeniture, hoped to be rewarded for their service in the wars. They rarely got what they desired.[81]

It could be said that Elizabethan concepts of duty made it possible to afford the Elizabethan state, since gentlemen were expected to absorb so much of the cost in time and money up front, hoping for future rewards, which, if they came, seldom came directly from the royal pocket. They had to take their reward in honor and opportunity.

Of course, this was the accepted system. In a world where a prime qualification for office-holding, voting for members of Parliament, and other things was his income—a justice of the peace had to have at least £20 a year—it was clear that with wealth came responsibility. It was much easier for the state to trade on honor and responsibility than it was to tax this wealth. It was only when an inheritance made wealth truly visible that the Queen had a chance of profiting from it, but not through taxation. She used her feudal rights.

[77] TNA SP 63/52 fol. 99.   [78] TNA SP 63/59 fol. 131v.

[79] Michael B. Pulman, *Elizabethan Privy Council in the 1570s* (Berkeley: University of California, 1971), 169–72.

[80] Officers of Courts of Revenue and Exchequer ca. 1579. HEH EL 1198.

[81] Rory Rapple, *Martial Power and Elizabethan Political Culture: Military Men in England and Ireland, 1558–1594* (Cambridge: Cambridge University Press, 2009), 58–9.

THE COURT OF WARDS AND LIVERIES

As Master of the Court of Wards (see Fig. 7.2) since 1561, Burghley saw to it that the land held *in capite* for knight service always returned to the Queen if the family line failed and there was a minor heir. The Court of Wards had the management of the property during the minority of the heir. Moreover, Burghley enforced the law that royal lands should not be granted, as was popular in Edward VI's reign, in socage tenure, free of knight service. Land granted for knight service could return to the Crown, and it was an important incidental source of revenue, yielding a net income of between £12,000 and £14,000 most years of Elizabeth's reign.[82]

Fig. 7.2. *A View of the Court of Wards and Liveries, with the Officers, Servants, and Other Persons there Assembled* by George Vertue, line engraving, 1747, from an original *c.*1585. NPG D10999. © National Portrait Gallery, London.

[82] Bell, *Wards*, Appendix A.

The anonymous biographer, who seems to have known the working of the Wards well, noted that Burghley increased the revenue by raising the sales price of wardships when he took office. Previously, a male ward had sold for one year's income, and a female sold for two years' income. Burghley raised this to one and a half for males and "raised much" the rate for females. Similarly, he insisted that the feodaries of the Court of Wards reappraise lands before they were leased. Apologetically, the biographer insisted that Burghley could have raised the rates even more "if he had not respected her Majesty's honor, and regarded the ease of the subject, seeking rather to win their loves to their Prince by indifferent gain, than by drawing more from them, to procure their curse and hatred."[83]

The Court of Wards and Liveries was given form by two statutes. Henry VIII, c. 46 (1541) established it as a court of record, with a seal and a master. The monarch's wards were placed under the new court, and accounts of their lands and revenues were directed to the court, rather than to the Exchequer. No ward of the King could take delivery of his lands (livery, as it was called) without action by the Court of Wards. Having created a logical inconsistency, since there was already a Master of the Liveries, Parliament passed 33 Hen. VIII, c. 22 (1542), uniting the Court of Liveries with the Court of Wards, forming a powerful new revenue court, the Court of Wards and Liveries.

The Court of Wards and Liveries was the logical outgrowth of the efforts of Henry VII to enforce the collection of feudal dues owed to the King. Anyone owing knight service to the Crown would have his lands returned to the Crown upon his death. His minor heirs became wards of the monarch, and their properties were kept and managed on their behalf until they reached their majorities. In practice, this usually meant that the care of the heirs and their lands was sold to a third party for some fraction of the predicted value of the minority. With the guardianship went the heir's marriage—the right to marry the child to the person of the guardian's choice. The guardian recouped the purchase price through the profits of the lands, and through the less tangible but very important disposal of the heir and the property through marriage.

The dissolution of the monasteries had released large amounts of land into secular hands and, by the Act creating the Court of Augmentations in 1536, none of that land could be granted without preserving the Crown's right to knight service. This vastly increased the number of tenures held by knight service, which, in turn, increased the work of the Court of Wards and Liveries.[84] The Augmentations was dissolved in 1554 and its records and duties transferred to the Exchequer, but the Exchequer was not granted power over wardships and liveries. Although the Exchequer looked after the Crown's revenues, the money brought in through wardships continued to pass through the Court of Wards and Liveries.

Although in the reign of Edward VI there was a trend toward selling land outright in socage tenure—service commuted to a fee, without wardship—much better management of the feudal dues under Queen Mary meant that the revenues from wards and liveries rose sharply in the late 1550s. Elizabeth inherited this, and

[83] Collins, 32–3.   [84] Bell, *Wards*, 14–15.

in 1561 Sir William Cecil became the Master of the Wards, holding the office until he died in 1598. In essence, he was presiding over a court that controlled the future of the ruling classes' estates and of their families. When Lord Burghley became the Lord Treasurer in 1572, he consolidated in himself the revenue arms of the Crown: the Wards and the Exchequer.

How he managed the Wards is murky. Evidence in the records of the court suggest that in the early years he took an active role, countersigning the sales of wardships. This practice stopped after a few years, so we seldom see his direct influence except in politically important cases, such as when Lettice Knolles, the widowed countess of Essex, sued her son Robert Devereux, earl of Essex, for her dower in 1576.

It was a celebrated, complicated case, since she had remarried, to Robert Dudley, earl of Leicester, under scandalous circumstances, provoking Queen Elizabeth to great anger. In that case Burghley, who had corresponded with Lettice about the issue, personally oversaw the drafting of the order of the Master and Council of the Wards that enforced her dower rights, and ordered Robert to provide her access to the "evidences" of the income from her dower lands. Burghley actually signed the draft, as well as providing her a parchment "subscribed under the hand of the said Lord Treasurer whereof the one part remaineth with the said countess and the other with the said lord Treasurer and the others" that specified her property.[85]

Unusual cases apart, he seems to have left it to professionals to run the Wards, while he himself played a greater role as a judge in the court. His activities there are harder to see, but we catch a glimpse in a 1594 letter to Robert Cecil written by a secretary, where he added at the bottom, "I am forced to spare my hand, having notwithstanding more [need] to spare my head." He dictated, "This day I have been in the Court of Wards, with small cause and much pain. This afternoon I have appointed divers of her Majesty's causes to be heard; And tomorrow by special appointment, I am to be in the Exchequer chamber about writs of error, which without my presence can hardly be ended. And upon Wednesday it is the Star Chamber where I think I may be spared."[86] Like many good managers, he was constantly active, but often invisible.

As a venal office, the mastership of Wards and Liveries was very profitable. Burghley was the default guardian of all the Queen's wards, so we do not find him purchasing and paying for many wardships, but he appears to have shared in the revenues generated by wards he chose not to sell to others.[87] The Master of the Court of Wards was officially given a fee and diet of £233/6/8 a year when he took on the office, but he clearly made a fortune off the job, with the Queen's approval.[88] Joel Hurstfield argues that the real value of the post was in the fees paid by grateful suitors to Burghley and other members of the court in order to get the ward or license sought.[89]

[85] TNA WARD 1/3/1, fols 1–14.   [86] TNA SP 12/248 fol. 194.
[87] Joel Hurstfield, "Lord Burghley as Master of the Court of Wards, 1561–98," *Transactions of the Royal Historical Society*, 4th ser., 31 (1949), 104.
[88] TNA WARD 9/369, fol. 318.   [89] Hurstfield, "Burghley as Master," 107–8.

Of course, since the offices in the Wards were all venal, there were many ways of profiting from them. Everyone took fees of one sort or another. For instance, there is a note at the end of one enrolled lease that reads: "This lease was enrolled for six dozen of larks at Michaelmas next to be bestowed on us clerks."[90]

A letter written by Thomas Cecil, Burghley's son, in 1578 helps us see how the very complex world of wardship worked both as a financial tool and a political tool. Burghley had written to tell Thomas of an offer "made of late by Mr. Dyer from Lord Leicester, of his good-will for buying the wardship of Lord Sheffield" for one of Thomas Cecil's daughters. Edmund Sheffield, third Lord Sheffield, was born in 1565, and orphaned in 1578, so he was about fourteen when this was proposed. His mother, Lettice Knolles, was married to Robert Dudley, the earl of Leicester when this offer was made. The wardship of Lord Sheffield belonged to his mother, and was valued at £640/10/– a year.[91] Thomas Cecil had eight daughters from his 1564 marriage, so it is hard to know if a particular child was in mind, but none of them was very old at the time it was proposed to acquire the wardship and marry Lord Sheffield to one of them.

Thomas was not anxious to marry a child so young, but he was especially concerned about the cost. The wardship was owned by "my Lady," Lettice, the dowager countess of Essex who had recently married Dudley,

> who holdeth the wardship at two thousand pounds, which money, I hope, when I shall be better able hereafter, will procure my daughter, though perhaps not so noble a marriage, yet it may be in living more present and in match more assured, for that my daughter being young, the adventure of the money will be great, and a hazard whether the match shall take place, or no, to both their likings. And yet, I must confess, the house being noble and in that country which I count a neighbor to your Lordship's living and mine, I would be loath to overship a match that might be hereafter a strengthening to your posterity. And, therefore, I beseech your Lordship the matter may be entertained from conclusion as long as may be.[92]

Although he could not afford to buy young Sheffield at the moment, he was anxious to acquire the property that came with him. Thomas may have been sent a copy of a document his father's clerks had prepared, showing the value of Lord Sheffield's lands in several counties. Burghley himself had annotated the list of manors in Lincolnshire that would be joined to the Cecil holdings in Lincolnshire if such a marriage took place. They were worth, in his estimation, £888/8/2.[93]

In the end, Thomas did not purchase Lord Sheffield's wardship and the children married others. Perhaps Thomas was not excited by the idea of owning another ward of the Crown, since, in the same letter, his father (who seldom approved of anything Thomas did) had informed him that people were complaining that he was trying to sell a ward his father had given him for too high a price. Indignantly, Thomas replied he never asked for more than £400 for young Randolph, and that he has since offered to sell the child to his mother for only £300—a bargain, given

90 TNA WARD 9/118, fol. 146.   91 BL Lansd. 13, fols 107–11.
92 CP 161/52.   93 BL Lansd. 27, fol. 56.

what he would inherit at his majority. True to his word, he, and his partners, eventually sold Randolph to Roger Cave for £400.[94]

The fact that William Cecil used the system well in his own interest suggested that he was not surprised when he, and his clerks, became the center of a patronage maelstrom. The reality was that the system of wardship and livery could be highly profitable, and it was hated, since it put children of the ruling classes on the market. As Sir Thomas Smith observed in *De republica Anglorum*, it made it so that "a freeman and gentleman should be bought and sold like an horse or an ox." "Others," he continued, "do but seek which way they may make most advantage of him, as of an ox or other beast." Consequently, those who buy wards are not at pains to educate them, so they are "evil brought up touching virtue and learning." Worse, a young man whose father kept a good house will find, when he reaches his majority at twenty-one, "woods decayed, houses fallen down, stock wasted and gone, land let forth and plowed to the bare and to make amends, shall pay yet one year rent for relief and *ouster le main* [livery fees paid to the Court of Wards] besides other charges, so he may never recover his fortune."[95]

Smith ties his discussion of the Court of Wards to the portrayal of wives and marriages, since one of the important reasons for acquiring a ward was the marriage potential of the minor. Girls could be legally married at age twelve, and, once married, their property passed entirely to their husbands. "Hers," he noted, "no moveable thing is by the law of England *constanti martimonio*, but as *peculium servi aut filii familias*: and yet in movables at the death of her husband she can claim nothing, but according as he shall will by his testament..." In short, a ward could be acquired and married off to the man of the guardian's choice, ensuring that her property would become her husband's property.[96] It was a convenient way of building a family's fortune. Alternatively, a boy could be acquired and married to the daughter of the guardian, ensuring that the girl's family made a powerful connection. This is what William Cecil did for his daughter Anne, when he kept the wardship of Edward de Vere, seventeenth earl of Oxford. He approved a marriage between them that he regretted, but which gave his grandchildren impressive social status. At the same time, Oxford had to purchase his marriage from the Court of Wards, incurring a debt that he never paid and which gave his father-in-law/guardian a chance to sue him in the Queen's name for debt and seize part of his lands.[97]

As a patron, Cecil was buffeted by demands. There were many people hoping to buy and sell orphans, and he received constant requests. One, from Arthur Hall, the first ward he himself acquired, contains a pointed, whining, comment on the process of grants of wardship.[98] Hall had petitioned for a ward, and had been

---

[94] TNA WARD 9/107 fols 295v–296.
[95] Thomas Smith, *De republica Anglorum*, ed. Mary Dewar (Cambridge: Cambridge University Press, 1982), 128–9.
[96] Smith, *De republica*, 130–3.
[97] Joel Hurstfield, *The Queen's Wards: Wardship and Marriage under Elizabeth I* (London: Longmans, Green and Co., 1958), 252.
[98] TNA WARD 9/369 fol. 171v. He bought Hall in the first year of Edward VI's reign.

denied. Frustrated, he wrote his former guardian a letter which may have been blunter because he was a part of Burghley's *familia*. "I little feared my request should have been put back," he wrote, "because the mother should have him, if it please you to make that the cause; it falls out often that always mothers are not guardians to their children." But the mother did not get the child, "for that my Lord of Bedford is suitor therein; but whether I, a poor man, have preferred you before earls and their greater, my dealings more than once or twice are my good witnesses. I might have craved the lease of the ward's lands, but shall content myself with your liking." Hall was clearly not content, for his patron had let him down in order to grant a favor to an earl. In the market for wards, there were many players.[99] And because there were many suitors, it gave Burghley the power to reward or deny. As Hall said so bitterly, there were earls to be placated before poor men were seen to.

Although he had asked him not to take it amiss, Hall received a singeing reply from Cecil, who had underlined the most egregious bits of Hall's letter. Hall cowered and begged forgiveness, promising eternal friendship and loyalty. "You can have no more of the cat but the skin," he wrote, but Cecil had always had that. Hall knew it was not a good idea to undermine the links with his patron, just as Burghley understood the necessity of placating earls.[100] Cooperation had its price.

Hall was disappointed, but he was not alone. In 1580 he reported to Burghley that George Bowes was complaining that the Master of the Wards had lied to him. Petitioning for the heir of Mr Medcalf, Bowes was dismissed by Burghley, who, he said, had given the wardship to the earl of Rutland. Bowes asked Rutland if this was true, and was told it was not. Wroth, he returned to Burghley, who this time told him he had bestowed it on one of his own servants. Bowes said this with "evil terms," and Hall was happy to tattle.[101] Obviously, Burghley could lose friends when wards were awarded, since acquiring an orphan was often important to the petitioners' future successes.

However, Burghley was also guardian of the wards' property, so he had to deal with legal challenges to their possessions. In 1567 Archbishop Parker made a claim for the earl of Oxford's manor at Flete in Kent. Cecil, as Oxford's guardian and Master of the Wards, found this legally unusual, but he was forced to recognize the validity of the suit. The archbishops of Canterbury had a claim on Flete stretching hundreds of years back. In the first year of Henry VII's reign an inquisition post mortem had noted that the archbishop held three quarters of it, by a knight's fee and a half.[102] The Court of Wards was forced to issue a debenture by decree granting Archbishop Parker a third of the value of the manor, backdated to the date of the sixteenth earl's death.[103]

---

[99] CP 5/59.   [100] CP 5/60.   [101] CP 162/32.

[102] *Calendar of Inquisitions Post Mortem, Henry* VII (London: HMSO, 1898), vol. 1, 51.

[103] This case has been noted by Daphne Pearson, *Edward de Vere (1550–1604): The Crisis and Consequences of Wardship* (Aldershot: Ashgate, 2005), 26. Pearson treats the assignment of the revenue to Parker as using Oxford's inheritance to placate someone important to the Queen, abusing Oxford's estate. I read this as a genuine legal claim that recognized the archbishopric's ancient right. However,

And so the Court of Wards was a source of power, wealth, contention, and influence. Its operation was important to the Crown's revenue, and it gave Cecil, as its Master, tremendous patronage power and influence. This may explain some of Cecil's obsession with genealogy. His anonymous biographer asked rhetorically, "what nobleman or gentleman and their dwellings, matches and pedigrees, did he not know?" He could, said the biographer, describe the locale of a gentleman's home better than the gentleman himself. He continues: "He took great pains and delight in pedigrees, wherein he had great knowledge, and wrote whole books of them with his own hand, which greatly augmented his knowledge both abroad and at home."[104]

The Court of Wards and Liveries depended on the willingness of local gentlemen to participate in its taxing activities. As in the valuing of property for subsidies, a jury of local gentlemen was assembled to determine the nature and extent of the estate of the deceased father. In theory this was the job of the escheator, the Queen's officer who "took back" the Queen's property for the Exchequer. However, there was another county officer, the feodary, whose job it was to find the wards and report them to the court. These officers were often in conflict, and both worked with the reluctant neighbors, who dragged their feet when it came to defining the Queen's rights over the wards' properties. The gentlemen of the county, noblesse oblige, were drawn in to aid a process many of them detested.

The Docket of Writs in the Court of Wards suggests the scale of local involvement as writs were sent to local gentry to conduct inquisitions post mortem and other tasks. For example, when Burghley's father-in-law, Sir Anthony Cooke, died in 1576, four gentlemen from Essex and one from Surrey were called to investigate his holdings. But his was a simple case. When John Everarde died in 1573 four commissions were created to deal with all the land he had in four different counties.[105]

The death of John Gamage and the marriage of his daughter, Barbara, give us a glimpse of the powers and responsibilities of the Master of the Wards. Like most good stories from the archives, we know this one because it became complicated and required Burghley himself to intervene in '*Wallia Australis*', Glamorganshire.[106]

It began with the death of John Gamage of Coity, Glamorganshire on September 8, 1584, leaving Barbara as his only heir. Among the great families of Wales and the Welsh Marches, there was considerable interest in Gamage's estate because it was large—his heiress was worth more than £1,000 a year—and Barbara was

the citation provided by Pearson to Cecil's reply to Parker is not found where she says it is located. She cites TNA WARD 9/129 fol. 145. An inspection of WARD 9/129 finds no trace of it. However, that the decree was made is not in doubt, since Parker was being paid by the Wards. See TNA WARD 9/380 fol. 67.

[104] Collins, 65–7.

[105] TNA WARD 9/171 Docket of Writs 15–30 Eliz. These are not paginated. They are arranged by legal term, county, day, and month of the commission. Cooke's commission is at Trinity Term 18 Eliz., Essex, 12 July. Everarde's are at Hilary, 15 Eliz., 6 Feb. Middlesex and Sussex; Suffolk 14 Feb.; Suffolk 22 Feb.

[106] Wallia Australis and Wallia Borealis were record divisions in the Court of Wards. TNA WARD 9/157, fol. 215v.

unmarried. Contention over her hand and estate became instantly heated as the ruling families in the Marches, the Stradling, Croft, Herbert, Howard, and Sydney clans, asserted their claims.[107]

At her father's death, she was taken into the custody of her maternal uncle, Sir Edward Stradling, Sheriff of Glamorganshire. It was believed that she was held against her will, prompting a threatening letter from Sir James Croft:

> your wife hath taken the gentlewoman forcibly from Herbert Croft, and as a prisoner doth so detain her as he cannot have access unto her: which injury, considering how the case stands betwixt them, is very strange. Whereof...I hope you will do that which shalbe for your worship and credit in the face of the world. And, so doing, I shall think myself beholden to you, yielding such friendship and courtesies as such worshipful and honest dealings deserve: otherwise I must seek courses I would be loath to do to any of your reputation.[108]

The imputation that his honor was at stake did not move Stradling, and neither did Barbara's friends and relatives at Court. Sir Walter Raleigh and Sir Francis Walsingham became involved, as did Lord Chamberlain Howard. The crux of the complaints was that Barbara and her fortune should not be disposed without the consent of her friends and near kin. Sir Walter Raleigh asked Stradling, "that you suffer not my kinswoman to be bought and sold in Wales, without her Majesty's privity, and the consent or advise of my L. Chamberlain and myself, her father's cousins german: considering she hath not any nearer kin nor better; her father and myself came of two sisters..."[109]

Walsingham and the council wrote to the Sheriff of Glamorganshire, to Sir William Herbert, and to others, telling them the girl was to remain with "some of them." Then they changed their minds and asked she be sent to the court.[110]

Lord Burghley, as Master of the Court of Wards, also intervened. Burghley was moved to draft Stradling a letter, in his own hand, removing Barbara from his custody and placing her and her possessions in the keeping of *one* Carne, *either Sir John or his father Thomas Carne, the sheriff*.[111]

It is an interesting letter because it highlights his responsibility as Master and the difficulties of managing the frictions between great families. It appears that he did the genealogy of the families involved, as he prepared to write. Although the pedigree, entirely in his hand, is undated, it relates to the case, which contained a genealogical snarl of claims to kinship. It shows how the Gamage, Stradling, Herbert, Vaughan, and Cecil families were intermarried—perhaps enforcing his right to interfere as a kinsman as well as Master.[112] But it was as Master of the Wards and Liveries, the guardian of the Queen's interest, that he wrote to Stradling.

"I have not to do with mine office to intermeddle with the state of the marriage of the daughter and heir of Mr John Gamage late deceased . . . she is of full age and

---

[107] Penry Williams, *The Council in the Marches of Wales under Elizabeth I* (Cardiff: University of Wales Press, 1958), 242–6.
[108] John M. Traherne, ed., *The Stradling Papers* (London: 1840), 41–2.
[109] Traherne, *Stradling*, 22–3.   [110] Traherne, *Stradling*, 27.
[111] Williams, *Council of Wales*, 243.   [112] CP 143/16.

at her own liberty to marry where she shall best like with advise of her near kin folks," he wrote. Nonetheless, it was his duty to protect her property, since she had not yet sued livery from the court. He was empowered to ensure that she, and all wards, "may have their lands and possessions preserved from waste, or from any interference by any strangers, and specially from all entries of parties that may have any pretense or color of title to any part of the said lands."

Her kinfolk could dispose of her person in marriage, but Stradling, Burghley understood, had entered her house and seized the "evidences of her lands," before an inquisition post mortem could be conducted, "by my direction, and an office found after the death of her father, who was the Queen Majesty's tenant *in capite*, whereby she may according to the laws of the realm sue her livery." This was unjust and unlawful, and Stradling could not do it. Burghley ordered him to "permit some other persons more indifferent to take the charge of the house, and to cause all places where the evidences are to be sealed up, until I shall cause" a writ to be issued in the case.

In the meantime, he was to turn Barbara over to Sir Thomas Carne, the neighbor nearest her house, and Stradling and his wife were to refrain from coercing her. Stradling and Carne were enemies, which may have been a subtle way of snubbing him.[113]

Burghley was asserting his right as Master of the Queen's Wards and Liveries to control her property until she sued for it and paid her entry fine. Gamage's lands belonged to the Crown, so, until livery was sued, their income belonged to the Queen, even though Barbara was of age. Stradling was threatening to deprive Elizabeth of that income. It seems doubtful that Burghley really expected to realize the revenue, but the Queen's fiscal interest was being protected.

He had a weak hand. As in many things in the realm, he was a long way from the local action and he had very few tools to work with other than loud claims to authority. When he informed Carne that he was to go get Barbara from Stradling, he said it was "service, being agreeable to justice, a neighborly part for you, and a charitable deed for the saving of the gentlewoman's inheritance." Interestingly, he sent this letter to Stradling so he could deliver it to Carne. And he reserved Barbara's right to reject Carne as her protector and name some other party as long as it was not Stradling, and if Carne agreed to it. In short, they were to work it out face to face.[114]

Croft portrayed Stradling as dishonorable and untrustworthy if he did not release the girl. The Privy Council and Sir Francis Walsingham, speaking in the Queen's name, demanded that she be sent to court. Burghley ordered her turned over to Carne. But the Sidney family had other ideas. Sir Henry Sidney was President of

---

[113] BL Lansd. 102, fols 215–215v. Penry Williams identifies this as Sir John Carne, but it is more likely Thomas Carne of Ewenny, Glamorganshire, the father of John. Thomas was sheriff of the county three times, most lately in 1581. The Carnes had a running feud with John Gamage of Coity. Carne was attempting to enforce his feudal rights as successor to the priors of Ewenny over lands of Gamage, and the two were locked in a dispute in the Exchequer. Thomas Carne was a well-known recusant, but he sat in the Parliament of 1586 and again in 1589. HPT sub Carne, Thomas. Gamage's seat at Coity Castle was less than three miles from Thomas Carne's home at Ewenny.

[114] BL Lansd. 102, fol. 216.

the Council of the Marches of Wales, and was married to the earl of Leicester's sister, Mary Dudley. A member of the Privy Council, too, he also had a son, Robert, in need of a wealthy wife. Soon Walsingham wrote Stradling, "being now secretly given to understand that for the good will you bear unto the Earl of Pembroke [Henry Herbert], you mean to further what you may young Mr Robert Sidney," he encouraged him to move in that direction. He knew, he averred, that the Queen, Lord Chamberlain Howard of Effingham, Sir Walter Raleigh, and the rest of her kinfolk would be pleased by it.[115] Henry Herbert, the second earl of Pembroke, was married to Mary Sidney, the daughter of Sir Henry Sidney and Mary Dudley, so Stradling's affection for Pembroke meant affection for his brother-in-law, Robert Sidney, too.

John Gamage had died on September 8, 1584. Two weeks later, on September 23, 1584 Barbara Gamage wed Robert Sidney, and went on to a happy marriage, becoming the countess of Leicester on her husband's succession.

In January 1585, the Court of Wards issued a commission for an inquisition post mortem on John Gamage. As was customary, five local men were appointed to the commission to appraise his property. After all the kerfuffle, Sir Edward Stradling headed the list of commissioners.[116]

Of course, the reason Burghley was concerned, ultimately, had to do with the working of government. The Council of the Marches was dysfunctional enough without another reason for the great families to quarrel. Naturally, he was also concerned about money. The price of Barbara Gamage's livery was depended on the appraised value of her father's estate. He knew that its value might conveniently drop as deeds and other documents disappeared from her house.

This was an extreme case, but a visible one. For the hundreds of others the process ran more smoothly. A sampling of the patent rolls for 1558–72, 1576–90, and 1592–3 found 1225 grants of wardship enrolled. Seventeen percent were given to repeat suitors, with William Tooke, the Auditor of the Court of Wards from 1544 until 1588, leading the pack with sixteen Elizabethan wards. Altogether Tooke's family alone accounted for twenty-seven wardships. Clearly, the Auditor was well placed to acquire wards, and probably sold them on to others. But if we look at the list of those who acquired multiple wardships we can see many of the same names we saw in the Gamage case. Cecil, Dudley, Walsingham, Sidney, Howard, and Croft all had multiple grants. The others were pillars of the Elizabethan state, such as: Francis Knowles (Treasurer of the Household), Christopher Hatton (Receiver of First Fruits and Tenths, then Lord Chancellor), Francis Russell (earl of Bedford), Henry Clinton (earl of Lincoln), Thomas Sackford (Master of Requests), the earls of Arundel, Robert Freke (Teller of the Exchequer), and Robert Keilway (Surveyor of the Court of Wards).[117]

[115] Traherne, *Stradling*, 29.

[116] *Calendar of Patent Rolls, 27 Eliz. I*, item 209, 31, Jan. 30, 1585. TNA C 66/1256 m. 6d.

[117] Elizabeth B. Woolcott, "Maternity's Wards: Investigations of Sixteenth Century Patterns of Maternal Guardianship" (unpublished MA thesis, Utah State University, 2003), 26–8. http://digital-commons.usu.edu/cgi/viewcontent.cgi?article=1000&context=etd_history.

The Wards, customs duties, fees, patents, offices, and other possessions gave Burghley and Elizabeth resources that, because they were episodic, could be sold, granted, and leased as favors, as rewards, as punishments, and as sources of revenue, all of which were useful. It appears that Burghley did not maximize the yield to the Queen on these things. He preferred to use them as tools to secure cooperation, reward effort, and influence behavior. The desire of honorable men for offices and titles prompted them to take on tasks that might, or might not, lead to royal rewards. They could not even be sure they would have their expenses paid by the Crown, but they took the gambles out of duty, honor, and hope for reward.

Money was at the heart of the royal government, but it was seen more as a tool of persuasion and influence than as a good in itself. The Queen needed real cash, but, as Burghley's memo of 1595 and his handling of the Wards suggests, he saw its influence as more important than its possession. Taxes collected with sensitivity, fiscal burdens eased, captains rewarded, and wards handled at a reasonable price kept the magisterial classes working with the Queen. When Burghley's son Robert took over the Court of Wards he failed to understand this and, under intense pressure from military costs, he could not afford to continue his father's generous approach. Raising the price of ward to four times the appraised value, he set off a reaction among the Queen's tenants that led to the dissolution of wardship.

Money was a sensitive issue for the magisterial classes. Squeeze too hard and they might not provide it, but war required them to find it.

8

Managing War

Since my last coming, I have earnestly spoken to sundry gentlemen to raise some lancers for defense of the realm against invasion, and found at first many willing, though a service strange to these countrymen, and never required of any here before. But I perceive since that they are most loath to enter into that charge, because they fear they should always hereafter be charged for all kind of service, as other parts of the realm be; if assured that they should only serve towards Scotland, as in former times, they would neither shrink much at this, nor be so backward at the muster of light horsemen. The number of good geldings is much decayed in these North parts, but yet it is far greater than I can get to be seen at any muster, do what I can; and one principal cause is that they are unwilling to come into the muster book, lest they should be called upon for any service in Ireland, or other parts than towards Scotland.

Henry, earl of Huntingdon, Lord President of the North,
to Secretary Walsingham, April 28, 1588[1]

Defense was a primary job of the monarch, and the records of attempts to maintain the realm's military readiness are voluminous. Burghley and his colleagues worried constantly about musters, training, equipment, ships, and other necessities. Elizabeth's and Burghley's conservatism did not prevent them from evolving tools to improve defense, even though it did prevent them from radical solutions such as creating a standing army. Expanding the use of lords-lieutenant, trained bands armed with guns, and royal commissions empowered to interfere when local magnates undermined their tenants' abilities to provide for defense, they quietly made changes to the system they had inherited. They did nothing radical, but as they confronted particular problems, they worked on solutions that, over time, took small steps toward a more centralized state.

The defense of the realm was tended by the Queen's managers, but the machinery of command was poorly developed. The people at the very top engaged with issues they would never have known about in a more elaborated system. On August 28, 1588, during the Armada crisis, we find Burghley sending instructions, "post haste, haste, haste, post haste for life," to the Lord Admiral concerning two ships engaged with a Spaniard in the road at Newhaven, detailing the number of culverin shot, sacre shot, minion shot, and barrels of powder that should be distributed to each. At the same time, he told the Lord Admiral that he left it to him to do what he thought fit. The post riders raced from London south to the coast at a

---

[1] TNA SP 15/30 fol. 194v.

rate of four miles an hour, so it was just short of a day later when the admiral received the order.[2] Of course, by the time his letter reached the admiral, Captain Fenner of the *Aide* and his fellow captains had concluded that they lacked shot, powder, and food to fight it out with the great Spanish ship and so had returned to base to resupply.[3]

Like the letter from the earl of Huntingdon that begins this chapter, this story catches the dependence of the state on the local powers to "do as you shall think fit" in the cause, as well as the council's attempts to be in command. Although Burghley and other officers could attempt, at a distance, to direct defenses, they needed a great deal of local cooperation, a cooperation that required persuasion and sensitivity to local concerns. If the men on the borders of Scotland were unwilling to register in a muster book for fear of being drafted and sent to Ireland or the Low Countries, their concerns had to be heard.[4]

Likewise, if the Bishop of Chester said his poor clergy could not afford or find men to hire for the Irish war, reporting "there is an old vain speech" that was "better to be hanged at home than die like dogs" in Ireland, it was necessary for Burghley to parley with him over what his clerics could afford. The bishop not only wanted to compound for the cost, he wanted out of the recruiting business. He urged the creation of a royal commission with authority to compel men, rather than expecting the bishop and his colleagues to recruit them.[5] The bishop's desire for a commission, using the power of the Queen to relieve him from his duty to raise troops, matched Burghley's realization that more coercion and persuasion was necessary. However, this was ad hoc. The system would remain highly contingent on local circumstances and men. As Neil Younger has said, it was "more a case of construction of a network —an alliance, even—to meet short-term needs," than of state formation.[6]

In Ireland, where those networks were very difficult to maintain, the captains became laws unto themselves, resorting to whatever means were necessary to maintain their rule.[7]

The long wars in the Low Countries, the Armada crises, and the running sore of Irish conflicts created huge military managerial problems. The Privy Council tried to convince men to provide what was required, but orders and laws could not fix the inadequate system based on traditional levies. As John McGurk observed about the Nine Years War in Ireland,

> The queen, the privy council and the high command might issue proclamations, orders, rulings, instructions, and codes of discipline and articles of war (many clauses in the latter carrying the death penalty) and all to be carried out by a hierarchy of administrators—muster masters, clerks of the check, commissaries for apparel, for

[2] Folger Shakespeare Library, Ms. X.d.494.   [3] TNA SP 12/215 fols 133–133v.
[4] TNA SP 15/30 fol. 194v.   [5] TNA SP 63/187 fol. 77.
[6] Neil Younger, *War and Politics in the Elizabethan Counties* (Manchester: Manchester University Press, 2012), 46–7.
[7] Malcolm Smuts, "Organized Violence in the Elizabethan Monarchical Republic," *History* 99 (2014), 434–7.

victuals, for arms and munitions—and yet rules were honored in the breach or ignored as corruption and chaos at every level...[8]

Problems of control on the borders, in Ireland, and in expeditionary forces were exacerbated by the deficiencies in the royal administrative system. The Crown expected local men to do their duty, while pretending to be able to exert central control. A system of government designed for southern England did not work in places like Kildare and Cumberland, where sparse populations and lack of resident gentry with deep pockets made it falter.[9]

It did not work very well in southern England, either, if we are to believe the complaints that Burghley, Bacon, and others made about justices of the peace and other officers, but in military affairs it was immediately obvious because the needs were most pressing. From the beginning of the reign, there were discussions about how to improve the system of local musters run by local magnates, who were expected to fund arms, oversee training, find horses, and generally create their own local army and navy. Over the length of the reign, some changes were made. The increasing importance of lord-lieutenants and their deputies in regional power structures was one sign. Another was the spread of regional trained bands, on London's model, across the country. Some of this was driven by new technologies, as bows were replaced by guns, and some of it was a managerial response to the pressing needs of a nation that was at war on land and sea for the last half of Elizabeth's reign.

Growing out of the need to muster troops efficiently in times of crisis, the appointments of the lords-lieutenant began under Henry VIII, who used them as temporary royal representatives. They began to be regularized in the 1550s, but it was not until the later 1580s that the entire realm had lord-lieutenants in place. The outbreak of the war with Spain in 1585 made their appointments pressing. By later in Elizabeth's reign there were regular districts for them, not always corresponding with shire boundaries. Each lord-lieutenant was expected to organize the mustering, arming, and commanding of the militia in his district. He also had the unpleasant job of levying men for the wars abroad and seeing to it that they were paid "coat and conduct" money, the costs of clothing and transporting them. Informally, the office became an important connection between the court and the localities, since the lord-lieutenant served longer than the sheriff and could be expected to undertake other royal commissions as needed. The office was often held by aristocrats who already had great power in their localities, such as the earl of Pembroke in Somerset, Wiltshire, and all the counties under his presidency in the Welsh Marches.[10] But no matter what their title and authority, they still had to

---

[8] John McGurk, *The Elizabethan Conquest of Ireland* (Manchester: Manchester University Press, 1997), 194.

[9] Steven G. Ellis, *Tudor Frontiers and Noble Power: The Making of the British State* (Oxford and New York: Oxford University Press, 1995), 258.

[10] Neil Younger, "Henry Herbert, Second Earl of Pembroke and Noble Leadership in Elizabethan Provinces," in Peter Iver Kaufman, ed., *Leadership and Elizabethan Culture* (London: Palgrave Macmillan, 2013), 121.

work with their gentry colleagues to achieve results, using all of the formal and cultural tools at their disposal.[11]

This system worked well in places where the ruling elites were dominated by a single local magnate. In Cambridgeshire, for instance, Roger Lord North's dominance of the county in the 1590s tied a "restricted and intricately connected rump of the elite together to govern the shire" through the lieutenancy. Burghley did the same in Hertfordshire, and Huntingdon did it in Leicestershire. The lords Stanley did it in Cheshire and Lancashire, while the earl of Shrewsbury made it work in Derbyshire.[12] In areas lacking dominant aristocrats, where factions struggled for control, the lieutenancies worked less well because the established regional power structures were weak.

Naturally, the lord-lieutenant nominated deputy lieutenants, who had to be local gentlemen approved by the council, to carry out the real work. The deputies had to interpret the Privy Council's general orders to suit local conditions. Concerned about a Spanish invasion, they ordered all the ports and havens defended, and requested information about the men available to muster near the coasts (see Fig. 8.1). These orders had to be interpreted locally, and that created at best confusion, and at worst ways of evading the orders. In 1586 the deputy lieutenants of Hertfordshire wrote to the council a belated response to some articles and instructions their lord-lieutenant, the earl of Leicester, had forgotten to give them. Once they had the documents, they were confused, because the orders talked about guarding the coast, and, as they truthfully reported, Hertfordshire had no coast. They apologized for not mustering the militia because harvest time and bad weather made it inconvenient. Although the justices of the peace on the quorum were ordered to provide a horseman armed with a carbine, the deputies were sure the council was mistaken, since they were already paying for units of lancers and could not afford to support more troopers. Therefore, the deputies sought clarification from the council. Told to keep careful watch on papists, they responded, "God be thanked for it," that there were no willful recusants in the shire.[13]

The deputy lieutenants and the captains that reported to them were, by late in the reign, organizing "trained bands" who were replacing the feudal levies as the main force. Although every man was still expected to own arms, and to practise regularly with the longbow, select companies were armed with more modern weapons and taught how to use them. Beginning in 1577 there was a fitful effort to create them in every county. By 1588, about a tenth of the militia was in these bands so that the nation had an army of about 26,000 men with some level of training at the time of the Armada crisis.

The reason for the expansion of the lieutenancy structure is not hard to find. An undated memorandum on the defense of the realm from the middle of the 1580s, probably related to the confusing orders complained about by the deputy lieutenants of Hertfordshire, identified the key issue: "it is to be doubted that without

---

[11] Younger, *War and Politics*, 14–47.

[12] Eugene J. Bourgeosis II, *The Ruling Elite of Cambridgeshire, England, c.1530–1603* (Lewiston, NY: The Edwin Mellen Press, 2003), 279–80.

[13] TNA SP 12/86, fols 148–9.

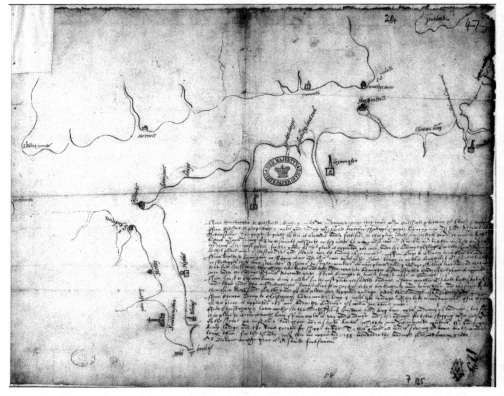

Fig. 8.1. Survey of the landing places on the coast of Hampshire from Portsmouth to Bournemouth; with the numbers of men appointed to guard at particular spots, and names of gentlemen commanding them, document ref. SP 12/199 fol. 47. National Archives of the UK.

lieutenants in respect of the factions and equality between the commissioners in the several counties, the service will be greatly hindered both in the speedy and well performing of the same."[14]

The lord-lieutenant, then, was a conduit and tiebreaker. Orders sent directly to the justices of the peace to muster the forces were often poorly executed, since there was no local commander. The lord-lieutenant, with his superior social authority, gave the Queen a single point of contact. The lord-lieutenant's deputies gave him tentacles in the locales. And, at least in theory, these appointments stood outside the normal social hierarchies within the lieutenancy. Thus Burghley, by choosing the right lord-lieutenant (or appointing himself as a lord-lieutenant), had a firmer grip on the military in each area.

This grip was especially important because of the danger posed by powerful Catholic gentlemen. They might be the natural leaders in their locales, and appointing a lord-lieutenant was a way of ensuring that the command structure was made of

[14] TNA SP 12/176/1 fol. 235.

religiously loyal men.[15] Neil Younger has linked the revival of the lord-lieutenants to the Bond of Association of 1584, with its panicked fear of a Catholic succession should Elizabeth be assassinated. Although the Queen rejected the bond and all the plans for an interregnum that swirled around it, Burghley and his colleagues still sought a way to ensure the safety of the state during a succession crisis. Standing lord-lieutenants might make that possible. New appointees and more of them could, Younger suggests, ensure loyal forces in all regions if the Protestant state was threatened. It was, he says, "the most significant change in the machinery of local government of the reign."[16]

In this model, orders could go to the lord-lieutenant, and he would oversee their distribution and enforcement within his area of jurisdiction. For example, in April 1588 the Lord-Lieutenant of Lancashire, the earl of Derby, issued an order to his deputy lieutenants to command the constables in every parish to inform the gentlemen and freeholders, who were "charged by statute or otherwise" to have arms and armor, to muster. They were to bring the armed men of their parishes to be viewed by Sir Edward Stanley at Worcester eighteen days later. These same gentlemen and freeholders, many of whom would have also been justices and other officeholders, were also to bring with them the money collected in the parishes to pay the soldiers 8d each for their "conduct" money.[17]

The lord-lieutenant and his deputies were still tied into the social hierarchy, since it was almost unthinkable that an officer would come from the lower orders. In 1592 the deputy lord-lieutenants of Hertfordshire made a report to their lord-lieutenant, Lord Burghley, about the trained bands of the shire, many of which were serving abroad. They were in need of new equipment and officers. In Sir John Cutts's band there was a particular problem. Cutts had not been in the shire in two years, so the leadership of the band fell to his lieutenant. However, they noted what appeared to them to be an issue: "charge upon any occasion of service resteth only upon his lieutenant who although he be a gentleman of birth, yet is he but a mean man to supply a place of such credit."[18]

In the very first month of the reign, Sir James Croft and his fellows had provided Cecil with advice on the organization of the Marches against Scotland, making clear the importance of social standing for officers. Advising that a lord-lieutenant should be created, they defined him as

> a man of authority and experience, so in favor and in counsel with the Queen's Majesty that the nobility there being shall not have cause of disdain to serve under him and such one, as men have hope that upon his report of their service may be able to stand them in [good] stead.

---

[15] Younger, *War and Politics*, 43.

[16] Neil Younger, "Securing the Monarchical Republic: The Remaking of the Lord Lieutenancies in 1585," *Historical Research*, 84, 224 (2011), 252.

[17] HEH EL 6284–9. Multiple copies of the same order.

[18] TNA SP 12/241 fol. 136. Cutts had moved from Hertfordshire to Cambridgeshire, where he became a deputy lieutenant to Lord North. Apparently, he did not bother to resign his captaincy in Hertfordshire. HPT, sub Cutts, Sir John (1545–1615), of Horham Hall, Essex; Shenley Hall, Herts and Childerley, Cambs, <http://www.historyofparliamentonline.org/volume/1558-1603/member/cutts-sir-john-1545-1615>. Accessed Oct. 23, 2014.

They went on to explain that anyone appointed a warden of the Marches should be a man of lesser social standing than the lord-lieutenant, laying out a command structure that echoed social precedence and recognized the tensions borne of social competition. There could be no effective shared governance among men of equal rank, they said, "for when two at one time remain in one country in authority any while together, equal in birth and estimation, they cannot but have some secret inclination to disdain each at other, and think the well doing of them to be derogation to the other's honor and renown."[19] As Michael Braddick has observed, the rhetoric of national defense cut across that of social authority. It made it nearly impossible to create a tight, focused military system.[20]

Sir John Cutts's absence from Hertfordshire raised another question. What if the officers were not present in their counties when crises arose? Who then would lead the defense? The same memo on the defense of the northern Marches demanded a reform that would correct this. It suggested that the lieutenant there be required to be resident from August until Christmas (elsewhere defined as "from harvest" until Christmas), the season when the Scottish enemy was the most active.[21]

The increasing use of lords-lieutenant helped solve the problem of communication between the center and the shires, giving Burghley at least the illusion that orders might be carried out, but he himself had to fulfill orders and answer questions from the Queen about military matters. Of course, he also had to find the money to pay for any military decisions that exceeded normal expectations of supply from the men who owed service.

In the fall of 1592 there is an interesting example of how these issues came together for Burghley. By then, England's unhappy intervention in Brittany in support of Henri of Navarre had been running for a long time and bearing little fruit. Spanish troops were threatening French ports on the English Channel, and the expedition led by the earl of Essex and Sir John Norris had not relieved them. Burghley believed continued intervention necessary, while Elizabeth was reluctant to commit further resources. Only after a defeat of the Anglo-French army in May 1592 was Elizabeth convinced to increase to 5,000 the number of troops she was willing to send.[22] Shortly after, she changed her mind. As the debate between the Queen and her council over Brittany continued, she propounded questions she wanted answered about the war there.

Burghley listed them as "considerations to be had" in a document he himself endorsed as "A Memorial of causes proposed by her Majesty." Then he scrawled answers in the margins. It is one of the rare moments when the oral interaction with the Queen was caught on paper.

Elizabeth wanted to know if she should continue aiding the French king in Brittany, considering the loss of her people, the expense, and the fact that Henri

[19] TNA SP 59/1 fols 49, 50, 53–53v.

[20] Michael Braddick, "'Uppon This Instante Extrordinarie Occasion': Military Mobilization in Yorkshire before and after the Armada," *Huntington Library Quarterly*, 61 (1998), 454–5.

[21] TNA SP 59/1 fol. 49.

[22] John S. Nolan, *Sir John Norreys and the Elizabethan Military World* (Exeter: University of Exeter Press, 1997), 180–203.

was not doing his best to eject the Spanish. She was worried, too, about the expense of the army in the Low Countries, and she was contemplating withdrawing them. However, if the English troops left, how would Ostend and Bergen be defended? Clearly, she feared, as Burghley feared, a pro-Spanish revolt of the recusants, "namely in Lancashire," and wondered how to prevent it. Lastly, she wanted to know what the border commissioners advised on strengthening the border against "papists and Spanish" invaders.

Burghley's marginal and interlinear responses are hard to read, but he put the issues of expenses, recusants, and continuing the war into a single category. He suggested that if the recusants could be squeezed hard enough, they could be made to pay for the troops needed in Brittany. He thought he could get another 4,000 foot and 1,000 horse this way, especially if he renegotiated the loans taken in the City of London to help pay the debts already incurred.[23]

Over the next weeks and months we see the council working on these projects, while Burghley himself battled ill health. A few days after he started thinking about the problem, he scribbled a draft concerning the numbers of men to be sent to Brittany and the Low Countries, where they might come from, and how many would be needed.[24]

Meanwhile, attention was focused on recusants, consulting the Warwickshire "Book of Recusants" for 1592.[25] He got a list of nine persons in Lancashire that "keep popish priests."[26] He received and annotated a list of popish persons, priests, and vicars in Lancashire, noting their hundreds and jotting a note about the fines they owed.[27] It is not clear if he was proposing new levies on them, identifying their existing fines as a source of money that could be diverted to support the operation in France, or tracking possible rebels. The council launched new investigations into known Catholic gentry, asking that any armor they had be seized by the justices.

But recusants were not the only group targeted for extra taxes to support troops. Clergy and lawyers were on the list, too.[28]

While they worked on this particular need, the usual heavy flow of reports on imprests of men, the movement of troops, coat and conduct, and costs associated with the wars continued to reach the council. Sir Thomas Shirley, Treasurer at War in the Low Countries, steadily supplied information on money gathered and funds disbursed for the forces on the continent.[29] In trying to answer the Queen's concerns, Burghley, old and ill, was acting on many fronts at once.

Revolts in Ireland were especially difficult and expensive. The Queen did not like the expense of her Irish kingdom, and pressured Burghley to fix it. For example in 1581 Lord Deputy Grey was getting instructions to suppress the

[23] TNA SP 12/243 fol. 136. The *Calendar* does not note Burghley's endorsement indicating these are Elizabeth's questions.
[24] TNA SP 12/243 fol. 143. [25] TNA SP 12/243 fols 202–16.
[26] TNA SP 12/243 fol. 158. [27] TNA SP 12/243 fol. 194.
[28] Younger, *War and Politics*, 189.
[29] Shirley's reports were sent in frequently and can be easily found in the Calendar of State Papers Domestic for 1591–4. For instance, TNA SP 12 243/fol. 160.

Irish rebellion because it was too expensive. It prompted Burghley to rework the way the army there was supplied, centralizing the victualing process under a single surveyor-general of the victuals. It cut the Queen's expenses in half.[30]

Supply in support of war was a game that Burghley played his entire life as a royal servant. When Lord Warden Ralph Eures was indicted in 1597 for raising the fines on his tenants, making them too poor to keep horses, Burghley probably gave a wry sigh born of frustration with an ancient argument. He had heard the same complaint from Eures' father's tenants in 1580, along with many similar laments. His whole career had been a running battle with the men wealthy enough to keep horses for the militia. Burghley and his colleagues had spent many administrative days trying to find ways to make them supply the horses and armor that the law required them to keep. Statutes, proclamations, and commissions were devoted to the problem. And still the number of horsemen available was never as great as the muster books said there should be.

The horses, furniture, and arms were for the common defense of the realm, "wherein every good and faithful subject is interested," but apparently many loved the Queen too little to devote resources to feeding a war horse. By 1580, there were ten statutes in force concerning the requirements.[31]

In 1559, Cecil tried to ensure the supply of horses by reviving a Henrician statute making the unlicensed conveying of horses, mares, and geldings into Scotland a felony. Horses had to be kept in the country to ensure the defenses.[32] It seemed a simple and sensible law. People were exploiting a loophole that allowed export of horses for personal use. Apparently, many, many horses needed to go with travelers, so an Act was passed to plug the leak of horses into Scotland.[33]

Just before Parliament met in 1562/3, the council issued a proclamation concerning the increase and breeding of big horses for war. It demonstrated an understanding of bloodlines, and worked to keep puny horses from breeding. Small "unprofitable beasts" were to be killed.

Defining "unprofitable," the council declared it wanted mares of at least thirteen "handfuls" in height, and every deer park was to keep brood mares commensurate with the size of the park: one square mile required two mares; four square miles required four. Stallions had to stand at least fifteen handfuls tall (at four inches to the handful) if they were to be pastured in any common or waste ground. Horses that did not measure up could be seized by the person who found them.

The proclamation encouraging promoters to seize horses that were too small backfired in East Anglia. In the fen country the stumpy stallions did not come up to the standard height, so they were being taken, to the distress of their owners. In the Parliament of 1566 a bill was launched to stop this, pointing out that horses of the size required by the law would drown in the fens. The completed new Act allowed stallions of thirteen hands in those watery places.[34]

---

[30] Christopher Maginn, *William Cecil, Ireland, and the Tudor State* (Oxford: Oxford University Press, 2012), 135–7.

[31] H&L, vol. 2, 463–4. "Enforcing Statutes for Maintaining Horse, Armor," April 14, 1580.

[32] 1 Eliz. I, c. 7.   [33] 6 Eliz. I, c. 19.   [34] 8 Eliz. I, c. 8.

This same proclamation reviewed the rules about who had to keep horses, arms, and armor. Anyone worth £1,000 had to keep six heavy horses for demi-lances (armored troopers with lances) and ten light horses, with the furniture of harness and weapons requisite for their service. Gradations of wealth beneath that were each assigned a number of horses and a list of equipment down to an income of 100 marks. Persons of that income were required to have one gelding fit for light horsemen, with harness and weapons, along with a collection of pikes, longbows, arrows, steel caps, and other military tools.

The proclamation finished with a reminder that horses could not be exported to Scotland without a license. Naturally, the justices of the peace were to ensure that everyone had the horses and equipment assigned each according to his income.[35]

The same day, May 7, 1562, another proclamation was issued, enforcing the statutes of apparel. This, too, was ultimately about horses. The Queen, it says, has noticed the "monstrous abuse of apparel" and the decay and "disfurniture" of horses for service. These issues commingled because sumptuary laws sorted costumes according to ranks and wealth, using categories like those for horses and armor, making dress a ready indicator of wealth. Therefore she announced the creation of special commissions in every county to discover "what persons shall not have…according to the statute, by reason of their wives' apparel…horses according to the statute." It was her intention to conduct these reviews every six months until the number of horses necessary for defense was reached.[36]

It is likely that William Cecil was the one behind this plan. He admitted to Elizabeth in 1560 that he was known for speaking out against excess apparel, and he certainly understood the need for more horses. Tellingly, an abstract of the statutes concerning apparel exists with Cecil's own corrections. Its purpose was to "induce" the Queen's subjects to observe the laws, suggesting that the latest subsidy lists be used to determine who could wear what.[37]

Certainly, the council was thinking about creating commissions to enforce a number of penal statutes. It may be that this proclamation was the first tried to see if it would work.[38]

The Privy Council began issuing commissions for investigation of women's dress and big horses. Soon reports were coming in from around the country about women seen wearing silk, cloth of gold, or velvet. The commissioners interviewed them about their husbands' horses. It must have been an uncomfortable process.

In Cambridgeshire several wives were reported wearing "toga Sirica" and "habilimento operis aurifabri" despite their husbands' lack of land of sufficient value. A few horses might be found there.[39] In Winchester the commissioners reported that to their knowledge no man's wife had, since mid-August, worn any gown of silk, any French hood or bonnet with any "bylyment", poste or edge of gold, pearl, or

---

[35] H&L, vol. 2, 196–201.   [36] H&L, vol. 2, 193–4.
[37] TNA SP 52/4, fol. 29. The abstract of statutes is TNA SP 12/23 fol. 20.
[38] D. R. Lidington, "Parliament and the Enforcement of Penal Statutes: The History of the Act 'In Restraint of Common Promoters' (18 Eliz. I, c. 5)," *Parliamentary History*, 8, 2 (1989), 310.
[39] TNA E178/469.

stone, or any chain of gold about her neck or in the "parlletts," nor in any apparel of her body. Nor had they any velvet in the lining or other part of their gowns other than in the cuffs and "purfells." Nor were they wearing silk petticoats. In short, there were no new horses to be added to the muster in Winchester.

In Portsmouth one woman was found wearing velvet on her kirtle, and her husband had no horse or armor. In Alton Hundred a woman was seen wearing a French hood with a billment, but she explained that her husband had his horse and armor in London, whence they came.[40]

In Huntingdonshire eight wives were detected wearing silk, but all their husbands had horses. The commissioners swore there were no other women wearing silk in their county.[41] No one at all in Durham wore silk, while in Northumberland every woman who wore silk had horses and armor according to her husband's station—but the commissioners did not report on Newcastle, since it was not a part of the county.[42]

In Sarum and New Sarum, the fashion was clearly to wear a black or russet gown or cassock with black velvet guards or hoods. The inquest held there turned up a number of offenders, dressed in the same way, whose husbands had no horses. They were referred to the justices of the Exchequer for determination of their guilt.[43]

Down in Cornwall seven women in silks were interviewed, and all were found to have matching horses. For instance, the wife of John Arundell of Longherne had, since August 15, worn "a gown of silk and hath a trotting gelding with armor and furniture for the same."[44]

It appears that the attempt to use women's clothes against their husbands failed to produce many horses, and, despite the official warning that the investigation would be repeated every six months, there was never another one.

The cherished belief about the waste engendered by excess apparel had been tested and found wanting. Maybe it was untrue, or perhaps the commissioners were unwilling to inspect their neighbors' wives' clothing too closely. An alternative theory now gained popularity: landlords had increased the rents and fines on their properties to such an extent that their horse-providing tenants could not afford horses any more. This theory, however, came from the same moral universe in which unvirtuous behavior undermined the state. William Harrison linked abuses in apparel to rising rents—"unreasonable exactions made upon rich farmers and of poor tenants where with to maintain" expensive, vain fashions. The greed of the landlords, Harrison contended, was engrossing the wealth of England into their hands, "leaving the commonality weak or as an idol with broken or feeble arms, which may in a time of peace have a plausible show but when necessity shall enforce have an [sic] heavy and bitter sequel."[45]

[40] TNA E178/2004.   [41] TNA E178/1052.

[42] TNA E178/733 Durham; NA, E178/3058 Northumberland, Newcastle on Tyne.

[43] E. Margaret Thompson, "Some Wiltshire Wives," *Wiltshire Notes and Queries, 1899–1901*, 3 (1902), 323–8.

[44] TNA E 178/512.

[45] William Harrison, *The Description of England: The Classic Contemporary Account of Tudor Social Life*, ed. Georges Edelen (Washington, D.C. and New York: Folger Shakespeare Library and Dover Publications, 1994), 204.

Still certain that it was covetousness that kept men from keeping horses, but no longer sure it was the fault of their wives, the Privy Council was more willing to believe the complaints of tenants who blamed their equine poverty on increasing rents and fines. They could not afford to pay rent and keep horses, too. In a period of high inflation, these adjustments to rents and fines may have been economically necessary, but they became the standard excuse when a muster failed to produce enough horsemen.

In 1579 the council made another attempt to address the shortage of horse soldiers on the Scottish border where the open country of the long border made cavalry essential. Maps in Burghley's possession displayed their attempts to understand the problems there (see Fig. 8.2). The analysis of the cause was familiar—almost traditional. The raising of rents and fines, the depredations of Scots raiders, absentee officeholders and landlords, unfit keepers of castles and forts, the quarrels between the border families, especially the Herrons and Carrs, and the long peace were all given credit for the decay of the defenses. As one analyst put it,

> in this long peace they have rather sought their greatest profit, taking of their tenants great fines for leases. For payment whereof the tenants have sold their horses and furniture. And now such possessioners may not charge their tenants with keeping of horses and furniture as they were wont; neither do the tenants provide so carefully for horses, as for cattle to store their farms thus dearly obtained, to the general decay and want of horse and furniture through the whole Marches.[46]

Lord Hunsdon, Warden of the East Marches, concurred. Fines and great rents made keeping horses impossible; worse, land was being let to Scots, who were not required to keep horses for defense against the Scots, because they paid higher rents to the landlords. Absentees were, he said, a big problem, citing the example of Sir Henry Percy, keeper of Norham Castle who lived in Tynemouth.[47]

The Warden of the Middle Marches, Sir John Forester, informed the Privy Council that, in his opinion, the shortage of horses was primarily the result of the raising of rents and fines. He asked the council to intervene to stop the increases, encouraging the tenants to provide the horses and armor needed. He also noted that many horses were being sold over the border, reducing the supply.[48]

Sir John's muster book bears witness to the problems he was finding. William Lord Eures' tenants at Sturton Grange, summoned to muster against Scottish sheep thieves in 1580, came on foot. Asked why they had no horses, contrary to order, they pointed out that Lord Eures had raised their rents from 40s to £5.[49]

All of these complaints and concerns came together in a brief outlining how a new statute for defense of the border against Scotland could be drawn. Burghley was clearly managing it, and it has his extensive revisions written at its foot.[50] This turned into a draft called "An act for the maintenance of horse and armor upon

---

[46] TNA SP 59/20 fol. 80.   [47] BL Cotton, Caligula, B. VIII. fol. 214.
[48] TNA SP 59/20 fol. 115.   [49] TNA SP 59/20 fol. 121.
[50] TNA SP 59/21 fols 10–13. TNA SP 12/148 fols 87–8 is a set of his notes outlining the content of the bill.

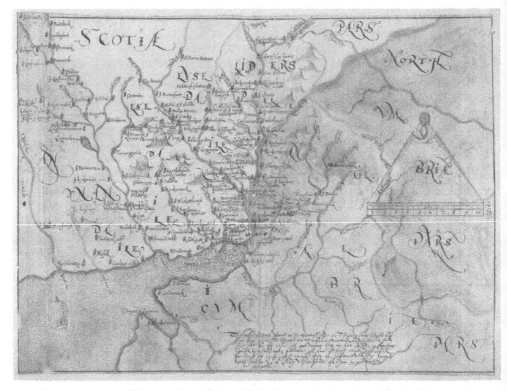

Fig. 8.2. A map of the English and Scottish borders, 1579, Lord Burghley's Atlas, British Library, Royal 18 D. III, fol. 76. © The British Library Board.

the Borders of Scotland." Once again, Burghley's hand is throughout, improving and correcting.[51]

After the bill was introduced into the Lords in 1581, it hit a wall of resistance. It called for a commission to "reform" lords whose rent increases made it impossible for their tenants to provide horses, armor, and munitions. Committed in the Commons, the original Lords' bill was thrown out and a new bill written. The *nova billa* added language that actually sharpened the Act against absentee landlords.

It went further than the Lords liked. By writing a new bill the Commons had broken with procedure. The peers cried foul, claiming the Commons had acted in a way "derogatory to the Superiority of the Place, and contrary to the ancient Course of both Houses."[52]

At the heart of this was the issue of national defense placed against the rights of the border lords. The bill empowered royal commissioners to step between lords and their tenants if the lords were raising rents and fines to such an extent

[51] TNA SP 59/21 fols 1–4.

[52] "House of Lords Journal Volume 2: 8 March 1581," in *Journal of the House of Lords: vol. 2: 1578–1614*, 45–7, ‹http://www.british-history.ac.uk/lords-jrnl/vol2/pp45-47›. Accessed March 15, 2015.

that the tenants could not maintain their horses and armor for defense of the border. Burghley clearly saw this as an Act in the interest of the nation. Those who objected saw it as depriving them of their rights. "It abbridgeth the subjects," said an objector, "of the right they have both by the law of god, nature, and man to dispose of their lands and goods as they think good." It undermined the lords' control of the lesser sort, too, generally encouraging them to believe that every time a rent was raised, an appeal could be made to the Queen. This encouraged people to question their betters and rebel. "The most part of the inferior sort of these parts are bondmen," it was said, "and therefore no cause the Lords should be bridled for their sakes."

In response, supporters of the bill alleged both national interest and legal safeguards. Force on a frontier was a national necessity, and sacrifices had to be made for the public good. Moreover, defending the God-given rights of the lords over their tenants would reduce the farmers to desperation. If the borderers knew what was thought of them they would be incensed, for "by this rule no common people may understand that their complaints ought to be heard." Besides, the commissioners would only act if military preparedness was threatened.

Burghley worked on the details, responding to the objections voiced and the changes made by the Commons. He tried to make it clear that the commissioners would not be arbitrary, that their work would be to investigate before acting, and that their actions could be checked by law. But he insisted on the necessity of national defense taking precedence over local privileges. He was convinced that the border lords were extorting too much from their tenants, although a provision blaming landlords for reducing manpower by converting farms to pasturage did not make it into the Act.[53]

It passed in the end, and commissions were issued to ensure sufficient horsemen on the border.[54] However, by the 1590s the Queen was subsidizing the borderers so they could afford their war horses. They were receiving 12d a day.[55] As it was doing at Berwick, Elizabeth's administration had concluded it could not squeeze enough support from the local inhabitants to cover the cost of securing the northern border.

Horses were a constant problem, and so were weapons. As the military balance shifted away from the longbow, traditional English militias fell behind their continental enemies in weaponry. Without a national army, however, the council had to command and cajole the counties and towns to buy guns and train men in their use. In 1570, for instance, William Cecil drafted an order from the Queen to the deputy lieutenants of Kent, Essex, and Hampshire, commanding them to buy harquebuses and train at least five or six hundred men in their use, apportioning the cost so that everyone paid, not just the people living near the coast where more

---

[53] G. R. Elton, *The Parliament of England, 1559–1581* (Cambridge: Cambridge University Press, 1986), 69 n. 34.

[54] Hartley, vol. 1, 536–7, 539, 542. "House of Lords Journal Volume 2: 8 March 1581," *Journal of the House of Lords: vol. 2: 1578–1614*, <http://www.british-history.ac.uk/lords-jrnl/vol2/pp45-47>. Accessed March 15, 2015. Elton, *Parliament*, 68–9. 23 Eliz. I, c. 4.

[55] CP 53/78.

men were needed. They also warned the deputy lieutenants to prevent the harque-busiers from hunting rabbits with the guns.[56]

As equipment changed, the council tried to improve the arms of the realm's cavalry by specifying the sorts of weapons that were to be provided by the gentlemen of wealth. In August 1586, with the Babington plot unfolding, they wrote to authorities around the country, ordering every justice of the peace of the quorum to provide two horsemen armed with petronells, also known as carbines. Those JPs not of the quorum were to provide one rider with the same arms.[57]

Unable to directly tax and command, the council did what it could to make it easier for local units to be equipped with guns and powder. An indignant letter from the Privy Council to the Lord President of the North complained that York and Hull had never sent anyone to London to collect the powder and matches pro-cured for them by Henry Dale.[58]

Responses to these sorts of orders were typically reluctant. In the north, where the earl of Huntingdon was constantly negotiating downward the number of horsemen he could be expected to raise, the answer was not one the council liked. As Huntingdon told Secretary Walsingham, "as for petronels or carbines, as some call them, many may be raised, but not in that sort as my Lords directed... for many in the commission of the peace are not able to furnish both a light horse and two petronels, and yet for the service of the country as justices of peace, they are men not to be spared."[59] Men too poor to pay for horses and equipment were still needed to govern the country.

In Hertfordshire, the deputy lieutenants insisted they did not understand what the council meant. Were justices who already supplied demi-lances to supply horsemen armed with petronels in addition to lancers? Did the petronel men replace the lan-cers or supplement them? They would not act until their lord-lieutenant, the earl of Leicester, found out more.[60]

These questions from the deputy lieutenants were not idle, since the lancer was being replaced on the continent by armored pistoleers. In France at the Battle of Coutras in 1587, 1,300 men equipped with petronels routed 2,000 heavy lancers.

The nearly constant attempts by the council to ensure a sufficient supply of horses and arms were matched with efforts to supply sufficient ships and mariners for naval defense. The "Act for Politic Constitutions made for the Maintenance of the Navy" of 1563 was designed to encourage investment in fishing and the wine trade, so that there would be sufficient ships and men to be mobilized if a navy was needed. The bill had begun with a motion by Admiral Sir William Winter. The first draft was committed to a committee chaired by Cecil, which produced a new one containing a "political Lent." A proviso in the Act required that fish be eaten every Wednesday, "to be used and kept" as every Saturday in the week ought to be.

---

[56] TNA SP 15/18 fol. 235.

[57] TNA SP 15/29 fol. 210v. This is the letter sent to the Lord President of the North. Similar instructions went to lord-lieutenants and others.

[58] HEH, HM 30881, fol. 21.   [59] TNA SP 15/30 fol. 194.

[60] TNA SP 12/186 fols 148–9.

The uproar this caused among Protestant members who thought they had been freed of papist fish days is well rehearsed elsewhere, but Cecil's logic had nothing to do with penance and everything to do with the need for a strong defense. The decline in shipping caused by wars in the Mediterranean and the Baltic, the decay of the spice trade as the Iberians dominated it from "their Indies," the sharp drop in demand for fish caused by the Reformation, and foreign competition all contributed to the shortage of ships.[61]

The nature of these interventions shows the limits of the tools in the hands of the council. To manage defense, it had to find ways to encourage private individuals and groups to purchase military equipment. Proclamations, acts, and commissions all had their uses. But all of them required vigilance and negotiation.

We can see this at work in the attempts to repair the fortifications at Kingston upon Hull. In a long series of letters between the city and the Privy Council, the two sides fell out over the question of who would pay for repairs. The Privy Council, having received a plea for relief from the cost of repairs, pointed out that Kingston upon Hull had been given land by Edward VI, which was supposed to generate revenue to maintain the forts. They asked for information about how the profit from the land was being employed. As they negotiated back and forth, over several years, the need, the cost, and who should pay hung in the balance. It appears that the aldermen were willing to pay for the repairs if they could pull down part of the fortifications and use the spoil to repair the existing ones. The council, which took expert advice, was not willing to do this, and the conversation, which began in 1576, ran until 1583.[62]

Burghley kept track of these sorts of things in his pocket notebooks. In one for 1592 we can see the military needs of the realm sketched onto his "to do" lists. Notes on the stations of ships, the numbers of men needed, the repairs to ports and forts, were all jumbled in with his other concerns. Sometimes an action is clearly foreshadowed in his notes, such as the March 1592 scrawl: "A proclamation ag. making of any iron ordnance above a minion."[63] By early September this became a proclamation prohibiting the export of iron ordnance of sizes greater than that of a 1,500 pound "minion" canon.[64]

In all of these things, the council was working with military leaders, men who bridged the gap between the political culture of the ruling classes and the distinctive culture of the soldiers. Military leadership in Elizabeth's state was very much about social standing, and so her great admirals and generals were often men of high station: Robert Devereaux, earl of Essex; Robert Dudley, earl of Leicester; Ambrose Dudley, earl of Warwick; Thomas Radcliffe, earl of Sussex; Lord Admiral Edward Fiennes de Clinton, first earl of Lincoln; Lord Admiral Charles Howard, second Baron Howard of Effingham and first earl of Nottingham. But the Elizabethan state had at its core a tension between the aristocratic soldiers and their bureaucratic fellows.

[61] Hartley, *Proceedings*, vol. 1, 103–7.
[62] Helen Good, ed., *Kingston upon Hull Records 1, Letters 1576–1585* (Hull: 1997), 2, 4, 5, 6–7, 8, 10. Transcription of BRL 17, 19, 20, 21, 26, 28, 29.
[63] BL Royal App 67, fol. 12.   [64] H&L, vol. 3, 107–8.

Naunton, in his *Fragmenta regalia*, had sorted Elizabeth's great courtiers into two groups, the *togati* and the *militia*; all served at the Queen's pleasure, but their origins and roles were different. Most of the soldiers in the *militia* were related to Elizabeth by blood, and were of the proper class for military leadership. Earls and younger sons of earls mostly, they were the sort of men Elizabeth, "as she loved martial men," trusted and promoted.[65] Familial links were important to her, and many of her military leaders had their commands because they were of her blood. The exception was Sir Walter Raleigh who, as the earl of Oxford said of him, was a "jack and an upstart."

First among the *togati* was Lord Burghley. He and his fellows had risen by talent and were the managerial heart of government.

At its core, the managerial problem confronting the council when it came to military affairs was, like the rest of its administrative activity, one of judgment and trust. Admirals at sea or generals deployed to Ireland, the north, or the Low Countries were beyond control. The council might bombard them with letters, but most of the time they could not wait for orders. They made decisions on their own.

The value system used to make these decisions was often not the one preferred by virtuous managers like Burghley. Although, or perhaps because, Burghley had seen combat at the Battle of Pinkie Cleugh during the English invasion Scotland in 1547 (and had, it appears, been saved from a canon shot by a comrade who lost his arm thrusting Cecil out of the way of the ball) he distrusted soldiers and did not like war. He famously advised his son Robert not to bring up his sons for the wars because a soldier can "hardly be an honest man or a good Christian."[66]

Burghley and his mistress watched the purse and thought about the ends more than some of their more militant colleagues, whose value systems were not so aligned with the civic humanism that made military glory less important than service to the commonwealth.

The miles gloriosus was a stock figure known to all Elizabethan schoolboys, and it was assumed to be true to life. The egos among Elizabeth's commanders seemed to prove the rule. Leicester and Sussex were mortal enemies, while Essex and Sir John Norris competed for glory in Ireland, the young earl treating the old general as if he was ignorant—"Imberbes docere sense," the "beardless teaching the old," as Naunton observed.[67]

Rory Rapple has spelled out these tensions, noting that Elizabethans commonly expressed their belief that the honor of the martial profession was being neglected. The virtues praised by Sir William Cecil, Sir Thomas Smith, Sir Roger Ascham, and other humanist lights of the state did not include the *sprezzatura* and boldness of a soldier. The chivalric ethos was devalued in the first half of Elizabeth's reign, says Rapple, because foreign policy avoided costly military engagements. Elizabeth, too, contributed to the decline of chivalry because a woman could not be a man. Failing to marry someone who could be the focus of military glory, or seek the

---

[65] Naunton, 84.   [66] Francis Peck, *Desiderata curiosa* (London: 1732), vol. 1, 65.
[67] Naunton, 76.

bubble of reputation in the cannon's mouth, as her father had, Elizabeth's court had little place for men of war.[68]

On the other hand, the Elizabethan military leaders did have a sense of their own virtue, even if it conflicted with that of the civilians. The earl of Essex, for instance, who had been educated in humanist ideals of service at Cambridge, was greatly concerned with his own virtue. He saw himself in the chivalric role of the "perfect Protestant knight," who, like Sir Philip Sidney, his role model, gained glory through self-sacrifice in war. For him, boldness led to honor and profit—a self-conception guaranteed to put him at odds with Burghley.[69]

Shortage of wars in the first half of the reign created little opportunity for the younger sons of the nobility who dominated captaincies. Too much peace meant too little employment, and no chances for the sort of service that brought men the attention and rewards from the Queen. This led many to look for service abroad. Serving other kings was not shameful for those bred in the culture of chivalric military service, and it confused them when Elizabeth demanded that they not serve her enemies. Worse, they were often not committed to the new sectarian divisions among European states. Fighting to ensure religious victory was not high on their agenda; fighting for glory and reward were.

Politically, military officers did not share in the sort of commonwealth values of the *togati*. Instinctually, they were used to command, and that made them more comfortable with absolute authority than with the sort of parliamentary mixed government that Sir Thomas Smith described so lovingly in *De republica Anglorum*. Rapple shows how Sir Humphrey Gilbert, in Parliament in 1571, argued for a constitution that was based upon the monarch's absolute authority. Growing from his experience in Ireland, where captains personified the royal power, he saw anything that undermined it as dangerous. Gilbert was drawing on French arguments and experience too, which taught that a regularly paid standing army was best for ensuring the safety and strength of the Queen.[70]

It appears that such a thing never entered into Burghley's many ruminations on how best to defend Elizabeth. He probably agreed that a standing army would strengthen the Crown, but how could it be paid for? The English system of taxation and militias had a very different fiscal base than the one the French monarchy enjoyed. Moreover, English government depended on the participation of gentlemen; they shared responsibility and cost.

However, he did use the tools available within traditional English governance to pressure the ruling classes into doing their military duty. The expansion of the use of commissions, notable from the very beginning of the reign in the area of military preparedness, continued throughout Burghley's regime. The willingness of at least some men to enforce the Queen's demands on their fellows gave them a chance to rise in the royal service, while it continued undermining regional

[68] Rory Rapple, *Martial Power and Elizabethan Political Culture: Military Men in England and Ireland, 1558–1594* (Cambridge: Cambridge University Press, 2009), 61.

[69] Paul Hammer, *The Polarisation of Elizabethan Politics: The Political Career of Robert Devereux, 2nd Earl of Essex, 1585–1597* (Cambridge: Cambridge University Press, 1999), 399–400.

[70] Rapple, *Martial Power*, 193–9.

exceptionalism based on aristocratic power. A process begun in the reign of Henry VIII, which expanded English-style government into the borders, the Marches, and the Kingdom of Ireland, it was continued by Burghley, though more subtly.

As observed in chapter 7, in Elizabeth's reign central participation in funding for the common defense was expanded. As money was sent to Berwick, Portsmouth, and other places to ensure their maintenance, Burghley and his colleagues were slowly, and perhaps not even consciously, increasing the reach of the Queen in the name of the commonwealth. Undermining local power, finding ways to manage the conflicts between great families, and seeking certainty about the supply of horses, weapons, men, and ships, Burghley was willing to use the existing tools of the state. By the end of the reign, the center was stronger, but there had not been much official change in the system. Burghley and Elizabeth got away with these incremental changes; the Stewart kings, not understanding how to manage within the system, provoked constitutional confrontations.

Keeping the peace and defending the realm in the latter sixteenth century prompted an expansion of royal power that was quiet, hard to see, and welcomed by most of the ruling groups because it helped them in their efforts to carry out their duty. There probably never were enough horses for defense of the border, and the problem disappeared in March 1603, but rule by royal commissions entrusted to the local gentlemen and overseen by the nationally great and important was by then a well-established thing. It gave the Crown more power, it eased the burdens on the magisterial classes, and it empowered them.

These developments were subtle, and they did not amount to a military revolution that prompted the emergence of a modern state. The Elizabethan military system remained firmly fixed in fiscal feudalism. It did not provoke sweeping measures to create a new revenue system to support the wars. Instead, it encouraged what Younger calls "tiny acts of government" that let local officials see themselves as a part of a national system. Since the Queen lacked direct coercive power, the regime could only operate militarily with the support of the magisterial classes, and its military possibilities were limited by their willingness to gather the money and muster the forces. The fact that this system broke down under the Stewart kings indicates that it was conscious acts of management that maintained the Elizabethan system.[71]

[71] Younger, *War and Politics*, 239–41.

9

Managing the Protestant State

That knowledge be had who they are in every country, that have office either
spiritual or temporal, that do not resort to their churches, and who they are
and, though they do resort sometime to their churches, be either condemners
or deriders of the order of religion established by act of parliament.

Lord Burghley's memo on legal reforms, c.1572[1]

In its traditional role as defender of the realm and dispenser of justice, the Crown
did not have an established bureaucratic system for managing religion. In the
traditional worlds of the Exchequer, the Wards, and the central courts, a "course"
was followed that was understood, under the oversight of royal officials who
came together in the Star Chamber and the Privy Council on a regular basis. In
this world, Lord Burghley was the pole star of administration. But the Elizabethan church had a different orbit, retaining a medieval structure that was apart
from the state except for its dependence on the Queen. This left the church
leaders and Burghley in an uneasy position. They had influence but not full control. Elizabeth, sure of her divine prerogative, was always capable of disrupting
their intentions.

Burghley's job, when it came to religion, was to ensure conformity and safety for
the Queen's church. He could not, however, perform the usual dance of favor and
influence that kept the localities working with him. His tools in religion were
much more heavy-handed, and he had difficulty in responding to the local needs
and preferences. The Queen's desire for conformity ignored local conditions and
preferences, creating tensions that the bishops and the council struggled to abate.

Daniel Nexon, writing about the continental Reformation, observed that the
Reformation caused terrible stresses in the composite states of early modern Europe
by giving a new ideological dimension to political disputes that were already hard
to resolve. Burghley and Elizabeth clearly recognized this, and their efforts concerning religion were often designed to blunt and defeat these religious tensions
that might make governing impossible.[2]

Elizabeth had two managerial goals when it came to religion. The first was to
please God. The second was to keep the religious peace. It was assumed that
pleasing God would have a positive outcome; displeasing Him would not. God

---

[1] BL Lansd. 104/fol. 27v.
[2] Daniel H. Nexon, *The Struggle for Power in Early Modern Europe: Religious Conflict, Dynastic Empires, and International Change* (Princeton: Princeton University Press, 2009), 6.

was best pleased when He was worshiped properly, and it was the job of the church, under the management of the Queen, to see that this was done. At the same time, enemies of the church had to be prevented from disrupting the proper worship of God and obedience to His anointed handmaiden Elizabeth.

The church had been amalgamated with the state in the reign of Edward VI, when it was decided to create "common" worship and national religious uniformity under the royal supremacy. Using the English tongue, the Edwardian council sought to edify England and reduce it to God's true worship. The Elizabethan leaders, who had experienced Edward's reign, remembered the Protestant squabbles over the Book of Common Prayer, with its 1549 and 1552 versions, and how that Reformation failed. Marian restoration of Catholic worship and papal obedience, they were sure, was a sign of God's displeasure. After four forms of worship in twelve years, the Elizabethan settlement returned the church in England to the Edwardian status quo ante of 1552, rejecting the Pope once again, and again placing the church's property under royal control. Going through all this, they had learned a few lessons about the power of ideology and how it could turn against the state.

As Principal Secretary in 1559, William Cecil confronted two managerial problems. One was the actual shape and function of the Elizabethan church. Henry and Edward had kept the episcopal structure of the church, and the canon law, in so far as it was not "repugnant" to the authority of the monarch. Cecil had to integrate this structure with the Queen's government. The other problem was keeping theological conflict from destroying the nation, while ensuring the victory of the Protestantism embodied in Elizabeth. He had a secular role in protecting the ecclesiastical structure.

Because the church had a quasi-autonomous status, managing it was really about influencing the appointments of bishops and archbishops. Unlike the secular aristocrats, who were often born to their places, churchmen could be selected for their talents and their ideological positions. Reporting to Elizabeth, the Supreme Governor of the Church in England, the bishops were a distinct tool of government, required to please God and the Queen, while playing roles as magistrates within their dioceses.

The bishops, however, did not always agree that Elizabeth was their governor. They inherited 1,500 years of episcopal authority, believing they were charged with managing the spiritual lives of their flocks. The separation of church and state that had caused so much heartburn in the later Middle Ages still underpinned many bishops' self-conception.

Elizabeth, on the other hand, believed that obeying God meant obeying her. She saw herself as the *auxilia domini*, the handmaiden of the Lord. Thinking her primary duty was to secure domestic peace, religious order, and proper worship, she required her subjects to recognize her total responsibility to God for her church. If they honored God, they had to honor the Queen.

The Elizabethan settlement of religion, enacted in 1559, created the church and defined its relationship to the Queen. I argue elsewhere that the recreation of a Protestant settlement in England was easier because Elizabeth accepted the

Edwardian settlement of religion as valid.[3] Accordingly, before Parliament met in late January 1559 a committee met to revise the 1552 Book of Common Prayer. Samples of the new book were assembled, mostly from sheets printed in 1552, signed by the Privy Council, and made available as a template.[4]

Despite resistance from the Catholic bishops in the Lords, the Edwardian settlement was revived, with small changes. The slightly revised Book of Common Prayer of 1552 was reimposed on the nation, the Queen was recognized as Supreme Governor of the Church in England (a concession to many factions who resisted the idea of a female "head" of a church), and its traditional structures were maintained. From the very beginning, it was clear that Cecil was managing the process, even though it did not go smoothly.

The 1559 legislation greatly increased the Queen's authority over her church. An Act was passed granting to her the right to appropriate temporal property in vacant episcopal sees, swapping temporal for spiritual goods in the form of tenths and impropriated parsonages.[5] This was most likely part of a plan to reduce the pomp and wealth of the bishops. Cecil, a good Protestant Commonwealth man, believed episcopal wealth would be better used for enriching the Crown, maintaining ministers, and educating youth. Over the years, this would prove to be a great aggravation to the bishops, since it made it very difficult for them to get full access to the assets of their bishoprics.[6] Moreover, although they lost wealth, they did not see a reduction in their duties and expenses.

Another Act returned to her the clerical tax of first fruits and tenths. This old tax consisted of the first year's income of a benefice, plus 10 percent of its value annually. Collected by the bishops, it was paid into the Exchequer. As we have seen in chapter 7, this was both a burden on the bishops and a lucrative source of income to the Queen. When added to the clerical subsidies, these church taxes benefited Elizabeth a great deal, and gave her a separate power over the bishops.

Most importantly, the 1559 Parliament created the Ecclesiastical High Commission, a mixed oversight body for the Queen's church. It allowed the Queen to appoint by letters patent a group of people empowered

> to visit, reform, redress, order, correct and amend all such Errors, Heresies, Schisms, Abuses, Offences, Contempts and Enormities whatsoever, which by any Manner of Spiritual or Ecclesiastical Power, Authority or Jurisdiction, can or may lawfully be reformed, ordered, redressed, corrected, restrained or amended, to the Pleasure of

---

[3] N. L. Jones, *Faith by Statute: Parliament and the Settlement of Religion, 1559* (London: Royal Historical Society, 1982).

[4] My thanks to Cyndia Susan Clegg for allowing me to see the manuscript of her article "The 1559 Books of Common Prayer and the Elizabethan Reformation," forthcoming in *The Journal of Ecclesiastical History*, in which she demonstrates the existence of this pre-Parliamentary copy of the 1559 Book of Common Prayer. Her discovery ends the speculation about Elizabeth's supposedly conservative religious values.

[5] 1 Eliz. I, c. 19.

[6] Jones, *Faith by Statute*, 165–6. Felicity Heal, "The Bishops and the Act of Exchange of 1559," *Historical Journal*, 19 (1974), 233–4. N. L. Jones, "Profiting from Religious Reform: The Land Rush of 1559," *Historical Journal*, 22, 1 (1979), 279–94.

Almighty God, the Increase of Virtue, and the Conservation of the Peace and Unity of this Realm…[7]

This undefined group had authority over "all Manner of Jurisdictions, Privileges and Preeminences, in any wise touching or concerning any Spiritual or Ecclesiastical Jurisdiction, within these your Realms of *England* and *Ireland*."

Based on earlier models of ad hoc commissions, issued by letters patent, this new high commission was an evolving form.[8] At first, commissions were issued for particular causes, but, beginning about 1565, the Ecclesiastical High Commission began to change into a standing court of law. In the beginning it acted like a common law court, using trial by twelve jurors in its cases, but by about 1580 it had become a canon law court, and dropped common law pleading procedures. Instead, it used the oath *ex officio mero*, to the horror of common law judges. Nonetheless, there was no question that it was a parliamentary creation under the Queen's control.[9]

Because the ecclesiastical commissions were royal appointments, William Cecil, Lord Burghley had a great deal of influence over who served on them, even though he could not directly control them. As Archbishop Parker told him, when suggesting members for a new commission, "ye may allow of these or of any other whom your wisdom shall think meet either to remove or to add."[10]

Managing the church was something that Burghley found difficult because the Queen took a personal interest in its affairs, jealous of her prerogative over it. Moreover, its archbishops could be hard to control and were often at odds with Elizabeth or with Burghley and powerful in their own right. Archbishop Parker had depended upon Burghley's help; Archbishop Whitgift was stronger because of his personal relationship with the Queen.

In the most unsettled period of the Elizabethan settlement, the 1560s, Cecil, the bishops, and the Queen explored the possibilities and limitations of the new state church, badgered by religious enthusiasts from all sides, demanding and resisting changes, all claiming to know what God wanted. The Supreme Governor and her servants did not easily find a modus vivendi. They disagreed about church discipline, who had the authority to interpret ecclesiastical law, and who should enforce it.[11]

Having been brought within the statutory system, the church leaders expected the Crown to support them, and sometimes it did. The Act for enforcing of the writ *de excommunicato capiendo*, 5 Eliz. 1, c. 23, lent secular strength to punishment of excommunicated persons. It required the sheriffs to return the writs against excommunicates to the Chancery, giving the church courts the support of the secular arm, because the Queen's subjects "are grown into such license and con-

---

[7] 1 Elizabeth I, c. 1.19.   [8] Cal. Pat. Rolls, Ed. VI, III. 347.

[9] Roland G. Usher, *The Rise and Fall of the High Commission* (Oxford: Oxford University Press, 1913), 149–57. Coke makes it clear that the Queen could not alter religious law using the commission, and that they could not invent new heresies. Edward Coke, *The Twelfth Part of the Reports of Sir Edward Coke* (1656), 19–28. Wing/958:13.

[10] *Parker Correspondence*, 369.

[11] Norman Jones, *The Birth of the Elizabethan Age* (Oxford: Blackwell, 1989), 17–47.

tempt of the laws ecclesiastical...that unless it were for fear of the temporal sword and power they would altogether despise and neglect the same...[which are] often times slowly and negligently executed."[12]

In the same Parliament, laws were proposed requiring episcopal officers to have university degrees, and attempts were made to improve the income of the clergy. One, giving the bishops the right to amalgamate small livings, was defeated. It was replaced by a bill for the augmentation of livings too small to support an incumbent minister. This bill was drafted by William Cecil, and, had it passed, it would have granted the Chancery the power to help poorer ministers, taking it away from the bishops. No one in Parliament was anxious to give the episcopate more power over property.[13]

The bishops' duty to God was colliding with the Queen's belief in her authority over the church. Clashes continued throughout the reign as the bishops, caught between their duty, Protestant enthusiasts, and the Queen's prerogative, were battered from all sides. This battle created managerial problems. The bishops could not be dismissed or ignored, so the Queen had to work with them without seeming to remove their authority. This is where Cecil came in. He had friends, clients, and savvy magnified by his connection to the Queen, making him the broker between the bishops and their Supreme Governor. He could play the mediator.

We can watch this at work in the letters exchanged by Archbishop Matthew Parker and Cecil in the 1560s and 1570s. Theirs was an old friendship, stretching back to their youth in Cambridge. Parker once described Cecil as "of long time my special good friend and master," and it is clear that they had known each other since the time Sir John Cheke had been their friend and tutor at Cambridge.

Archbishop Parker and his fellows were dependent upon Cecil and Bacon for their appointments, and they used this patron/client relationship to get them to influence the Queen. We see Parker's reliance upon Cecil in numerous letters in which he vents his frustrations. In 1563 we find him writing to Cecil, "I cannot be quiet till I have disclosed to you, as to one of my best willing friends, in secrecy, mine imperfection, which grieveth me not so much to utter in respect of mine own rebuke, as it grieveth me that I am not able to answer your friendly report of me."[14]

All of this becomes important when we remember how Elizabeth related to Parker and his fellow bishops. She depended upon the terror of her office to keep them obedient to her supremacy. The bishops knew that the Reformation, their jobs, even their lives, depended upon the success of the Elizabethan settlement, and they were born into a society that held the majesty of monarchy in great awe.

But as ministers of the church, they also held that the Queen was their spiritual child, and they were heirs of a very long history of ecclesiastical independence from secular rule. Putting all this together could produce moments like Archbishop Grindal's famous rebuke of the Queen that got him suspended from office. Therefore, Elizabeth and her bishops sparred over their conflicting roles.

---

[12] Corpus Christi College, Cambridge, Ms. 121, 280.
[13] Jones, *Faith by Statute*, 178–80.   [14] *Parker Correspondence*, 199–201.

In the 1560s this relationship was tested in a series of moves made by the bishops and rescinded by the Queen. Startling scenes of her anger sent them running to Cecil for solace and help. When, in 1561, Elizabeth declared that she would not tolerate clerical wives in colleges and cathedral closes, Parker, a married man, was horrified. The Queen, he told Cecil, "expressed to me a repentance that we were thus appointed in office, wishing it had been otherwise." He was "in horror to hear such words to come from her mild nature and Christianly learned conscience." Convinced that the Devil must be at work, he turned to Cecil for help. To him he felt he could pour out his anguish—he even wished he could die, "in amaritudine animae meae [in the bitterness of my soul]." But he also felt he could tell Cecil that the clergy were duty-bound to serve their consciences, commenting, "I would be sorry that the clergy should have cause to shew disobedience, with *oportet Deo obedire magis quam hominibus* [it behooves one to obey God more than men]."[15] It is striking that he could talk to Cecil this way, and he clearly expected that his prayers for God to change Elizabeth's heart were more effective if they reached the ears of the Principal Secretary. Cecil, he knew, had influence with God's handmaiden.

The bishops' belief in their right to discipline the church was disabused as they learned that, in the Queen's eyes, they did not have the power to enact a new church discipline. The 1563 convocation, led by Archbishop Parker and acting out of duty, had prepared a slate of further reforms, a set of articles of faith, and a renewed commission to reform the canon law. Episcopal working parties had drafted various documents on discipline that were turned into bills for parliamentary ratification but, when they were introduced in Parliament, they were stopped by royal wrath.[16] The attempt to have the measures passed in the 1566 Parliament met with the same fate. A petition from the bishops to the Queen, begging her to allow the bills to proceed in parliament, stressed that they advanced the cause of Almighty God and identified "divers and sundry errors...such as have been in this realm wickedly and obstinately by the adversaries of the Gospel defended." The passage of these Articles of Religion, they said, would allow her to reduce all her subjects to unity in religion. It was signed by all the bishops.[17]

Elizabeth was not impressed. Ignoring the issue of ecclesiastical discipline, she demanded to know why Parker and his brethren had introduced the bills without her permission, against her express order. The archbishop denied it to the Queen and immediately wrote Cecil, commenting that "Your presence with the Queen's Majesty wanteth; whereby her Highness may be the more disquieted with informations," reflecting the importance of the Court's oral culture.[18] In the speech from the throne at the closing of Parliament, the Lord Keeper, speaking in the Queen's name, announced the Queen's goals: to ensure that God was truly wor-

---

[15] *Parker Correspondence*, 156–60.
[16] David J. Crankshaw, "Preparations for the Canterbury Provincial Convocation of 1562–63: A Question of Attribution," in Susan Wabuda and Caroline Litzenberger, eds, *Belief and Practice in Reformation England* (Aldershot: Ashgate, 1998), 60–93. Norman Jones, "An Elizabethan Bill for the Reformation of the Ecclesiastical Law," *Parliamentary History*, 4 (1985), 171–87.
[17] *Parker Correspondence*, 293–4.   [18] *Parker Correspondence*, 291.

shiped, to see that her subjects "do no injury one to another, and specially to make quietness among the ministers of the church."[19]

As an alternative to the suspended legislation, Archbishop Parker and his colleagues drew up "advertisements" on church discipline and asked Cecil to seek the Queen's approval. She did not give it, and the bishops were forced to issue them under their own authority. As they began to enforce conformity, the bishops started a rift in their church that might not have occurred if their authority had been more certain. The Vestiarian controversy, breaking out in London, Oxford, and Cambridge, convinced some Protestants that the bishops were the enemy. Meanwhile Cecil tried to use his authority to stop the trouble where he could, forcing William Fulke, Master of St John's College, Cambridge to apologize for his support of the students who protested against "popish trumpery."[20]

Peace and conformity in the church continued to be Elizabeth's goal. When Parker died in 1575 he was replaced by Edmund Grindal, promoted from the archbishopric of York to be Primate of All England at Canterbury. Burghley, who had been his patron throughout his career and who would be an executor of his will, was behind his promotion, but it seems Elizabeth was not so certain that he was the right choice. He was unmarried, which she liked, but would he stick to the via media that kept the peace? In a letter telling Grindal of his impending election, Burghley waxed voluble about the need for a middle ground between ecclesiastical administration and precisian resistance. "I wish," he told the future archbishop, "there was more caution and circumspection in all their canonical jurisdictions and consistories, that the exercise thereof might be directly *ad edificationem* [for improvment], and not to make gain of that which was meant to punish or prevent sin."[21]

Grindal, however, was soon caught between loyalty and duty. The Queen, agreeing with the recently deceased Parker, saw the popular clerical gatherings known as prophesyings as a threat to good order. When, in 1576, a report of troublesome prophesyings in Northamptonshire and Warwickshire reached the Queen, Burghley and Leicester both tried to warn Grindal of her concerns, but he did not listen carefully. Even when ordered to suppress the meetings by the Queen herself, he demurred. Instead, he wrote her a "schoolmasterly reproof" defending the gatherings and asserting that he could not in good conscience suppress them. "Bear with me," he wrote, "if I choose rather to offend your earthly Majesty than to offend the heavenly majesty of God."[22] "Remember Madam," he lectured, "that you are a mortal creature," who must appear before the divine tribunal. In the bowels of Christ, he besought her to put God's majesty before her eyes when dealing in religious matters.[23]

She did not bear with him. Leicester delivered his letter, and for the next five months the Queen's anger mounted. Burghley told Grindal to stay away from the

---

[19] Hartley, vol. 1, 169.   [20] Jones, *Birth of the Elizabethan Age*, 55–60.
[21] Quoted in Patrick Collinson, *Archbishop Grindal, 1519–1583: The Struggle for a Reformed Church* (Berkeley: UCLA Press, 1979), 223.
[22] Collinson, *Archbishop Grindal*, 233–42.
[23] William Nicholson, ed., *The Remains of Edmund Grindal* (Cambridge, 1843), 389.

court, pleading sickness if necessary. Elizabeth sequestered Grindal in Lambeth Palace in May 1576, suppressing the prophesyings by a royal order directed to the bishops.

Elizabeth was so furious, she wanted Grindal removed. Burghley, Leicester, Bacon, and other men of influence attempted to protect him, but now the Queen turned it on them. She had been crossed in her policy and she would not let her servants undermine her position.

Sir Thomas Wilson informed Burghley that Elizabeth disliked his dealing with Grindal, "whom she would have deprived for his contempt committed." Burghley, suffering from her displeasure, could not work his usual trick of being the Queen's reasonable voice, since Grindal was not interested in being reasonable. Burghley wrote him a long letter in which he tried to demonstrate to Grindal how to approach the Queen for forgiveness without necessarily admitting she was correct. The archbishop was instructed to use "good speeches of her majesty as a prince that in all her public doings hath shown her wisdom, in doing nothing without good cause."[24] He invited him to set down his answer to the Queen in writing so that Burghley could correct it, but Grindal refused to follow his advice. To make matters worse, Leicester had disgraced himself by marrying, so he, too, had lost the Queen's favor and could not help Grindal. With or without his friends' support, Grindal could not escape the consequences of thwarting the Queen's policy.[25] Although he was never deprived of his office, he died in disfavor.

Elizabeth firmly believed that God made her sovereign, and that He required her to keep the peace in the church, suppressing any who would challenge her God-given authority. At the same time, she demonstrated the limits of the moderating influence of important courtiers. Neither Burghley nor Leicester, working behind the scenes, could deliver Grindal's obedience. Nor, therefore, could they protect him from the Queen's consistent strategy of requiring ecclesiastical obedience. At the same time, the crisis made the difficulty in managing the church as an arm of government manifest. The council could not command the bishops, but the Queen could. A close political relationship existed between Elizabeth and her established church, and she guarded it jealously.

Grindal was in trouble because he was tolerating exercises that were associated with religious insubordination, while being insubordinate himself. To Elizabeth, the threat from people who saw ecclesiastical authority arising from below was just as great as the threat from people who thought it resided in Rome. The early Elizabethan church contained many clergy who had more Genevan ideas of ecclesiology than their Queen liked. To give the laity power in the church was to undermine the authority that God had given his handmaiden and her bishops. Consequently, Elizabeth was not tolerant of Protestants who did not promote her church. They were a threat to the peace of the realm, not unlike the dissidents in Scotland who embraced Presbyterianism and ran their Queen out of the country.

[24] BL Lansd. 103, fols 14–15v.   [25] Collinson, *Archbishop Grindal*, 249–77.

Elizabeth's old-fashioned Protestantism was primarily about her place in God's plan; it was only secondarily about theology. Conformity was her watchword.[26]

In a speech to her bishops in 1585, Elizabeth used her chief weapon, rhetoric, to demand compliance from men who had great independence. Upbraiding them for permitting ministers to preach whatever they wanted and to minister the sacraments "according to their own fancies...to the breach of unity," she demanded that they be brought to "conformity and unity." "And we require you," she went on, "that you do not favor such men being carried away with pity, hoping of their conformity and inclining to noblemen's letters and gentlemen's letters; for they will be hanged before they will be reformed." She knew, she said, that some of her Protestant subjects "of late have said that I was of no religion, neither hot [nor] cold, but such a one as one day would give God the vomit."[27] These Protestants were to be treated as strictly as papists because they were enemies of the realm and the state of religion. Private conventicles, she pronounced, were destroying good order.

In place of erring sermons and servants with too much learning, Elizabeth recommended the reading of the Book of Homilies. Her bishops were clearly perturbed by this, since one sign of a properly reformed church was learned preaching, but they protested a shortage of educated men instead. When the Archbishop of Canterbury pointed out that there were 13,000 parishes in England and little hope of finding learned preachers for them all, Elizabeth was shocked. "Jesus!" she blasphemed, "thirteen thousand! It is not to be looked for. I think the time hath been there hath not been four preachers in a diocese. My meaning is not you should make choice of learned ministers only, for they are not to be found, but of honest, sober, and wise men, and such as can read the Scriptures and Homilies well unto the people."[28] As usual, she attacked and then moderated her attack, one of her managerial tricks.

Unity of doctrine and orderly service were clearly her political goals, and she was willing to sacrifice some religious ideals to get them. If maintaining unity and concord required silencing preachers or reading homilies, she was willing to take those steps. To those of her subjects who advanced God's cause above that of God's handmaid, she offered only gall and wormwood. Her purpose is summed up in another of her prayers:

> Father most high...who hast appointed me as monarch of the British kingdom, favor me by Thy goodness to implant piety and root out impiety, to protect freely willed religion, to destroy superstitious fear by working freely to promote divine service, and to spy out the worship of false idols; and further, to gain release from the enemies of religion as well as those who hate me—Antichrists, Pope lovers, atheists, *and all persons who fail to obey Thee and me.*[29]

---

[26] Peter Iver Kaufman, *Thinking of the Laity in Late Tudor England* (South Bend: University of Notre Dame Press, 2004), 103–38.

[27] Leah Marcus, Janet Mueller, and Mary Beth Rose, eds, *Elizabeth I: Collected Works* (Chicago: University of Chicago Press, 2000), 179. Elizabeth was paraphrasing Revelation 3:16, in which the Laodiceans are told that because they are neither hot nor cold, God will spew them out. Clearly, her contemporaries were applying the verse to her.

[28] *Elizabeth I: Collected Works*, 178–81.   [29] *Elizabeth I: Collected Works*, 163, emphasis added.

Elizabeth's government was clearly charged with controlling persons who failed to obey her. At the top of that list were bishops who wavered in doing their duty to the Queen. Cecil was the man Elizabeth expected to prevent their disobedience. Brett Usher's study of William Cecil and the episcopacy suggests that Cecil, though not in the beginning a supporter of prelacy, had, by the summer of 1562, "become the Church's One Foundation, its bulwark against pressures political, economic, and...doctrinal." "Henceforth," says Usher, Cecil's was "a voice of soothing moderation."[30]

I am not so sure that Cecil had been as opposed to bishops as Usher believes, but it is clear that he did see himself as a defender of the church's peace and prosperity, even though that sometimes led to conflict with the Queen, the bishops, or both. He was acting on lessons learned in the 1540s and 1550s, when he was deeply involved in the Edwardian religious reforms.

Having watched how the religious certainty of Edwardian religious legislation had been displaced by the religious certainty of Marian religious legislation, and undoubtedly scarred by his own Nicodemism, he was more comfortable with keeping the peace than asserting the truth. Therefore, no Elizabethan legislation contains the sort of arrogant theological certainty that underlay Edwardian and Marian reforms. This changed the relation between the Crown and God under Elizabeth. In neither the Elizabethan Act of Uniformity nor the Act of Supremacy nor the Act for Restitution of First Fruits is there any theological discussion. Instead, they are about restoring "good old laws" in order to suppress foreign usurpation and taxation. Returning to the status quo ante did not require theological assertions of the sort both Edwardian and Marian leaders felt it was necessary to provide. For Elizabeth, breaking with the Pope did not require denunciation of the Pope; it only required rectification of a legal mistake.

When Cecil became Principal Secretary to Elizabeth, and the chief draftsman of proclamations and legislation, raison d'état became the dominant theme, even when God's law was clear. We can see Cecil's administrative goals here. He was very afraid of the dissension religious disagreement could bring to the state. Elizabeth, and Cecil, had concluded that a state church that required conformity without defining belief would allow her to rule as God wanted her to rule.

Some of this grew from their sense of God's providence in giving the crown to Elizabeth. The deaths of Queen Mary and Cardinal Pole on November 17, 1558 was clear proof of divine intervention. Elizabeth was sent by God to give England another chance at true religion. As Steven Alford has observed, Cecil became heavily providential in his understanding of the dangers facing Elizabeth's regime.[31] The nation, he believed, could avoid God's just punishment by political actions that carried out God's mandate.

The ensuing Elizabethan settlement of religion is hard to place theologically. Although it revived Edwardian religion, with some small amendments, the

[30] Brett Usher, *William Cecil and Episcopacy, 1559–1577* (Aldershot: Ashgate, 2003), 98.
[31] Steven Alford, *The Early Elizabethan Polity: William Cecil and the British Succession Crisis, 1558–1569* (Cambridge: Cambridge University Press, 1998), 26–8.

theological sympathies of the Queen were not displayed in it. A letter, written by a Dane in late February 1559 about the events in Parliament, suggests that Elizabeth was interested in the Lutheran style of reformation, a style that Cecil also admired, but that she was steering carefully past the Augsburg Confession.[32] Susan Doran believes Elizabeth was theologically Lutheran, and John Schofield has argued that Elizabeth was a Melanchthonian—attracted to the broad church position despised by more radical Protestants.[33]

It is reasonable to suspect that Cecil, too, was attracted to that sort of Protestantism, as moderated by Peter Martyr. A Lutheran—or prayer book—style fitted Cecil's and his queen's upbringing, and Cecil was clearly not a Calvinist of the John Knox sort. He undoubtedly agreed with Archbishop-elect Parker, who said to him: "God keep us from such visitation as Knox have attempted in Scotland; the people to be orderers of things."[34] Indeed, his emphasis on obedience was much closer to Lutheranism, with its Augustinian understanding of grace, than to Calvinism.[35]

This attraction to Lutheranism might explain the birth of the Ecclesiastical High Commission, too. In Lutheran states like Denmark, Sweden, and the German principalities, hybrid systems extended the authority of the secular ruler through superintendents, lay and ecclesiastical appointees who conducted ecclesiastical visitations of their appointed regions. In Württemberg, this took final form in 1559 in the Great Church Ordinance, which created a national system for oversight of the church that derived from the power of the Duke Christopher. In the Württemberg case, the duke was enforcing his ordinances of 1553, an equivalent to the Act of Uniformity. His Great Church Ordinance, drafted by his chancellery, put local superintendents in where bishops had once been; in England there were still bishops. What might have attracted Elizabeth and Cecil was the General Superintendents, a national oversight body much like the Ecclesiastical High Commission. The General Superintendents were there to restore peace and quiet by remedying contentions.[36]

---

[32] Simon Adams and David Scott Gehring, "Elizabeth I's Former Tutor Reports on the Parliament of 1559: Johannes Spithovius to the Chancellor of Denmark, 27 February 1559," *English Historical Review*, 128, 530 (2013), 35–54.

[33] Susan Doran, "Elizabeth I's Religion: The Evidence of Her Letters," *Journal of Ecclesiastical History*, 51 (2000), 712–13. John Schofield, *Philip Melanchthon and the English Reformation* (Aldershot: Ashgate, 2006), 182–204.

[34] *Parker Correspondence*, 105.

[35] Steven Alford has classified Cecil as "moderately Calvinist," but the evidence he uses to reach that conclusion is thin. Because Cecil believed in the need for a common front against the papacy, he did not seem to parse his Protestant theology strictly. If we ask if he accepted double predestination, I think the answer is no, and we cannot count him with the Calvinists. He could not have been sympathetic to Calvinist conceptions of empowered congregations, and he certainly was not sympathetic to their political forms. I side with Patrick Collinson's reading of the religion of Cecil and his peers, when he says they were not sympathetic to Calvinist predestinarian theology. I do agree it is impossible to believe that Cecil did not know what Calvinism was about until 1595. Alford, *The Early Elizabethan Polity*, 25–6. Patrick Collinson, "Sir Nicholas Bacon and the Elizabethan *via media*," *Historical Journal*, 30 (1979), 255–73. There were only two religious books in Burghley's office at his death, Peter Martyr's *Commonplaces* and an English Bible. TNA SP 12/268 fol. 65.

[36] James Martin, ed., *Godly Magistrates and Church Order: Johannes Brenz and the Establishment of the Lutheran Territorial Church in Germany, 1524–1559*, Renaissance and Reformation Texts in Translation, no. 9 (Toronto: Victoria University Press, 2001), 11, 192.

The lessons about the political dangers of religion from the 1550s for rulers everywhere were obvious, whether in Württemberg, Rome where the Inquisition was introduced, or in England. Those lessons were sharpened by outbreaks of civil wars over religion in France, the Low Countries, and Scotland in the early 1560s.

To Cecil, it was obvious that good laws and severe enforcement were essential to the health of the church. It must have been frustrating that Elizabeth was so unwilling to press her subjects on their religious discipline, even preventing the administration of the oath of supremacy, the one secular tool he had, to most people.[37] Not wanting to use what power she had, the Queen's reluctance to provide more law for the church made it hard to defend the religious settlement. Cecil blamed this laxness for the crisis in 1569, the Northern Rebellion.

In the spring of 1569 he drafted, as we have seen before, "A necessary consideration of the perilous state of this time." His propositions were two. First, that all nations who accept the authority of the Bishop of Rome feel it is their duty, in conscience, to persecute "with all violence" the recusants in their midst. It follows that the same states that persecute their recusant Protestant citizens will also attack Protestant states.[38] Second, England, as the greatest Protestant state, was their natural target. What made England so galling to papists was the form of its religious settlement. He noted:

> no country is as established by laws in good policy, to remain in freedom from the tyranny of Rome, and in constancy and conformity of true doctrine, as England is, wherein no person of any state is by law admitted to profess openly the contrary without some punishment provided for the same, by good order of laws, and such like [straight?] policy to all purposes is not found in Christendom.[39]

"And herein the first and principal mean to prevent these perils with the assistance of Her Majesty," he says, must "altogether use the speedy force of her own assured good subjects," by boosting their readiness

> to avoid and shift out of the borders of this whole land the miserable spectacle and captivity of slaughter, murder, spoils, rapes, burnings, drowning, sieges, prosecuting and sudden death, of which the sounds only and reports as they daily now do come from all foreign parts in France, Flanders, Spain and their appendants do bring sufficient terror to all wise and sensible persons…

Later, he expatiated on the threats facing England. Because the Queen was unmarried and childless, the nation had no foreign allies. Therefore, he proposed that England ally with all those who had a quarrel with the supporters of the tyranny of Rome. And he meant *all* of those for, as he said, this should be done without "daintiness"—meaning without theological scruples—as a defensive league.

Internally, the line of defense available to him was the earnest execution of the laws and ordinances concerning religion. England had, he said, "enjoyed, by God's goodness, a certain singular privilege of peace, when no other had it; so ought

---

[37] Leslie Ward, "The Treason Act of 1563: A Study of the Enforcement of Anti-Catholic Legislation," in Norman Jones and David Dean, eds, *Interest Groups and Legislation in Elizabethan Parliaments: Essays Presented to Sir Geoffrey Elton. Parliamentary History*, 8, 2 (1989), 289–308.
[38] TNA SP 12/51/fols 9–13.   [39] TNA SP 12/51/fol. 9v.

men to fear, for the displeasure of Almighty God against the abundance of sin and irreligion," that God would send civil and foreign war as a chastisement. Of course, besides God's just displeasure, there were many other practical reasons to be afraid that rebellion on behalf of Mary, Queen of Scots or foreign invasion might happen, and he lays them out, with remedies. But ultimately, he returns to pleasing God by enforcing the law as the first defense against condign punishment.[40]

Enforcement was, of course, the one tool the secular state had to defend the church. It could not depend on the clergy, for there was no secular, central way of controlling them, as the godly frequently pointed out. Ministers, ordained by bishops and appointed by owners of impropriated livings for their lifetimes, were not good tools of statecraft. Livings and advowsons were a form of property, and they could be defended as property in common law, making it nearly impossible for either the bishop or the Crown to remove a man from his living, or take a church away from the person or institution that owned the right of presentation.[41]

Practically, this meant that the best the council could do was to remove religious foes from positions of influence. In 1569 the Inns of Court were ordered either to make their benchers attend church or expel them. All of the justices of the peace were ordered to take the oath of supremacy, forcing them to declare their allegiance to the Queen. The laws concerning religion were to be systematically enforced, really for the first time since Elizabeth assented to them. After all, enforcing conformity required judges who accepted the Queen's supremacy.

In this "Short Memorial" we can see a defensive position emerging. Fearing God's punishment, the law must be enforced. Fearing the papal tyranny, alliances must be made with all who resist the Pope, even if they are not good theological matches. The outbreak of the Northern Rebellion, Elizabeth's excommunication by the Pope, and Philip II's endorsement of the "enterprise of England" confirmed his beliefs. The state was the bulwark against all that Cecil feared.

By 1573 he was clearly adumbrating this position as a policy. Addressing the justices in a speech that survives in his own hand, Burghley spoke of ministers who were young in years, and over-young in learning and discretion. These ignorant youths were, contrary to the "public order established by law," altering the forms of service and enticing their congregations into error. Their crime was

> condemning the whole government of the Church and order ecclesiastical, and in moving her Majesty's good subjects to think it a burden of conscience to observe the orders and rites of the church established by law; a matter so pernicious to the state government, that her Majesty cannot, for the charge committed to her by almighty God, but by speedy good means procure the stay of the dangers that must needs follow.[42]

---

[40] "A Short Memoryall of the State of the Realme," in Samuel Haynes and William Murdin, *A Collection of State Papers, Relating to Affairs in the Reigns of King Henry VIII, King Edward VI, Queen Mary, and Queen Elizabeth, Transcribed from Original letters and Other Authentick Memorials, Left by William Cecill Lord Burghley*, vol. 1, *1542–1570* (London: 1740) #606, pp. 579–88. TNA SP 12/51 fols 9–14. A short version of the "Perils" was copied and published by John Strype, who says the one he copied had been sent to the duke of Norfolk. Strype, *Annals*, I.2, 309–10.

[41] Jones, *English Reformation*, 61–70.

[42] BL Cotton Titus B ii, fol. 249. Printed in John Strype, *The Life and Acts of Matthew Parker* (Oxford: 1821), 350.

England was likened to a ship in a storm, which, if the crew refused to follow orders, would be wrecked and the crew drowned. The justices had the responsibility of preventing the shipwreck.

Underneath this statist attitude toward religion was a theological position that left the secrets of men's hearts to God, accepting that no church could be totally purified by human law. The price of theological dispute was too high. Burghley, like Elizabeth, performed his duty rather than explaining himself, but there is one startling discussion of religion, in his own hand, in the State Papers Domestic. It is a long letter, written in December 1574, to Sir Thomas Copley, Cecil's cousin by marriage. Copley had been a reformer, imprisoned under Mary, but in the mid-1560s he converted to Catholicism. Refusing, as a JP, to take the oath of supremacy, he went into self-imposed exile in 1570, after publishing two books seeking Christian unity over issues of faith and works.

Cecil's letter is a thoughtful discussion of religion sent to a kinsman he clearly liked, and who he was trying to persuade of the error of his position. Rather than launching a Gospel-slinging attack, he admitted some room for temporizing—perhaps as he had allowed himself under Mary.

In long Ciceronian sentences he asked Copley to consider the cost of exile, arguing:

> that no church in earth shall be (until the day of judgment …) so clear and free either in doctrine ceremonies or manners from errors, superstitions, and corruptions, but that there must be a conversation of the good with the evil, so as the good must alwise contend, by teaching, and example to amend and correct the evil, and this exercise of the good must continue to the end of the world, for otherwise men should do, as the persons do that being in a ship whereunto the church of Christ is resembled, and perceiving some evil conditioned person, will, for misliking of them, leave the ship to their own peril.

This case for the imperfection of all churches, a paraphrase of St Augustine's *De civitate Dei*, rests on the fact that the people of the heavenly city live with diverse secular governments. "It therefore is so far from rescinding and abolishing these diversities that it even preserves and adopts them, so long only as no hindrance to the worship of the one supreme and true God is thus introduced." Cecil invited Copley to think about whether foreign Catholics were any better than English Protestants:

> But in this ship of England do you find such offenders, as are not in the like [ship] abroad? Be there in this our ship blasphemers, heretics, irreligious advoweters [owners of advowsons], and such like? And be there not the like in other, yea, in all places of Christendom, the more is to be lamented? And be there not here also, think you, in this your native country, numbers that reverence and believe in the same God, the father the son and the Holy Ghost, as you and others where you are do? That receive and uphold the same articles of the apostolic creed that you and others do? That prefer all moral virtues and condemn all vices as far as you and others do? That labor to preserve public peace by administration of justice, with as great care as others do?[43]

---

[43] TNA SP 12/99 fol. 31.

The letter to Copley was not persuasive enough to get him to return to England, or to get him to send Burghley the information about Catholic books printed in France that would betoken his obedience. It is, however, a nicely articulated statement of his views about the imperfection of all churches and times. In a nation that had just been through the Northern Rebellion, had executed the duke of Norfolk for plotting for a Catholic succession, and that was being harangued by the *Admonition to Parliament*, Burghley must have been very aware of the perceived imperfections. To side with any was to lose the peace that God required the City of the World to provide, so he kept emphasizing the law, with its fixed positions and clear expectations.

It appears that he and his mistress had realized, by the early 1570s if not before, that they were boxed in by religious savagery that could only be dampened, never extinguished. Unlike in the heady days of Edward and Mary, when both sides seemed sure of their victory, the Elizabethan management could only hope to prevent religious violence. If their choices were between clinging to the law of England, the establishment of an inquisition, or massacres like that of St Bartholomew's Day, they chose forced conformity to the church established by law.

In the early 1560s there was hope that gentle persuasion might work; by the 1570s the Elizabethan state had arrived at its own particular middle way, a *via media* of legally defined conformity that permitted a distinction between personal theology and public conformity. Only by stressing obedience and ignoring theology could the factions be kept from one another's throats.

We see Burghley's management of this position emerging at Cambridge, in the battles with Thomas Cartwright, the Lady Margaret Professor of Divinity at St John's. When Cartwright preached sermons that supported a Presbyterian ecclesiology, he was seen as a threat to good order. Matthew Hutton, the dean of York, responding to a request from Burghley, the Chancellor of Cambridge University, for his opinion on the controversies over "things indifferent' in the church, wrote a long letter musing on the troublemakers and their impacts. He dated the troubles from "about" nine years earlier, when questions were asked that undermined the authority of the church and the Queen. "I saw then," he wrote, "that the gospel was like thereby to be hindered, the golden quiet of the church disturbed and a great occasion given to the Adversary to rejoice ..." The motives were not all the same—theologians, who knew better, secret papists, and those greedy for the goods of the clergy all contributed—"yet they please themselves best when they talk of matters of council, maintenance of commonwealths, of the office of princes, of councilors, of platforms of churches, of the duty of bishops and of parliaments." He greatly respected John Calvin, but Calvin was writing theology for a "popular" state, not a monarchy, and was therefore not to be used as a guide in a monarchy. St Paul said all must obey the magistrates, and the Queen is God's vicegerent, and so she must be obeyed, and her laws must be enforced by the lesser magistrates, for conscience's sake. He advised that dissidents be sharply reined in by the magistrates because they were attempting to overthrow the Queen's authority over the church.[44]

44 CP 7/109.

As Dr William Redman said, the duty of the people was to obey the Supreme Governor and her magistrates. There was no need for consultation or consent. *Nihil a plebe*; they needed only to obey.[45]

Many agreed, and the statutes of Cambridge University were revised in 1570, removing the power of the young regent masters who had governed it, and transferring authority to the heads of colleges. Leading the charge for the change were Andrew Perne, the Vice-Chancellor, who famously changed his religion every time the regime changed, and John Whitgift, Master of St John's. Cartwright was expelled, just as Hutton suggested, and Whitgift went on to become Vice-Chancellor, later an authoritarian Bishop of Worcester and then Archbishop of Canterbury. In university government, as in parish government, the lesser folk need only obey their betters.[46]

Whitgift, in his dispute with Cartwright and other Presbyterians during the admonition controversy, was arguing like Hutton, but with more nuance. He made use of Augustine's distinction between the worldly church and the invisible church, agreeing that it was impossible to separate the two. God governed the invisible church, but "The visible and external government is that which is executed by man and consisteth of external discipline and visible ceremonies practiced in that church that containeth in it both good and evil."[47] Moreover, because good and evil were commingled in the church, the Christian magistrate had the job of providing discipline "according to the kind and form of government used in the commonwealth."[48]

Whitgift and Burghley were both casting the church in England in Augustinian terms that made the support of the royal supremacy and the established order a divine mandate. It is not surprising that Burghley liked this. After the turmoil at the beginning of the 1570s, he can hardly be blamed for developing a new, more inclusive yet more authoritarian sense of the church within the state. Obedience to the prince became easily linked with obedience to God using this approach. Any leader saddled with a Thomas Cartwright or an Edward Dering would find it attractive.

The controversy over Cartwright, who was an eloquent exponent of Presbyterian organization, irritated Burghley. A finger-wagging letter from Edward Dering, suggesting that Cartwright be allowed to read the Hebrew lecture at Cambridge, caused an eruption from the Lord Treasurer. Dering had publicly subjected Elizabeth to a similar chastisement, and Burghley's patience was exhausted.

He told Dering that he, at first, had not intended to respond to his biting letter, since it would waste his time and encourage Dering's evil humor. But he could not help himself. To be imputed a pagan was more than Burghley could stand. He wrote: "Indeed, on the contrary of your hard speeches, through God's goodness, I do affirm, that I have not to my knowledge conceived or held *obstinata consilia*." By God's grace and a good education, he continued,

---

[45] Kaufman, *Laity*, 111.

[46] Patrick Collinson, *Richard Bancroft and Elizabethan Anti-Puritanism* (Cambridge: Cambridge University Press, 2013), 17. Kaufman, *Laity*, 109–13.

[47] John Whitgift, *Works*, ed. John Ayre (Cambridge: Parker Society, 1851), vol. 1, 183.

[48] Whitgift, *Works*, vol. 2, 263.

I have beheld the gospel or evangel of Christ, that son of God…with such inward feeling of God's mercy by Jesus Christ revealed to me in his Gospel, and confirmed to me by his sacraments, as I trust I may say with the Church, *Pater noster, sanctificetur nomen tuum.* And though I am made of worldly elements, as other creatures are, and thereby, while I live in this tabernacle, subject to sin and infirmities, so as I may not glory of any perfection, wherein others think themselves to excel their brethren; yet I will confidently use St. Paul's speech, *non erubesco evangelium,* i.e. I am not ashamed of the gospel; and why? *Virtus enim Dei est in salutem omni credenti,* etc. For it is the power of God to shew salvation to every one that believeth.[49]

He goes on to ask Dering how he dared to presume to judge his brother's faith or religion. "I must say to you, as St. Paul said to the Corinthians, *Qui me judicat, Deus est;* i.e. he that judgeth me, is God." He signed himself "Yours to be taught, but not to be condemned."[50]

Burghley's assertion that he had a personal testimony of his Lord and Savior Jesus Christ is uncompromising. This is no mild response. But it is also clear that he took seriously the command to judge not lest you be judged and not to remove the speck from your brother's eye until you had removed the log from your own. Perhaps he actually did not want to make windows into men's souls, and his job did not demand it.

Dering's accusation of paganism was excessive, but Burghley was equally perturbed by Dering's earlier, nasty, accusation that he was mismanaging Cambridge, contrary to law.[51] To be accused of being a bad Christian and a lawbreaker were the two charges that struck at the heart of his identity.

Burghley's own religious practice was punctiliousness.[52] He is described as never missing a sermon, and as one who, as master of his household, ensured that his servants did not, either. Everyone was expected to attend morning and evening prayer, and to hear a sermon in the chapel every Sunday. When he created ordnances for his almshouse in Stamford, he thoughtfully prescribed their religious duties, tightening the rules as he drafted the charter:

Every of these poor men shall resort to Common Prayers [go *struck through*] <[every seven day *struck through*]> to St. Martin's church and shall sit or kneel together <[*Margin*] in some place appointed by the church warden> and so shall they do upon Wednesday and Fridays, [and if any *struck through*] <at Morning Prayers>/ and shall be absent without just cause <every next day [?]> by the rules to be notified to the parish clerk …

Those who were absent without excuse were docked 2d from their week's wages, which were paid at Sunday evensong.[53]

It was this sort of methodical legalism that provoked his dislike of those who would tamper with the established order of worship, and of Catholic missionaries.

---

[49] BL Lansd. 102, fol. 156.   [50] BL Lansd. 102, 132.
[51] BL Lansd. 12, fols 190–191v.   [52] Collins, 56.
[53] My thanks to Jon Culverhouse, Curator at Burghley House, for supplying me with a transcription of this "Draft Scheme for Lord Burghley's Hospital, Stamford," found at Burghley House in Burghley's own hand.

Their disobedience threatened divine wrath, and, more practically, civil war. Catholics who denied the authority of statutes made by the Queen in Parliament were traitors. To disobey was to threaten the state. Therefore, disobedience had to be punished, while conformity was to be encouraged.

That Burghley embraced this managerial goal is demonstrated by the rhetorical approach of his *Execution of Justice in England* (1583). An apologia addressed to those who accused England of persecuting Catholics, in the aftermath of the execution of Edmund Campion, he denied the charge. Instead, England was punishing disobedience to the law. Throughout the short work the noun "queen" is constantly modified by "lawful" and the "religion" is the one "by law enacted." The traitors are people who, though bound by the law of God to obey their prince (1 Romans 13), seek to persuade their fellows that what the Pope has done is lawful. They have unlawfully denied that she was the lawful queen of England. The "bloody questions," used to clarify a Catholic's allegiance, turn around whether it is treason to deny the lawful authority of the queen.[54]

After all, as it asks in Spangenberg's Catechism, "Who is a tyrant?" He who does not govern according to law. Elizabeth did. Therefore, she must be obeyed.[55]

By the time he published *The Execution of Justice in England*, Burghley had transsubstantiated Catholics who obeyed the Pope into traitors who could be punished for disobedience, rather than their belief.

Once he concluded that papists were inherently disobedient, he was happy to exert pressure on them. Tucked into one of his memos on things to be done, between Ireland and controlling new building in London, was a list of actions to be taken against recusants. Written about 1580, it summarized his approach to controlling the danger. Up until that time, he seemed to muse, their treatment had been too gentle. The papists who had been deprived had been living under house arrest. Now, he wrote, "all the deprived ecclesiastical Papists, be collected together, and sent to divers castles, as some to Wisbeach and Banbury."

Gentlemen who had refused the oath of supremacy had been, until now, allowed to give their bonds for good behavior. Now he thought "that all the principal lay men being manifest recusants remaining on bonds may be sent for by the Commissioners, and bestowed into some convenient places near London under sure guard." These same gentlemen had, until then, been expected to arm the militia, as suited their stations. That was to end, and their armor was to be seized. All the other recusants, "that generally... will not come to the church," he thought should be fined and imprisoned by the ecclesiastical commission.[56]

Coming from Burghley, these were not idle threats. He began acting on them. The deprived leaders of Mary's church were moved to prison, and in Parliament

---

[54] William Cecil, *The Execution of Justice in England for Maintenaunce of Publique and Christian Peace, against certeine stirrers of sedition, and adherents to the traytors and enemies of the realme, without any persecution of them for questions of religion, as is falsely reported and published by the fautors and fosterers of their treason. Xvii. Decemb. 1583* (London: 1583), sig. Fiij [STC (2nd edn)/4902].

[55] Johann Spangenberg, *Margarita theologica continens praecipuos locos doctrinae Christianae per quaestiones breuiter & ordine explicatos* (1570), fol. 67 [STC (2nd ed.)/23002].

[56] TNA SP 15/27/2 fols 46–46v.

that year a new treason law increased the fine for not coming to church from a shilling each Sunday to £20 a month—a huge fine.

It is clear that Burghley, however ardently Protestant he may have been in his heart, saw papists (as distinct from Catholics) as "dissident oppositional expressions of religious motive, linked by a common reliance on Rome."[57] This left room for obedient Catholics in the Elizabethan state.

Moreover, he recognized that there was no "Catholic community"; there were instead leading papist gentlemen who had to be watched. Given the hierarchical reality of Tudor England, and the way power was distributed in localities, it was these men, not common recusants, who presented the central risk. But because the risk was political, the prosecution of Catholics was also highly political.[58]

As Peter Lake has noted, struggles within the Privy Council often were accompanied by anti-Catholic campaigns. In response to the attack on Archbishop Grindal for refusing to suppress the prophesyings, Bishop Aylmer and Secretary Walsingham prompted a survey of the bishops to discover how many recusants there were and how much they were worth. They were whipping up a papist scare to counter the fear of Puritans, insisting that the rebuff to good Protestants represented by the suppression had encouraged Catholics, so recusancy was on the rise. The effort was successful enough to set off an anti-Catholic backlash in defense of the Protestant cause. It was, says Lake very correctly, a form of intense, court- and queen-centered politics, in which ideological parties struggled, but none was victorious.[59] This shows us Burghley's attitude for what it was: he was seeking to keep the peace between the factions in order to keep Elizabeth secure.

We can see this in the response to the Queen's other subjects who, though Protestants, were disobedient on religious grounds. How did he respond to people who argued for Protestant reasons that conscience might require disobedience? Who believed in Presbyterian ecclesiology? Were they allies like foreign Protestants might be? How were they to be managed?

In the 1570s Burghley made common cause with Cambridge leaders who repressed the Presbyterian agitators. By the mid-1580s Burghley and Whitgift, who became Archbishop of Canterbury in 1583, had evolved differing philosophies about how to control dissenters. After Archbishop Grindal's disgrace and house arrest, Whitgift clearly saw it as his duty to obey the Queen's demand that Protestant dissenters be repressed. Moreover, he had learned of the dangers of letting the Queen's officers take too much authority over religious enforcement. If the church was to thrive, it had to prove it was able to keep its house in order. As Bishop of Worcester in 1581, Whitgift demonstrated the tension between the secular and ecclesiastical officers of the Queen when he protested against the request from the Lord President

[57] Michael Braddick, *State Formation in Early Modern England, c.1550–1700* (Cambridge: Cambridge University Press, 2000), 300–1.

[58] Susan Cogan, "Catholic Gentry, Family Networks and Patronage in the English Midlands, c.1570–1630" (University of Colorado, unpublished PhD dissertation, 2012), 23–4.

[59] Peter Lake, "A Tale of Two Episcopal Surveys: The Strange Fates of Edmund Grindal and Cuthbert Mayne Revisited," The Prothero Lecture, *Transactions of the Royal Historical Society*, 6th ser., 18 (2008), 129–63.

of the Marches of Wales for a renewal of the Ecclesiastical High Commission for hunting recusants. He did not want the Lord President instituting the commission. It was, he said, just a ploy to take recusant fines from the church and divert them into the coffers of the Council of Wales. It was a trick to get more power over the clergy. Worse, he had heard that the Queen had granted the Lord President the right to appoint clergy to lapsed advowsons, which would work terrible mischief and inconvenience on honest men. He asked Burghley not to further burden the Queen's subjects with a commission, and then went on to talk of the people being prosecuted by him for non-attendance at church and brought to conformity.[60]

As archbishop, Whitgift found the Ecclesiastical High Commission useful for prosecuting clergy who did not fully conform, having transformed it into a canon law court. Burghley had recently argued to the world that England allowed freedom of religion to everyone who accepted the Queen's authority. Whitgift was disproving this by insisting that all clergy agree to twenty-four non-statutory articles, as well as signing a statement confirming the religion established by Parliament and the Queen. This was aimed at clergy inclined to Presbyterianism, and it had a sting in its tail. The high commission could now demand that the accused take an oath *ex officio mero*, promising to answer all questions put to them without knowing what the questions might be. Then, if the person swearing confessed to a crime, he could be tried by the same people who had offered him the oath.[61] It was a neatly constructed trap, and Burghley, like many others, was horrified by what he considered its extra-legal nature.

His concerns turned around a practical worry and a legal scruple. His practical worry was that the nation was besieged by seminary priests who were stirring revolt, and to attack the ardent Protestant preachers now encouraged the papists. It was introducing schism and division among Protestants at a time when it could not be afforded.[62]

Worse, the archbishop was using a procedure in canon law that was contrary to English legal process. "I desire the peace of the Church," he wrote Whitgift, "I desire concord and unity in the exercise of our religion. To favor no sensual and willful recusants. But I conclude that according to my simple judgment, this kind of proceedings is too much favoring of the Romish Inquisition: And is rather a device to seek for offenders, than to reform any. This is not the charitable instruction that was intended ..." It may be, he said, that the canon lawyers could defend the procedure in canon law, "but though *Omnia licent*, yet *Omnia non expedient*."[63] "All is permitted, yet not all is expedient" became Burghley's mantra.

---

[60] BL Lansd. 34 fol. 25.

[61] Leo Solt, *Church and State in Early Modern England, 1509–1640* (Oxford: Oxford University Press, 1990), 113.

[62] Peter Lake has argued for a sort of dialectic between anti-Puritanism and anti-popery and the deployment of those by the government depending on the situation from about the 1570 onward. See his "The Monarchical Republic of Queen Elizabeth I (and the Fall of Archbishop Grindal) Revisited," in John F. McDiarmid, ed., *The Monarchical Republic of Early Modern England: Essays in Response to Patrick Collinson* (Aldershot: Ashgate, 2007); and "A Tale of Two Episcopal Surveys," 129–63.

[63] John Strype, *The Life and Acts of the Most Reverend Father in God, John Whitgift, D.D.* (Oxford: 1822), vol. 3, 9, appendix, 104–7.

Here speaks a judge who believed in common law procedure. Demanding blind oaths offended him. He believed in the right of the accused to know the accusation. Moreover, as a friend of Chief Justice Dyer of the Court of Common Pleas (who he sometimes cites) Burghley knew the case law. The justices of Common Pleas had held, in 1569, that one Leigh, suspected of hearing Mass, could not be examined upon his oath by the high commission. He was released from the Fleet prison by their order.

In 1577 a man named Hind refused to swear an oath *ex officio mero* in a usury investigation before the Ecclesiastical High Commission. It imprisoned him for contempt, but he, too, was released from the Fleet under a writ of habeas corpus, since he was jailed for refusing to incriminate himself.[64]

Burghley recognized that the use of these oaths evoked the procedures used against the Marian martyrs. The oath *ex officio mero* had been limited to cases involving matrimony and wills until the reign of Mary, when it was used to interrogate people charged with heresy. The Act of 2 Henry IV on which it had been based was declared void in 10 Elizabeth, and the common law procedure, which refused to demand self-incrimination, was asserted to be victorious.[65]

The Lord Treasurer was in a peculiar spot, since he had to uphold the authority of the bishops by law, but their authority was not clear.[66] It was possible, as some were arguing at the time, that the archbishop had exceeded his authority by creating a new oath and articles that had not been approved by Parliament. The positive law of England, they contended, did not permit the church to override statute law, since it, too, was divinely ordained. But that is what Whitgift was doing.[67] In Parliament in 1588 a petition from the Commons attempted to force Whitgift into line; it failed. Burghley was bombarded with letters from people like Sir Francis Knolles, the Chamberlain of the Household and the Queen's cousin, demanding that the bishops be curbed.

Knolles, a member of the Privy Council and longtime colleague of Burghley's, was campaigning against the bishops and what he took to be their *jure divino* claims of authority.[68] In one of his letters to Burghley he expressed his pleasure that Burghley agreed with his argument that all bishops and ministers had the power of the keys from the Word of God equally. Any difference in rank between them was merely a positive human ordinance to avoid confusion. Any bishop claiming that his authority over the clergy came from God, and demanding clerical subscription,

---

[64] Coke, *Twelfth Part*, 27 [Wing 958:13].   [65] Coke, *Twelfth Part*, 28.

[66] It was a problem that Richard Hooker was tackling at the same time. He was informed by his reading of William Staunford, who held that statute laws were rooted in common laws, and that those, in turn, were rooted in natural law. See his "Ad lectori" in *Les plees del coron diuisees in plusiours titles & common lieux, per queux home plus redement et plenairement trouera, quelq chose que il quira, touchant les ditz pleez, composees lan du grace, 1557* (London, 1557) [STC (2nd edn)/23219]. Notice that at the bottom of the "Ad lectori" Staunford makes the point that statute law is derived from common experience. Richard Hooker cites this in the *Laws of Ecclesiastical Polity*, vol. 1, X.10. Richard Hooker, *Works*, ed. Issac Walton (Oxford: 1845), vol. 1, 248.

[67] Hooker, *Works*, vol. 1, 272–5.

[68] W. D. J. Cargill Thompson, "Sir Francis Knollys' Campaign against the *jure divino* Theory of Episcopacy," in C. R. Cole and M. E. Moody, eds, *The Dissenting Tradition: Essays for Leland H. Carlson* (Athens, OH: Ohio University Press, 1975), 39–77.

manifestly prejudiced "Her Majesty's supreme government."[69] Knolles, appealing to Burghley's belief in law, argued that the bishops had to be forced to acknowledge that their authority derived only from statute law.[70]

Some bishops' willingness to prosecute dissident non-Catholics was obvious by the early 1590s, and it forced Burghley into trying to moderate them in the interest of religious peace and broad conformity. One technique was to stir up renewed fear of Catholics, if we read the proclamation of October 18, 1591 as part of a campaign against what Burghley considered Whitgift's ill-considered attacks on Protestants in a time of national crisis. The proclamation, "establishing commissions against seminary priests and Jesuits," stressed that Philip II was intent on destroying England, as was manifestly true. Philip and his ally the Pope were sending Jesuits into England to support that intent. That was why only Catholics loyal to the Pope were being indicted for high treason, while other Catholics were allowed their lands, lives, goods, and liberties for payment of a "pecuniary sum." Linking the Spanish threat to the Catholic threat, commissions were ordered to hunt for these traitors, such as the Jesuit Robert Parson, "arrogating to himself the name of the King Catholic's [Philip II] Councilor," who was promoting sedition. What Philip did not win with the Armada was to be delivered to him by revolting English Catholics.[71]

There followed a national hunt for Jesuits by commissioners instructed to gather every forty days to compare notes and make a quarterly report to the Queen on their findings. They were to examine suspects under oath, using a prescribed list of questions about their allegiance and their knowledge of attempts to stir up revolt.[72] When Burghley drafted the warrant, in the Queen's name, to the Lord Chancellor to set up the commissions he put the issue succinctly. The Queen knew that these traitors were diverting her subjects from their natural allegiance to her and to the religion established, so agreeable to the Gospel. They had to be found and prosecuted.[73]

This very public campaign made life difficult for Catholics, but it did not stop the prosecution of recusant Protestants by Whitgift and his allies on the council, though Burghley tried.

In April 1593 Burghley, despite having refused to have anything to do with them and their cause, tried to prevent the hanging of Henry Barrow and John Greenwood for publishing seditious, if Protestant, books.[74] Thomas Phellipes reported that they

> were to have been executed last week, but as they were ready to be trussed up, they were respited; but the day after the Lower House [of Parliament] had showed their dislike of this bill [against Barrowists and Brownists], they were hanged early in the morning. The reprieve was through a supplication to the Lord Treasurer, that in a land where no Papist was put to death for religion, theirs should not be the first blood shed who concurred about faith with what was professed in the country, and desired conference to be convinced of their errors. The Lord Treasurer spoke sharply to the Archbishop of

---

[69] BL Lansd. 61/fol. 174.   [70] BL Lansd. 64/fol. 86.   [71] H&L, vol. 3, 86–93.
[72] H&L, vol. 3, 93–5.   [73] CP 20/57.   [74] CP 167/102.

Canterbury, who was very peremptory, and also to the Bishop of Worcester, and wished to speak to the Queen, but none seconded him.[75]

Perhaps he, like the members of the House of Commons, was concerned that the legislation going through Parliament against ill-defined sectaries was going to be used by the bishops to sweep up dissidents of all kinds. The execution occurred on the day the House voiced these fears. The bishops, some thought, killed Barrow and Greenwood because of their "much hatred of the common people."[76]

Burghley sought to keep attention focused on papists and Spaniards, adding to his armory the argument that divine providence had blessed Elizabeth through the destruction of the Armada. But that logic ensured that all the schismatic whining of Puritans and papists should be stopped in the interest of national security and in recognition of Elizabeth's providential survival. Through the period attitudes toward all dissenters were hardening. Papists and Puritans alike were troublemakers, and a danger to the nation. By the middle of the 1590s the troubles heralded by Edward Dering had ripened into full-blown battles over soteriology. The question of grace, as understood by Calvin and his followers, became the grounds for debates over when election occurred and what, if any, contribution an individual made to his salvation. The disputes were shaking Cambridge. Peter Baro, the Lady Margaret Professor of Divinity, and William Barrett, a fellow of Caius, held that it was possible to lose one's election, infuriating the heads of several colleges, who, led by William Whitaker, denied this position.[77]

Humphrey Tyndall, the Archdeacon of Ely, described Chancellor Burghley's reaction to the debate. Writing to Whitgift, in response to an angry demand to know who leaked the draft of the Lambeth articles to Burghley and the Queen, he reported his interview. Whitaker, believing Burghley needed to know of them, "lest if he should understand of it after, it might be taken in evil part," had written Burghley and "sent a copy of his Sermon *ad Clerum*, and that he was purposed to go to his honor, and so signify what had been done in these late controversies, I said I would then accompany him, so accordingly I went, and we delivered to his Lordship a copy of those conclusions."

Burghley read them, and indicated that he had also read Whitaker's sermon, but the elderly Chancellor of their university commented

> that the matters were too high mysteries for his understanding, and seemed to dislike of the propositions concerning predestination, and did reason somewhat against Dr. Whitaker in them, drawing by a similitude a reason from a earthly prince, inferring thereby they charged god of cruelty and might cause men to be desperate in their wickedness.

[75] TNA SP 12/244 fol. 219.

[76] TNA SP 12/244 fol. 219. David Dean, *Law-making and Society in Late Elizabethan England* (Cambridge: Cambridge University Press, 1996), 67–70.

[77] Peter Lake, *Moderate Puritans and the Elizabethan Church* (Cambridge: Cambridge University Press, 1982), 201–13.

Whitaker, "seeing then his Lordship's weakness," did not argue with him, "so saying that these matters were too deep for him, his Lordship bad us farewell, and gave us thanks that we made him acquainted with those things."[78]

Whether or not Burghley inclined toward the Arminian position on salvation, the university's expulsion of Peter Baro for his proto-Arminian preaching was equally repugnant to him, but, true to his word, he did not lecture the dons on theology. Lawyer-like he noted the flaws in their procedure. The heads of his response were summarized:

> Omnia licent: at omnia non expedient ...
> Ye may punish him if ye will, but ye shall do it for well doing in holding the truth in mine opinion.
> Ye sift him with interrogat[ories] as he were a thief this seemeth [some?] of stomack amongst you.
> The witnesses do not agree.
> If he have done contrary to order and commandment in renewing therein he hath not done well. I will write to him myself and charge him as chancellor, etc.[79]

Here we see Burghley, citing once again the maxim that though some things are permitted, they are not all expedient, injecting his lawyerly sense of right into a religious debate. However, we can also see his distaste for the political implications of strict election. A God or monarch who ruled without justice did not deserve obedience. Besides, in his certainty of Christ's grace he probably found the Calvinism of his colleagues' beliefs about election to be personally repugnant.

Burghley had a certain faith in Christ and an equally strong faith in the providential nature of Elizabeth's governance of the church in England, but he looked at religion through the tired eyes of an administrator who was trying to keep the peace between fanatics and enthusiasts, using the tools available to the state. To do that, he found the law, that other revelation from God, to be his most certain guide. In his youth he and his colleagues had reveled in the Edwardian spring of Protestant victory, only to lose their innocence and certainty of providence's linearity under Mary. As the years went by and religious enthusiasts of all sorts demonstrated that they were a danger to the Queen, he became more and more insistent that the law be observed. Rather than worry about theological certainty, he tried to keep the English in one boat, conforming to one faith by law established, so they would not tear themselves apart.

By the middle years of the reign, however, the ecclesiastical leadership itself was split over how this could be done, and was seeking new tools for enforcing conformity on people of all theological bents. Burghley's willingness to tolerate practices he deemed unnecessary to salvation was not shared by everyone. Moreover the Queen's insistence on her own personal authority over religion kept ecclesiastical control separate from regular secular authority, complicating matters. These tensions explain why the battles over religious conformity were so long and bitter. There were too many different authorities trying to manage religion, and the secular side of the state had limited tools. Treason it could try; heresy was not its province.

---

[78] Cambridge, Trinity College, MS. B.14.9, 127–8.
[79] Cambridge, Trinity College, MS. B.14.9, 129.

However, religious peace and proper worship of God were the regime's pole stars. Both were best served by obedience to the Queen and participation in God's church in England by law established. This was the belief that guided Burghley's and Elizabeth's responses to bishops, dissidents, and the religious fanatics alike. Elizabeth had less patience than he, so she sided more with Whitgift's enthusiasm for enforcement of the rules on Protestants, but they did keep the peace. Treasonous papist priests might be executed, and the occasional Protestant fanatic as well, but it was for the good of the commonwealth.

The thanks they got were meager, since all those with greater theological certainty and less political sagacity saw Burghley and Elizabeth as their enemies. As far as William Cecil, Lord Burghley was concerned, however, his job was to manage England in ways that served God by serving his Queen, enforcing the law to preserve the church and keep the peace. That was what she and he wanted.

10

Managing within the Possible

Atque haec coniunctio confusioque virtutum tamen in philosophis ratione quadam distinguitur. Nam cum ita copulatae connexaeque sint ut omnes onmium participes sint nec alia ab alia possit separari, tamen proprium suum cuiusque munus est, ut fortitudo in laboribus periculisque cernatur, temperantia in praetermittendis voluptatibus, prudentia in delectu bonorum et malorum, iustitia in suo cuique tribuendo.[1]

Cicero, De finibus bonorum et malorum, V, xxiii, 67

Managing the Elizabethan state was a matter of finding the possible, separating it from the ideal and the impossible. It was about what worked to achieve the ideals of peace, security, and the honor of God. The ideals of virtuous rule were never abandoned, but in practice the virtues were, as Cicero says, conjoined together and enacted on the stage of the human community. That community, for Burghley, was defined by law and custom, personalities, and plain technical possibility. All the high-minded policy in the world did no good if a courier could not get through the mud. Consequently, he could aspire to a grand strategy, but events would dictate just how, and how far, that policy could be carried out. His daily grind shackled him to process, even as he kept rolling the Sisyphean rocks of order and defense up the historical mountain.

Moreover, the conservatism of Elizabeth and of the system meant that he was constantly putting new wine into old wine skins. As Jesus warned, it meant that the wine often leaked out, but the leaky old skins of the Exchequer, the management structure of the church, the model of knight service, and other systems defined his range of possible choices. Certainly, he changed things, using the tools he had. But when he flirted with remodeling the system, he had to pretend he was not changing anything. *Semper eadem.*

Of course, ideas and structures were used by Elizabeth, Burghley, and the rest of the magistracy to fulfill their mutual interests and to meet daily demands. The values that shaped the behavior of the Elizabethan magistracy were the product of their life experiences, shaped by the conditions of government and by education and cultural expectations. They had to be flexible, since life was variable, but values informed their choices.

---

[1] "For although the virtues are so closely united that each participate in every other and none can be separated from any other, yet on the other hand each has its own special function. Thus courage is displayed in toils and dangers, temperance in forgoing pleasures, prudence in the choice of goods and evils, justice in giving each his due."

The state Elizabeth inherited was a complex composite, a reinforced form of late feudal monarchy. Henry VIII had revived and reinvented some key features of an old system. He had restored and strengthened the role of Parliament in order to wrest authority from the church, but he had not dismantled his church. Nationalizing the English church but leaving its managerial structure intact, he had appropriated huge tracts of real estate to the Crown. Rejecting the theology embodied in monasteries and chantries for the dead, he and his son undertook a wholesale redistribution of real estate that had belonged to the dissolved institutions.

This redistribution looked back to the traditional system of English royal government for its structure. Rather than giving free title to land, Henry VIII granted it for knight service, *tenans in capite*, making the recipients pay a fee for its use to the Crown. Grants in this form guaranteed that the King retained the title, so the property escheated to him if the tenant died without an heir. If the tenant did have an heir, there were other fees to pay, and, if the heir was under age, he or she became a ward of the Crown. New courts, of Augmentations and Wards and Livery, were created in the 1540s to manage all of this. Folded together in Mary's reign, these courts enhanced both the revenue and the power of the monarchy. Thus the "new men" prospering from the Reformation (and the "old men" who became richer and more powerful as a result of it) were bound more tightly to the monarchy than ever. More and more people had the King as their direct lord because they owed him service and fees.

The gentlemen within this structure accepted the idea of service that came with tenancy as a natural part of their world. The feudal system had always had at its heart contractual obligations of service to one's direct lord. But their understanding of service was colored by religious debates raging around them when they were young. Children of the early Reformation, Elizabethan rulers probably could not remember a time when Europe was not convulsed by religious debate and violence. William Cecil was born the same year Martin Luther defined the key elements of what became Protestantism, carrying within it ideas developed by humanist theologians and thinkers that secularized vocation and service just as Henry VIII was secularizing ecclesiastical authority, claiming the right to act as an emergency bishop like the nobility of the German nation. The first Bible in English appeared at that time, with Tyndale copying Luther's intention to make scripture the only guide to a Christian life.

It was a heady, frightening time, but it contained powerful ideas about what men who had been given rule by God could be expected to do. The leading Edwardian preachers associated with the "commonwealth men" explicated their duty in powerful ways. As Edward came to the throne, the generation that would lead Elizabethan England had just come to manhood, and it clearly heard the message about their duty to the commonwealth.

Their conception of that duty was not purely Christian, however. The revival of classical learning known as the Renaissance was slow to reach England. Its full impact was not really felt until the reign of Henry VIII, when great teachers like Erasmus brought the idea that good princes were good men, bolstering it with the exciting learning of the ancients. This new curriculum, stressing the *vita activa*, was seen by thinkers like Sir Thomas Elyot as the perfect education for the English magistracy, and the generation after him put it into effect. Good Latin and Greek were transformative for people like Sir William and Mildred Cecil, Sir Nicholas and Anne Bacon, and Elizabeth Tudor. Opening a world full of rhetorical beauty, political example, and alternative ways of thinking about power, it gave them a new vocabulary, and new political shorthand. It taught them the power of history; it taught them the importance of language; and it taught them to borrow its leadership tools when confronted with a problem. Good leaders were to imitate great leaders like Cato the Elder and Cyrus the Great. As Cicero had worried about how one could live with *virtu* when buffeted by *fortuna*, so the Elizabethan leaders sought to emulate the Stoic virtues of the late Roman Republic and early Empire.

Reading the Greeks and Romans also taught them to appreciate their own history, and to use it as a tool for understanding themselves, their state, and their place in the world.

They brought this Weltanschauung to their tasks as local and national rulers. Living within a revivified late feudal system, they used and improved the system within their understanding of their duty. It is remarkable that it worked, since it was inchoate, but the values of these rulers held it together and pointed them at their common goals well enough for the system to stumble along. And its success was largely due to the stability of the regime. Elizabeth and Burghley shared these values and kept using them across her whole reign. By late in the reign, youngsters who did not have this common background were pushing restlessly against it, less committed to the commonwealth and more interested in individual good, so this world view slowly receded. It had been the key to the Elizabethan state, in which an old system of government was refurbished and kept running thanks to the way its leaders understood their roles, and the way its complex networks operated together in the real world.

Spend enough time in Burghley's archive and you come to see the management of the Elizabethan state as multi-dimensional and indirect. He, his sovereign, and his colleagues were running the nation using a combination of methods and tools based upon privilege, tradition, wealth, position, and personal preference. Shaped by English legal assumptions and customs, they were using many of the methods of a late feudal state while talking about it in the language of Christian civic humanism. They knew where God expected them to put their effort, and how it should prove their virtue. But when it came to day-to-day operations, it was about who you knew, who owed favors to whom, who married who, and how personal interests could be made to coincide with a safe conscience.

Ultimately, they were participating in the culture of the governing classes, that compound of assumptions, learned values, and self-interest that made governance possible and limited its possibilities. Elizabeth, Burghley, and his colleagues understood what management theorists have dubbed "positive linking," the idea that decision-making is made in a context, and is influenced by group values and interactions. "It is," says Paul Ormerod, "the subtle concepts of social norms, of what constitutes reasonable behavior in the relevant peer groups" that leads to acceptance of ideas and actions.[2]

In order to make use of this system of linked relationships, they had to project the community's ideals while converting their goals into a rhetoric that transcended the particulars of those relationships, binding people into a shared community. As Peter Bearman perceptively named his book *Relations into Rhetoric*, so Burghley and his colleagues were validating and tinkering with the existing system of governance, trying to get it to provide what they knew it should.

Slowly, the governing classes developed new ways of thinking and talking about themselves, which were thrown into relief when King James VI & I failed to learn their code.

One of the things Burghley practiced was conscious, gentle persuasion of the powerful. Burghley, and Elizabeth, recognized that in order to get cooperation, they had to give cooperation. Elizabeth was careful about calling Parliaments, revising the tax rolls, or doing other things that offended the leading members of society, who were expected to do the work of government. The state could be ruthless, but it could only be as ruthless as its cooperating ruling class permitted it to be. Better to collect less money than to lose cooperation.

If Elizabeth did not ask more of her magistracy than she could get, that did not mean they had carte blanche. Left to rule their manors, towns, and counties in loose relation to the central authorities, they were expected to keep the peace and participate in governing at all levels, as commissioners of sewers and justices of the peace, as muster masters and arbiters of local disputes. It was their calling and social place, and most of them accepted their duty and did what honor required— within their self-defined limits. Some were doing what their fathers and grandfathers before them had done, proving their gentle lineage through service. Others, new to the upper echelons of society, were happy to do their duty for the same reason—it was proof of their social standing. How well they did it is questionable, but that most tried is unquestionable.

A careful policy was followed in religion. The new religious settlement had created mechanisms for ruling the church, and they were exploited, but the Elizabethan managerial limitations and philosophy reduced religious resistance because it did not ask the ruling classes to choose sides too harshly. Burghley's irritation with Whitgift's enthusiasm for controlling Puritans was matched by his careful handling of Catholic aristocrats. He was not a friend of Catholics, and he hated and feared the Pope, but his "bloody questions" emphasized that he was seeking cooperation, not hunting heretics. It was remarkable that Elizabeth and Burghley agreed on this most of the time. Conformity was their goal, because they so feared civil war over religion, and because the Queen's church pleased God. As times changed, the ways in which conformity was encouraged and enforced changed, but it remained their goal. And perhaps it was the only thing they could reasonably hope for, since their control over religion was tenuous.

[2] Paul Ormerod, *Positive Linking: How Networks Can Revolutionise the World* (London: Faber and Faber, 2012), 59.

This balancing act made many reforms, whether in church or state, hard because they could not be managed safely and easily. The case of the justices of the peace is a good example of a system that was deeply flawed, since it let the local gentlemen have so much discretion, but there was no easy way to fix it. A good sermon, and maybe a Star Chamber case, might help, but ultimately the Queen's power was hostage to the local gentlemen. It maddened Lord Keeper Bacon, and he and Burghley worked hard to harness the chaos, but he could only patch the system, not replace it with something better suited to serving a centralized state.

The Queen's mandate from Heaven required that she provide justice and peace to her subjects. Although her instruments—the magisterial classes, the venal office holders, the justices, and others—were very blunt, she could use law, religion, and propaganda to hedge in their more chaotic tendencies. Here Burghley was aggressive in his attempts to shape the public understanding of royal policy, often using the language of the virtuous commonwealth. He rushed into print his carefully edited versions of major events; he and the council crafted proclamations for clarification, instruction, and prohibition; and the Queen in Parliament made law, just as royal justices "found" it on their benches. It is in projecting the image of a strong, reasonable state that Gloriana's regime was the most successful in its management of the realm. Keeping the peace and ensuring justice led to innovations that permanently shaped the English-speaking world, legally and otherwise.

This legislative activity did not arise from ideological enthusiasm—Burghley and Elizabeth were as careful to avoid enthusiasm as any *philosophe*, since enthusiasm arose from the very passions that those educated in Stoicism and English law distrusted. Instead, legislation grew from attempts to provide laws that solved problems. The process of law-making could be messy, since it could not easily be controlled, but Elizabethan use of statutes and proclamations went hand in hand with the usefulness of the law for dealing with all sorts of concerns. Developing the language that would underpin the "old constitution," the Elizabethans were participating in myth-making that sanctioned the independence of the law in the face of royal authoritarianism. It was used by Elizabeth because it was the price of cooperation.

The military crises of the second half of the reign were met by adapting old institutions to solve new problems. A major new administrative structure was born in the persons of the lord-lieutenants, but out of an old office. Relying on the men born to rule, it recognized the validity of regional power structures and made use of them in defense of the monarchy. But there, too, it was assumed that the men entrusted to oversee the regional military arrangements were the ones who should be doing so anyway. Appointments as lord-lieutenant formally gave authority to men chosen for their combination of social rank and Protestant commitment. The old tool of royal commissions was brought in as a check on these same ruling aristocrats, but these commissioners were men of correct social standing.

Ironically, small changes wrapped in tradition and law slowly increased the authority of the Queen, creating the conviction on the part of many Elizabethans that their institutions were older and greater than they were. As John Pocock appositely said, in a different context, "short-term actions are...sometimes undertaken in contexts stabilized by structures having a longer durée behind them, and...changes in such structures are...sometimes slow and continuous enough to merit the name of 'processes.' "[3]

Although the rhetoric of monarchy obscured it, there was much that the Queen did not know, and did not need to know. She was dependent on her favorites and councilors, expecting them to do their duties. Burghley, however, sought to know as much as he could, informing his decisions and putting him in a good position to inform the Queen. The notable thing about the later sixteenth century, across Europe, was the rise of a managerial class of royal servants who aspired to expand the royal control through knowledge. Geoffrey Parker once asked if Philip II had a "grand strategy," and wrote a book about the difficulty of having one. The king of Spain embroiled his empire in continuous wars while trying to make decisions at too great a distance, asserting a control he could not achieve.[4] In his attempt at control, he demanded more and more information, more and more paper, better maps, and better spies. Burghley did the same, and Spain and England look much alike in this period. But Philip failed by trying to be too much an absolute king.

What about Elizabeth? Did she have a grand strategy? One that would guide Burghley in his duties? It appears that Elizabeth, as seen through Burghley's archive, understood how her small state worked better than Philip understood his complex empire. Elizabeth's motto of *semper eadem* embodied a conservative philosophy that gave Burghley his marching orders. Keep the peace, maintain justice, and do not let things get out of hand. It was not so much a strategy as a preference for stasis.

But maintaining stasis was not easy. Threats to stability were all around, and he tried very hard to track and counter them. Preventing religious civil war, defending the realm from foreign enemies, collecting the revenues, honoring God with proper worship, and dispensing justice were all part of ensuring things remained as much the same as possible.

Put another way, what innovations to the English state did Elizabeth permit or demand? The Elizabethan settlement of religion was a major, lasting change, but it came at the commencement of the reign and Elizabeth treated it as eternally correct, *saecula saeculorum*. It was, like the whole Reformation, an attempt at returning the church to the status quo ante of primitive purity, not an endorsement of eternal evolution.

The complex system of mutual responsibility allowed leaders at all levels a great deal of independence and therefore innovative responses to local issues. Burghley was concerned about national security, about revenues, and about obedience, but he had a weak grasp, despite his best efforts, on the details. Local government was, unless it became too abusive, generally left to look after itself. Only when the behaviors of the governors became egregious did the Queen, Burghley, and his colleagues on the Privy Council take note of it. When it did become abusive, or when

---

[3] J. G. A. Pocock, *The Ancient Constitution and the Feudal Law: A Study of English Historical Thought in the Seventeenth Century. A Reissue with a Retrospect* (Cambridge: Cambridge University Press, 1986), 278.

[4] Geoffrey Parker, *The Grand Strategy of Philip II* (New Haven: Yale University Press, 1998).

the great families that dominated a place began quarreling with one another, undermining government, the council and the Queen might step in, first through personal interventions and then, if those failed, with heavier tactics. These quarrels, in this interbred world, were often treated like family disputes.

This allowed the state to function without much cost and without requiring much infrastructure. Would greater centralization have made it work any better? Perhaps not, because its aims were limited.

Defense, worship, and justice were its goals. As long as those needs seemed to be met, all was well. Of course, the council knew that many of the Queen's local managers did a poor job. The constant harping on the justices of the peace makes that certain. But they accepted that they had few tools for correction, other than rhetorical, and that the ruling classes were generally content with the system.

It was this reality—the Queen's dependence on the magistracy—that made the government through individual virtue so important. The "republicanism" of this monarchy was based in the magistracy's acceptance of its duty to rule England on behalf of their God-given Queen.[5]

And so the Elizabethan managers of England took a composite state with weak communications, powerful local lords, urban oligarchs, and abstruse laws and did what they could with it. But in doing it for so long, the Elizabethan era became a bridge toward a stronger sense of national identity and royal authority. The commonwealth was slowly turning into a nation defined by values that were shared across its elites. Their "ancient constitution" was mostly made of Elizabethan habit, which, when affronted by a monarch who truly believed in absolutism, appeared to them as something good because it was ancient and as divinely established as any kingship.

---

[5] Markku Peltonen, *Classical Humanism and Republicanism in English Political Thought, 1570–1640* (Cambridge: Cambridge University Press, 1995) argues that this mid-Tudor conception of duty based on humanist thought continued as an important theme in English political thought up to the civil war. However, his concentration on thought rather than action, for men committed to *vita activa*, obscures the value of these ideas to Elizabethans.

Bibliography

MANUSCRIPT SOURCES

Burghley House
BKS 16611
"Draft Scheme for Lord Burghley's Hospital, Stamford"
MUN 18518

The British Library
Add. 33,271; 62,540
Cotton, Caligula B.VIII; X
Cotton, Titus B.II
Egerton 2603
Harleian 260; 6990
Lansdowne 7; 10; 12; 13; 14; 26; 27; 28; 33; 34; 43; 53; 61; 63; 64; 68; 94; 101; 102;
    103; 104; 107; 109; 115
Royal App 67
Stowe 162; 362

The Cecil Papers, Hatfield House
CP

Corpus Christi College, Cambridge
MS 121
MS 582

Folger Shakespeare Library, Washington, D.C.
Folger MS V.a.460, II
L.a.309
L.b.194

Henry E. Huntington Library, San Marino, CA
EL 1198; 1404; 1522; 1538; 2219; 2653; 6284–90
HEH 267
HM 1418
HM 30881

Inner Temple Library, London
Petyt Ms. 538/10; 47

Lambeth Palace Library, London
Talbot Papers MS. 3200; 3206

The National Archives
E 178

PC 2/12; 2/20
PROB/11/63; 92
SP 10/15; 18
SP 12/1; 3; 13; 17; 19; 23; 39; 46; 48; 49; 51; 59; 60; 69; 74; 75; 85; 86; 90; 92; 99; 105;
114; 122; 148; 152; 176; 181; 186; 199; 207; 215; 241; 243; 244; 248; 255; 256; 262; 268
SP 15/12; 18; 19; 20; 23; 24; 27/2; 29; 30; 32
SP 52/4
SP 53/11
SP 59/1; 20; 21; 26
SP 63/20; 32; 52; 59; 110; 187
SP 78/7
SP 83/4; 5
SP 99/1
WALE 30/51/16
WARD 1/3/1; 9/107; 9/118; 9/129; 9/157; 9/171; 9/369; 9/380

Trinity College, Cambridge
MS. B.14.9

Yale University, Beinecke Library, New Haven, CN
Osborn Shelves Fb 6

PRIMARY SOURCES

Adams, Simon and David Scott Gehring. "Elizabeth I's Former Tutor Reports on the Parliament of 1559: Johannes Spithovius to the Chancellor of Denmark, 27 February 1559," *English Historical Review*, 128, 530 (2013), 35–54.

Allen, Gemma, ed. *The Letters of Lady Anne Bacon. Camden Society*, 5th ser., 44 (2014).

Ascham, Roger. *The Scholemaster*. 1570. STC (2nd edn)/835.5.

Ascham, Roger. *The Whole Works of Roger Ascham*, ed. Dr Giles. London, 1865.

Ayre, J. ed. *The Sermons of Edwin Sandys*. Cambridge: Parker Society, 1842.

Bacon, Francis. *Essayes. Religious Meditations. Places of Perswasion & Disswasion. Seene and Allowed…* 1597. STC (2nd edn)/1137.5.

Bacon, Francis. *The Works of Francis Bacon*, ed. James Spedding, Robert Leslie Ellis, and Douglas Denon Heath. 15 vols. Boston: Houghton Mifflin and Company, 1900.

Baker, J. H., ed. *Reports from the Lost Notebooks of Sir James Dyer*. London: Selden Society, 1994.

Bateson, Mary. "Collection of Original Letters from the Bishops to the Privy Council, 1564, with Returns of the Justices of the Peace and Others Classified According to their Religious Convictions," *Camden Society*, new ser., 53, *Camden Miscellany*, 9. London, 1895.

Bavande, William, trans. *A Woorke of Ioannes Ferrarius Montanus, touchynge the good orderynge of a common weale wherein aswell magistrates, as priuate persones, bee put in remembraunce of their dueties, not as the philosophers in their vaine tradicions haue deuised, but according to the godlie institutions and sounde doctrine of christianitie* [1559].

Becon, Thomas. *The Gouernaunce of Vertue Teaching al Faithfull Christians, howe they oughte dayly to leade their lyfe, [and] fruitefully to spend their tyme vnto the glorye of God and the health of their owne soules*, in *The Early Works of Thomas Becon*, ed. John Ayre. Cambridge: Cambridge University Press, 1843.

Belleforest, Francois de. *Harangues militaires, et concions de princes, capitaines, ambassadeurs, et autres manians tant la guerre que les affaires d'estat.* Geneva, 1595.

Birch, Thomas, ed. *Memoirs of the Reign of Queen Elizabeth from the Year 1581 until her Death…from the original papers of his intimate friend, Anthony Bacon…* London, 1754.

Bracton, Henry. *De legibus et consuetudinibus Angliae.* <http://bracton.law.harvard.edu/>. Accessed Feb. 8, 2011.

Broughton, Hugh. *A Treatise of Melchisedek Prouing him to be Sem, the Father of all the Sonnes of Heber, the Fyrst King, and all Kinges Glory: by the generall consent of his owne sonnes, by the continuall iudgement of ages, and by plentifull argumentes of scripture.* (1591). STC (2nd edn)/3890.

Bruce, John and T. T. Perowne, eds. *Correspondence of Matthew Parker.* Cambridge: Parker Society, 1853.

Cabala, sive Scrinia sacra mysteries of state and government. 1663. Wing/C185.

Calendar of Inquisitions Post Mortem, Henry VII. London: HMSO, 1898.

Calendar of the Patent Rolls Preserved in the Public Record Office. Elizabeth I, vol. 7, *1575–1578,* ed. J. H. Collingridge. London: HMSO, 1982.

Calendar of Patent Rolls 27 Elizabeth I (1584–1585), C 66/1254–1270, ed. Louise J. Wilkinson. *List and Index Society,* 293 (2002).

Calendar of Patent Rolls 27 Elizabeth I (1585–1586), C 66/1271–1285, ed. Simon R. Neal. *List and Index Society,* 294 (2002).

Cecil, William. *The Execution of Justice in England for Maintenaunce of Publique and Christian Peace, against certeine stirrers of sedition, and adherents to the traytors and enemies of the realme, without any persecution of them for questions of religion, as is falsely reported and published by the fautors and fosterers of their treason. Xvii. Decemb. 1583.* London, 1583. STC (2nd edn)/4902.

Cecil, William. "The Preface," Catharine Parr, *The Lamentacion of a Synner, made by the moste vertuous lady Quene Caterine, bewailyng the ignoraunce of her blind life: set foorth & put in print at the instant desire of the right gracious lady Caterine duchesse of Suffolke, and the ernest request of the right honourable Lord William Parre, marquesse of Northampton.* 1548. No pagination. STC (2nd edn)/4828.

Certain Sermons or Homilies Appointed to be Read in Churches in the Time of Queen Elizabeth of Famous Memory. London: SPCK, 1846.

Cheke, Sir John. *The Hurt of Sedicion howe greueous it is to a commune welth.* 1549. Sig. Aiiij. STC (2nd edn)/5109; 1569, STC (2nd edn)/5110; 1576, STC (2nd edn)/5111; 1641, Wing/C3778.

Cicero, Marcus Tullius. *De officiis,* trans. Walter Miller. Cambridge, MA: Harvard University Press, 2001.

Cicero, Marcus Tullius. *The Familiar Epistles of M. T. Cicero Englished,* trans. J. Webbe. 1620. STC (2nd edn)/5305.

Cicero, Marcus Tullius. *Letters to Friends,* ed. D. R. Shackleton Bailey. Cambridge, MA: Harvard University Press, 2001.

Cicero, Marcus Tullius. *Paradox stoicorum ad M. Brutum,* in J. G. Baiter and C. L. Kayser, eds, *Opera.* Leipzig. Tauchnitz, 1865.

Cockburn, H. S., ed. *Calendar of Assize Records. Hertfordshire Indictments Elizabeth I.* London: HMSO, 1975.

Coke, Edward. *The Twelfth Part of the Reports of Sir Edward Coke.* London, 1656. Wing/958:13.

Collins, Arthur, ed. *The Life of the Great Statesman William Cecil Lord Burghley.* London, 1732.

Cooper, J. Chris, ed. and trans. *Eustache de Refuge, Treatise on the Court. The Early Modern Management Classic on Organizational Behaviour*. Boca Raton, FL: Orgpax Publications, 2008.

The Declaracyon of the Procedynge of a Conference, begon at Westminster the last of Marche, 1559 concerning certaine articles of religion and the breaking vp of the sayde conference by default and contempt of certayne bysshops, parties of the sayd conference. STC (2nd edn)/25286.

Elyot, Thomas. *The Book Named the Governor*, ed. S. E. Lehmberg. New York, Dutton, 1970.

The English Reports. Edinburgh: W. Green and Sons, 1900–.

Fitzherbert, Sir Anthony. *The Nevve Boke of Iustices of Peace Made by Anthonie Fitz Herbert Iudge, lately translated out of Fre[n]ch into Englishe and newlye corrected. The yere of our Lorde. 1554*. 1566. STC (2nd edn)/10977.

Fitzherbert, Sir Anthony and Richard Crompton. *L'Office et aucthoritie de justices de peace 1584*. London, 1972.

Fletcher, John M., ed. *Registrum annualium collegii Mertonensis, 1567–1603*. 3 vols. Oxford: Clarendon Press for the Oxford Historical Society, 1976.

Friedberg, Aemilius, ed. *Decretum magistri Gratiani*. Graz, 1959.

Fry, E. A., ed. *Inquisitions Post Mortem Relating to the City of London Returned into the Court of Chancery*. London: London and Middlesex Archaeological Society, 1980.

Furnivall, Frederick J., ed. *Child-marriages, Divorces, and Ratifications, &c. in the Diocese of Chester, A.D. 1561–6*. London: Early English Text Society, 1897.

Gifford, George. *A Sermon Preached at Pauls Crosse the Thirtie Day of May 1591*. London, 1591. STC 11862.3.

The Harleian Miscellany. London, 1744–6.

Harrison, William. *The Description of England*, ed. Georges Edelen. Washington, D.C. and New York: Folger Shakespeare Library and Dover Publications, 1994.

Hartley, T. E., ed. *Proceedings in the Parliaments of Elizabeth I*. 3 vols. Leicester: Leicester University Press, 1981–95.

Haynes, Samuel and William Murdin. *A Collection of State Papers, Relating to Affairs in the Reigns of King Henry VIII, King Edward VI, Queen Mary, and Queen Elizabeth, Transcribed from Original Letters and Other Authentick Memorials, Left by William Cecill Lord Burghley*. Vol. 1, *1542–1570*. Vol. 2, *1571–1596*. London, 1740, 1759.

Historical Manuscripts Commission. *Manuscripts of Lord Montagu of Beaulieu*. London, 1900.

Historical Manuscripts Commission. *Report on the Manuscripts of the Family of Gawdy*. London, 1885.

Hooker, Richard. *The Laws of Ecclesiastical Polity*, ed. Isaac Walton. 3 vols. Oxford, 1845.

Hughes, P. L. and J. F. Larkin, eds. *Tudor Royal Proclamations*. 3 vols. New Haven: Yale University Press, 1969.

Good, Helen, ed. *Kingston upon Hull Records 1 Letters 1576–1585*. Hull, 1997.

Jewel, John. *The Apology of the Church of England*. London: Cassell, 1888.

Kingdon, Robert, ed. *The Execution of Justice in England by William Cecil, and A True, Sincere, and Modest Defense of English Catholics by William Allen*. Ithaca, NY: Cornell University Press, 1965.

Lambarde, William. *Eirenarcha, or Of the office of the iustices of peace in two bookes: gathered 1579 and now reuised*. 1581. STC (2nd edn)/15163.

Latimer, Hugh. *Seven Sermons before Edward VI*, ed. Edward Arber. London, 1824.

Leslie, John. *A Treatise of Treasons against Q. Elizabeth, and the Croune of England Diuided into Two Partes: whereof, the first parte answereth certaine treasons pretended, that neuer were intended: and the second, discouereth greater treasons committed, that are by few percei-ued: as more largely appeareth in the page folowing.* 1571. STC (2nd edn)/7601.

Livy, Titus. *The History of Rome, Vol. 1.* Ernest Rhys, ed. London: J. M. Dent, 1912.

Marcus, Leah, Janet Mueller, and Mary Beth Rose, eds. *Elizabeth I. Collected Works.* Chicago: University of Chicago Press, 2000.

Martin, James, ed. *Godly Magistrates and Church Order. Johannes Brenz and the Establish-ment of the Lutheran Territorial Church in Germany, 1524–1559.* Renaissance and Refor-mation Texts in Translation, no. 9. Toronto: Victoria University Press, 2001.

May, Steven W. ed. *Queen Elizabeth I. Selected Works.* New York: Washington Square Press, 2004.

Mayer, Thomas, ed. *Correspondence of Reginald Pole.* 4 vols. Aldershot: Ashgate, 2002–8.

More Molyneux Family of Loseley Park, Historical Correspondence. Surrey History Centre. <http://www.nationalarchives.gov.uk/a2a/records.aspx?cat=176-6729&cid=10-46#10-46>. Accessed March 12, 2009.

Naunton, Robert. *Fragmenta regalia, or Observations on Queen Elizabeth Her Times and Favorites,* ed. John S. Cerovski. Washington, D.C.: The Folger Shakespeare Library, 1985.

Nevinson, Charles, ed. *The Later Writings of John Hooper.* Cambridge: Parker Society, 1852.

Nicholson, William, ed. *The Remains of Edmund Grindal.* Cambridge: Parker Society, 1843.

Nowell, Alexander. *A Catechisme, or First Instruction and Learning of Christian Religion. Translated out of Latine into Englishe.* 1570. STC (2nd edn) /18708.

Overall, W. H. and H. C. Overall, eds. "Offices and Officers." *Analytical Index to the Series of Records Known as the Remembrancia: 1579–1664.* British History Online. London: E. J. Francis, 1878.

Owen, G. Dyfnallt, ed. *Calendar of the Manuscripts of the…Marquess of Bath…vol. 5, Talbot, Dudley and Devereux Papers, 1533–1659.* Historical Manuscript Commission 58. London, 1980.

Peacham, Henry. *The Compleat Gentleman fashioning him absolute in the most necessary & commendable qualities concerning minde or bodie that may be required in a noble gentleman.* 1622. STC (2nd edn)/19502.

Peck, Francis. *Desiderata curiosa.* London, 1732.

Pricke, Robert. *The Doctrine of Superioritie, and of Subiection, contained in the fift comman-dement of the holy law of Almightie God. Which is the fundamental ground, both of all Christian subiection: and also of like Christian government, as well in church, and common-wealth, as in very schoole and private familie.* [1609]. Sig. C6. STC (2nd edn)/20337.

Rainolde, Richard. *A Booke Called the Foundacion of Rhetorike because all other partes of rhetorike are grounded thereupon, euery parte sette forthe in an oracion vpon questions, verie profitable to bee knowen and redde.* 1563. STC (2nd edn)/20925a.5.

Ramsay, G. D., ed. *John Isham Mercer and Merchant Adventurer. Two Account Books of a London Merchant in the Reign of Elizabeth I.* Northampton: Northamptonshire Record Society, 1962.

Read, Conyers, ed. *William Lambarde & Local Government. His "Ephemeris" and Twenty-nine Charges to Juries and Commissions.* Ithaca, NY: Cornell University Press, 1962.

Reynolds, John, trans. *A Treatise of the Court or Instructions for Courtiers: Digested into two books. Written in French by the noble, and learned iuris-consull Monsr Denys de Refuges, Councellor of Estate, and many tymes ambassador (in foraigne parts) for ye two last French kings his masters.* London, 1617. STC (2nd edn)/7367.

Salutem in Christo. Good Men and Evil Delite in Contrarities. 1571. STC (2nd edn)/11506.

Saunders, H. W., ed. *The Official Papers of Sir Nathaniel Bacon of Stiffkey, Norfolk as Justice of the Peace, 1580–1620.* Camden Society, 3rd ser., 26 (1915).

Sidney, Philip. *The Defence of Poesie.* 1595. STC/904:16.

Smith, A. Hassell, ed. *The Papers of Nathaniel Bacon of Stiffkey,* vol. 1, *1556–1577.* Norwich: Norfolk Record Society, 1979.

Smith, Thomas. *De republica Anglorum,* ed. Mary Dewar. Cambridge: Cambridge University Press, 1982.

Smith, Thomas. *De repvblica Anglorum: The Maner of Gouernement or Policie of the Realme of England.* London, 1584. STC (2nd edn)/22858.

Spangenberg, Johann. *Margarita theologica continens praecipuos locos doctrinae Christianae per quaestiones breuiter & ordine explicatos.* 1570. STC (2nd edn)/23002.

Staunford, William. *Les plees del coron diuisees in plusiours titles & common lieux, per queux home plus redement et plenairement trouera, quelq chose que il quira, touchant les ditz pleez, composees lan du grace, 1557.* London, 1557. STC (2nd edn)/23219.

Tawney, R. H. and E. Power, eds. *Tudor Economic Documents.* 3 vols. London: Longmans, 1963.

Traherne, John M., ed. *The Stradling Papers.* London, 1840.

A True and Plaine Declaration of the Horrible Treasons, practised by William Parry the traitor, against the Queenes maiestie. The maner of his arraignment, conuiction and execution, together with the copies of sundry letters of his and others, tending to diuers purposes, for the proofes of his treasons. Also an addition not impertinent thereunto, containing a short collection of his birth, education and course of life. Moreouer, a fewe obseruations gathered of his owne wordes and wrytings, for the farther manifestation of his most disloyal, deuilish and desperate purpose. STC (2nd edn)/19342a.

Venn, John, ed. *Biographical History of Gonville and Caius College, 1349–1897.* 3 vols. Cambridge: Cambridge University Press, 1901.

Vermigli, Pietro Martire. *The Common Places of the Most Famous and Renowmed* [sic] *Diuine Doctor Peter Martyr: diuided into foure principall parts: with a large addition of manie theologicall and necessarie discourses, some neuer extant before. Translated and partlie gathered by Anthonie Marten.* London, 1583. STC (2nd edn)/24669.

West, William. *Symbolaeography which may be termed the art, description or image of instruments, extra-iudicial, as couenants, contracts, obligations, conditions, feffements, graunts, wills, &c. Or the paterne of praesidents. Or the notarie or scriuener…* [1592]. STC (2nd edn)/25267a.

Whetstone, George. *A Remembraunce of the Precious Vertues of the Right Honourable and Reuerend Iudge, Sir Iames Dier, Knight, Lord Cheefe Iustice of the Common Pleas who disseased at great Stawghton, in Huntingdon shire, the 24. of Marche, anno. 1582.* [1582]. STC (2nd edn)/25345.

Whitaker, William. *A Disputation on Holy Scripture: against the papists, especially Bellarmine and Stapleton.* Cambridge: Parker Society, 1849.

Whitgift, John. *Works,* ed. John Ayre. 2 vols. Cambridge: Parker Society, 1851.

Wigand, Johann. *De neutralibus et mediis. Grossly Englished, Jacke of both sides. A Godly and necessary Catholic admonition, touching those that be neuters, holding by no certain religion or doctrine, and such as hold with both partes, or rather of no parte, very necessarye to stay and stablish Gods elect in the true Catholic faith against this present wicked world,* trans. Anon. 1562. STC (2nd edn)/ 25612.

Wilson, Thomas, trans. *The Three Orations of Demosthenes Chiefe Orator among the Grecians, in fauour of the Olynthians, a people in Thracia, now called Romania with those his fower orations titled expressely & by name against King Philip of Macedonie: most nedefull to be redde in these daungerous dayes, of all them that loue their countries libertie, and desire to take warning for their better auayle, by example of others. Englished out of the Greeke* ... 1570. STC (2nd edn)/6578.

SECONDARY SOURCES

Adams, Simon. "The Dudley Clientele and the House of Commons, 1559–1584," in N. Jones and D. Dean, eds, *Interest Groups and Legislation in Elizabethan Parliaments. Essays Presented to Sir Geoffrey Elton. Parliamentary History*, 8, 2 (1989), 216–39.

Alford, Stephen. *Burghley. William Cecil at the Court of Elizabeth I.* New Haven: Yale University Press, 2008.

Alford, Stephen. *The Early Elizabethan Polity. William Cecil and the British Succession Crisis, 1558–1569.* Cambridge: Cambridge University Press, 1998.

Alford, Stephen. *Kingship and Politics in the Reign of Edward VI.* Cambridge: Cambridge University Press, 2008.

Alford, Stephen. *The Watchers. A Secret History of the Reign of Elizabeth I.* London: Penguin, 2013.

Allen, Douglas. *The Institutional Revolution. Measurement and the Economic Emergence of the Modern World.* Chicago: University of Chicago Press, 2011.

Allen, John C., Susan E. Dawson, Gary E. Madsen, and Chih-Yao Chang. "A Social Relationship Response to a Proposed Coal-Fired Power Plant. Network Theory and Community Change." *Community Development Journal*, 39, 1 (2008), 35–49.

Alsop, J. D. "Exchequer Office-Holders in the House of Commons, 1559–1601," in N. Jones and D. Dean, eds, *Interest Groups and Legislation in Elizabethan Parliaments. Essays Presented to Sir Geoffrey Elton, Parliamentary History*, 8, 2 (1989), 240–75.

Alsop, J. D. "William Fleetwood and Elizabethan Historical Scholarship," *The Sixteenth Century Journal*, 25 (1994), 155–76.

Baker, John. *The Oxford History of the Laws of England*, vol. 6, *1483–1558.* Oxford: Oxford University Press, 2003.

Bearman, Peter S. *Relations into Rhetorics. Local Elite Social Structure in Norfolk, England, 1540–1640.* Rutgers, NJ: Rutgers University Press, 1993.

Bell, H. E. *An Introduction to the History and Records of the Court of Wards and Liveries.* Cambridge: Cambridge University Press, 1953.

Bellamy, J. G. *Bastard Feudalism and the Law.* Portland, OR: Areopagitica Press, 1989.

Bland, D. S. "Henry VIII's Royal Commission on the Inns of Court," *Journal for the Society of Teachers of Law*, 10 (1969), 178–94.

Bodkin, E. H., "The Minor Poetry of Hugo Grotius," *Transactions of the Grotius Society*, 13 (1927), 95–128.

Bourgeois II, Eugene J. *The Ruling Elite of Cambridgeshire, England, c.1530–1603.* Lewiston, NY: The Edwin Mellen Press, 2003.

Braddick, Michael. *State Formation in Early Modern England, c.1550–1700.* Cambridge: Cambridge University Press, 2000.

Braddick, Michael. "'Uppon This Instante Extrordinarie Occasion.' Military Mobilization in Yorkshire before and after the Armada," *Huntington Library Quarterly*, 61 (1998), 429–55.

Braddick, Michael J. and John Walter, eds. *Negotiating Power in Early Modern Society. Order, Hierarchy and Subordination in Britain and Ireland.* Cambridge: Cambridge University Press, 2001, 1–42.

Braddick, Michael J. and John Walter, eds. *Negotiating Power in Early Modern Society. Order, Hierarchy and Subordination in Britain and Ireland*. Cambridge: Cambridge University Press, 2001.

Brooke, Christopher W., *Law, Politics and Society in Early Modern England*. Cambridge: Cambridge University Press, 2008.

Bryson, W. H. *The Equity Side of the Exchequer. Its Jurisdiction, Administration, Procedures and Records*. Cambridge: Cambridge University Press, 1975.

Carter, Patrick. "Parliament, Convocation and the Granting of Clerical Supply in Early Modern England," *Parliamentary History*, 19 (2000), 14–26.

Carter, Patrick. "Royal Taxation of the Elizabethan Church," in Susan Wabuda and Caroline Litzenberger, eds, *Belief and Practice in Reformation England*. Aldershot: Ashgate, 1998, 94–112.

Clegg, Cyndia. "Censorship and Propaganda," in Susan Doran and Norman Jones, eds, *The Elizabethan World*. Oxford: Routledge, 2011, 165–81.

Cogan, Susan. "Catholic Gentry, Family Networks and Patronage in the English Midlands, c.1570–1630." University of Colorado, unpublished PhD dissertation, 2012.

Coleman, Christopher. "Artifice or Accident? The Re-organisation of the Exchequer of Receipt, c.1554–1572," in C. Coleman and D. Starkey, eds, *Revolution Reassessed*. Oxford: Oxford University Press, 1986, 163–98.

Collinson, Patrick. *Archbishop Grindal, 1519–1583. The Struggle for a Reformed Church*. Berkeley: UCLA Press, 1979.

Collinson, Patrick. "De republica Anglorum, or History with the Politics put back," in Patrick Collinson, *Elizabethan Essays*. London: Hambledon Press, 1994, 1–30.

Collinson, Patrick. *Elizabethan Essays*. London: Hambledon Press, 1994.

Collinson, Patrick. "The Monarchical Republic of Queen Elizabeth I," in Patrick Collinson, *Elizabethan Essays*. London: Hambledon Press, 1994, 31–58.

Collinson, Patrick. *Richard Bancroft and Elizabethan Anti-Puritanism*. Cambridge: Cambridge University Press, 2013.

Collinson, Patrick. "Sir Nicholas Bacon and the Elizabethan *via media*," *Historical Journal*, 30 (1979), 255–73.

Cooper, J. P. D. *Propaganda and the Tudor State. Political Culture in the Westcountry*. Oxford: Clarendon Press, 2003.

Cooper, John. *The Queen's Agent. Francis Walsingham at the Court of Elizabeth I*. London: Faber and Faber, 2011.

Crankshaw, David J. "Preparations for the Canterbury Provincial Convocation of 1562–63. A Question of Attribution," in Susan Wabuda and Caroline Litzenberger, eds, *Belief and Practice in Reformation England*. Aldershot: Ashgate, 1998, 60–93.

Cromartie, Alan. *The Constitutional Revolution. An Essay on the History of England, 1450–1642*. Cambridge: Cambridge University Press, 2006.

Cust, Richard. "Earls Marshall and the Defence of Honor in Elizabethan England," unpublished paper presented at Rethinking Politics in Sixteenth Century England, University of Warwick, April 18, 2009.

Cust, Richard. "Honour and Politics in Early Stuart England. The Case of Beaumont v. Hastings," *Past and Present*, 149 (Nov. 1995), 57–94.

Davies, Catharine. *A Religion of the Word. The Defence of the Reformation in the Reign of Edward VI*. Manchester: Manchester University Press, 2002.

Dean, David. *Law-making and Society in Late Elizabethan England*. Cambridge: Cambridge University Press, 1996.

Dean, David and Norman Jones. *Parliaments of Elizabethan England*. Oxford: Blackwell, 1989.

Descimon, Robert. "Power Elites and the Prince. The State as Enterprise," in Wolfgang Reinhard, ed., *Power Elites and State Building*. Oxford: Clarendon Press, 1996, 101–21.

Dickinson, Janet. "Nobility and Gentry," in Susan Doran and Norman Jones, eds, *The Elizabethan World*. London: Routledge, 2011, 285–300.

Dietz, Frederick C. *English Public Finance, 1485–1641*, vol. 2, *1558–1641*. London: Frank Cass & Co., 1964.

Doran, Susan. "Elizabeth I's Religion. The Evidence of her Letters," *Journal of Ecclesiastical History*, 51 (2000), 699–720.

Elliott, J. H. "A Europe of Composite Monarchies," *Past and Present*, 137 (1992), 48–71.

Ellis, Steven G. "Centre and Periphery in the Tudor State," in Robert Tittler and Norman Jones, eds, *A Companion to Tudor Britain*. Oxford: Blackwell Publishing, 2004, 133–50.

Ellis, Steven G. *Tudor Frontiers and Noble Power. The Making of the British State*. Oxford and New York: Oxford University Press, 1995.

Elton, G. R. "The Elizabethan Exchequer. War in the Receipt," *Studies in Tudor and Stuart Politics and Government Papers and Reviews 1946–1972*, vol. 1, *Tudor Politics Tudor Government*. Cambridge: Cambridge University Press, 1974, 355–88.

Elton, G. R. "Government by Edict?" *Historical Journal*, 8 (1965), 266–71.

Elton, G. R. "Lex Terrae Victrix. The Triumph of Parliamentary Law in the Sixteenth Century," in D. M. Dean and N. L. Jones, eds, *The Parliaments of Elizabethan England*. Oxford: Basil Blackwell, 1990, 15–36.

Elton, G. R. *The Parliament of England, 1559–1581*. Cambridge: Cambridge University Press, 1989.

Elton, G. R. "Reform and the 'Commonwealth-Men' of Edward VI's Reign," in G. R. Elton, *Studies in Tudor and Stuart Politics and Government*, vol. 3, *Papers and Reviews, 1973–1981*. Cambridge: Cambridge University Press, 1983, 234–53.

Enis, Cathryn. "The Dudleys, Sir Christopher Hatton and the Justices of Elizabethan Warwickshire," *Midland History*, 39, 1 (2014), 1–35.

Evenden, Elizabeth. "The Michael Wood Mystery: William Cecil and the Lincolnshire Printing of John Day," *Sixteenth Century Journal*, 35, 2 (2004), 383–94.

Fisher, R. M. "Thomas Cromwell, Humanism and Educational Reform," *Bulletin of the Institute for Historical Research*, 50 (1977), 151–63.

Fritze, Ronald H. and William B. Robison, "Age and Magistracy—An Ambiguous Connection? The Situation of the Justices of the Peace of Hampshire and Surrey, 1485–1570," *Lamar Journal of the Humanities*, 20 (1994), 47–8.

Gleason, J. H. *The Justices of the Peace in England, 1558 to 1640*. Oxford: Clarendon Press, 1969.

Goldie, Mark. "The Unacknowledged Republic. Office Holding in Early Modern England," in Tim Harris, ed., *The Politics of the Excluded, c.1500–1850*. Basingstoke: Palgrave, 2001, 153–94.

Gordon, M. D. "The Invention of a Common Law Crime: Perjury in the Elizabethan Courts," *American Journal of Legal History*, 24 (1980), 145–70.

Gordon, M. D. "The Perjury Statute of 1563. A Case History of Confusion," *Proceedings of the American Philosophical Society*, 126, 6 (1980), 438–54.

Grafton, Anthony. *What was History? The Art of History in Early Modern Europe*. Cambridge: Cambridge University Press, 2007.

Graham, Kenneth J. E. *The Performance of Conviction. Plainness and Rhetoric in the Early English Renaissance*. Ithaca, NY: Cornell University Press, 1994.

Graves, Michael A. R. *Thomas Norton the Parliament Man*. Oxford: Blackwell, 1994.

Guth, DeLloyd J. "Law," in Norman Jones and Robert Tittler, eds, *A Companion to Tudor Britain*. Oxford: Blackwell Publishing, 2004, 77–97.

Guy, J. A. *The Court of Star Chamber and its Records to the Reign of Elizabeth I*. Public Record Office Handbooks no. 21. London: HMSO, 1985.

Hammer, Paul. *The Polarisation of Elizabethan Politics. The Political Career of Robert Devereux, 2nd Earl of Essex, 1585–1597*. Cambridge: Cambridge University Press, 1999.

Hasler, P. W., ed. *The House of Commons, 1558–1603*. 3 vols. London: HMSO, 1981.

Heal, Felicity. "The Bishops and the Act of Exchange of 1559," *Historical Journal*, 19 (1974), 227–46.

Heal, Felicity. "Food Gifts, the Household and the Politics of Exchange in Early Modern England," *Past and Present*, 199 (2008), 41–70.

Heal, Felicity. "Reputation and Honour in Court and Country: Lady Elizabeth Russell and Sir Thomas Hoby," *Transactions of the Royal Historical Society*, 6th ser., 6 (1996), 161–78.

Heal, Felicity and Clive Holmes. *The Gentry in England and Wales, 1500–1700*. Stanford: Stanford University Press, 1994.

Hindle, Steven. "County Government in England," in Robert Tittler and Norman Jones, eds, *A Companion to Tudor Britain*. Oxford: Blackwell Publishers, 2004, 98–115.

Hindle, Steven. *The State and Social Change in Early Modern England, c.1550–1640*. New York: St Martin's Press, 2000.

Hudson, Winthrop S. *The Cambridge Connection and the Elizabethan Settlement of 1559*. Durham: University of North Carolina, 1980.

Hurstfield, Joel. "Lord Burghley as Master of the Court of Wards, 1561–98," *Transactions of the Royal Historical Society*, 4th ser., 31 (1949), 95–114.

Hurstfield, Joel. *The Queen's Wards. Wardship and Marriage under Elizabeth I*. London: Longmans, Green and Co., 1958.

Hurstfield, Joel. "Was There a Tudor Despotism after all?" *Transactions of the Royal Historical Society*, 5th ser., 17 (1967), 83–108.

Jack, Sybil M. "English Bishops as Tax Collectors in the Sixteenth Century," *Parergon*, 14, 1 (1996), 129–63.

James, Mervyn. "The Concept of Order and the Northern Rising," in Mervyn James, *Society, Politics and Culture. Studies in Early Modern England*. Cambridge: Cambridge University Press, 1986, 270–307.

Jones, N. L. "Profiting From Religious Reform. The Land Rush of 1559," *Historical Journal*, 22, 1 (1979), 279–94.

Jones, Norman. *The Birth of the Elizabethan Age*. Oxford: Blackwell, 1993.

Jones, Norman. "David Lewis, the Founding Principal of Jesus College," *The Jesus College Record* (2009), 33–42.

Jones, Norman. "An Elizabethan Bill for the Reformation of the Ecclesiastical Law," *Parliamentary History*, 4 (1985), 171–87.

Jones, Norman. *The English Reformation. Religion and Cultural Adaptation*. Oxford: Blackwell Publishing, 2002.

Jones, Norman. *Faith by Statute. Parliament and the Settlement of Religion, 1559*. London: Royal Historical Society, 1982.

Jones, Norman. *God and the Moneylenders. Usury and Law in Early Modern England*. Oxford: Basil Blackwell, 1989.

Jones, Norman. "William Cecil and the Making of Economic Policy in the 1560s," in P. Fideler and T. Mayer, eds, *The Commonwealth of Tudor England*. London: Routledge, 1992, 169–93.

Jones, W. J. *The Elizabethan Court of Chancery*. Oxford: Clarendon Press, 1967.

Kaufman, Peter Iver. *Thinking of the Laity in Late Tudor England*. South Bend: University of Notre Dame Press, 2004.

Kesselring, K. J. *The Northern Rebellion of 1569. Faith, Politics, and Protest in Elizabethan England*. London: Palgrave Macmillan, 2007.

Kirby, Torrance. "Peter Martyr Vermigli's Political Theology and the Elizabethan Church," in Polly Ha and Patrick Collinson, eds, *The Reception of the Continental Reformation in Britain*. Oxford: Oxford University Press, 2010, 83–106.

Kishlansky, Mark. *Parliamentary Selection. Social and Political Choice in Early Modern England*. Cambridge: Cambridge University Press, 1986.

Koenigsberger, H. G. "Monarchies and Parliaments in Early Modern Europe. *Dominium Regale* or *Dominium Politicum et Regale*," *Theory and Society*, 5, 2 (1978), 191–217.

Lake, Peter. *Moderate Puritans and the Elizabethan Church*. Cambridge: Cambridge University Press, 1982.

Lake, Peter. "The Monarchical Republic of Queen Elizabeth I (and the Fall of Archbishop Grindal) Revisited," in John F. McDiarmid, ed., *The Monarchical Republic of Early Modern England. Essays in Response to Patrick Collinson*. Aldershot: Ashgate, 2007, 129–48.

Lake, Peter. "The Politics of 'Popularity' and the Public Sphere. The 'Monarchical Republic' of Elizabeth I Defends Itself," in Peter Lake and Steven Pincus, eds, *The Politics of the Public Sphere in Early Modern England*. Manchester: Manchester University Press, 2007, 59–94.

Lake, Peter. "A Tale of Two Episcopal Surveys. The Strange Fates of Edmund Grindal and Cuthbert Mayne," *Transactions of the Royal Historical Society*, 18 (2008), 129–63.

Lake, Peter and Steve Pincus. "Rethinking the Public Sphere in Early Modern England," *Journal of British Studies*, 45, 2 (2006), 270–92.

Lidington, D. R. "Parliament and the Enforcement of Penal Statutes. The History of the Act 'In Restraint of Common Promoters' (18 Eliz. I., c. 5)," *Parliamentary History*, 8, 2 (1989), 309–28.

Little, David. *Religion, Order and Law*, 2nd edn. Chicago: University of Chicago Press, 1984.

Loades, David. *Elizabeth I*. London: Hambledon and London, 2003.

MacCaffrey, Wallace. *Elizabeth I*. London: Edward Arnold, 1993.

MacCaffrey, Wallace. *The Shaping of the Elizabethan Regime*. Princeton: Princeton University Press, 1968.

MacCaffrey, Wallace T. "Talbot and Stanhope: An Episode in Elizabethan Politics," *Bulletin of the Institute of Historical Research* 33, 87 (1960), 73–85.

McDiarmid, John F., ed. *The Monarchical Republic of Early Modern England. Essays in Response to Patrick Collinson*. Aldershot: Ashgate Publishing, 2007.

McGurk, John. *The Elizabethan Conquest of Ireland*. Manchester: Manchester University Press, 1997.

McIntosh, Marjorie Keniston. *Controlling Misbehavior in England, 1370–1600*. Cambridge: Cambridge University Press, 1998.

Maclean, Paul D. *The Art of the Network. Strategic Interaction and Patronage in Renaissance Florence*. Durham, NC: Duke University Press, 2007.

MacLure, Millar. *Register of Sermons Preached at Paul's Cross, 1534–1642*. Revised and edited by Peter Pauls and Jackson Campbell Boswell. Ottowa: Dovehouse Editions, 1989.

Maginn, Christopher. *William Cecil, Ireland, and the Tudor State*. Oxford: Oxford University Press, 2012.

Mears, Natalie. "The Council," in Susan Doran and Norman Jones, eds, *The Elizabethan World*. London: Routledge, 2011, 59–75.

Milward, Peter. *Religious Controversies of the Elizabethan Age. A Survey of Printed Sources*. Lincoln, NE: University of Nebraska Press, 1977.

Morrissey, Mary. *Politics and the Paul's Cross Sermons, 1558–1642*. Oxford: Oxford University Press, 2011.

Muldrew, Craig. *The Economy of Obligation. The Culture of Credit and Social Relations in Early Modern England*. London: Macmillan Press, 1998.

Neale, J. E. *The Elizabethan House of Commons*. Harmondsworth: Penguin, 1963.

Nexon, Daniel H. *The Struggle for Power in Early Modern Europe. Religious Conflict, Dynastic Empires, and International Change*. Princeton: Princeton University Press, 2009.

Nolan, John S. *Sir John Norreys and the Elizabethan Military World*. Exeter: University of Exeter Press, 1997.

North, Douglass C. *Violence and Social Orders. A Conceptual Framework for Interpreting Recorded Human History*. Cambridge: Cambridge University Press, 2009.

Ormerod, Paul. *Positive Linking: How Networks Can Revolutionise the World*. London: Faber and Faber, 2012.

Overell, M. A. "Vergerio's Anti-Nicodemite Propaganda and England, 1547–1558," *The Journal of Ecclesiastical History*, 51 (2000), 296–318.

Palmer, William. "Scenes from Provincial Life. History, Honor, and Meaning in the Tudor North," *Renaissance Quarterly*, 53 (2000), 425–48.

Parker, Geoffrey. *The Grand Strategy of Philip II*. New Haven: Yale University Press, 1998.

Pearson, Daphne. *Edward de Vere (1550–1604): The Crisis and Consequences of Wardship*. Aldershot: Ashgate, 2005.

Peltonen, Markku. *Classical Humanism and Republicanism in English Political Thought, 1570–1640*. Cambridge: Cambridge University Press, 1995.

Pocock, J. G. A. *The Ancient Constitution and the Feudal Law: A Study of English Historical Thought in the Seventeenth Century. A Reissue with a Retrospect*. Cambridge: Cambridge University Press, 1986.

Pollock, Linda. "Honor, Gender, and Reconciliation in Elite Culture, 1570–1770," *Journal of British Studies*, 46, 1 (2007), 3–29.

Pulman, Michael B. *The Elizabethan Privy Council in the 1570s*. Berkeley: University of California, 1971.

Quintrell, B. W. "Government in Perspective. Lancashire and the Privy Council, 1570–1640," *Transactions of the Historic Society of Lancashire & Cheshire*, 131 (1982 for 1981), 35–62.

Ramsay, G. D. "The Life of John Isham," in G. D. Ramsay, ed., *John Isham Mercer and Merchant Adventurer. Two Account Books of a London Merchant in the Reign of Elizabeth I. Northamptonshire Record Society*, 21 (1962).

Rapple, Rory. *Martial Power and Elizabethan Political Culture. Military Men in England and Ireland, 1558–1594*. Cambridge: Cambridge University Press, 2009.

Read, Conyers. *Mr Secretary Cecil and Queen Elizabeth*. London: Jonathan Cape, 1955.

Read, Conyers. *Lord Burghley and Queen Elizabeth*. London: Jonathan Cape, 1960.

Redwood, Pamela. "The Games Family versus the Borough of Brecon, 1589–1606," *Brycheiniog*, 25 (1992–3), 67–78.

Risse, Thomas. "Vertrauen in Räumen begrenzter Staatlichkeit. Eine politikwissenschaftliche Analyse," in Jörg Baberowski, ed., *Was ist Vertrauen? Ein interdisziplinäres Gespräch*. Frankfurt: Campus, 2014, 127–46.

Roebuck, Derek. *Mediation and Arbitration in the Middle Ages. England, 1154–1558*. Oxford: Holo Books, the Arbitration Press, 2013.

Russell, Conrad. *The Causes of the English Civil War.* Oxford: Oxford University Press, 1990.

Schofield, John. *Philip Melanchthon and the English Reformation.* Aldershot: Ashgate, 2006.

Schofield, Roger. "Taxation and the Political Limits of the Tudor State," in Claire Cross, David Loades, and J. J. Scarisbrick, eds, *Law and Government under the Tudors.* Cambridge: Cambridge University Press, 1988, 227–55.

Shuger, Debora Kuller. *Habits of Thought in the English Renaissance. Religion, Politics and the Dominant Culture.* Berkeley: University of California Press, 1990.

Sinclair, David. *The History of Wigan.* Wigan: Wall, 1882.

Skelton, R. A. "The Maps of a Tudor Statesman," in R. A. Skelton and John Summerson, *A Description of Maps and Architectural Drawings in the Collections Made by William Cecil First Baron Burghley now at Hatfield House.* Oxford: The Roxburghe Club, 1971, 3–35.

Smith, Alan G. R. *Servant to the Cecils. The Life of Sir Michael Hickes.* London: Jonathan Cape, 1977.

Smith, Alan G. R. *William Cecil. The Power behind Elizabeth.* New York: Haskell House Publishers Ltd, 1971.

Smuts, Malcolm. *Culture and Power in England, 1585–1685.* London: Macmillan, 1999.

Smuts, Malcolm. "Organized Violence in the Elizabethan Monarchical Republic," *History,* 99 (2014), 418–43.

Snow, Vernon F., ed. *Parliament in Elizabethan England. John Hooker's Order and Usage.* New Haven: Yale University Press, 1971.

Solt, Leo. *Church and State in Early Modern England, 1509–1640.* Oxford: Oxford University Press, 1990.

Stern, Virginia. *Gabriel Harvey. His Life, Marginalia and Library.* Oxford: Clarendon Press, 1979.

Strype, John. *Annals of the Reformation and the Establishment of Religion,* 4 vols. Oxford, 1824.

Strype, John. *The Life and Acts of Matthew Parker.* Oxford, 1821.

Strype, John. *The Life and Acts of the Most Reverend Father in God, John Whitgift, D.D.* Oxford, 1822.

Strype, John. *The Life of John Cheke.* Oxford, 1821.

Sutton, James. *Materializing Space at an Early Modern Prodigy House: the Cecils at Theobalds, 1564–1607.* Aldershot: Ashgate, 2004.

Syme, Ronald. *The Roman Revolution.* Oxford: Oxford University Press, 1939.

Tawney, R. H. "The Rise of the Gentry. A Postscript," *The Economic History Review,* 2nd ser., 7 (1954–5), 91–7.

Thirsk, Joan. *The Agrarian History of England and Wales, 1500–1640.* Cambridge: Cambridge University Press, 1967.

Thompson, E. Margaret. "Some Wiltshire Wives," *Wiltshire Notes and Queries, 1899–1901,* 3 (1902), 323–8.

Thompson, W. D. J. Cargill. "Sir Francis Knollys' Campaign against the *jure divino* Theory of Episcopacy," in C. R. Cole and M. E. Moody, eds, *The Dissenting Tradition. Essays for Leland H. Carlson.* Athens, OH: Ohio University Press, 1975, 39–77.

Tittler, Robert. "Elizabethan Towns and the 'Points of Contact.' Parliament," *Parliamentary History,* 8, 2 (1989), 275–88.

Tittler, Robert. *Nicholas Bacon. The Making of a Tudor Statesman.* London: Jonathan Cape, 1976.

Usher, Brett. *William Cecil and Episcopacy, 1559–1577.* Aldershot: Ashgate, 2003.

Usher, Roland G. *The Rise and Fall of the High Commission*. Oxford: Oxford University Press, 1913.

Vasaly, Ann. *Representations: Images of the World in Ciceronian Oratory*. Berkeley: University of California Press, 1993.

Wake, Joan. *The Brudenells of Deene*. London: Cassell, 1953.

Wall, Alison. "'The Greatest Disgrace': The Making and Unmaking of JPs in Elizabethan and Jacobean England," *English Historical Review*, 119, 481 (2004), 312–32.

Ward, Leslie. "The Treason Act of 1563. A Study of the Enforcement of Anti-Catholic Legislation," in Norman Jones and David Dean, eds, *Interest Groups and Legislation in Elizabethan Parliaments. Essays Presented to Sir Geoffrey Elton. Parliamentary History* 8, 2 (1989), 289–308.

Warnicke, Retha. "Family and Kinship Relations at the Henrician Court," in Dale Hoak, ed., *Tudor Political Culture*. Cambridge: Cambridge University Press, 1995, 653–65.

Williams, Penry. *The Council in the Marches of Wales under Elizabeth I*. Cardiff: University of Wales Press, 1958.

Williams, Penry. *The Tudor Regime*. Oxford: Clarendon Press, 1979.

Woodward, Donald. "The Background to the Statute of Artificers. The Genesis of Labour Policy, 1558–63," *The Economic History Review*, new ser., 33, 1 (1980), 32–44.

Woodworth, A. "Purveyance for the Royal Household in the Reign of Queen Elizabeth," *Transactions of the American Philosophical Society*, new ser., 35, 1 (1945).

Woolcott, Elizabeth B. "Maternity's Wards. Investigations of Sixteenth Century Patterns of Maternal Guardianship." Unpublished MA thesis, Utah State University, 2003. <http://digitalcommons.usu.edu/cgi/viewcontent.cgi?article=1000&context=etd_history>.

Wrightson, Keith. "Two Concepts of Order. Justices, Constables and Jurymen in Seventeenth-Century England," in John Brewer and John Styles, eds, *An Ungovernable People. The English and their Law in the Seventeenth and Eighteenth Centuries*. London: Hutchinson, 1980, 21–46.

Younger, Neil. "Henry Herbert, Second Earl of Pembroke and Noble Leadership in Elizabethan Provinces," in Peter Iver Kaufman, ed., *Leadership and Elizabethan Culture*. London: Palgrave Macmillan, 2013, 121–39.

Younger, Neil. "Securing the Monarchical Republic. The Remaking of the Lord Lieutenancies in 1585," *Historical Research*, 84, 224 (2011), 249–65.

Younger, Neil. *War and Politics in the Elizabethan Counties*. Manchester: Manchester University Press, 2012.

Youngs, Frederic A., Jr. *The Proclamations of the Tudor Queens*. Cambridge: Cambridge University Press, 1976.

Index